T0360646

ROUTLEDGE LIBRARY EDITIONS:
FOOD SUPPLY AND POLICY

Volume 9

AFRICAN FOOD SYSTEMS IN CRISIS

AFRICAN FOOD SYSTEMS IN CRISIS

Part One: Microperspectives

Edited by
REBECCA HUSS-ASHMORE AND
SOLOMON H. KATZ

Routledge
Taylor & Francis Group

LONDON AND NEW YORK

First published in 1989 by Gordon and Breach

This edition first published in 2020
by Routledge
4 Park Square, Milton Park, Abingdon, Oxon OX14 4RN
605 Third Avenue, New York, NY 10017

Routledge is an imprint of the Taylor & Francis Group, an informa business

British Library Cataloguing in Publication Data
A catalogue record for this book is available from the British Library

ISBN: 978-0-367-26640-0 (Set)
ISBN: 978-0-429-29433-4 (Set) (ebk)
ISBN: 978-0-367-27582-2 (Volume 9) (hbk)
ISBN: 978-0-429-29678-9 (Volume 9) (ebk)

Publisher's Note
The publisher has gone to great lengths to ensure the quality of this reprint but points out that some imperfections in the original copies may be apparent.

Disclaimer
The publisher has made every effort to trace copyright holders and would welcome correspondence from those they have been unable to trace.

AFRICAN FOOD SYSTEMS IN CRISIS
Part One: Microperspectives

edited by

REBECCA HUSS-ASHMORE

Department of Anthropology
University of Pennsylvania

and

SOLOMON H. KATZ

The W. M. Krugman Center
for Child Growth and Development
University of Pennsylvania

GORDON AND BREACH SCIENCE PUBLISHERS
New York   London   Paris   Montreux   Tokyo   Melbourne

Gordon and Breach Science Publishers

Post Office Box 786
Cooper Station
New York, New York 10276
United States of America

Post Office Box 197
London WC2E 9PX
United Kingdom

58, rue Lhomond
75005 Paris
France

Post Office Box 161
1820 Montreux 2
Switzerland

3-14-9, Okubo
Shinjuku-ku, Tokyo 169
Japan

Private Bag 8
Camberwell, Victoria 3124
Australia

Library of Congress Cataloging-in-Publication Data

African food systems in crisis / edited by Rebecca Huss-Ashmore and Solomon
    H. Katz.
        p.   cm. — (Food and nutrition in history and anthropology ;
    v. 7)
    Includes bibliographies and index.
    Contents: pt. 1. Microperspectives.
    ISBN 2-88124-306-1 hardcover; 2-88124-332-0 paperback
    1. Food supply—Africa.   2. Produce trade—Africa.
3. Agriculture—Africa.   4. Famines—Africa.   5. Africa—Economic
conditions—1960-   I. Huss-Ashmore, Rebecca.   II. Katz, Solomon H.,
1939-   .   III. Series.
HD9017.A2F65 1988
363.8'096—dc19   88-25949
                                                                      CIP

CONTENTS

FOREWORD

Of the world's continents, only Africa remains under the constant shadow of massive acute and chronic shortages of food. A complex pattern of possible global climatic change has produced steadily increasing desertification across sub-Saharan Africa, and agricultural productivity has dropped to dangerously low levels on at least two occasions in the last generation. Although this process alone has had an enormous impact on the agricultural potential of the land, desertification may be further catalysed by some traditional farming practices, such as those leading to overgrazing and loss of ground moisture. However, climatic change and agricultural practices are only a part of the emerging picture of food shortage.

The continued growth of population size in regions with economic bases limited principally to agriculture, together with the demographic trend toward rapid urbanization, has further exacerbated the socioeconomic problems of agricultural productivity by creating political policies that favor the lowering of food prices in the cities to avoid social unrest, at the expense of higher prices and greater incentives to farmers. Westerners interested in helping to assist farm productivity by long-term individual investment in the land often have been baffled by the social organization of tribal life, where the chief frequently owns the land and the farmers more often than not can only use it. This situation limits the usefulness of western models of land ownership as a source for long-term incentives for labor-intensive investment.

With the wide-ranging local, regional, and international power struggles for political allegiance and economic influence, various political movements and warfare enormously exacerbate already strained resources for free production and distribution of agricultural products. In some countries the political instability caused by unsteady economic growth, and coups and countercoups, or even the more devastating effects of civil warfare, continues to produce an enormous toll on the basic capacity to respond to food emergencies. This results in true famine situations throughout those various regions with very limited infrastructures to distribute even the food which is donated by international agencies.

There is still another reality that needs to be added to this list of economic woes and political instability. It is the reality of an ecosystem that is still heavily burdened by a series of deadly and/or debilitating endemic parasitic diseases, such as river blindness, malaria, and schistosomiasis, and more recently the specter of AIDS, which is rising in Africa. Where these chronic endemic diseases have generally limited the productive capacity of the rural areas in which they are not controlled, AIDS appears to be producing an opposite effect. In fact, if current estimates in urban areas for the number of newborn children infected with AIDS contracted from their mothers are correct, then several of the African countries are likely to undergo substantial urban depopulation in the next decade, from this cause alone.

Although new varieties of high-yielding cereal grains have been developed for Southeast Asia and Asia proper as a result of sophisticated collaboration among developed and Third World countries in the Pacific, the infrastructure of most African universities has limited the potential for the development of a sophisticated African equivalent of the International Rice Research Institute of the Philippines. A start has been made with the four African agricultural centers supported by the Consultative Group on International Agricultural Research. However, there is a serious need to develop and maintain the educational infrastructure in the universities that could supply local and regional intellectual talent to become a part of future endeavors to improve agricultural productivity. This means ultimately that the environmental, social, political, economic and medical factors mentioned above, that are thought to influence agricultural productivity, must also be built into the educational infrastructure necessary to overcome these problems.

Having confronted the emerging reality of a worsening crisis of development and famine in much of sub-Saharan Africa, I proposed the formation of a Task Force on African Famine to the newly emerged "General Unit" of the American Anthropological Association at its first meeting, held in Denver in 1984. The concept of forming a Task Force to look into and make recommendations on how the members of our organization could help with this deeply troubling human tragedy was appealing to many of our members. Although I am not an "Africanist", I remained sufficiently committed to the concept of launching the Task Force on African Famine to agree to my appointment by the president of the General Unit, Dr. Jane Lancaster, as its first director until someone else with more appropriate experience emerged to take my place.

The response to an appeal for help was remarkably encouraging. Especially helpful was Dr. Rebecca Huss-Ashmore, who helped plan a series of comprehensive symposia on the African famine, which led to the concept of this two-volume series on the subject. Many of our professional colleagues joined the process of sharing the best of their knowledge bases with one another and with the many "PVOs" (private voluntary organizations) and "NGOs" (non-government organizations) who, along with several US agencies, were invited to send representatives to our symposia held in Washington, DC. With the information and interaction from these symposia, the Task Force began to take on a more permanent shape.

Professionals representing both traditional anthropological interests and applied areas, who had not personally and publicly exchanged knowledge for many years, now willingly became committed to doing so. Thus, results of the exchange of knowledge at these symposia had a real impact that went beyond the highly synthetic and important products presented in the pages of these volumes. This is because they demonstrated the real potential of the field to move forward in a unified mode to examine global problems confronting modern humanity, in ways that are just not as available to other fields of knowledge.

Perhaps the most important issue that arose consistently throughout the symposia came from the attempt to identify those aspects of the anthropological perspective that were best able to contribute to the overall problem of chronic and acute shortage of food in Africa. In doing this, we searched other fields looking for scholars with applied and theoretical interests who might assist us in filling in the natural lacunae that inevitably result from any collection of essays, so that we could present an integrated perspective on the problems. However, we found that most of the perspectives offered by other fields (with, of course, the notable exceptions provided in these volumes) were not sufficiently focused on the microperspective that the integrated and holistic anthropological knowledge-base offered.

Time and time again the problems of Africa, including economics, agricultural practices, nutrition and health, demographics, and history, are presented and understood in terms of macroperspectives. In one sense, the kind of broad-brush explanations used in the beginning of this preface serve the important purpose of informing the reader about the general issues, but they do not provide the necessary details on how to solve the problem. However, to apply these macroperspectives to what really happens at the local level requires keen understanding of the interacting variables. How these local and even household practices impinge on the macro-level policies and practices is just not known. This is exactly the area that anthropological approaches to integrated and holistic microstudies are best able to cover. Hopefully, as these anthropological approaches begin to fulfill their promise, the macroperspective will no longer be forced to make assumptions that will not be borne out and that result in the local chaos and hardship that comes from potentially oversimplified regional and national policies, however well-intentioned. It is with these thoughts in mind that we respectfully dedicate this book to the peoples of sub-Saharan Africa.

Solomon H. Katz

PREFACE

This book is the first of two volumes dealing with the long-term and ongoing food crisis in Africa. It presents a series of anthropological and ecological perspectives on the causes of the current problem and the coping strategies used by both indigenous people and development planners. It is the first book produced by the Task Force on African Famine of the American Anthropological Association, and represents that group's commitment to share their specialized knowledge with a wider audience.

It is generally accepted in the late 1980s that efforts to develop Africa have not succeeded. Quality of life has improved little in the last 20 years, and population growth has outstripped the increase in food production in many areas. Political economists have pointed out that much of this failure can be attributed to colonial policies which deliberately under developed Africa. While this can hardly be denied, the failure of more recent development efforts is not such a simple matter. Failure to account for habitat fluctuation and ignorance of social and political complexities have certainly hindered change.

Indigenous peoples have continued to cope with the unpredictable and fragile African environment. Over thousands of years, they have developed social and subsistence systems which help to minimize risk. Often these local strategies are in direct contradiction to the strategies advocated by programs of development and modernization. For programs of development to succeed, they will have to take account of these local strategies. They will have to assure Africans that the changes they invoke will not simply destroy traditional systems of survival, leaving the population even more vulnerable to famine.

These two volumes deal with the problems of food in Africa primarily at the level of the local producer. There is no shortage of books and articles dealing with African famine on the macro-policy level. Economists, planners, agronomists, and ecologists have generally preferred to deal with macro-systems. These have given us a very useful overview of the forces which constrain African food production and distribution at the national or regional level. However, changes in food production ultimately depend on changes at the level of the individual producer and the household production-consumption unit. These volumes look specifically at constraints and strategies which operate at that level. They adopt, in other words, a *micro*perspective.

These volumes address our general ignorance of the way in which local-level societies in Africa cope with the unpredictability of their environment. They attempt to fill gaps in our knowledge of local-level food supply problems and how these are solved under conditions ranging from normal to severe adversity. Many of the authors address the problems of change, citing specific instances of ways in which systems imposed from the outside during development programs have interacted in unsuspected ways with local systems. This is an important and relatively new approach to analyzing development problems. By their emphasis on the small and the concrete, studies such as these provide data necessary to the building of workable models for change.

This first volume is divided into three sections. The introductory section reviews current explanations for food problems in Africa. While environmental and macro-economic explanations have dominated the dialogue up to this point, there is an increasing awareness that these models do little to improve the situation. Researchers in a variety of disciplines (from Farming Systems to nutrition) have begun to concentrate on production and consumption problems at the household level, and to view food stress and responses to it from this perspective.

The second section provides a series of perspectives on the context (environmental, historical, political and economic) of food stress in Africa. The first three articles discuss environmental factors that heighten uncertainty in food supply. In his initial article, Glantz points out that drought is only one aspect of the African environment which has the potential to disrupt food supplies. Variability inherent in African climates makes them risky for food production, but does not, by itself, lead to famine. In the following two extended articles, Mabbutt and Spooner present very different views of the problem of desertification. Published here for the first time, Mabbutt's impressive data show that desertification is a growing and quintessentially African problem. Spooner, however, argues that it is also a social and political problem, and will require social and political change to solve.

The social and political aspects of food availability are discussed in detail in the article by Messer. She shows convincingly that food production is influenced not only by local ecological and social systems, but by larger political agendas, including those involved in famine prevention and relief. Robson's article concentrates specifically on the problems of famine prevention, arguing that both a comprehensive theory of famine etiology and an international organizational structure are necessary for success in this area. Finally, the article by Martin, Armelagos, and Henderson documents the time depth of food stress for one of the arid areas of Northeast Africa, Sudanese Nubia. In this area, prehistoric populations show patterns of periodic and chronic malnutrition similar to those found in the region at the present time.

The third section of this volume presents a series of case studies showing the ways in which Africans have responded to the threat of drought and hunger. Fleuret gives a detailed account of traditional and modern responses to drought in Taita (Kenya), emphasizing the importance of wage labor. Curry takes up this theme, showing that for the Hausa of Niger, wage labor is a seasonal strategy which becomes exaggerated during times of stress. For pastoral groups in northern Kenya, Legesse shows that traditional demographic and economic structures still operate as adaptive mechanisms. Where these are disrupted, land degradation and social disintegration may follow. Sukkary-Stolba shows how famine also strains traditional coping responses. As Dirks argues, not only hunger, but relief from hunger may be experienced as stressful. His cross-cultural analysis indicates that quarreling and disruptive behavior are predictable responses to refeeding and famine relief. In the final article, Hitchcock, Ebert, and Morgan explain how modernization has changed the traditional coping strategies for foraging groups in Botswana. Increasing competition from herders for traditional "famine" resources has increased Basarwa dependence upon the government. While the government has instituted relatively far-sighted programs of drought warning and relief, the life-style change which they impose may be irreversible.

The production of these volumes has proven to be a rather lengthy process. This is partly because the problem of food supply in Africa is complex, multi-disciplinary, and frustratingly contradictory. All of us who have worked on this project have had to learn a great deal in order to speak responsibly on the subject. That learning has been facilitated by a number of people and institutions, to whom we are indebted. The editors are particularly indebted to the members of the Task Force on African Famine, and to the American Anthropological Association for supporting its efforts. In particular, we would like to recognize Jane Lancaster, Sylvia Forman, and Roy Rappaport for their continued encouragement. Anne Fleuret and Stephen Reyna have taken over the direction of the Task Force, and continue to expand its effort to communicate.

The initial symposia on which these volumes are based owe a great deal to the efforts of Antoinette Brown. Helpful comments and suggestions on the format of the books (and their individual papers) were offered by David Cleveland, Ralph Faulkingham, Michael Glantz, Art Hansen, Michael Horowitz, Francis Johnston, Edward Robins, Brooke Thomas, and William Torry. A series of anonymous reviewers read and commented on the manuscripts. Janis Goodman provided able editorial assistance. Clerical help in a variety of guises was supplied by Linda Lee, Sophie Luzecky, and Robin Ashmore.

Rebecca Huss-Ashmore

INTRODUCTION

Perspectives on the African Food Crisis

Rebecca Huss-Ashmore

Department of Anthropology
University of Pennsylvania
University Museum
Philadelphia, PA 19104-6398

During the last fifteen years, famine in Africa has twice captured public attention and galvanized relief efforts on a global scale. The scope of these disasters and the intensity of media coverage surrounding them has lent a drama to the entire concept of African famine. In the 1980's, as in the 1970's, images of starving cattle and starving children became publicly symbolic of the African condition. Africa, a continent long romanticised, feared, and misunderstood, was suddenly and visibly in difficulty.

Despite the sudden intrusion of African food problems into the consciousness of developed countries, these problems are not new, nor are they limited to famine. Rather, these are problems with a recognizable time depth, and varying severity continent-wide. The depth of the problem and the intricacy of the factors underlying it have only begun to be explored. However, there is a growing concensus that sub-Saharan Africa has been left behind in the global push toward food sufficiency. For example, undernutrition and subclinical malnutrition are estimated to affect between 10% and 60% of African children (Grant 1985). Per capita food production has declined by 1.5% annually over the last two decades, compared with an annual population growth of approximately 3% (Lemarchand 1986, Lofchie 1986). Africa now imports approximately 10 million tons of grain a year; despite this, the World Bank estimates that 20% of the population may receive insufficient food (Lofchie 1986:3).

These signals of a complex crisis in African food systems are now well documented. They include disappointing agricultural performance, increasing foreign debt, increasing food imports, growing population, environmental degradation, and persistently high rates of malnutrition and infant mortality. Together, these problems imply an increasing uncertainty in future food supply for the continent. However, because they represent long-term, gradually cumulative problems, such proximal indicators of food system failure have attracted little general attention. Famine, by its very visibility, may have served to deflect attention from the more general underlying dilemma.[1]

Ironically, famine is often seen as the more tractable problem. It is dramatic, it is limited in space and time, and it is theoretically amenable to intervention. As Robson notes (this volume), people in developed countries are comforted by the knowledge that food can be directed *toward* the problem. However important it might be, alleviating immediate starvation can not improve future food security for Africa. Widespread starvation is merely the final indicator of food system collapse.

Even within the scientific community, recognition of the complex and obstinate nature of African food problems has been very recent. This recent interest in the persistence of African food crisis is reflected in a variety of publications (see, for example, Commins, et.al. 1986, Glantz 1987a, Hansen and McMillan 1986, Moses 1986). These document the dimensions of the agricultural crisis, and discuss the constraints to greater productivity and food security. It is apparent from these writings that a great deal is already known about economics and food policy in sub-Saharan Africa. However, the operation of food systems, especially the integrated working of local-level production and consumption systems, has only begun to be explored. The impact of those systems on the nutritional status and biological well being of the human population is virtually unknown.

In this book, we are interested not only in the short-term crisis of African famine, but also in the continuing crisis of African food supply. Understanding these crises means that we have to look beyond the conventional wisdom of any given discipline. Data and methods from economics, agronomy, anthropology, public health, climatology, and nutritional science (among others) are necessary for an integrated understanding of both the long-term and short-term dynamics of food

---

[1]There is a growing and specialized literature on famine which has appeared since the Sahelian drought of the 1970's. See especially Franke and Chasin 1980, Mellor and Gavian 1987, Robson 1981, Sen 1981, Torry 1979, 1984, 1986, Watts 1983.

in Africa. We are also interested not only in the conditions underlying food shortage, but in the effects of those on the human population. Thus we are interested in the strategies by which humans cope with shortage or the threat of shortage, factors which constrain those strategies or cause them to fail, and evidence for the health and demographic effects of such failure. Data on this last point are almost nonexistent, but constitute an important research priority (Seaman, et al. 1978, Watkins and Menken 1985).

This paper outlines some of the major perspectives which have emerged from the study of African food problems. It is not meant as a comprehensive review of these perspectives, but rather as an introduction to the arguments involved. Environmental, economic, sociopolitical, and biological factors leading to food stress and famine are briefly reviewed. I then discuss an alternative perspective which I feel may be useful in understanding the basic dynamics in African food systems. Throughout I argue the need for integrated, interdisciplinary research, and an attention to history. Creative solutions to the current crisis will require an understanding of its roots.

Historical Aspects of African Food Stress

Randall Baker has argued (1987:149) that Africa is a continent "trapped by its own history." Yet in dealing with the current food problems, Africa has often been treated as if it *had* no history. Many who responded to the Ethiopian crisis in 1985 were unaware that there had been a major famine in Ethiopia some ten years earlier. While most of the world was surprised by the recent evidence for failing food systems in Africa, the roots of the crisis have a long and visible past (Bryceson 1981). For many Africans, and for those Western experts with a sense of history, the Sahelian famine of the 1970's was neither the beginning nor the end of the problem. Like the current crisis, it was merely one event in a long sequence of ecological and economic difficulties.

Evidence for Drought and Famine

Both Africa's history and its prehistory show a record of recurring social, economic, and climatic disruption, accompanied by food stress. The record is of course clearer and more detailed for the colonial and post-colonial periods. However, archeological, geological, and historical evidence suggests periodic difficulties with food supply over the last several thousand years. While unpredictable climate is frequently implicated in these episodes, it is increasingly clear that major famines and epidemics of malnutrition are linked to political and economic change (Independent Commission on International Humanitarian Issues 1985, Messer, this volume).

While problematical, the Nile flood chronologies and Old Kingdom records present probably the earliest evidence of African famine linked to rainfall failure and political discontinuity (Butzer 1984). Beginning with the third millenium, B.C., periods of economic and political decline in Egypt can be linked to significantly lowered levels of the Nile flood. These episodes frequently coincide with accounts of increased grain prices, uprisings and food riots by the poor, and when government did not intervene, outright famine (Butzer 1984: 108–109). This documents the nutritional risk associated with early systems of intensified agriculture.

Such risk has been observed archeologically in societies from many geographic locations (Cohen and Armelagos 1984). The shift from mobile foraging to sedentary agriculture is associated with an increase in skeletal indicators of infection and nutritional stress. While data from Africa are sparse, agricultural intensification in Sudanese Nubia appears to have led to both population growth and declining health (Armelagos, et al. 1984, Martin, et al. 1984). As agricultural technology improved during the Meroitic phase (350 B.C.-A.D. 350), there was an increase in dental caries, iron deficiency anemia, growth retardation, and premature osteoporosis. The concentration of these problems in children and in women of childbearing age agrees well with patterns of malnutrition still seen in the area (Martin, et al., this volume).

Apart from these early records from the Northeast, precolonial information on food supply and its consequences is frustratingly scarce. In a few places, oral histories or the chronicles of early Arab geographers have provided a glimpse of local conditions (Watts 1983). These have been supplemented by climatological data, in order to reconstruct a chronology of drought and food supply.

One of the more complete such chronologies has been constructed for the Sudano-Sahelian zone. Watts, for example, documents a series of food shortages in Hausaland and the Central Sudan, going back to the mid-sixteenth century (Watts 1983:102). Fourteen local famines are recorded between 1543 and 1795 alone, associated with drought, epidemics, and warfare. Using climatological data and early geographical chronicles, Nicholson (1979, 1986) pushes the record of fluctuating climate and economic activity in this area back to the eighth century. While earlier periods are generally agreed to have been wetter than the present, major cycles of prolonged drought are evident from the early nineteenth century.

Records for Southern Africa show a similar pattern of short-term wet and dry cycles, superimposed on a long-term pattern of increasing dessication (Cooke 1979). Dendrochronology and oral histories show a record of periodic drought and migration extending back to the fourteenth century (Webster 1979). Populations moving into the Lake Malawi littoral for refuge during dry periods appear to have come from as far away as Ethiopia, Natal, and Central Africa. For the historic period (ca. 1550 on), detailed records from Angola show repeated episodes of drought, disease, agricultural pests, and political disruption, many of which resulted in famine and more-or-less permanent migration (Dias 1981, Miller 1982). The most severe of these episodes gave rise to institutionalized banditry and kidnapping, disturbances exploited by the Portugese in establishing the slave trade in that area.

In East Africa, the chronicle of famine extends with certainty back to the thirteenth century, and by inference, beyond. Degefu (1987), following Wood (1977) and Shove (1977), records eight droughts or famines in Ethiopia prior to 1800, and 20 since that time. Several of these involved the whole of Ethiopia, and extended into neighboring areas of Somalia and Kenya. Drought and food shortage became particularly visible in Somalia and Tanzania in the twentieth century (Cassanelli 1981, 1982, Shao 1986). Despite higher average rainfall from 1860–1890 (Nicholson 1986), frequency of reported famine and food stress rose from the middle of the nineteenth century in all areas studied. This is partly due to an improvement in record-keeping, but also reflects locally unstable climate and changing political-economic patterns (Watts 1983, Dias 1981). In Angola, increasing European demands for ivory, wax, and cash crops changed local patterns of production, resulting in food shortage and epidemic disease (Dias 1981). Comparable changes in Hausa relations of production were not seen until the twentieth century, but the resulting instability of food supply was equally castastrophic. Watts (1983) argues that the shift from local food shortages to large-scale regional famines was a result of colonial extraction and commoditization. Similar arguments have been made for Ethiopia and Somalia (Cassanelli 1982, Koehn 1979, Kloos 1982, Swift 1977).[2]

Perspectives on Food Stress

Even from this imperfect record, it seems probable that the scope and severity of African food crises has increased over time. Given the time depth of the problem, its public invisibility is unexpected. This invisibility certainly relates to a lack of documentation of biological and social events on a continent with chronically underdeveloped infrastructure. However, it may also result from the structure and paradigms of disciplines dealing with Africa. The colonial image of Africa as exotic and dangerous, basically *different* from Europe and America, has led to a widespread trivializing of its problems (Smiley 1982). Unfortunately, early anthropologists and geographers often unwittingly reinforced this image, by concentrating on the arcane in their data. In addition, the normative and synchronic approach of these and other sciences applied to Africa has obscured its inherent temporal variability. Glantz, for example, has argued that a normative approach to African climate has deflected attention from its seasonal and inter-annual fluctuation (Glantz 1987 and this volume). Assuming that conditions would return to "normal" following a drought, planners were unprepared for future shortfalls in rainfall and production.

If there is one group that is not surprised by food insecurity, it is the "African peasant."[3] Africans have always known that they lived an unpredictable habitat, and have developed social, economic, and perhaps biological methods of coping with it (Campbell and Trechter

---

[2]In Ethiopia, increasing commercialization and taxation by the monarchy may have played the same role as colonial extraction did elsewhere in Africa. For a contrasting view of events in Tanzania, see Bryceson 1981.

[3]There is a continuing controversy in social science literature as to what constitutes a peasant, especially outside of Europe. I refer here merely to farmers and herders, individuals producing primarily for their own use, whose market relationships are mediated by the state (Payne, et al. 1987).

1982, Colson 1979, Fleuret 1986, Kjekshus 1977, Watts 1983). As the papers in the second part of this volume show, social networks, storage, crop diversity, and mobility have traditionally served to even out food supply in all but the most extreme circumstances. Slow growth and efficient metabolism may reinforce these strategies by reducing the energy requirements for the population (Stini 1975). With modernization, wage labor has increasingly become the strategy of choice for obviating risk. While effective in the short run, resulting shortages of agricultural labor may have negative long-term consequences for African food supplies (Huss-Ashmore and Thomas 1988).

From an historical perspective, the roots of Africa's food crisis are increasingly visible. Hindsight shows us a sequence of interrelated and escalating environmental and political-economic problems. In much of Africa, decades of inept economic policy based on centuries of European extraction have been superimposed on millenia of unstable climate and worsening cycles of drought. Modern political upheavals, commodity prices, and population growth are merely the proverbial last straw.

The following section outlines some of the major perspectives which have been used to account for the modern crisis in African food supply. Most of the writing since 1984 blames current problems on one or more of five major factors. These factors are 1) the physical environment, 2) external economic forces, 3) internal economic policies, 4) social and political factors, and 5) biological factors, encompassing both the human population and its cultigens. These factors are obviously interrelated, and few authors would argue for a single explanation. Because most of these approaches are concerned with explanation on a national, regional, or continental level, I refer to them here as *macroperspectives*.

Macroperspectives

The Physical Environment

Physical features of the African environment have often been mentioned as both proximal and remote causes of famine and food prolems. Unpredictable climate and fragile soils make many areas of

Africa highly risky for sustained agricultural or pastoral production. Attempts at agricultural development have intensified or changed patterns of land use, with resulting degradation of soil structure and fertility. Consequent loss of soil moisture and plant cover have been implicated in increasing desertification in Africa (Charney 1975, Mabbutt, this volume).

African soils constitute a definite constraint to production. Because Africa is geologically old, many of its soils are highly weathered, acidic, and low in nutrients (Okigbo 1986, Popenoe 1986). The distribution of soil types is related to climate, with sandier, more fertile soils found in drier regions. These soils are unfortunately highly subject to both sheet and gulley erosion (Mabbutt, this volume). Soils in more humid areas are higher in clay, but are generally deficient in nutrients, particularly nitrogen and phosphorus. These elements can be replaced by the use of either chemical or organic fertilizers, but other soil problems are not so easily remedied. Iron and aluminum toxicity are common in certain areas (Moran 1987), and prolonged irrigation may exacerbate soil crusting and salinity (Popenoe 1986). Removal of vegetative cover from lateritic tropical soils results in rapid leaching of nutrients and serious compacting of the surface. Traditional methods of land management, such as shifting cultivation and controlled burning, may act to minimize some of these constraints.

While the quality of African soils is a critical factor in food shortage, perhaps the most frequently cited causes are climate and meterological factors, particularly drought. Drought in the last two decades has often seemed to observers to be of unprecedented severity and unusually widespread in sub-Saharan Africa. As noted above, this impression is partly due to the paucity of historical records and awareness. However, many researchers (Bryson 1974) feel that recent droughts in Africa are the result of global climatic processes that are manifest locally as a long-term trend toward increasing aridity.

The role of humans in amplifying this trend has been amply debated. Bryson (1974) cites the effects of atmospheric dust and carbon dioxide in changing climate. Charney (1975) argues that changing albedo (surface reflectance) due to human activity may have lowered rainfall in arid areas, increasing the risk of drought and desertification. By contrast, Nicholson (1986) feels that drought is an inherent aspect of African climate, and finds little evidence that current conditions are unique.

Human activity has been implicated not only in temporary climatic change, but in long-term degradation of the African habitat. Desertification, or the spread of desert-like conditions, appears to be increasing in Africa, both in terms of land area and of population affected (Mabbutt, this volume). Causes commonly cited include overstocking of rangelands, concentration of stock around boreholes, monocropping, shortened fallows, increased irrigation and siltation of water sources, and increased demand for fuelwood. While many of these processes are directly connected to population increase, others may be the result of changing economic pressures and land use practices connected with development of drought-prone areas (Horowitz and Salem-Murdock 1987, ICIHI 1985, Vermeer 1981).

While drought has often been seen as synonymous with famine, there is growing evidence that the two are not isomorphic. As Glantz (this volume) notes, 1982–83 was a period of drought for many regions of the world, but famines occurred only in Africa. Fluctuating climate increases the risk of crop failure, but does not by itself constitute a crisis. Thus the relationship of drought to famine cannot be assumed, but must be assessed on a case by case basis. Similarly, while desertification places major constraints on African production systems, it is only one of many processes underlying food system failure. The articles here by Glantz and by Spooner both underline the complexity of the interactions among climate, environmental degradation, and famine.

External Economic Forces

Next to climate, the most common explanation for the current African food crisis is the operation of external economic forces. Proponents of this point of view assign primary responsibility for poor productivity to the international economic system and poor terms of trade (Lofchie 1986). They point out that post-colonial African governments have relied on export revenues to generate the surplus needed for development. Given current world markets, this strategy has proven risky.

Poor terms of trade for Africa countries are seen as the result of rising prices of imports and falling or static prices for exports (Lofchie 1986). Overall, the demand for primary agricultural products, Africa's main exports, has risen little in the last decade. Coffee, tea, and cocoa have been particularly sluggish, but cotton, rubber, and sugar have also been affected (Lofchie 1986). Demand for many of these products has been affected by surplus production elsewhere in the world, but also by the development of synthetic substitutes. Countries where agricultural development is dependent on petroleum imports (for fuel, fertilizer, and pesticides) are particularly vulnerable. For such countries, the ratio of debts to exports has risen precipitously in the last ten years (Baker 1987).

Many aspects of this externalist view rely implicitly on dependency theory. This point of view holds that current economic problems can be traced to economic policies implemented under colonial rule (Alpers 1975, Amin 1981, Frank 1969, Shaw 1987, Watts 1983). African countries, like those of Latin America and Asia, were incorporated into the world capitalist system through colonial exploitation. Agriculture and mining were developed to provide raw materials for the core industrial countries, but little was done to build up infrastructure. Instead, indigenous economies and political structures were disrupted and rendered dependent on Europe for markets and technology (Kraus 1986). Baker (1987) emphasizes the degree to which change in Africa is still seen as dependent on help from outside.

Because of this external orientation, development in Africa is peculiarly un-African. Failure of export revenues to adequately finance needed programs has led African governments to an increasing reliance on outside donors. The impact which these donors have on economic policy should not be underestimated (Lofchie 1986). Aid frequently consists not only of capital and equipment, but expertise and manpower as well. Thus projects designed outside and financed from outside are frequently staffed with outsiders. As a result, such projects rarely take into account either the concerns or the constraints of the rural African producer (Commins 1986).

Historically, agricultural development in Africa has not been concerned with food production. Reflecting development theories current at the time, the majority of African agricultural projects have emphasized cash crops as a basis for financing industrial growth (Staatz and Eicher 1986). The most efficient strategy was seen to be the wholesale transfer of large-scale, mechanized, scientific Euro-American agriculture to the African continent. Assumptions underlying this strategy were numerous, but included the need to overcome innate peasant conservatism and the availability of surplus labor (Weaver and Jameson 1981). Because African farming systems are frequently female farming systems, male labor was seen to be underemployed.

Boserup (1970) has pointed out the consequences of this Euro-centric bias for African farming systems. Accustomed to male farming systems, European and American advisors perceived female agricultual labor as inefficient. Consequently, they recruited men into cash-cropping schemes, providing them with technological inputs and extension support. Resulting crops were often purchased at subsidized prices. The result was the marginalization of women as producers, and the neglect of women's crops. Spring (1986 and these volumes) emphasizes the need to focus on the role of women in African production systems. Because women are frequently the producers of household subsistence, improvement of the food supply may have to begin with them.

Externally derived development has achieved some notable successes in Africa (for example, in Kenya and the Ivory coast), but in general is seen as a qualified failure. Agricultural technology has not diffused, partly because it had little to do with peasant needs, and partly because farmers were unable for economic reasons to employ higher-cost modern methods (Commins 1986). Many such projects pushed producers to accept increased innovation, but also increased risk. Given the peasant strategy of spreading risk, such projects were likely to be rejected as irrelevant or dangerous (Berry 1986b, Colson 1979). In addition, many have proven to be ecologically unsound, with increased probability of erosion, silting, or desertification.

Given the failure of large-scale "project-oriented" development, agricultural programs in the 1980's have shifted to an emphasis on the resource-poor small farmer (Staatz and Eicher 1986). Farming systems projects in many parts of Africa have attempted to increase production by introducing technology congruent with the farmer's needs. Integrated development projects have emphasized the need to concentrate simultaneously on agriculture, health, and income generation (P. Fleuret, these volumes). These are commendable approaches, but they require a long-term commitment on the part of donors and of African governments. In the past, donors have often proven impatient, changing strategies when results were not forthcoming in two or three years.

Even the most enlightened and committed donor policies are not likely to succeed if they do not have the support of the African producer. Change imposed from outside runs the risk of being ignored if Africans find it irrelevant to their own goals. This is equally true of internal policy change, in that African governments may have goals as alien to peasant producers as those of foreign donors (Commins 1986). Democratization of the development process, that is, involvement of the producer in planning, seems essential if food security is to be increased (Baker 1987, Seidman, these volumes).

Internal Economic Policies

Although world markets and donor agencies obviously play an important role in Africa's current crisis, some authors see that role overshadowed by the effects of internal government policies (Asante 1986, R.H. Bates 1981, 1986; Berg 1981; Lofchie 1986, 1987). These writers feel that the single most important factor in Africa's economic decline is the tendency of governments continent-wide to control and suppress agricultural producer prices. This policy is designed to keep urban consumer prices low, while transferring resources from the agricultural sector to the state (Bates 1981). By artificially suppressing prices of farm goods, governments hope to forestall political unrest among their urban power base. Unfortunately, the result has been to reduce incentives for increased production. This effect has been compounded by the tendency toward currency overvaluation. Such overvaluation artifically cheapens the price of imported foods relative to those produced locally (Lofchie 1987). This problem has been less severe in francophone countries, where the currency is officially tied to that of France, than it has been elsewhere on the continent.

The creation of parastatal marketing boards (state-run corporations) as overseers of agricultural inputs and marketing has also had a negative impact on food production.[3] These parastatals are characterized throughout Africa as corrupt, inefficient, and poorly managed (Asante 1986). In some cases, the expenses of these corporations are higher than their returns from produce sales. This means that farmers

---

[4]The lack of private-sector marketing structures in much of Africa has meant that governments have taken over this function, through the creation of state-run corporations. These corporations are often staffed by political appointees, and may have a government-mandated monopoly over buying, selling, and processing specific agricultural goods.

are not paid for their crops, or are paid late and paid less than they were promised. This in itself can be seen as a powerful disincentive to commercial crop production. Weaver and Jameson (1981) noted that the parastatal system has provided developing countries with the bureaucracy and inefficiency of socialism plus the inequality of capitalism—in effect, the worst of both worlds.

Investment in industry at the expense of agriculture has also slowed the growth of food production in Africa. Fledgling urban industries have siphoned off capital which might have been used to introduce new high-demand crops or to develop new varieties of traditional ones (Lofchie 1986). Because of inefficiencies in production and management, goods produced by local industries are frequently expensive, putting them beyond the reach of the poor rural consumer and insuring the need for continued state support.

Given the focus on export crops to finance government agendas, food crops have received little attention. Similarly, livestock has been equated with exportable cattle, ignoring the small stock raised for subsistence. As noted above, much of this current agricultural policy is rooted in colonial history (Davis 1986). Even where government policy is now oriented toward food self-sufficiency, it may not be possible to overcome the tradition of neglect. For example, colonial policy in Lesotho explicitly discouraged agriculture, in order to create a reserve labor force for the mines in South Africa (Murray 1981). Rates of labor outmigration are now so high in that country that rural areas experience a labor shortage, at least seasonally (Huss-Ashmore 1984). As a result, despite government policies to promote food crops, agricultural production has declined.

Economic and political policies of African governments may affect agricultural producers in unforseen ways. Kenya's agricultural policies favoring large farmers have increased commodity output, but have also increased social differentiation (Peterson 1986). In Tanzania, the process of villagization increased government control over the rural population, but destroyed the system of shifting cultivation necessary to maintain productivity in less fertile areas (Shao 1986). After a brief period of increased output, both food and export crops declined. These examples suggest that the impact of policy can rarely be confined to a single sector. Social and biological outcomes of agricultural policy may be as important as economic ones, although more difficult to predict.

Social and Political Factors

A wide variety of social and political factors have been blamed for the current food crisis in Africa. These factors range from the highly visible and indisputable impact of warfare to the subtle and debatable effect of peasant attitudes. While social factors are certainly involved and probably critical in the overall determination of food supply, their exact role has proven difficult to document, particularly at the macrolevel. Aside from warfare, there are few data to directly support or refute the significance of socio-political factors.

For severe food crises such as famine, there is now a consensus on the importance of political factors (ICIHI 1985). The control of resources is inherently political, and in general, the elite do not starve. In the case of long-term food insecurity, political influences may be more complex, if no less important. In Africa, the instability of national governments is frequently cited as a factor constraining food production (R.H. Bates 1986, Shaw 1987). This instability may operate in several ways. First, frequent changes in leadership may preclude long-term continuity in policy, in that programs designed by one set of officials are often scrapped by their successors. Second, policies designed to placate one constituency may alienate another. As noted above, the need to defuse unrest in urban populations has led to pricing policies detrimental to farmers.

Inter-ethnic hostilities have also been a factor in constraining food production and distribution in many African nations (Aykroyd 1974). The colonial legacy in sub-Saharan Africa includes not only economic structures, but also a set of national political boundaries which have little to do with former ethnic divisions. European divisions of territory frequently separated single groups (such as the Hausa of Niger and northern Nigeria) into opposing nation states, while including disparate and traditionally antagonistic groups within a single polity. Traditional inter-ethnic rivalries have been expressed subtly, through discrimination in jobs and government appointments, and overtly, through civil wars. In the most serious cases, such as Nigeria, the Congo, Mozambique, and Ethiopia, warfare has led to famine through accidental or intentional disruption of food supplies. In the less obvious cases, such as Botswana, discrimination has led to increasing poverty and vulnerability of minority groups (Hitchcock, et al., this volume).

While many social factors contribute to food insecurity, those which have been most frequently cited in the African context include traditional land tenure arrangements and modes of production. In particular, systems of communal land tenure have been criticized for their negative impact on production. Such systems are widespread in Africa, where both grazing and farming land are often owned by the state or an ethnic group as a whole, and use rights assigned by a chief. Adults usually retain rights to land as long as it is in use, but may have it reassigned if it is abandoned. Critics of this practice argue that this system constitutes a disincentive to long-term investment in improving land quality and productivity. The World Bank, commenting on land tenure in Lesotho, stated this position succinctly:

"A succession of overseas economic missions . . . have without exception stated categorically that the traditional system of land tenure is quite unsuited to modern economic development. . . . The lack of the security of tenure made the farmer reluctant to make any permanent land improvements, and the absence of negotiable title to the land meant that farmers had no security to offer for credit for the purchase of implements, seed, fertilizer, and so forth" (IBRD 1975:8–9).

The case has been made even more forcefully for grazing lands. Following Garrett Hardin's (1968) argument for the "tragedy of the commons," proponents of land tenure change have cited the conflict between communal ownership of land and private ownership of livestock. They argue that this conflict leads to land degradation because the benefits of increased herd size accrue to the owners individually, while the costs are born by the community as a whole. Owners are thus motivated to increase the number of animals beyond the carrying capacity of the range.

Horowitz and Little (1987) have offered a persuasive criticism of Hardin's model. They give evidence that private ranges may in fact not be managed better than public ones. Citing Sandford (1983), they note that overstocking and environmental damage may be as bad where both livestock and land are privately owned as it is in traditional situations. More importantly, they argue that even in traditional societies, pastoralists are responsible to the community as a whole, which can be expected to check individual greed.

One of the most telling arguments against the destruction of traditional land tenure systems is the observation that increased social differentiation almost always ensues. In essence, privatization of public resources may lead not to resource conservation, but to the contentration of resources in the hands of an elite few. Lesotho's Grazing Lands Management Project provides an example of this process (Horowitz and Little 1987). This project granted exclusive grazing rights in the project area to an influential herder's association, whose affluent members used their political position to overstock with impunity. At the same time, changes in Lesotho's land tenure laws for peri-urban areas resulted in the rapid conversion of farmland into house plots on the outskirts of many towns. By 1982, these house plots were seen as potential investments and had begun to accumulate in the hands of many of these same elites. Rather than improving productivity, these changes in traditional land tenure may have contributed to the degradation of Lesotho's scarce agricultural lands.

In addition to land tenure, other aspects of the traditional African production system have been seen as detrimental to development. One of the most frequently cited such aspects is the role of kinship in the organization of production (Berry 1986a). The African emphasis on kin networks and obligations is often seen as a leveling mechanism which discourages entrepreneurial activity, and thus impedes capital accumulation (Weaver and Jameson 1981). Others (Colson 1979) have seen it as an appropriate strategy for distributing risk in an uncertain environment.

Debates on the organization of African production are part of a larger theoretical discourse on the relative importance of world capitalism and class conflict in changing local economic relationships. Much of this debate currently centers on the existence of "precapitalist modes of production" and their fate when confronted with capital (Meillassoux 1981). The practical importance of this debate for African food supplies lies in its ability to resolve several questions. First, what is the role of social relationships in determining food production? Second, is there something uniquely African about that role? Third, to what degree are those relationships susceptible to macroeconomic influences? The ability of governments to intervene directly in the production process depends on the answers to those questions.

Hyden (1980, 1986) has argued that social relationships are critical to the organization of African production. He contends that production in much of Africa is organized along lines that are neither capitalist nor socialist, but that constitute what he calls an "economy of affection." This term denotes "networks of support, communications and interaction among . . . groups that are connected by blood, kin, community or other affinities, e.g., religion (Hyden 1986:23)." He argues that this type of economy persists in Africa to a degree that it does not in Latin America or Asia. Unlike peasants elsewhere, African producers retain control over their own land and maintain a rural orientation, even as urban migrants. The household orientation of production, with its relatively unspecialized technology and division of labor, gives African peasants an autonomy and resistance to government intervention not found in most of the developing world.

The economy of affection has been criticised as overstating the case for peasant autonomy and for portraying African peasants as static and impervious to change (Lemarchand 1986). While such criticisms are justified, Hyden's formulation has a number of useful features. First, it points out the necessity of looking at the constraints and opportunities peculiar to African societies. Second, it emphasizes the importance of micro-processes and local-level organizations in peasant economic systems. Finally, it recognizes that macro-economic changes do not necessarily result in changes at the micro level. At the very least, those changes may be translated in imperfect and unpredictable ways. The interface between macro-level policy and micro-level production is a critical area of study for understanding Africa's food crisis, and is discussed further below.

Biological Factors

While social and economic explanations for Africa's current dilemma are plentiful, there is much less discussion of biological factors which may be involved. Among those authors who consider biological factors, two separate lines of evidence are mentioned. One has to do with factors affecting food sources, that is, the plant and animal resources of the continent, and the other is concerned with factors affecting the size and composition of the human population itself. In some cases, as in discussions of disease vectors, these two may be related.

Scholars concerned with African food resources cite the failure of the green revolution to transform African agriculture (Odhiambo 1987, OTA 1984). Reasons given for this failure include 1) the inappropriateness of the Asian model or "package" for African conditions, 2) the lack of research on crops important to Africa, 3) inadequate educational opportunities, both for researchers and farmers, and 4) disease and pest constraints. These problems affect not only crop production, but livestock management as well.

Woodhouse (1988) and Barton (1986) have questioned the appropriateness of the "green revolution" philosophy for Africa. The technological package, as it was constituted for Asia and Latin America, consisted of high-yielding varieties of grain, accompanied by high inputs of fertilizer and pesticides. It required a controlled water regime and intensive human care. This strategy was designed to optimize yield per hectare, in that it was based on the assumption that land was limiting, and that surplus economic and human resources were available (Barton 1986). Unfortunately, several of these conditions are lacking in most of rural Africa. First, rainfall is sparse and unpredictable in much of Africa, and irrigation is poorly developed. This makes investment in high-yielding varieties unacceptably costly. Farmers are reluctant to invest in expensive hybrid seed and fertilizer, when risk of crop failure due to inadequate rainfall is high. Second, for many African societies, land is less of a constraint than labor, particularly during periods of peak demand (Woodhouse 1988).

A further difficulty in transferring the green revolution to Africa lies in the crops on which it has been based. Much of the research on high-yielding plant varieties has been directed toward rice and wheat, crops which have limited applicability for Africa (Odhiambo 1987). Improved maize varieties have been developed for southern Africa, but the more traditional crops of cassava, sorghum, millet, and cowpeas have attracted scientific interest only recently (Beck 1982). Bananas, sweet potatoes, and other root crops have been all but ignored by the international research effort. Odhiambo (1987) notes that Africa has five banana researchers for a banana-dependent population of nine million. Livestock research has been similarly structured, with an emphasis on cattle to the exclusion of camels, donkeys, goats, and domestic fowl.

This dearth of research on African crops is partly an accident of history, in that the establishment of the international agricultural research centers occurred at a time when Asian food problems were highly visible. Research on rice and wheat was a direct response to recurring threats of famine throughout South and East Asia. However, the problem can also be traced to the lack of funds and facilities for training African researchers. African scholars are quick to point out the disincentives to agricultural research (Odhiambo 1987, Okigbo

1986). Not only are training facilities and libraries poor, but excessive bureacracy often stifles individual initiative. Further, the lack of educated manpower is so acute in many parts of Africa that anyone with a graduate degree, including research scientists, may be siphoned off into administrative positions.

The lack of education and training is a critical constraint to development of food resources, as well as to other aspects of development. The importance of increased education, not just for scientists, but for farmers, should not be underestimated. Not only the development of new technology, but also the application of existing technology, depends on sharing information (Njoku 1986). Increasing and improving agricultural extension services is one way in which the link between research and production can be strengthened (Barton 1986). However, for that relationship to be most productive, the flow of information should not go only one way. Peasants have repeatedly shown themselves to be keen observers of their environment, and peasant "science" has a store of information on which innovation might be based (Odhiambo 1987, Okigbo 1986, Richards 1985).

One of the most persistent biological constraints requiring scientific attention is the abundance of pests and pathogens in the African environment. Both pre-harvest and post-harvest losses are high (R.P. Bates 1986), due to birds, locusts, rodents, armyworms, fungus, and a host of microbes. Livestock populations are similarly vulnerable, with rinderpest, trypanosomiasis, brucellosis, foot-and-mouth disease, tick fever, and internal parasites causing high mortality and reduced productivity (Odhiambo 1987). The economic impact of these pests is difficult to calculate; trypanosomiasis alone accounts for the disuse of approximately 10 million square kilometers of land (Foulks 1981).

Disease is also an important constraint for the human population. All of the World Health Organization's priority diseases are found in Africa, with malaria, onchocerciasis, schistosomiasis, and trypanosomiasis among the most visible (Franklin, et. al. 1981). Tuberculosis, diarrheas, and other diseases of poverty and poor sanitation are abundant, while diseases of modernization (hypertension, heart disease) are increasing (Scotch 1960, Wyndham 1979). Reduced morbidity from onchocerciasis is expected to result from the donation of Mectizan to sufferers (Nyerges 1987), but continent-wide these gains are more than offset by the increasing prevalence of AIDS. While the eventual impact of AIDS is difficult to predict, some urban areas in East and Central Africa report an annual incidence of 500–1000 cases per million adults, leading to an eventual mortality rate of 0.1% per year (Piot, et al. 1988:578). While some heavily infected rural areas may be depopulated, the greatest impact is likely to be felt in urban areas and among educated elites. Changing life-styles for this group appear to have put them at greatest risk of infection (Piot, et al. 1988).

The current AIDS epidemic points up one of the essential ironies in the study of African food supply. Population, in particular, rapid population growth, is frequently cited as a cause of the current food crisis (Faruqee and Gulhati 1983, ICIHI 1985, Njoku 1986, OTA 1984). Current growth rates exceed 3% for Africa as a whole, such that the 1980 population of 359 million will have doubled by the end of the century (OTA 1984). Much of this growth is attributed to declining mortality as a result of improved public health and medical care. Despite this, labor shortages are frequently reported in rural areas, even in areas of high population density (Woodhouse 1988). In addition, shortages of skilled manpower seriously hamper research, education, industry, and government. Thus Africa's population problem becomes simultaneously one of too much and too little. By selectively removing educated urban adults, the AIDS epidemic can only compound this problem.

Limitations to Macroperspectives

As Netting (1987:240) wryly notes, " 'Everybody' knows that the food crisis in Africa is the almost irresistable outcome of burgeoning population pressing on limited natural resources in a situation where traditional farming methods are static, technologically primitive, and unproductive." The preceding discussion of macroperspectives shows that there is another group that knows with equal certainty that economic policies are in fact the motive force, having failed to "capture" the peasantry and draw them into the market. There are two difficulties inherent in both of these perspectives. The first is that they see the problem as solely one of production. Consumption, and the factors which constrain consumption, are conspicuously absent. While levels of food production in Africa are a legitimate concern, Sen (1981) has rightly pointed out that food entitlement is probably more germane than food supply in the genesis of current food crises.

The second problem with these macroperspectives is their scale. By using global models, they tend to obscure the variability in African food systems. They are, in effect, like satellite images, viewing African food problems from a great distance and through Western disciplinary lenses. Like such images, they reveal more about the *structure* of African food systems than about their function. While the long view is necessary for planning, it should be grounded in a knowledge of local behaviors and constraints.

Understanding these behaviors and constraints will require the co-ordinated effort of researchers with a number of theoretical tools and disciplinary perspectives. In Africa, the causes of food shortage are clearly bio-social, political-economic, and physio-geographic. Most current writers on Africa recognize that the situation is complex, and few would argue for a single point of view. However, macro-economic perspectives, whether internalist or externalist, have a tendency to dominate the present discussion, as climatic theories did before them. We have seen that climate, as a single variable, is necessary but not sufficient in explaining food insecurity. Similarly, economic policy change, while necessary, is unlikely to solve the problem alone.

The macroperspectives discussed here are important, but are insufficient by themselves to understand the operation of African food systems and their trajectory over time. Recognizing this, an increasing number of researchers in varying disciplines have begun to examine production and consumption at the micro level. While methods and questions differ somewhat by discipline, the convergence of approaches is intriguing. In the following section, I discuss some of these encouraging new directions and their relevance for African food questions. I also point out some potentially useful perspectives which have been relatively underutilized in African research.

Microperspectives

Traditionally the province of anthropologists and cultural geographers, microperspectives and micro-level research have become increasingly respectable outside of those disciplines. Recent discussions of famine early warning systems, for example, have stressed the need for micro-level data in predicting food crises (Borton and York 1987, Walsh 1988a). In addition, agronomists, agricultural economists, rural sociologists, demographers, historians, and nutritionists have all seen the value of small-scale intensive research on nutritional issues. While theory and emphasis obviously differ among disciplines, methodologies are widely exchanged. As a consequence of this cross-fertilization, interdisciplinary perspectives now emerging have the potential to provide a more comprehensive picture of African food systems than we have heretofore acquired.

Four perspectives are presented here that illustrate the range of approaches current in interdisciplinary studies of food in Africa. These are the household focus (an offshoot of the "new" household economics), ecological particularism, the Farming Systems perspective, and the bio-cultural approach. Although these approaches address different theoretical problems, they have three common elements. First, they are concerned with the operation of very small human systems—communities, households, and sometimes individuals. Second, they are ecological, in the broadest sense of that term. That is to say, they place human systems within the context of their particular natural and social environment. Third, these micro-perspectives are concerned with linkages, i.e., the channels by which one process affects another. This last concern is especially important for predicting the impact of change.

The Household Focus

Changes in agricultural policy can affect food supply only if they change the behavior of food producers. In Africa, these are primarily small-scale farmers and herders, relying on family and community labor. Understanding the responses of these producers has necessitated a study of economic decisions at the family or household level. The household focus is an approach to economic behavior which has its origins in the theory of consumer choice developed in the mid-1960's (Low 1986). This theory treats households as production and consumption units which make decisions about the uses of both market goods and household resources (time, labor, land) in generating maximum satisfaction or welfare for the unit. In its application, this theory has generally treated household economic behavior as a series of cost-benefit calculations undertaken by the unit as a whole, for the benefit of the whole. While this assumption ignores much of the variability among households, it calls attention to the dynamics of decision making at the micro-level.

Because of the diversity of economic arrangements in African households, understanding the production and consumption decisions of these units has necessitated some adjustments to the original approach. Guyer (1986), for example, points out that for much of Africa, production and consumption units within the household may not necessarily coincide. Thus an aggregate model of household behavior does not necessarily tell us who makes decisions about what. Individual household members frequently have separate incomes, and may have a high degree of individual control over other resources such as time. Consumption-oriented groups within the household may overlap with or be nested in production-oriented groups. The result is a complex web of rights and obligations by which labor and income are allocated.

Understanding this decision-making process within the household is a critical first step toward understanding change in African food systems. The second step is to identify the linkages between this household-level behavior and macro-policy (Josserand 1984). The common economic assumption has been that prices, agricultural extension services, and infrastructure are the only important variables mediating between government policy and household economic strategy (Berry 1986b). Berry points out that intra-household dynamics may alter the ways in which households respond to policy change.

Household-level studies in rural Africa show that, far from acting as a unit, individual household members may pursue conflicting economic strategies (Berry 1986b). Changes in technology or the availability of markets may lead to conflicts between men and women in the household, or between generations. In Liberia, for example, women responded to increased male cash cropping and migration in the 1970's by trying to gain more control over household rice production and marketing (Commins 1986). This diverted their labor from the commercial rice schemes which the government was trying to promote. If household conflicts over resource allocation are serious enough, they may totally block the response to new opportunities.

New economic opportunities may also change alliances within the household or between households, because they change the channels through which access to resources may be gained (Berry 1986b). Thus wages paid to young male migrants may alter the ability of old men to command labor and arrange marriages. Similarly, credit programs for women, tractor pools for progressive farmers, or even food aid to children can be expected to alter power relationships within the household and the community.[5] The outcome of these altered alliances may not be increased production, but increased social friction.

Changing social and economic alliances may also alter aspects of food distribution, particularly within the household. Increased energy needs by men involved in wage labor may divert food resources to them and away from women and children. Similarly, male control over cash resources may increase their control over the kind and amount of household food purchases. On the other hand, new economic opportunities for women may either increase or decrease dietary quality, through increased purchasing power and conflicting demands on time. The impact of economic change on household nutrition is a topic which will need more intensive study in the context of African food systems.

Ecological Particularism

The recent micro-focus in economics has been mirrored in human ecology by an interest in local environmental problems. Global ecosystems models of human-environment interaction have been increasingly replaced by descriptions of resource use and hazard avoidance in specific situations. Richards (1983) has called this approach "environmental particularism." In his recent work on deforestation in Indonesia, Vayda (1983) has used an analogous approach, calling it "progressive contextualization." Both of these approaches stem from a renewed interest in and awareness of local habitat complexity. They also reflect a new awareness that land use practices are determined by politics and ideology, as well as by climate and vegetation. The emerging picture is a mosaic of highly variable local knowledge and practice.

---

[5] The introduction of the Social Security Program in the United States provides a pertinent, if whimsical, example of this type of shift in social alliances. A folksong popular at the time maintained, "I'll put the flapper on the shelf, get a grandma for myself, when that old-age pension check comes to her door."

Richards (1983) makes a case for the use of ecological particularism in the study of African production systems. He argues that attention to local land use is necessary to properly appreciate the historical achievements of African agriculture. These achievements include finely tuned techniques of soil preparation, moisture control, and cultigen selection. Intercropping, long discouraged by Western advisers as inefficient, may prove to be one of the most important of these local African technologies.

In Africa, maintenance of soil physical properties and moisture retention are primary land management goals (Richards 1983). Breakdown of soil structure is far more difficult to reverse than loss of fertility, and results in both severe compacting and erosion (Lal 1979). Traditional methods of land preparation and cultivation act to conserve or improve soil structure. These include ridging, terracing, mulching, and zero or minimum tillage, techniques which have only recently been introduced into mechanized agriculture. Many of these techniques also promote moisture retention.

Selection of appropriate cultigens includes both drought and pest-resistant plants, as well as complementary plant combinations. Indigenous African crops, such as millet and sorghum, may yield less per hectare than introduced maize, but they are much more drought tolerant. Multiple plantings of a single cultivar, and planting of several varieties, are also practices designed to decrease risk where rainfall is unpredictable. Intercropping, the combining of several compatible crops in the same field, may be an even more effective strategy for risk avoidance.

By now, the benefits of intercropping are familiar to most observers of tropical agriculture. These benefits include reduced erosion and increased moisture conservation, but also more efficient use of available sunlight, reduced disease spread, and suppression of weeds (Okigbo 1986, Richards 1983). This last consideration is critical, in that weeding is a major constraint in tropical agriculture. Intercropping has been criticized by development agronomists accustomed to Euro-American farming systems, in that it cannot easily be mechanized. However, when yields for all crops in a single plot are considered, this form of cropping produces significantly higher yields than monocropping (Odhiambo 1987). For example, in Kenya, a sorghum-maize-cowpea tricrop can produce 65% higher yields than a monocrop. It also produces higher yields per unit of labor, a more important consideration in the African context (Norman 1977).

As Richards (1983) has argued, an attention to local strategies for coping with the environment can suggest productive new research directions. One obvious approach is to search for specific multi-crop combinations which increase productivity. However, the potential inherent in African agriculture is unlikely to be realized as long as African farming systems are perceived as primitive. As agronomists have begun to discover, the environmental knowledge and management practices involved in these systems are quite sophisticated. They are also the result of long periods of trial and error under local conditions. Therefore, improvements in food production are more likely to come from enhancements to the system in place, rather than from imported replacements.

Farming Systems Research

Farming Systems Research (FSR) is an approach to agricultural development that starts with the environmental conditions and management practices of the small farmer. In theory, its aim is to increase the welfare of farm households as defined by the goals of the farmers themselves (Frankenberger 1985). In practice, its focus has been the generation and transfer of agricultural technology to increase production of resource-poor rural households. As practiced in Africa, FSR is one of the major avenues by which the micro-approach in both economics and ecology has been translated into practice. Because it is concerned with the adoption of innovation, FSR is necessarily concerned with economic decisions within the farm household (Moock 1986). Similarly, its focus on local agricultural practices has made it more sensitive than other development approaches to indigenous resources and hazards.

While a variety of practices and philosophies are currently included under the general Farming Systems label, all of them share common elements. First, they are concerned less with individual crops and commodities than with the whole farm as a system. Second, they are concerned with understanding the farmer's circumstances, including the social and economic goals and constraints of the farm household. Third, they are interested in adapting existing agricultural technology to increase production within those constraints.

Of the micro-approaches discussed here, FSR is the only one with a clearly developed methodology. In its most widely practiced variant, the research is divided into five stages (Gilbert, et al. 1980). These include informal and formal surveys to assess farmers' attributes and problems, hypotheses about how to improve productivity given these circumstances, testing of new technology or strategies on farmers' fields, and evaluation of the long-term potential for adoption or success of innovations. Finally, those technologies which appear successful are made available to other farmers through extension information and services.

Although the emphasis in FSR is on adaptation of existing technology, situations arise in agricultural research where new technologies are called for. Both national and international experiment stations have played an important role in developing new products and techniques, including improved crop varieties (Low 1986). In Africa, the failure of foreign crop technologies has led to an increasing interest in indigenous plants and management methods (Walsh 1988b). Research on appropriate African cultigens has begun to concentrate on ways of suiting those crops to the rigors of the African environment. This means a program of breeding, not for high yields, but for early maturity, drought tolerance, and disease and pest resistance (Woodhouse 1988). There is also an emerging interest in the productive potential of *wild* foods, many of which play an important role in the diet of African agriculturalists (A. Campbell 1986, Fleuret and Fleuret 1980, Huss-Ashmore and Curry 1986, Ogle and Grivetti 1985).

While the traditional emphasis in agricultural development (including FSR) has been on production, some Farming Systems theorists have recently seen the need to examine food consumption. This recent interest stems from the realization that diet and nutritional status are basic indicators of the well-being of rural families (Huss-Ashmore and Curry 1986). In addition, food consumption goals constitute a priority for farming households, and may therefore be important in influencing production decisions. Finally, it is increasingly clear that the process of agricultural production is itself linked to food consumption in rural households.

Frankenberger (1985) has characterized the relationship between food consumption and agricultural production as a set of six linkages. These are 1.) seasonality of production, which includes seasonal patterns of food availability, work requirements, and terms of trade for the poor, 2.) crop mix and minor crops, including production of subsistence vs. cash or non-food crops, 3.) income—regularity, kind, and recipients, 4.) the role of women in production, 5.) crop labor requirements, and 6.) market prices and their seasonality (Frankenberger 1985:8–9). All of these factors act as channels whereby production decisions and constraints can affect rural diet.

Farming Systems projects in Sierra Leone and Swaziland are two of the very few agricultural projects in sub-Saharan Africa to have included food consumption concerns within their goals or plans of research. In the case of the Swaziland Cropping Systems Project, research on food consumption addressed concerns that new herbicide recommendations (designed to relieve weeding bottlenecks) might endanger the supply of nutritionally important intercrops, including wild greens (Huss-Ashmore and Curry 1986). Dietary records showed a high seasonality to food availability, with late winter a time of potential nutritional stress. This information has led project agronomists and horticulturalists to search for appropriate crops which might fill in this production and consumption gap.

By linking production and consumption concerns, Farming Systems Research has the potential to describe not only how food strategies work, but how they affect the population which employs them. This is an important step if we are to understand the current African food crisis, much less solve it. Since increased production does not necessarily mean increased consumption, particularly for those portions of the population at nutritional risk, the consumption impacts of agricultural development are critical. In addition, since food consumption is not the only factor determining nutritional status, future research should begin to include those factors such as disease which affect health outcome.

At present, very few agricultural projects have committed themselves to examining consumption issues, and even fewer to examining nutrition. Since food consumption is at least phrased in the vocabulary of economics, it is more likely to be incorporated into future agricultural projects. However, the total biological impact of production and consumption systems is currently seen as beyond the scope of Farming Systems Research (Frankenberger 1985). New approaches will have to be developed if the impact of changing food systems is to be reliably assessed.

The Biocultural Approach

One approach which has traditionally been concerned with the linkages between human behavior and biology is the bio-cultural approach in anthropology. This approach has tried to trace connections between environmental stressors and resources, human cultural behavior, and biological outcomes. This perspective has proven to be especially useful in studying nutrition and disease, and is now being applied to problems in developing countries (Huss-Ashmore and Johnston 1985).

While bio-cultural linkages have been implicit in American anthropology since Boas, the explicit development of this perspective has been associated with anthropologists interested in adaptation (Bennett, et al. 1975, Watts, et al. 1975). Studies employing this perspective have emphasized the role of phenotypic plasticity, rather than genetic change *per se,* in the human adaptive pattern (Thomas, et al. 1979). Behavior, including cultural behavior, has been seen as a specific form of non-genetic adjustment to rapidly changing conditions.

Many bio-cultural studies have been concerned with identifying adaptive strategies. These studies have taken two general forms, either 1) identifying biological traits which are useful in a particular cultural context, or 2) showing how people use culture to overcome environmental constraints. Thus the association of various genetic polymorphisms with malaria and agriculture has been seen as evidence of adaptation (Livingstone 1958). Similarly, small body size may be a developmental adaptation to energy-limited nutritional environments (Stini 1975). On the other hand, Thomas (1973) has shown that behavioral strategies, including division of labor by age and sex, are important adjustments to these same environments. Katz and his colleagues have also argued for the adaptive value of various traditional culinary practices, including alkaline processing of maize, soybean fermentation, and the use of fava beans in certain malarial areas (Katz 1987, Katz et al. 1975, Katz and Schall 1979).

Studies of adaptation, including bio-cultural studies, have traditionally been criticized for misconstruing correlation as cause and for emphasizing homeostasis and equilibrium (Vayda and McCay 1975). This has probably been true only in the worst of cases. However, these studies have been criticized more recently for their tendency to assume that humans act as free agents in interactions with their environments, that is, that human solutions to environmental challenges are *optimal* (Huss-Ashmore and Thomas 1988). As a result of these criticisms, bio-cultural research has begun to pay more attention to the impacts of change, and to the historical and political-economic constraints under which populations operate.

Rather than emphasizing adaptation, these recent studies have been more concerned with methods of coping. This shift in emphasis reflects a greater sensitivity to the conflicts inherent in any strategy for dealing with resources and hazards. As Berry (1986b) noted in dealing with household economics, individuals within a household may have conflicting goals and pursue strategies which benefit themselves rather than the household as a whole. Similarly, short-term solutions to resource problems may conflict with long-term goals. As Leatherman and Thomas (1987) have shown for Nuñoa, coping with family illness by the use of child labor may interfere with educational achievement. In the worst case, no acceptable solution may be available, such that coping strategies reflect a least-harm principle.

The potential of this bio-cultural approach for addressing the African food crisis lies in its ability to do two things. First, it has the ability to link change in economic systems with changes in the biological well-being of rural populations. Second, it has the potential to show how this biological well-being (or lack of it) affects cultural and economic patterns. Studies of either sort are rare in Africa. Research on the first problem has begun to appear, conducted less often by anthropologists than by economists and nutritionists. For example, Josserand (1984) showed that cash-cropping and income for Senegalese peanut farmers were related to household food consumption, but not to nutritional status of preschool children. Lawrence, et al. (1985) also showed that seasonal changes in work requirements for Gambian women had a significant effect on energy expenditure, body fat, and birthweight of offspring. While both use correlational approaches, the second study is more informative, in that it uses women's activity patterns as a link between economic decisions and biological outcomes.

Correlational studies are a valuable first step toward understanding the operation of African food systems. However, the full potential of a bio-cultural perspective will be realized only through indentifying and understanding the factors that link economic behavior and biology. Indentifying these intermediate factors requires the development of a comprehensive theory or explanatory framework. No such framework currently exists, but Frankenberger's (1985) work on production-consumption linkages is a potentially valuable model. As he and others (Huss-Ashmore and Johnston 1985, Townsend and Momsen 1987) have noted, women's work and time allocation may prove to be a critical factor in linking food production, food consumption, and health.

A comprehensive bio-cultural approach to African food problems will have to recognize that linkages go both ways. At present, the linkages between biological status and food production have been virtually ignored. Research in this area might include the direct effects of health on working capacity, but should also include the indirect effects of illness on production decisions. Strategies used to overcome the constraints of poor health may prove to be economically significant, just as strategies used to overcome economic constraints are important for health. Understanding the impact of these coping strategies will be critical for identifying points of intervention and effective economic change.

Conclusions

The microperspectives discussed here are but four of the possible theoretical and methodological approaches to African food systems and the current crisis in food supply. Their strength lies in their ability to uncover the dynamics of food production and consumption behavior at the household, intra-household, and community level. Their interdisciplinary focus and emphasis on linkages promise a better understanding of the ways in which policy affects production. They may also help to identify those economic changes that have a potentially negative impact on nutrition and health.

The weakness of these approaches lies in the specificity of their results, and in the time and effort which micro-level studies entail. Obviously, they are not meant as a substitute for global perspectives, but as a complement to them. The long-term alleviation of food stress for sub-Saharan Africa will undoubtedly require many different approaches, both to macro-policy and to changes in micro-level behavior. It will certainly require an increased sensitivity to the goals and knowledge of African producers.

One of the positive aspects of the current focus on African food problems is the realization that imported technology may not be the efficient solution that development theorists have thought it to be. The failure of foreign technology has begun to force an appreciation for the complexity and variability of indigenous African production systems. These systems have a long history of (sometimes marginal) success in managing an unpredictable habitat. Management strategies have centered on diversity—of cultigens, of cropping practices, and of labor organization. Micro-level research increasingly shows that African food systems are not static, but are capable of responding to new challenges and opportunities. Improving those systems without destroying their flexibility must be the essential development challenge.

References

Alpers, E.A. 1975. *Ivory and Slaves in East Central Africa: Changing Patterns of International Trade in the Late Nineteenth Century*. London: Heinemann.

Amin, S. 1981. Underdevelopment and dependence in Black Africa—origins and contemporary forms. In *Political Economy of Africa*, ed. by D.L. Cohen and J. Daniel. London: Longman. pp. 28–44.

Armelagos, G.J., D.P. Van Gerven, D.L. Martin, and R. Huss-Ashmore. 1984. Effects of nutritional change on the skeletal biology of Northeast African (Sudanese Nubian) Populations. In *From Hunters to Farmers: The Causes and Consequences of Food Production in Africa*, ed. by J.D. Clark and S.A. Brandt. Berkely: University of California Press. pp. 132–146.

Asante, S.K.B. 1986. Food as a focus of national and regional policies in contemporary Africa. In *Food in Sub-Saharan Africa*, ed. by A. Hansen and D.E. McMillan. Boulder: Lynne Rienner. pp. 11–24.

Aykroyd, W.R. 1974. *The Conquest of Famine*. London: Chatto and Windus.

Baker, R. 1987. Linking and sinking: economic externalities and the persistance of destitution and famine in Africa. In *Drought and Hunger in Africa*, ed. by M.H. Glantz. Cambridge: Cambridge University Press. pp. 149–170.

Barton, J. 1986. The new biotechnology and African agricultural development. In *Proceedings: African Agricultural Development Conference*, ed by Y.T. Moses. Pomona: California State Polytechnic University. pp. 81–84.

Bates, R.H. 1981. *Markets and States in Tropical Africa: The Political Basis of Agricultural Policies*. Los Angeles: University of California Press.

———— 1986. The regulation of rural markets in Africa. In *Africa's Agrarian Crisis*, ed. by S.K. Commins, et. al. Boulder: Lynne Rienner. pp. 37–56.

Bates, R.P. 1986. Postharvest considerations in the food chain. In *Food in Sub-Saharan Africa* ed. by A. Hansen and D. McMillan. Boulder: Lynne Rienner. pp. 239–253.

Beck, B.D.A. 1982. Historical perspectives of cassava breeding in Africa. In *Root Crops in Eastern Africa,* Proceedings of a workshop held in Kigali, Rwanda, 23–27 November, 1980. Ottawa: International Development Research Center. pp. 13–18.

Bennett, K.A., R.H. Osborne, and R.J. Miller. 1975. Biocultural ecology. *Annual Reviews of Anthropology* 4:163–81.

Berg, E. 1981. *Accelerated Development in Sub-Saharan Africa: An Agenda for Action.* Washington, DC: World Bank.

Berry, S. 1986a. Social science perspective on food in Africa. In *Food in Sub-Saharan Africa* ed. by A. Hansen and D. McMillan. Boulder: Lynne Rienner. pp. 64–81.

——— 1986b. Macro-policy implications of research on rural households and farming systems. In *Understanding Africa's Rural Households and Farming Systems.* ed. by J.L. Moock. Boulder, CO: Westview Press. pp. 199–215.

Borton, J. and S. York. 1987. Experiences of the collection and use of micro-level data in disaster preparedness and managing emergency operations. Report on a workshop held at the London School of Hygiene and Tropical Medicine. London: Relief and Development Institute.

Boserup, E. 1970. *Woman's Role in Economic Development.* New York: St. Martin's Press.

Bryceson, D.F. 1981. Colonial famine responses—the Bagamoyo district of Tanganyika, 1920–61. *Food Policy* 6(2):91–104.

Bryson, R.A. 1974. A perspective on climatic change. *Science* 184:753–760.

Butzer, K.W. 1984. Long-term Nile flood variation and political discontinuities in Pharaonic Egypt. In *From Hunters to Farmers: The Causes and Consequences of Food Production in Africa.* ed. by J.D. Clark and S.A. Brandt. Berkely: University of California Press. pp. 102–112.

Campbell, A. 1986. The use of wild food plants, and drought in Botswana. *Journal of Arid Environments* 11:81–91.

Campbell, D.J. and D.D. Trechter. 1982. Strategies for coping with food consumption shortage in the Mandara Mountains region of North Cameroon. *Social Science and Medicine* 16:2117–2127.

Cassanelli, L. 1981. Drought and famine in Somalia: Pastoral strategies through the twentieth century. Paper presented to the Seminar on Food Production Systems and Environmental Rehabilitation in Somalia, National Academy of Sciences, Washington DC.

——— 1982. *The Shaping of Somali Society.* Philadelphia: University of Pennsylvania Press.

Charney, J.G. 1975. Dynamics of deserts and drought in the Sahel. *Quarterly Journal of the Royal Meterological Society* 101:193–202.

Cohen, M.N. and G.J. Armelagos, eds. 1984. *Paleopathology at the Origins of Agriculture*. New York: Academic Press.

Colson, E. 1979. In good years and bad: Food strategies in self-reliant societies. *Journal of Anthropological Research* 35(1): 18–29.

Commins, S.K. 1986. Peasants and rural development in Liberia. In *Africa's Agrarian Crisis*, ed. by. S.K. Commins, et. al. Boulder: Lynne Rienner. pp. 133–152.

Commins, S.K., M.F. Lofchie, and R. Payne, eds. 1986. *Africa's Agrarian Crisis: The Roots of Famine*. Boulder, CO: Lynne Rienner.

Cooke, H.J. 1979. Botswana's present climate and the evidence for past change. In *Symposium on Drought in Botswana*, ed. by M.T. Hinchey. The Botswana Society. Hanover, NH: University Press of New England. pp. 53–8.

Davis, R.H., Jr. 1986. Agriculture, food, and the colonial period. In *Food in Sub-Saharan Africa*, ed. by A. Hansen and D.E. McMillan. Boulder: Lynne Rienner. pp. 151–168.

Degefu, W. 1987. Some aspects of meteorological drought in Ethiopia. In *Drought and Hunger in Africa*, ed. by M.H. Glantz. Cambridge: Cambridge University Press. pp. 23–36.

Dias, J.R. 1981. Famine and disease in the history of Angola c. 1830–1930. *Journal of African History* 22:349–378.

Faruqee, R. and R. Gulhati. 1983. *Rapid Population Growth in Sub-Saharan Africa: Issues and Policies*. World Bank Staff Working Papers No. 559. Washington DC: World Bank.

Fleuret, A. 1986. Indigenous responses to drought in Sub-Saharan Africa. *Disasters* 10:224–229.

Fleuret, P. and A. Fleuret. 1980. Nutrition, consumption, and agricultural change. *Human Organization* 39:250–60.

Foulks, J. 1981. Human trypanosomiasis in Africa. *British Medical Journal* 283:11722–1174.

Frank, A.G. 1969. *Latin America: Underdevelopment and Revolution*. New York: Monthly Review Press.

Franke, R.W. and B.H. Chasin. 1980. *Seeds of Famine: Ecological Destruction and the Development Dilemma in the West African Sahel*. Montclair, NJ: Allenheld.

Frankenberger, T. 1985. *Adding a Food Consumption Perspective to Farming Systems Research*. Washington, DC: USDA.

Franklin, R.R., C.F. Jacobs, and W.E. Bertrand. 1981. Illness in Black Africans. In *Biocultural Aspects of Disease*, ed. by H.R. Rothschild. New York: Academic Press. pp. 484–530.

Gilbert, E.J., D.W. Norman, and F.E. Winch. 1980. *Farming Systems Research: A Critical Appraisal*. MSU Development Paper No. 6. East Lansing: Michigan State University.

Glantz, M.H., ed. 1987a. *Drought and Hunger in Africa: Denying Famine a Future.* Cambridge: New York: Cambridge University Press.

―――― 1987b. Drought and economic development in Sub-Saharan Africa. In *Drought and Hunger in Africa,* ed. by M.H. Glantz. Cambridge: Cambridge University Press. pp. 37–58.

Grant, J.P. 1985. *The State of the World's Children 1985.* UNICEF. Cambridge: Oxford University Press.

Guyer, J.I. 1986. Intra-household processes and Farming Systems Research: Perspectives from anthropology. In *Understanding Africa's Rural Households and Farming Systems,* ed. by J.L. Moock. Boulder: Westview Press. pp. 92–104.

Hansen, A. and D.E. McMillan, eds. 1986. *Food in Sub-Saharan Africa.* Boulder, CO: Lynne Rienner.

Hardin, G.J. 1968. The tragedy of the commons. *Science* 162:1243–8.

Horowitz, M.M. and P.D. Little. 1987. African pastoralism and poverty: some implications for drought and famine. In *Drought and Hunger in Africa,* ed. by M.H. Glantz. Cambridge: Cambridge University Press. pp. 59–82.

Horowitz, M.M. and M. Salem-Murdock. 1987. The political economy of desertification in White Nile Province, Sudan. In *Lands at Risk in the Third World,* ed. by P.D. Little and M.M. Horowitz, with A.E. Nyerges. Boulder, CO: Westview Press. pp. 95–114.

Huss-Ashmore, R. 1984. Food, health, and agricultural underdevelopment in Lesotho. Paper presented to the American Anthropological Association, Annual Meeting, Denver.

Huss-Ashmore, R. and J.J. Curry. 1986. Nutritional consequences to on-farm research in Swaziland. In *Farming Systems Research and Extension: Food and Feed,* ed. by C.B. Flora and M. Tomaceck. Farming Systems Research Paper No. 13. Manhattan, KS: Kansas State University.

Huss-Ashmore, R. and F.E. Johnston. 1985. Bioanthropological research in developing countries. *Annual Reviews of Anthropology* 14:475–528.

Huss-Ashmore, R. and R.B. Thomas. 1988. A framework for analysing uncertainty in highland areas. In *Coping with Uncertainty in Food Supply,* ed. by I. DeGarine and G.A. Harrison. London: Oxford University Press. pp. 452–468.

Hyden, G. 1980. *Beyond Ujamaa in Tanzania.* Berkely: University of California Press.

―――― 1986. The invisible economy of smallholder agriculture in Africa. In *Understanding Africa's Rural Households and Farming Systems,* ed. by J.L. Moock. Boulder, CO: Westview Press.

Independent Commission on International Humanitarian Issues. 1985. *Famine: A Man-Made Disaster?* New York: Vintage Books.

International Bank for Reconstruction and Development. 1975. *Lesotho: A Development Challenge.* Washington, DC: World Bank.

Josserand, H.P. 1984. Farmer's consumption of an imported cereal and the cash/food-crop decision. *Food Policy* 9:27–34.

Katz, S.H. 1987. Food and biocultural evolution: A model for the investigation of modern nutritional problems. In *Nutritional Anthropology*, ed. by F.E. Johnston. New York: Alan R. Liss. pp. 41–63.

Katz, S.H., M. Hediger, and L. Valleroy. 1975. The anthropological and nutritional significance of traditional maize processing techniques in the New World. In *Biosocial Interrelations in Population Adaptation*, ed. by E. Watts, F.E. Johnston, and G.W. Lasker. The Hague: Mouton Press. pp. 195–232.

Katz, S.H. and J. Shall. 1979. Fava bean consumption and biocultural evolution. *Medical Anthropology* 4:459–77.

Kjekshus, H. 1977. *Ecology Control and Economic Development in East African History*. Berkely: University of California Press.

Kloos, H. 1982. Development, drought, and famine in the Awash Valley of Ethiopia. *African Studies Review* 25: 21–48.

Koehn, P. 1979. Ethiopia: Famine, food production, and changes in the legal order. *African Studies Review* 22:51–71.

Kraus, J. 1986. The political economy of agrarian regression in Ghana. In *Africa's Agrarian Crisis*, ed. by S.K. Commins, et. al. Boulder: Lynne Rienner. pp. 103–132.

Lal, R. 1979. The role of physical properties in maintaining productivity of soils in the tropics. In *Soil Physical Properties and Crop Production in the Tropics*, ed. by R. Lal and D.J. Greenland. Chichester: Wiley.

Lawrence, M., F. Lawrence, T.J. Cole, W.A. Coward, J. Singh, and R.G. Whitehead. 1985. Seasonal pattern of activity and its nutritional consequences in the Gambia. IFPRI/FAO/USAID Workshop on Seasonal Causes of Household Food Insecurity, Policy Implications and Research Needs. Annapolis, MD.

Leatherman, T., and R.B. Thomas 1987. Patterns of illness and work disruption in a rural Andean population. *American Journal of Physical Anthropology* 72(2):223.

Lemarchand, R. 1986. The political economy of food issues. In *Food in Sub-Saharan Africa*, ed. by A. Hansen and D.E. McMillan. Boulder: Lynne Rienner. pp. 25–42.

Livingstone, F.B. 1958. Anthropological implications of sickle cell gene distribution in West Africa. *American Anthropologist* 60:533–62.

Lofchie, M.F. 1986. Africa's agricultural crisis: An overview. In *Africa's Agrarian Crisis*, ed. by. S.K. Commins, et.al. Boulder: Lynne Rienner. pp. 3–18.

———— 1987. The decline of African agriculture: an internalist perspective. In *Drought and Hunger in Africa*, ed. by M.H. Glantz. Cambridge: Cambridge University Press.

Low, A. 1986. On-farm research and household economics. In *Understanding Africa's Rural Households and Farming Systems*, ed. by J.L. Moock. Boulder: Westview Press. pp. 71–91.

Martin, D.L., G.J. Armelagos, A.H. Goodman, and D.P. Van Gerven. 1984. The effects of socioeconomic change in prehistoric Africa: Sudanese Nubian case study. In *Paleopathology at the Origins of Agriculture*, ed. by M.N. Cohen and G.J. Armelagos. New York: Academic Press. pp. 193–216.

Meillassoux, C. 1981. *Maidens, Meal, and Money*. Cambridge: Cambridge University Press.

Mellor, J.W. and S. Gavian. 1987. Famine: Causes, prevention, and relief. *Science* 235:539–544.

Miller, J.C. 1982. The significance of drought, disease, and famine in the agriculturally marginal zones of West-Central Africa. *Journal of African History* 23: 17–61.

Moock, J.L., ed. 1986. *Understanding Africa's Rural Households and Farming Systems*. Boulder, CO: Westview Press

Moran, E.F. 1987. Monitoring fertility degradation of agricultural lands in the lowland tropics. In *Lands at Risk in the Third World*, ed. by. P.D. Little, M.M. Horowitz, with A.E. Nyerges. Boulder, CO: Westview Press. pp. 69–91.

Moses, Y.T., ed. 1985. *Proceedings: African Agricultural Development Conference*. Pomona: California State Polytechnic University.

Murray, C. 1981. *Families Divided: The Impact of Migrant Labour in Lesotho*. Johannesburg: Ravan.

Netting, R.M. 1987. Book review: *Indigenous Agricultural Revolution*, by P. Richards. *American Anthropologist* 89(1):240–1.

Nicholson, S.E. 1979. The methodology of historical climate reconstruction and its application to Africa. *Journal of African History* 20(1):31–49.

———— 1986. Climate, drought, and famine in Africa. In *Food in Sub-Saharan Africa*, ed. by A. Hansen and D.E. McMillan. Boulder: Lynne Rienner. pp. 107–128.

Njoku, J.E.E. 1986. *Malthusianism: An African Dilemma*. Metuchen, NJ: Scarecrow Press.

Norman, D.W. 1977. The rationalization of intercropping. *African Environment* 2 and 3:97–109.

Nyerges, A.E. 1987. Development in the Guinea Savanna. *Science* 238:1637–8.

Odhiambo, T.R. 1987. The innovative environment for increased food production. Address presented at the International Colloquium on World Food Issues on "Science, Ethics, and Food," Washington, DC: The Smithsonian Institution.

Office of Technology Assessment. 1984. *Africa Tomorrow: Issues in Technology, Agriculture, and U.S. Foreign Aid*. Washington, DC: OTA.

Ogle, B. and L.E. Grivetti. 1985. Legacy of the chameleon: edible wild plants in the Kingdom of Swaziland, Southern Africa. A cultural, ecological, nutritional study. Part IV—Nutritional analysis and conclusions. *Ecology of Food and Nutrition* 17:41–64.

Okigbo, B. 1986. The African condition and the need for urgent and appropriate action. In *Proceedings: African Agricultural Development Conference*, ed. by Y.T. Moses. Pomona: California Polytechnic University. pp. 25–37.

Payne, R., L. Rummel, and M.H. Glantz. 1987. Denying famine a future: Concluding remarks. In *Drought and Hunger in Africa*, ed. by M.H. Glantz. Boulder, CO: Westview Press. pp. 433–43.

Peterson, S. 1986. Neglecting the poor: State policy toward the smallholder in Kenya. In *Africa's Agrarian Crisis*, ed. by S.K. Commins, et. al. Boulder: Lynne Rienner. pp. 59–83.

Piot, P., F.A. Plummer, F.S. Mhalu, J-L. Lamboray, J. Chin, and J.M. Mann. 1988. AIDS: an international perspective. *Science* 239:573–9.

Popenoe, H. 1986. African soils: Opportunities and constraints. In *Food in Sub-Saharan Africa*, ed. by A. Hansen and D.E. McMillan. Boulder, CO: Lynne Rienner. pp. 169–176.

Richards, P. 1983. Ecological change and the politics of African land use. *African Studies Review* 26(2):1–72.

———— 1985. *Indigenous Agricultural Revolution: Ecology and Food Production in West Africa*. Boulder: Westview Press.

Robson, J.R.K., ed. 1981. *Famine: Its Causes, Effects, and Management*. New York: Gordon and Breach.

Sandford, S. 1983. *Management of Pastoral Development in the Third World*. Chichester: John Wiley and Sons.

Scotch, N. 1960. A preliminary report on the relation of sociocultural factors to hypertension among the Zulu. *Annals of the New York Academy of Sciences* 84: 1000–9.

Seaman, J., J. Holt, and J. Rivers. 1978. The effects of drought on human nutrition in an Ethiopian province. *International Journal of Epidemiology* 7(1):31–40

Sen, A. 1981. *Poverty and Famines: An Essay on Entitlement and Deprivation*. Oxford: Clarendon Press.

Shao, J. 1986. Politics and the food production crisis in Tanzania. In *Africa's Agrarian Crisis*, ed. by S.K. Commins, et.al. Boulder: Lynne Rienner. pp. 84–102.

Shaw, T.M. 1987. Towards a political economy of the African crisis: Diplomacy, debates, and dialectics. In *Drought and Hunger in Africa*, ed. by M.H. Glantz. Cambridge: Cambridge University Press. pp. 127–47.

Shove, D.J. 1977. African droughts and the spectrum of time. In *Drought in Africa*. 2. African Environment Special Report 6, ed. by D. Dalby, R.J. Harrison Church, and F. Bezzaz. London: International African Institute. pp. 38–53.

Smiley, X. 1982. Misunderstanding Africa. *The Atlantic Monthly* (September):70–79.

Spring, A. 1986. Women farmers and food in Africa: Some considerations and suggested solutions. In *Food in Sub-Saharan Africa*, ed. by A. Hansen and D.E. McMillan. Boulder: Lynne Rienner. pp. 332–348.

Staatz, J.M. and C.K. Eicher. 1986. Agricultural development ideas in historical perspective. In *Food in Sub-Saharan Africa,* ed. by A. Hansen and D.E. McMillan. Boulder: Lynne Rienner. pp. 43–63.

Stini, W.A. 1975. Adaptive strategies of human populations under nutritional stress. *Biosocial Interrelations in Population Adaptation,* ed. by E.S. Watts, F.E. Johnston, and G.W. Lasker. The Hague: Mouton Press. pp. 19–42.

Swift, J. 1977. Pastoral development in Somalia: Herding cooperatives as a strategy against desertification and famine. In *Desertification: Environmental Degradation in and around Arid Lands,* ed. by M.H. Glantz. Boulder, CO: Westview Press. pp. 275–306.

Thomas, R.B. 1973. *Human Adaptation to a High Andean Energy Flow System.* Occasional Papers in Anthropology, No. 7. Department of Anthropology, Pennsylvania State University, University Park.

Thomas, R.B., B. Winterhalder, and S.D. McRae. 1979. An anthropological approach to human ecology and adaptive dynamics. *Yearbook of Physical Anthropology* 22: 1–46.

Torry, W.I. 1979. Anthropological studies in hazardous environments: Past trends and new horizons. *Current Anthropology* 20(3):517–538.

_____ 1984. Social science research on famine: A critical evaluation. *Human Ecology* 12(3):227–252.

_____ 1986. Economic development, drought, and famines: Some limitations of dependency explanations. *GeoJournal* 12:5–8.

Townsend, J. and J.H. Momsen. 1987. Towards a geography of gender in developing market economies. In *Geography of Gender in the Third World,* ed. by J.H. Momsen and J. Townsend. Albany: State University of New York Press. pp. 27–81.

Vayda, A.P. 1983. Progressive contextualization: methods for research in human ecology. *Human Ecology* 11(3):265–81.

Vayda, A.P. and B.J. McKay. 1975. New directions in ecology and ecological anthropology. *Annual Reviews of Anthropology* 4:293–306.

Vermeer, D.E. 1981. Collision of climate, cattle, and culture in Mauritania during the 1970's. *Geographical Review* 71(3):281–297.

Walsh, J. 1988a. Famine early warning wins its spurs. *Science* 239:249–250.

_____ 1988b. Second chance for rice research center. *Science* 239:969–70.

Watkins, S.C. and J. Menken. 1985. Famines in historical perspective. *Population and Development Review* 11(4):647–676.

Watts, E., F.E. Johnston, and G.W. Lasker, eds. 1975. *Biosocial Interrelations in Population Adaptation.* The Hague: Mouton.

Watts, M. 1983. *Silent Violence: Food, Famine, and Peasantry in Northern Nigeria.* Berkely: University of California Press.

Weaver, J. and K. Jameson. 1981. *Economic Development: Competing Paradigms.* Washington, DC: University Press of America.

Webster, J.B. 1979. Drought and migration: The Lake Malawi Littoral as a region of refuge. In *Symposium on Drought in Botswana*, ed. by M.T. Hinchey. The Botswana Society. Hanover, NH: University Press of New England. pp. 148–157.

Wood, C.A. 1977. A preliminary chronology of Ethiopian droughts. In *Drought in Africa*—2, African Environment Special Report 6, ed. by D. Dalby, R.J. Harrison Church, and F. Bezzaz. London: International African Institute. pp. 68–73.

Woodhouse, P. *The Green Revolution and Food Security in Africa: Issues in Research and Technology Development*. DPP Working Paper No. 10. Milton Keynes: The Open University.

Wyndham, C. 1979. Mortality from cardiovascular diseases in the various population groups in the Republic of South Africa. *South African Medical Journal* 56:1023–30.

THE CONTEXT OF
FOOD STRESS IN AFRICA

Drought, Famine, and the Seasons in Sub-Saharan Africa

Michael H. Glantz

Environmental and Societal Impacts Group
National Center for Atmospheric Research*
Boulder, Colorado 80307

> The essential point is that country life is
> potentially rich with signals of crisis, but
> these are seasonal.
> —ICIHI, 1985, p. 40

Introduction

The dominant view of climate held within the development community, as late as the early 1970s, was that of a fixed boundary condition; that is, a constant given about which society could do little (Glantz 1987). As one report questioned,

> By any rational definition of 'underdeveloped country' most of them are entirely—or partially—in the tropics. Is [a hot tropical] climate the common factor that keeps them underdeveloped? (Greenwood 1957:vii)

Those who held this view contended that the climatic characteristics of a region set the stage for its economic and social development. As such, climate was considered a major, if not dominant, constraint to economic and social development in many locations around the world. The view was that either a region received enough rain for agricultural production and yields and production would be high, or it did not and yields and production would be low and erratic. It was believed that local populations had adjusted their agricultural activities to prepare for the perceived average seasonal conditions that their societies faced.

---

*The National Center for Atmospheric Research is sponsored by the National Science Foundation.

Recently, however, there have been two periods of intensified worldwide climate anomalies, especially drought. The first occurrence of widespread drought took place in 1972–73 (Fig. 1). This shattered the perception of climate as a fixed boundary condition, for it made clear that climate was not a steady unchanging state. After the climate-related food shortages of 1972 and 1973, climate variability and climate change became the important foci of attention for scientific researchers and policymakers (WMO 1979).

Climate is now coming to be viewed by climate impacts researchers as constantly changing from monthly to decadal and longer time scales. Since 1972, attention has focused on the interannual variability of climate, how such variability affects society, and how a society might prepare itself for coping with climate-related surpluses and shortfalls in food production. The variability of precipitation and temperature is of great importance to all societies, but especially to those dependent on agriculture. This became clearer once again during the second set of devastating droughts which occurred in 1982–83 (Fig. 2).

Although there were major droughts and climate-induced food shortages around the globe—in various parts of Africa, India, China, Indonesia, Brazil—famines occurred only in Africa. Whereas in the early part of this century people spoke about China as the land of famine, and later they referred to India in the same way, both of these countries have recently been successful in dealing with food production and distribution problems. Today, sub-Saharan Africa is considered the land of famine, with several famines having occurred, coincidentally, in the post-independence period. There has been considerable speculation about the causes of these famines with "blame" being attributed either to purely physical phemonena, such as drought, or to purely social, political, or economic factors.

Some of the recent regional droughts in Africa began as early as 1968 and apparently continued into the mid-1980s, as suggested by the following regional rainfall index (Fig. 3) for the West African Sahel (Lamb 1985; Lamb, personal communication).

Concern about African droughts, however, declined abruptly in 1974 with the apparent return to near-normal rainfall. Even though the meteorological conditions for that period had not really returned to "normal," a general belief existed that the Sahelian and Ethiopian droughts had ended and that life at the village level and among the

DROUGHTS

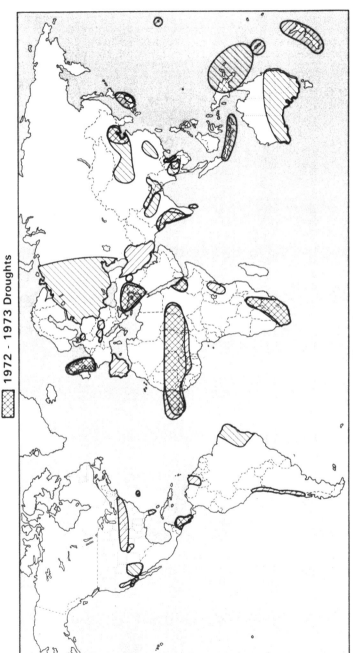

1972 Droughts (March - December)

1973 Droughts (January - August)

1972 - 1973 Droughts

Figure 1

CLIMATE IMPACTS MAP
DROUGHTS

1982 Droughts (January - December)

1983 Droughts (January - August)

1982 - 1983 Droughts

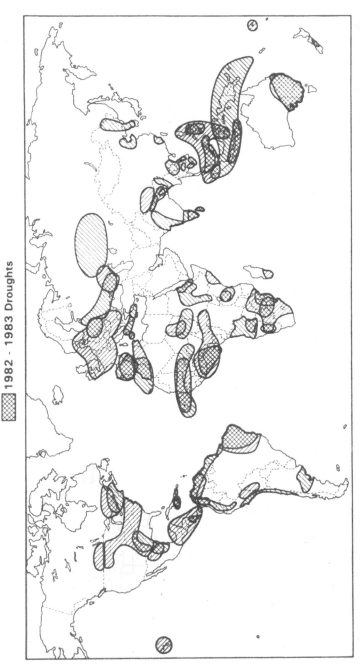

pastoralists would return to the relatively favorable predrought levels. Recently, Nicholson (1979, 1983:1986) commented on this apparent end to drought in the Sahel in the mid-1970s, noting that

> rainfall in 1974 and 1975 was still 15–20% below normal . . . but compared to the previous years [1968–73], conditions had dramatically improved and drought was generally presumed to have ended. The apparent return of 'normal' economic and human conditions supported this assumption.

SUB-SAHARAN RAINFALL INDEX

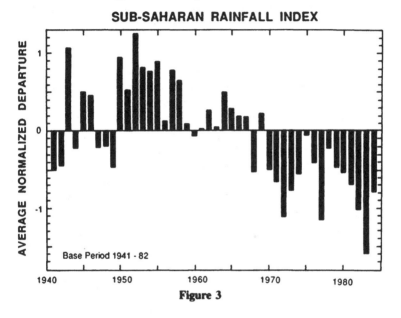

Figure 3

Yet, once again in the early 1980s much of Africa seemed to be plagued by a run of intensified drought conditions, sparking a call for emergency food relief from governmental and nongovernmental organizations alike.

The initial (and still prevalent) popular view has been that severe drought conditions in Africa have caused widespread famines, mass migrations, environmental degradation, and internal unrest. However, evidence strongly suggests that, while drought may have been an important factor in each of these processes, and especially in the recent food crises in various African countries, it was but one of several factors (Glantz 1987). As Morse (1987:xiv), former Director of the United Nations Development Program, has suggested,

> . . . drought itself is not the fundamental problem in sub-Saharan Africa. . . . The present drought has, however, intensified the interaction of the factors impeding development in Africa; it has laid bare the African development crisis.

A recent report on famine goes a step further, noting that

> At each stage from its genesis in rural poverty and food-production failures through to the reduction of communities to destitution and starvation, famine is avoidable. More than that, its causes are much more complex than just bad luck with the weather. The simple assumption that, if the rains fail . . . , less food will be grown and people will inevitably starve, may be a comfortable abdication of any human responsibility for what has happened (ICIHI 1985:24).

Drought's contribution to recent food (and agrarian) crises can be properly evaluated only along with consideration of other coexisting internal political, economic, fiscal, military, and demographic factors as well as external factors such as the mounting international debt burden, worsening terms of trade, and international involvement such as in Ethiopia, Mozambique, and Angola. Perhaps what is equally important as drought and other factors that generate food shortages and famine is a consideration of seasonality and a consideration of how drought affects (most often exacerbates) the existing linkages between the seasons, food production, and various aspects of rural poverty.

The purpose of this paper is to explore in a preliminary way some of the linkages between drought, desertification, famine, and the seasons. The stress that the different seasons produce for farmers in sub-Saharan Africa is explored. Different types of drought are then considered, as well as the effects that droughts might have on the seasonal rhythm of agricultural activities and thus on the usual hardships that farmers and their families face. Finally, the relationship between drought and desertification and drought and famine are briefly examined. An attempt is made to integrate the effects of seasonality into these relationships. It is important to note that this is an exploratory study. Therefore the relationships suggested require further multidisciplinary investigation.

The Seasons

The rhythm of the seasons is something to which every developed and developing society has had to accommodate its climate-dependent activities. The onset and duration of the rainfall as well as its distribution within the seasons and between seasons represents an important but often neglected aspect of climate and of food production in sub-Saharan Africa. A relatively small number of scholars have addressed the impacts of the seasons on rural well-being and rural poverty in general (Chambers et al. 1981) and in a specific local context (e.g., Watts 1983a, b). Yet, I believe that the annual progression of the seasons and its effects on rural poverty must be integrated into the existing literature on drought, desertification, famine and development. While the latter processes are highly visible and often spectacular, taking on a crisis mode, those processes only worsen the effects of an already existing, less spectacular, but potentially equally devastating climatic process, the changing of the seasons.

A rainfall seasonality index (Fig. 4) was presented in Chambers et al. (1981). This index essentially highlights the contrast between seasons of rainfall amounts in different regions of sub-Saharan Africa. It does not separate different types of rainfall regimes, such as one annual rainfall peak (unimodal) or two such peaks (bimodal). The

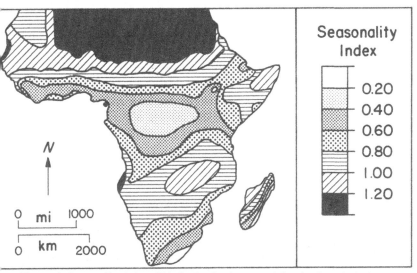

Figure 4 Seasonality index. This is simply the sum of the absolute deviations of mean *monthly* rainfall from the overall mean, divided by mean *annual* rainfall. In theory this index can vary between 0.00 (if all months have equal amounts of rain), and 1.83 (if all rain is concentrated into a single month). (Walsh 1980, as quoted in Chambers et al. 1981).

chart, in fact, is quite similar to one for interannual rainfall variability which indicates that the higher the interannual rainfall variability, the higher the probability of drought occurrence. Societies in such regions are most at risk from the vagaries of climate, although societies subject to lower interannual variability are not immune from such vagaries.

The progression of the seasons is a climatic characteristic that interacts with drought and famine, as, for example, suggested in a UN FAO report which noted that "preharvest shortages are sometimes acute and lead to famine conditions in years when crops fail as a result of drought" (1962:29). Preharvest shortages are a common occurrence in many African societies. Such shortages have been referred to as periods of seasonal hunger, that is, periods during which the nutritional condition of rural population declines. Such periods paradoxically occur during the wet season and become acute just prior to harvest.

The importance of rainfall seasonality has been explicitly recognized by scientists in specific areas of research such as human health (e.g., Huss-Ashmore 1982, Schofield 1974), but those dealing with broader issues of economic development have generally given little attention to how such seasonality might act as a constraint upon this development.[1] There are, of course, some notable exceptions (e.g., Chambers et al. 1981, Watts 1983a). Chambers et al. (1979:3) recently summarized the disparate works that have addressed the issue of seasonality as it relates to various aspects of rural poverty in the Third World, noting that

> besides climate, seasonal patterns are also found in labour demand in agriculture and pastoralism, in vital events, in migration, in energy balance, in nutrition, in

---

[1] While much of this paper is geared toward the agricultural population, similar considerations apply to pastoral communities. There are many reports and articles that discuss the process by which pastoralists have become more vulnerable to the vagaries of climate. Many of these reports point to political and economic factors, including few if any incentives from their governments to cull herds, pressure to maintain herds that are often larger than the exploited ecosystems can maintain in periods of climatic stress, the unplanned and uncontrolled construction of deep wells, low prices offered for meat in the urban centers, and so forth. All of these actions and more increase the vulnerability of pastoral populations to lengthy drought episodes (see, for example, Monod 1975; Dahl and Hjort 1976).

tropical diseases, in the condition of women and children, in the economics of agriculture, and in social relations, and in government interventions.

One of the most important issues related to seasonality and poverty is food production. Moreover, there is a seasonal cycle to food availability as well (e.g., Watts 1983a; Chambers et al. 1981).

Some regions have more pronounced seasonality than others. Some have a short rainy season which coincides with summer and the highest annual monthly mean temperatures. Others have rainfall in the winter months which is important to agricultural activities (e.g., Morocco). Still others have high amounts of rainfall all year long (e.g., the Brazilian Amazon). Seasons vary in the timing of their onset, in length, in temperature extremes, in rainfall amounts, and in rainfall distribution within the season. Even in years where the total amount of annual precipitation appears to be average, an agricultural drought may occur because of an irregular distribution of rainfall within the rainy season (see, for example, Dennett et al. 1985, on intraseasonal changes in rainfall distribution in the West African Sahel). The inhabitants of the different regions in sub-Saharan Africa have, in general, attempted to adjust their agricultural activities and practices to prepare for what might be considered average seasonal conditions.

Some societies are clearly less vulnerable, for a variety of reasons (including technological factors), to climate anomalies than are others. A drought in the U.S. Great Plains, for example, no longer leads to widespread malnutrition, migration, food shortages, and famine as was the case in the 1930s and earlier, but recent droughts in African countries such as Ethiopia and Mozambique still had devastating effects on the well-being of their populations (e.g., Hagman et al. 1984: 13). Moreover, not all segments of society are equally affected. For example, some groups (usually the poorer ones) pursue activities such as dryland farming in climatically marginal agricultural areas that provide them with little flexibility in responding to the vagaries of climate. On this point Sen (1981:43) noted that

> Indeed it is by no means clear that there has ever occurred a famine in which all groups in a country have suffered from starvation, since different groups typically do have very different commanding powers over food, and an over-all shortage brings out the contrasting powers in stark clarity.

Some members of society benefit from seasonality (e.g., rich peasants, grain merchants) at the expense of the larger fraction of rural

Table 1. Possible societal responses to the cycle of the seasons during favorable and drought-plagued periods.

	(Usual) seasonal impact	Prolonged drought impact
Post-Harvest (early dry season)	• food available • food prices decline • migrant laborers return to villages • morbidity declines • mortality declines • nutritional status improves "Post-harvest food availability largely determines the size and distribution of village calorie suplies, not just at the time but until the next harvest" (Schofield 1974:23).	• food availability declines • food prices continue to rise • domestic food self-sufficiency jeopardized • families borrow from kin/friends • disposal of assets for money • migrants do not return • additional family members migrate • nutritional intake deteriorates • morbidity stays high or increases
Dry Season (late dry season)	• food becomes less available • food prices increase • nutritional status (especially women, children) declines • drinking water becomes scarce • dry season irrigation becomes more important	

	• food prices go even higher • little work available in rural areas to earn cash • distress sales increase: livestock, stored grain, household goods • food unattainable (due to lack of availability, high price) • food-gathering activities intensify • nutritional status declines • seeds eaten (reduces future production) • eat plants/leaves, etc., not usually eaten • children's illnesses increase • morbidity increases • mortality increases • irrigation becomes limited as stream-flow is reduced • call on wider networks; reliance on more distant kin, and on national and international agencies
Wet Season (early wet season)	• "hunger season" begins • wild food use begins • gathering added to agricultural labor • high food prices • poor families borrow agricultural inputs • distress borrowing/distress sales • draft animals in relatively weak condition • diseases more prevalent • morbidity increases "During the wet season itself when seasonal food shortages peaked, hardship could be partially alleviated by participation in communal work parties and short-distance migration making use of the variation in the onset of the rains (and hence in the timing of planting, weeding, and harvest)" (Watts 1983:49).
Pre-Harvest (late wet season)	• food prices are at seasonal high • food intake is lowest (especially women and children) • body weights decline • "hunger season" peaks "Peak-season labour inputs often coincide with seasonal food shortages, as on-farm grain stocks are running low before prices begin to be pulled down by the impending harvest" (Schofield 1974:23).

poor (especially during periods of cultivation when work demands are at a peak and the nutritional status of the peasant farmers, especially women and children, is at an ebb).

Keeping in mind that many social, economic, and political factors affect the ability of groups to cope with the societal impacts of seasonality, making it difficult to generalize, the following chart (Table 1) represents a generalized situation of the effects of seasonality on an agricultural community. It does not necessarily apply to any particular community. The first column of the chart is based on a scenario presented in Chambers et al. (1979). It is presented here to suggest to the reader how the "usual" rhythm of the progression of the seasons might affect the rural populations in a community faced with a wet season and a dry season. The second column of the chart suggests how drought might affect the seasonal rhythm of agricultural activities.

The impact of drought on society will vary in part according to its timing. If it occurs at the onset of the growing season, for example, those farmers in a position to do so might replant several times thereby using up their seed reserves. If drought occurs in midseason, the number of options available to farmers, such as the planting of varieties that require shorter growing seasons, would be much less, as the growing season would have already been considerably shortened. Recent research on rainfall in the West African Sahel (Dennett et al. 1985) has suggested that there had been a decline in midseason rainfall (August) over the last few decades, a decline which has exacerbated severe food shortages in that region.

Drought tends to intensify seasonal hunger and to spread it across other seasons. As a result of drought, grain prices in the marketplace rise sharply, as illustrated in the following graph (Fig. 5).

Prolonged drought at first will adversely affect the poorest elements of rural society and, as it continues, its effects will spread to the relatively more affluent segments of society. As the poorer elements put their energies into surviving from one season to the next, they become extremely vulnerable to the impact of any additional insult such as drought, disease, or war (Rebecca Huss-Ashmore, 1986, personal communication). Thus, the existence of seasonal hunger is a critical aspect with regard to the levels of vulnerability that might be induced in a population, as well as to the level of inability of those populations to buffer themselves from other problems. Drought can

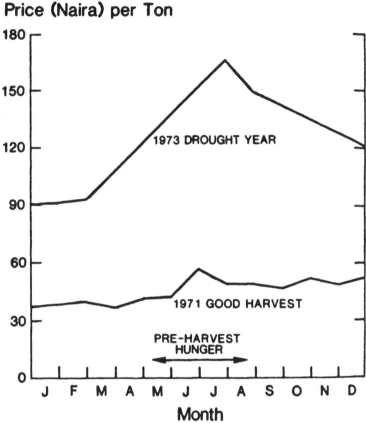

Figure 5. Interseason millet prices, from Kaita District Office (Nigeria) (Watts 1983a).

eventually convert the already existing widespread chronic malnutri- tion and seasonal hunger into full-fledged famine.

Drought

It is important to know the difference between meteorological, agri- cultural, and hydrologic droughts. Meteorological drought can be de- fined as a specified percentage reduction in precipitation over a given period of time. One view of drought is a 25 to 50% reduction in average annual precipitation. This information by itself is often not very useful to farmers because, although the amount of precipitation may be reduced in a given time period, it might fall at times favorable for crop growth and development.

The origin of the word "drought" in English can be found in the Anglo-Saxon word *drugoth,* meaning dry ground (Cooke 1978). This meaning corresponds best with an agricultural as opposed to a meteorological drought. Wang'ati (1985) captured the essence of an agricultural drought when he wrote that such a drought might be defined as "the lack of adequate soil moisture to sustain crop growth and production." He also observed that "the severity of agricultural droughts . . . depends on climatic and soil factors and the ability of the crops grown to adapt to the constraints of soil moisture availability" (1985:19).

A hydrologic drought occurs when a reduction in streamflow adversely affects human activities. Streamflow is obviously affected by seasonal precipitation. In many parts of sub-Saharan Africa farmers cultivate the area adjacent to rivers and standing bodies of water, from seasonal ponds to perennial lakes. During low streamflow irrigation becomes unavailable. The same situation occurs for standing bodies of water which, during drought, become greatly diminished or disappear completely, thereby reducing the area that might be put into cultivation.

Thus, reference to meteorological drought, by itself, does not fully explain production-related food shortages, nor does agricultural or hydrologic drought. The type of drought affecting food production must be identified in each particular case study, as its effect on the problems associated with seasonality will vary from one case to another.

As Table 1 suggests, drought (as well as average but poorly distributed intraseasonal rainfall) disrupts the normal rhythm of the seasons and the socioeconomic activities attuned to that seasonal rhythm. As mentioned earlier, a delay in the onset of the rainy season may shorten the length of the growing season. It can also cause repeated false starts in planting as seeds sown fail to receive enough moisture to germinate. This may prompt migration to neighboring agricultural areas that have received adequate early rains.

Drought can also accelerate the "normal" rates of seasonal migration of young men in search of wage labor to buy food for their families following the dry season. Severe and lengthy droughts can sharply increase the number of rural migrants to urban areas.[2] Such migration leaves even fewer people (often women, children, and the elderly) to produce food in the rural areas (Timberlake 1985:58). Drought can also leave local farmers who grow cash crops extremely vulnerable to food shortages. During prolonged droughts, they are unable either to grow enough food to subsist or to generate enough cash from the sale of their drought-decimated cash crops to buy food in the marketplace. Eventually they too migrate to other rural areas or to urban centers.

Drought also takes a heavy toll on draft animals, as it did in Ethiopia in the 1982–84 drought. The Ethiopian drought sharply reduced the draft animal population in much of the northern part of the country and, as a result, when the rains returned, fewer animals were available for tilling the soil. Thus, the amount of land that could be seeded was considerably less than it had been before the drought (McCann 1987).

There are numerous views about the role of drought in agricultural production. It is important to be aware of these differing views because each one warrants a different response by society to mitigate drought's impacts. An erroneous view can lead to erroneous actions by society. For example, one view within the U.S. Department of Agriculture of the effects of weather on the food balance situation in sub-Saharan Africa appears to be misleading, as suggested by the following chart (Fig. 6), which depicts weather (this must include

---

[2]Urban areas are frequently mentioned as the place toward which refugees go in times of severe droughts and prolonged food shortages. There is good reason for this. Urban areas are relatively protected from the direct effects of drought. Food imports and food aid usually pass through urban areas which are relatively well endowed with infrastructure. Most important is the fact that the urban populations are catered to by their governments because they are the base of their national political power which can easily be eroded by urban unrest. According to Lofchie (1987:102), "The evidence that rising food prices lead directly to urban unrest, and indeed, to critical problems of regime stability is overwhelming. The list of African cities where heightened food costs have been directly related to recent major episodes of political instability now includes such disparate locations as Khartoum, Cairo, Tunis, Rabat, Kampala, Nairobi and Monrovia. The relationship between urban inflation and political instability is so direct that it is not surprising that so few African governments have contemplated serious reforms in their food pricing systems. . . . ''

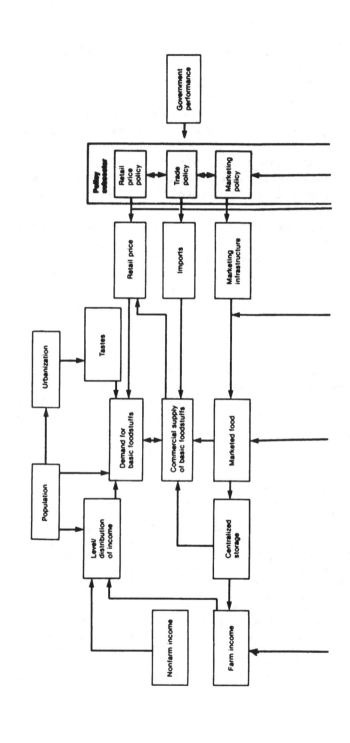

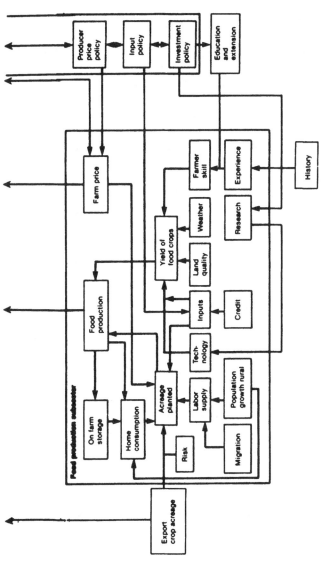

Figure 6. Interaction among food balance factors, sub-Saharan Africa

drought) as having a direct effect only on crop yields (USDA 1981). A reaction, therefore, might be to resort to costly irrigation or to the development of drought-resistant crop varieties. In fact, drought affects many factors (such as migration, storage, land quality, acres seeded, etc.) identified on the figure, and these effects are not simply the "indirect" effects from reduced crop yields.

While weather (drought) affects much more than crop yields, it is important to keep in mind that it is but one contributing factor in a multifaceted situation. Another view within the USDA, represented by the reports of the Economic Research Service (ERS), suggests this. In one of its annual situation and outlook reports the ERS notes, for example, that "drought and fertilizer import restrictions hampered food production"; that "drought and low prices paid to producers created a food shortage"; that "drought and the shift to cash crops left the rural populations vulnerable to shortfalls in food production"; that "drought and existing malnutrition decimated village populations"; and so forth (cf. USDA 1984).

The Famine-Drought Nexus

There are numerous reports, case studies, symposia, books and articles on the subject of famine, written from just about every disciplinary perspective. Yet, with all of this information, early warning systems still fail, famines still occur. Hundreds of thousands of people still die. Famines continue to plague developing societies in spite of all the technological advances that have been made with regard to food production, nutrition, and to global communication.

Famine refers to local, regional, or national problems related to the availability of or access to food that disrupt community well-being and place segments of the population at considerable risk to hunger-related increases in morbidity and mortality. According to Currey and Hugo (1984:1) "Famine is a community crisis: a syndrome with webs of causation through which communities lose their ability to support marginal members who consequently either migrate in families because of lack of access to food, or die of starvation-related disease." To Watts (1983a:13) famine refers "to a societal crisis induced by the dissolution of the accustomed availability of, and access to, staple foods on a scale sufficient to cause starvation among a significant number of individuals." Thus, as Apeldoorn (1981:15) concludes, famine is a social issue:

> . . . famine cannot be separated from the socio-economic system and the organization of production and distribution. Therefore, any meaningful discussion of potential or actual famine situations in the Third World is by definition concerned with the wider processes of underdevelopment, dependency relationships, and ownership and transformation of productive resources.

A review of the famine research literature (Torry 1984) has identified some important questions that arise: When does a famine begin? What criteria should be used to determine its onset; the number of deaths that take place following a food shortage, a particular level and magnitude of malnutrition for the general population, when food production declines sharply, when a particular socio-economic class becomes affected by food shortages?

Many observers believe that famines are a direct result of meteorological drought, arguing that a lack of rainfall reduces agricultural production which leads to reduced food availability in the marketplace which in turn leads to famine. When such a view is held by high-level decision-makers, they may propose to arrest the emergence of famine by applying technological solutions such as increasing the amount of acreage under irrigation, or planting more drought-tolerant crops, or even planting high-yield varieties on the most fertile land (perhaps under irrigation) in order to cover deficits that may occur in the country's drought-prone regions. Often, however, such technological solutions tend to favor cash crop production for export and not food crop production for domestic consumption. This leads to an increase in food imports. As Morse (1987:xv) noted, "Even Chad, with all its difficulties, had a record cotton harvest in 1984. The bias in favor of cash crops to generate foreign exchange prevails in many parts of Africa" (see also Lofchie 1975). Related to this issue, of course, is the take-over of productive agricultural land in use for subsistence food production by those (usually governments and international donors) interested in increasing cash crop exports.

Even a cursory review of the historical record of any drought-plagued region shows that famine does not necessarily follow drought. Most recently, for example, 31 countries in sub-Saharan Africa were declared to have drought-related food shortages. Only five of them, however, were plagued by famines. Each of those five (Mozambique, Angola, Chad, Ethiopia, and the Sudan) were also subjected to internal war (Timberlake and Tinker 1984). As Lofchie (1975:553) has suggested, "To the extent that there is a connection between drought and famine, it is mediated by the political and economic arrangements of a society. These can either minimize the human consequences of drought or accentuate its effects." This suggests that in order to determine the linkages between drought and famine, drought and its impacts must be looked at on a case-by-case basis.

Drought, however, can set the stage for famine, especially if there are runs of drought years. In general, most societies are prepared to withstand one poor food-production year. Social mechanisms at the local level in both farming and pastoral communities are geared to protect families from an occasional poor harvest resulting from meteorological or agricultural drought. A second year of drought, however, is considerably more difficult to survive. A third year is even worse (as was the case in Zimbabwe, Morocco and Mozambique) and a lengthy run of drought years, as has recently occurred in the West African Sahel and in Ethiopia, can be extremely devastating to families as well as to governments. Of course, it is somewhat difficult to compare the impacts of the early part of the so-called 17-year drought to the latter part because by the mid-1970s several governmental and nongovernmental international food aid agencies were in place in many of those drought-plagued countries.

There are underlying conditions in society that predispose it to food shortages and famine. There are precipitants that can convert those conditions into a famine situation. These vary from one region to another and from one time to another even in the same region. As has been discussed, food availability problems are not necessarily the result of climate-related food production problems (i.e., precipitants) but can result from the maldistribution of food resources within a country or from the inability of poorer segments of society to pay for food available in the local markets (i.e., underlying conditions). Amartya Sen (1981) identified underlying causes of famine as a function of "entitlement" to food within a society by disparate social groups within that society. His examples, drawn from Latin America, Asia, and Africa, assert that poor, malnourished people are converted into famine victims not because of supply problems induced by climate anomalies such as drought, but because of lack of access to food in the marketplace. He has noted that

> the common predicament of mass starvation does not imply any one common fundamental cause. Droughts, floods, general inflationary pressure, sharp recessional loss of employment, and so on, can all in their own way deprive large sections of the population of entitlement to adequate food (Sen 1986:2).

With regard to the role of drought, Bush (1985:60) wrote that "Drought clearly accelerates the permanent impoverishment of the most needy among Africa's peasantry. . . ." Sen also addressed this point, asking "Why is it that producers of food are the first and most seriously affected by drought and famine and why do so few town dwellers die from hunger while rural areas are decimated by starvation and death?" (Bush 1985:61). Sen noted that

> the importance of inter-group distributional issues rests not merely in the fact that an overall shortage may be very unequally shared by different groups, but also in the very recognition that some groups can suffer acute absolute deprivation even when there is no over-all shortage (1981:43-44).

The Drought-Desertification Nexus

Drought often highlights as well as exacerbates inappropriate land use activities and, in fact, is even very hard on land subjected to appropriate land-use practices. Meteorological drought conditions can lead to the destruction of crops during their growth stages, which in turn often leads to reduction in vegetative cover, eventually leaving the soils exposed to wind erosion. Wind-blown sand can also act to destroy crops in adjacent areas by covering them or by saltation processes. Dust in the atmosphere has also been blamed for futher suppressing rainfall thereby perpetuating the drought episode. Drought can in many instances accelerate, and in some cases initiate, desertification processes, though desertification also occurs in the absence of drought. As a recent *New York Times* article has noted, "Drought and desertification are intertwined. Progressive desertification over the centuries has rendered the whole region more vulnerable to drought. And drought, in turn, is accelerating the degradation of the land and increasing the rate of desertification" (1985:47).

Desertification is an all-encompassing (mega-) concept embracing virtually all types of land degradation, especially in arid, semiarid, and sub-humid areas. For example, wind and water erosion, soil salinization and waterlogging, and reduction in biological potential are all aspects of desertification.

The anthropogenic causes of desertification can generally be categorized as overgrazing, overcultivation, woodcutting, and improper irrigation practices. Grazing (and overgrazing) activities take place on a seasonal basis. In the West African Sahel, for example, the herders move their livestock in accordance with the seasonal availability of pasture grasses, following the seasonal movement of the rain-bearing Intertropical Convergence Zone (ITCZ). Drought disrupts this seasonal movement. If drought begins late in the rainy season, it can leave herders and their herds stranded in the drier (northern) reaches of their annual migratory routes with little pasture left between them and the wetter areas to the south. The areas where they are stranded become denuded of vegetation and susceptible to desertification.

In the past, irrigation has been used in various arid and semiarid areas to protect some Africans from the seasonal vagaries of the climate. These better watered, more fertile lands are less affected during drought episodes and so one sees the paradox of increasing crop exports during droughts when domestic food crops production sharply declines. Yet, improper irrigation practices such as poor drainage leads to the salinization of the soil thereby reducing its productivity. In time, such lands are abandoned and new irrigation sites are developed.

The best agricultural land is usually put into the irrigation of cash crops. As Timberlake, among others (e.g., Glantz et al., in preparation), has suggested, ". . . planting the best land in cash crops—which almost invariably use less [sic] labour than food crops—can push large numbers of subsistence farmers and herders onto more marginal land, resulting in desertification" (1985:69). These new lands were either agriculturally or climatically marginal areas and were, therefore, subjected to a higher frequency of drought than areas from which these farmers had moved.

During a run of drought years, as soil fertility declines, there is a need to bring more land into production in order to maintain the same total amount of production that had been obtained on the more fertile land or on the same land under favorable meteorological conditions.

This process expands the area of degradation and, ultimately, desertification. Grainger (1982) addressed the drought-desertification connection, noting that

> Drought can trigger rapid desertification and can make its effects more keenly felt by those living in the affected area, but most scientists are agreed that changes in climate are not responsible for the vast areas of land going out of production each year (1982:6).

Several authors have begun to address the direct and indirect connections between famine and desertification. If, as the students of desertification assert, relatively large areas of once-productive farmland and rangeland have been degraded to the extent that they are much less productive, or to the extent that they have been converted into barren fields, then it is not difficult to see how desertification can become a contributing factor to famine. The process would best be described as a downward spiral of land degradation that would result from the "catch-22" situation of an ever-increasing human and animal population having to be supported on an ever-dwindling resource base.

According to Timberlake (1985:38),

> After the 1968–73 Sahel drought, both donors and Sahelian governments pledged that their prime goal was to establish "food self-sufficiency" in the region. Donors had become aware of the links between environmental degradation and the famine, and promised to finance more projects which improved the environmental resource base. . . .

Timberlake then noted that, of the several billions of dollars that went into the region between 1975 and 1981,

> . . . only 4% of the aid went to growing rainfed crops. Only 1.5% went to ecological projects such as tree-planting and soil and water conservation, to improve the resource base upon which rainfed agriculture depends (1985:38).

Progress in combating desertification has not been apparent. Berry (1984:xi) suggested that continuing drought since 1978 has hampered the battle against desertification. His report, however, underscores the lack of understanding about desertification and how it links to famine. Timberlake concluded his book on the African crisis, explaining that he

> . . . tried to describe the environmental bankruptcy which is spreading insidiously across Africa, which has made Africans so vulnerable to the terrible famines of

1984 and 1985, triggered by the drought. Bankrupt environments lead to bankrupt economies and bankrupt nations, and could ultimately lead to a bankrupt continent (1985:224).

Conclusions

About twenty years ago, drought was viewed as primarily responsible for food shortages and famines in various parts of Africa, especially in the West African Sahel. With an apparent "break" in the drought of 1968–73, there was considerable opportunity for retrospective assessments of the role of drought in the development of food shortages and famines. As a result of those assessments and despite the fact that no general agreement has emerged on the causes and the impacts of widespread and prolonged drought, I have come to view drought as an aperiodic, recurring constraint on economic development in sub-Saharan Africa but not as the primary or sole source of the agrarian crisis existing in most countries on that continent. Drought is most often a contributing factor to other underlying problems plaguing societies that are dependent on agricultural production for their livelihood and welfare. The importance of drought as a contributing factor in any given situation must, however, be determined on a case-by-case basis from one region to the next and from one time to the next, even within the same region.

Another aspect of climate variability that affects the livelihood and welfare of various segments of different societies in sub-Saharan Africa is seasonality. Many researchers in a variety of disciplines take the seasons for granted. There is little we can do about the seasons; they come and they go on a regular basis, and they seemingly serve as a boundary constraint to agricultural activities. However, the way in which the recurrence of prolonged drought further distorts the effects of seasonality on the livelihood and welfare of rural populations is, I believe, of extreme importance for the understanding of how societies might best prepare for or mitigate the impacts of those prolonged drought episodes. If we do not look at the effects of seasonality when we are attempting to ascertain the effects of a drought on society, we will be focusing our attention only on the outlying extreme climatic events which occur relatively less frequently. By assessing seasonality and its impacts on human activities, we can then more properly determine the role that prolonged drought has played in the agrarian crisis in sub-Saharan Africa.

Acknowledgments

I would like to acknowledge the critical reviews of various drafts of this chapter by Maria Krenz (ESIG/NCAR) and by Lynette Rummel and Rhys Payne (UCLA African Studies Center and NCAR). I would also like to thank Jamie Monson (UCLA African Studies Center) for her interest in and comments on this chapter. A special thanks must go to Rebecca Huss-Ashmore, not only for her critical assessment of an earlier draft but for her suggestion to prepare such a chapter focusing on the interrelationship between drought, desertification, famine, and development.

References

Apeldoorn, G.J. van, 1981: *Perspectives on Drought and Famine in Nigeria*. London: George Allen & Unwin, Ltd.

Berry, L., 1984: *Assessment of Desertification in the Sudano-Sahelian Region 1978–1984*. United Nations Environment Programme, Background Paper No. 1, UNEP/GC.12.

Bush, R., 1985: Drought and famines. *Review of African Political Economy 33*, 59–64.

Chambers, R., R. Longhurst, D. Bradley, and R. Feachem, 1979: *Seasonal Dimensions to Rural Poverty: Analysis and Practical Implications*. Brighton, England: Institute of Development Studies, University of Sussex.

Chambers, R., R. Longhurst, and A. Pacey, Eds., 1981: *Seasonal Dimensions to Rural Poverty*. Towota, New Jersey: Allanheld, Osmun & Co., Publishers.

Cooke, H.J., 1978: The problem of drought in Botswana. In *Proceedings of the Symposium on Drought in Botswana*, M.T. Hinchey, Ed. The Botswana Society, Clark University Press.

Currey, B., and G. Hugo, Eds., 1984: *Famine as a Geographical Phenomenon*. Dordrecht: D. Reidel Publishing Co.

Dahl, G., and A. Hjort, 1976: *Having Herds: Pastoral Herd Growth and Household Economy*. Stockholm, Sweden: Department of Social Anthropology, University of Stockholm.

Dennett, M.D., J. Elston, and J.A. Rodgers, 1985: A reappraisal of rainfall trends in the Sahel. *Journal of Climatology 5*, 353–361.

Glantz, M.H., 1987: Drought and economic development in sub-Saharan Africa. In *Drought and Hunger in Africa: Denying Famine a Future*, Ed., M.H. Glantz. Cambridge, England: Cambridge University Press.

Glantz, M.H., R.W. Katz, R.L. Heathcote, A.R. Magalhaes, and L. Ogallo, in preparation: *Drought Follows the Plow*.

Grainger, A., 1982: *Desertification*. London: Earthscan, International Institute for Environment and Development.

Greenwood, D. 1957: Preface. In *Climate and Economic Development in the Tropics*, ed by D.H.K. Lee. New York: Harper & Brothers.

Hagman, G., H. Beer, M. Bendz, and A. Wijkman, 1984: *Prevention Better Than Cure*. Report on Human and Environmental Disasters in the Third World, Second Edition. Stockholm, Sweden: Swedish Red Cross.

Huss-Ashmore, R., 1982: Seasonality in rural highland Lesotho: Method and policy. In *A Report on the Regional Workshop on Seasonal Variations in the Provisioning, Nutrition, and Health of Rural Families*, Nairobi, 31 March-2 April 1982. The Ford Foundation.

ICIHI (Independent Commission on International Humanitarian Issues), 1985: *Famine: A Man-Made Disaster?* New York: Vintage Books.

Lamb, P., 1985: Rainfall in Subsaharan West Africa during 1941–83. *Zietschrift fur Gletscherkunde und Glazialgeologie 21*, 131–139.

Lofchie, M.F., 1975: Political and economic origins of African hunger. *Journal of Modern African Studies XIII(4)*, 551–567.

Lofchie, M.F., 1987: The decline of African agriculture: An internalist perspective. In *Drought and Hunger in Africa: Denying Famine a Future*, Ed., M.H. Glantz. Cambridge, England: Cambridge University Press, 85–109.

McCann, J., 1987: The social impact of drought in Ethiopia: Oxen, households, and some implications for rehabilitation. In *Drought and Hunger in Africa: Denying Famine a Future*, Ed., M.H. Glantz. Cambridge, England: Cambridge University Press, 245–267.

Monod, T., Ed., 1975: *Pastoralism in Tropical Africa*. Nairobi: International African Institute, Oxford University Press.

Morse, B., 1987: Africa beyond the famine: New hope. Foreword in *Drought and Hunger in Africa: Denying Famine a Future*, Ed., M.H. Glantz. Cambridge, England: Cambridge University Press, xiii-xx.

New York Times, 1985: Spreading desertification underlies famine. *Mazingira 8(4)*, 47.

Nicholson, S.E., 1979: Revised rainfall series for the West African subtropics. *Monthly Weather Review 107*, 620–623.

Nicholson, S.E., 1983: Sub-Saharan rainfall in the years 1976–80: Evidence of continued drought. *Monthly Weather Review 111*, 1646–1654.

Schofield, S., 1974: Seasonal factors affecting nutrition in different age groups and especially of pre-school children. *Journal of Development Studies 11(1)*, 22–40.

Sen, A., 1981: *Poverty and Famines: An Essay on Entitlement and Deprivation*. Oxford: Clarendon Press.

Sen, A., 1986: Food, economics, and entitlements. *Work in Progress* 9(3), 2–3. Tokyo, Japan: United Nations University.

Timberlake, L., 1985: *Africa in Crisis: The Causes, The Cures of Environmental Bankruptcy*. London: International Institute for Environment and Development, Earthscan.

Timberlake, L., and J. Tinker, 1984: *Environment and Conflict*. Earthscan Briefing Document 40. London: International Institute for Environment and Development.

Torry, W.I. 1984: Social science research on famine: A critical evaluation. *Human Ecology* 12(3), 227–252.

UN FAO (Food and Agricultural Organization), 1962: *FAO Africa Survey: Report on the Possibilities of African Rural Development in Relation to Economic and Social Growth*. Rome: FAO.

USDA (U.S. Department of Agriculture), 1981: *Food Problems and Prospects in Sub-Saharan Africa*. Washington: Government Printing Office.

USDA (U.S. Department of Agriculture), 1984: *Sub-Saharan Africa: Outlook and Situation Report*. Washington: Government Printing Office.

Walsh, R.P.D., 1980: Drainage Density and Hydrological Processes in a Humid Tropical Environment: The Windward Islands, Ph.D. thesis, University of Cambridge.

Wang'ati, F.J., 1985: Pattern and impact of drought in East Africa. In *Symposium on Drought in Africa*, held in Ottawa, Canada, 14–15 August 1985. Manuscript #IDRC-MR119e. Ottawa: International Development Research Centre.

Watts, M., 1983a: *Silent Violence: Food, Famine and Peasantry in Northern Nigeria*. University of California Press, Berkeley.

Watts, M., 1983b. The political economy of climate hazards: A village perspective on drought and peasant economy in a semi-arid region of West Africa. *Cahiers d'Etudes Africaines*, 89–90, 37–72.

World Meteorological Organization, 1979: *World Climate Conference*. A Conference of Experts on Climate and Mankind. Geneva: WMO.

Desertification:
The Public Record

J.A. Mabbutt

University of New South Wales (Emeritus)
Kensington, New South Wales, Australia

1. Status and Trends of Desertification in Africa: Introduction

These assessments were made for a global survey commissioned by the United Nations Environment Programme (UNEP) in the early 1980s as part of a report on progress in the first seven years of operation of the UN Plan of Action to Combat Desertification (PACD) (UNEP 1984). Information was drawn from country responses to a desertification questionnaire, from updates of reports and case studies offered to the UN Conference on Desertification (UNCOD) in 1977 and above all from a series of regional reports. These included a report on Mediterranean Africa by the Arab League Cultural and Scientific Organization (ALECSO), on the Sudano-Sahelian region by the UN Sudano-Sahelian Office (UNSO), and on African territories further south by the UN Economic Commission for Africa (ECA). Summaries of the regional assessments were annexed to the report by the Executive Director of UNEP to its Governing Council in 1984 (UNEP 1984) but they have not previously been published in full. To assist comparison with assessments made for UNCOD the concept of desertification used in the PACD has been retained, namely a trend towards a more desertic ecological status in the drylands, leading to diminished natural resources and lowered productivity. As in 1977, the assessments are based primarily on physical and biological indicators, including reduction in the area of woodland and forest, deterioration of rangelands, soil degradation and accelerated erosion of rainfed croplands, mobilization of dunes and sand sheets and attendant increase in airborne dust, reduction in amount and quality of water resources and waterlogging and salinization of irrigated lands. The definition of desertification in ecological terms has limited the

(Adapted from the United Nations

applicability of social indicators. In contrast with the 1977 estimates, these assessments have included the tropical subhumid regions, so increasing the areas and populations held to be at risk. These assessments of desertification status are at best rough estimates. No African country has the requisite information on land condition, nor is there yet a workable method of integrating such information within a quantitative classification of degree of desertification. Indications from various sources, at a range of scales and differing in quality, have been lumped together in making a qualitative assessment, ranging from moderate desertification, at which losses in production become significant, to very severe desertification where irreclaimable damage and loss of productive land have occurred. In general, information on deforestation and the condition of irrigated lands tends to be more satisfactory than for other indicators.

The situation regarding desertification trends is even worse, since there are no earlier benchmark surveys of desertification status to compare with the present. At UNCOD for example, the World Map of Desertification (Figure 1) and the accompanying estimates referred to *desertification hazard* rather than to the extent of desertified lands. Recourse has had to be made to consideration of current trends in the major factors held to be contributing to desertification, including land-use, rainfall, demographic and economic changes and even to political events.

Sudano-Sahelian Region

Background

The Sudano-Sahelian region contains the countries most severely affected by the drought of 1968–1973, which brought the problem of desertification to the attention of the world community. They are Benin, Burkina Faso, Cape Verde, Chad, Djibouti, Ethiopia, the Gambia, Guinea, Guinea-Bissau, Kenya, Mali, Mauritania, Niger, Nigeria, Senegal, Somalia, Sudan, Uganda, and United Republic of Cameroon. The United Nations Sudano-Sahelian Office (UNSO) was established in 1973 to assist the seven worst affected countries to combat the problem and in 1978 its mandate was widened geographically and environmentally to assist the 19 countries of the Sudano-Sahelian zone in the implementation of the Plan of Action.

Climate.

Climate differences identify the main ecological and land-use contrasts in the region and provide a convenient framework for the assessment. There are two main divisions. In West Africa, climatic patterns associated with the seasonal migration of the Inter-Tropical Convergence Zone run east-west and the following zonation is found, with diminishing and increasingly variable rainfall from south to north:

	Mean annual rainfall (mm)	Coefficient of variation (%)	Length of rainy season (mths)
Sahelo-Sahara	50–100	50	1–2
Sahel	100–400	30–50	2–3
Sudan	400–1200	20–30	3–5
Sudan-Guinea	1200–1600	15–20	5–8

The drylands extend from the Sahara southwards to the subhumid northern part of the Sudanian zone, with summer rainfall below 1000 mm, occurring on an average of between 20 and 40 days. Apart from seasonal variations, the distribution of individual rainfall events in time and space is also highly erratic, whilst high rainfall intensity adds to the desertification hazard through increased erosivity. In East Africa and the Horn the interaction of a monsoonal influence with the relief results in more complex patterns, with a roughly concentric arrangement about the moist and relatively cool Ethiopian Highlands. Arid climates occur in northern Sudan and on the Red Sea Coast and extend southwestwards from the Horn of Africa to Lake Turkana. Semi-arid and sub-humid climates are arranged within this arc and also on its outer margin to the south and west, where an equatorial regime of two rainy seasons is found.

The region as a whole is subject to periodic drought with a duration and spatial coherence not met with elsewhere. The view taken at UNCOD, that the Sahelian drought commencing in 1968 was terminated in the higher rains of 1975, has not proven justified. Much of the western area has since continued to receive annual rainfall well below the long-term average, and the distribution of falls within the season has also been generally unsatisfactory. Droughts were a feature of northern Kenya and parts of Uganda in the late 1970s and early

1980s, although no consistent pattern of unusually dry conditions prevailed in the area as a whole. However, dry conditions again became widespread in Ethiopia from 1979. The situation continues to be bad especially in Ethiopia, Chad, Cameroon, Cape Verde, Djibouti and Mali. Drought is affecting at least 18 African countries, with the difference that it now extends southwards beyond the Sudano-Sahelian region. Any sense, therefore, that the Sahelian crisis of 1968–73 has been resolved by natural processes is misleading. The original problems are still valid and urgent.

Changing land use.

The zonation of rainfall in West Africa is reflected in vegetation and land-use. There is a transition southwards from grass steppe through thorn scrub to savanna, with increase in height and density of woody plants and in the ground cover. There is a corresponding transition southwards from nomadic pastoralism on the seasonal pastures of the north to year-round grazing, and in the tree steppe and savanna zones of the south to rainfed cropping in swidden systems of agriculture. The climatic zonation in East Africa and the Horn is expressed in a similar range of vegetation from open desert to scrubland and savanna grasslands and in equivalent forms of land-use. But here the highlands form a settled agricultural core. Land-use changes in the region in the period 1977–1984 exhibit four main features: sedentarization of nomads, recovery of livestock numbers to pre-drought levels, continuing extension of rainfed cropping into marginal lands, and an expansion of the area under irrigation.

Apart from the impact of drought, a number of factors have disrupted traditional patterns of nomadic pastoralism in the rangelands of the region. These include the establishment of perennial man-made watering points in former seasonal pastures, political and legislative barriers to movement, continuing encroachment of agricultural settlement, and warfare. An important consequence has been the sedentarization of nomads, whether planned (as in the Sudan), spontaneous (as in general rural-urban migration, and in concentration around pumping stations in the Sahel), or forced (as in displacement to refugee camps). It is important to note that these changes constitute an increase in desertification hazard in rangelands, particularly when combined with a post-drought recovery in livestock numbers. For the region overall livestock numbers show a steady increase since 1977, with cattle now up to 61% above pre-drought numbers, and sheep and goats 31% and 17% above, respectively. This recovery has been more marked in and on the border of the agricultural zones than in those drier rangelands which were most severely affected by the earlier drought. For example, an update of the Niger case study produced for UNCOD shows cattle and camels at less than two thirds pre-drought numbers in the Sahelian zone, although small livestock now exceed pre-drought numbers.

The economic and demographic pressures for increased food production and additional cash cropping that drove the encroachment of rainfed cropping into former grazing lands during the relatively good rainfall years of the 1960s are still operative. The Niger Case Study update comments on continuing unchecked encroachment of millet fields into grazing lands 100 km north of the official limit for cultivation, and a comparable encroachment has also occurred in Northern Darfur. FAO figures (not uncontested) show a 19% increase in millet production over 1977 levels and an increase of 9% in cereals overall. This has been attained both through increased yields and increased acreages under cultivation. Yields vary annually according to the date of onset of the rains, the incidence of follow-up rains after sowing, and the adequacy of early-season (July) rains. Associated with these developments in staple crops is the increased adoption of cash cropping into mixed farming systems by small farmers, including groundnuts, cotton and potatoes. Individual countries show drops in production below the 1969–1977 baseline for certain years, among them Gambia, Guinea-Bissau, Mauritania, Senegal and Uganda. National production figures in several countries include output from more humid agricultural areas, but the trends in Sahelian countries dominated by drylands indicate that the generalization also applies in the area of lower rainfall.

In 1980 the area under irrigated crops in the region was somewhat in excess of 2.5 million ha, representing an increase of more than 10% over 1977. With population increase and rising consumption in the rapidly growing cities and towns, many countries in the region have become net importers of food in the last decade or two and there is considerable pressure to increase the area under irrigation. Traditional methods of seasonal flood irrigation have been increasingly supplemented by perennial basin irrigation from major storages.

Pressure for increased irrigation has also been associated with changes in food consumption, particularly in West Africa, where rice and to a lesser extent wheat have become staples for rapidly increasing and more affluent urban populations. The area under rice increased by almost 90% between 1977 and 1984, and production doubled. The main irrigation resources are the Senegal, Gambia, and Niger Rivers in West Africa, including the inland delta of the Niger as well as the lower Niger and its tributaries, the Nile system in the Sudan, and the Webi-Shabelle, Juba and Tana River in East Africa and the Horn. The principal irrigated areas are, therefore, found in Sudan, Nigeria, Upper Volta, Guinea, Mali, Senegal and Chad, but most countries have small to medium-scale projects. Production from *oualo* or flood-recession farming lands has been adversely affected by low rainfalls and low flood peaks since the mid-1970s, as in the Senegal River and in the inland delta of the Niger in 1977, when areas planted in Maurentania, Senegal, Niger and Mali were greatly diminished, aggravating shortages due to the failure of rainfed cropping in the same season.

Demographic trends.

The estimated population in the countries of the region in 1984 was 230 million, representing an increase of 23% since 1977. This reflects an annual growth of around 2.4% at which rate the population will exceed 400 million by the year 2000. East African and Horn countries generally show higher rates of increase than those of West Africa. The figures for Ethiopia, an exceptionally low 1.8% annual increase between 1975 and 1980, probably reflect out-migration as a result of warfare. By 1980 life expectancy in the region was between 47 and 48, compared with 56 over the developing world as a whole. Crude birth rates are in excess of 40 per thousand. On available data the dryland sections of the countries affected seem to have shared these regional trends. There is some evidence that rates of increase are slightly higher among crop-based than among animal-based communities. Population density within the region corresponds to rainfall patterns, ranging from less than 1 per km^2 in the driest areas to above 30 per km^2 in the subhumid districts.

In retrospect, droughts in the period 1968–1973 and in the years since 1975 seem to have had little effect on population growth in the region. The more obvious demographic response to drought and associated desertification has been migration, and the dryland areas participated fully in rural-urban migration which has accelerated in the region since 1960. Data for 16 countries show an average annual growth of urban population of 5.5%, indicating that 40–60% of this growth is due to in-migration which has involved pastoralists and farmers alike. A large proportion of it is in the capital cities, due to the concentration there of administrative apparatus and public sector employment.

Drought, desertification and political upheaval have also resulted in periodic large-scale movements of population within the rural areas. In northern Niger, Peul herdsmen who had moved into the region in the 1960s migrated southwards during the drought, but have since largely returned. In Ethiopia there have been large-scale population movements out of desertified parts of the densely settled highlands into the agriculturally marginal lowlands. In Sudan, thousands of herdsmen have abandoned their lands in Northern Kordofan to take up residence in the Butana area.

Economic trends.

Most countries within the region have gained political independence during the last 20 years, but their struggle for economic independence has been beset with difficulties. Among the critical factors are low incomes, lack of trained manpower, adverse terms of trade for economies oriented to the production of agricultural commodities, rising oil prices, problems of food balance aggravated by drought, and increases in defense budgets. Per capital GNP is below $400 for most countries of the region and remains below $500 for all except Nigeria and Cameroon. Literacy levels are mostly below 25%, Kenya and Somalia being exceptions with 50% and 60% respectively.

The balance of trade deficit for 10 countries in the region rose from $683 in 1977 to $3377 million in 1980. The oil bill for most African countries increased tenfold in the 1970s. There has been a continuing deterioration in the terms of trade since 1977, with commodity prices falling by 10–20% overall for the entire region, and as might be expected during this period of world economic recession there has been no significant expansion of exports. Even oil-producing Nigeria has suffered, because of the fluctuation in the world oil prices. These problems have been exacerbated by changes in exchange rates and by high and volatile interest rates, and are likely to persist for some time. Development of world markets may be important for some countries in the East African region but can only be of marginal help for the region as a whole. Also, given economic and political trends, massive increases in ODE are unlikely in the near future. There are prospects for mineral development, for example in recently-opened uranium deposits in Niger and in oil-exploration in the Sudan. Whilst such developments could relieve balance-of-payments problems, the benefits are likely to be delayed, particularly given the land-locked positions of many UNSO countries.

Political events.

During the period 1977–1984 many countries of the region have experienced civil unrest and war, as well as other political problems. These have detracted from the stability, continuity, organization and management needed to address the threat of desertification. They have reduced the availability of skilled manpower and financial resources, and in many ways they have aggravated the problem to desertification. As a consequence of political disruptions reinforcing the calamity of drought, most countries now have refugees, either from neighbouring territories or from within their own borders, which create an additional enormous financial burden.

Current Status of Desertification

At the time of UNCOD there was no systematic assessment of the status of desertification in the region. The World Map of Desertification shows a belt of high desertification hazard in the Sahelian zone bordering the Sahara, subject to accelerated wind and water erosion. This is followed southwards, in agricultural areas of the savanna zone, by a discontinuous belt of very high hazard associated with high densities of human and livestock populations and also subject to wind and water erosion. Moderate desertification hazard is depicted in intervening regions of lower land-use pressure, and southwards again in areas of higher rainfall. The Niger Case Study presented to UNCOD was valuable in substantiating the environmental and social consequences of desertification in the northern pastoral zone at the height of the drought, and also in showing how a potential imbalance in land use, which developed in the pastoral and agro-pastoral zones during the higher rainfalls of the 1960s, had contributed to eventual collapse under the stress of the ensuing drought. The present assessment is presented by sub-regions.

Sub-Sahelian West Africa. (Guinea-Bissau, Benin, Nigeria, Cameroon).

While parts of these countries suffer from periodic aridity, all have significant moist zones or are traversed by large rivers. In this subregion the subhumid and semiarid zones are used primarily for grazing, and have relatively dense human and livestock populations. Rangeland deterioration has continued and parts are now severely desertified. Desertification of rainfed croplands has also increased significantly since 1977, but their role in the economy is not sufficient for the problem to have become critical at the national level. Moderate desertification of irrigated lands through salinization is reported, but socio-economic problems arising from the introduction of large-scale projects into areas of traditional farming are more important (Adams and Grove, 1983). In Nigeria particularly, these have arisen from inadequate compensation for farmers displaced from inundated areas, disruption of traditional irrigation and flood-farming systems through changed hydrologic regimes below storages, and incompatibility between fragmented small holdings and the needs of modern irrigation and between traditional cropping and the needs of introduced crops. Most projects have significantly overrun their budgets due to delays and inflation (in some cases also due to inefficiency and corruption), targets for irrigated areas and yields have not been attained, and falls in commodity prices such as sugar have brought returns on investment far below expectations. Apart from their initial losses associated with the transformation in land use, subsequent returns to individual farmers have been disappointing. There has been much speculation in land, and benefits have accrued rather to urban entrepreneurs and the wealthier individuals than to the average peasant farmer, many of whom now rent land at inflated costs. The operation of the schemes, including watering schedules, is also commonly unsatisfactory. In large measure the welfare objectives of these projects have not been met. Perhaps the most serious manifestation of desertification in the sub-region, however, is that of deforestation, associated with the extension of cropping and the growing demand for fuelwood, which in the drier regions far exceeds the supply. The area subject to deforestation is steadily extending southwards towards the uplands of the Futa Djallon Massif.

Sahelian West Africa (Cape Verde, Senegal, Gambia, Mauritania, Upper Volta, Mali, Niger, Chad).

In this relatively dry zone with extensive aeolian sandy soils, sand-dune encroachment and sand drifting remain very serious problems, both in coastal areas and in the rangelands of the interior. So far there has been limited success in efforts to arrest dune migration. Some regeneration of rangeland pastures is observed on sandy soils in the more lightly-stocked areas, despite unfavourable rainfall, but there has been little recovery near the areas of closer settlement, where the destruction of woody vegetation by grazing and fuel-gathering continues. Complete destruction of vegetation and severe trampling of soils are reported from major watering points and the small settlements that have grown up around many of them. Such damage receives much attention because it is spectacular and accessible to outsiders. But its real significance rests in the fact that it indicates generally increased grazing pressure and fuel-gathering activity as a consequence of the development of centralized, permanent water supplies without compensating management regimes.

Desertification of rainfed croplands poses an even more serious threat. Increased cropping pressure and associated shortened fallow periods and reduced stubble-grazing by livestock have reduced soil fertility and crop yields and have led to soil crusting and increased runoff, accelerated water erosion and silting of bottom lands, and extensive deflation, sand drifting and localized dune encroachment on sandy soils. On irrigated lands salinization and siltation are critical problems, particularly in Niger, Gambia and Chad, where many projects have been abandoned or are at serious risk. Reduced flooding linked with low rainfalls of the past two decades has accentuated the salinization of floodplain soils. Depletion of woodlands and the widespread removal of all woody vegetation continue in the closer-settled areas and in expanding zones around the towns, where demand for fuelwood and timber far exceeds the local supply. There has been some over-exploitation of deep groundwater by pumping of boreholes, but a more serious problem is the deterioration of shallow wells and surface waters through the changed surface-hydrological balance.

Sudan.

A 1979 assessment shows an east-west belt of very high desertification hazard across northern Kordofan and Kassala provinces, southwards from Khartoum, with a smaller outlying area in the far west of Northern Darfur. A belt of high hazard intervenes between this zone and the desert to the north. To the south, the southern Darfur, southern Kordofan and Blue Nile and Upper Nile Provinces are largely depicted as being at moderate risk. Sand-dune encroachment is a continuing problem in the northern area, where it threatens agricultural lands along the Nile. In the arid and semiarid rangelands, deterioration of pastures and accelerated wind erosion are continuing, due to increased livestock numbers and the concentrations of herds following the provision of boreholes. Deterioration of rainfed croplands, attributed to unsuitable cropping practices on poor soils and rough terrain, has resulted in declining soil fertility, soil crusting and accelerated erosion and has caused lowered yields and some abandonment of agricultural lands. In the irrigated lands, salinization is a problem mainly in the tract of pump irrigation flanking the White Nile, particularly towards the north. In the Gezira the problems are linked with unsatisfactory operations and maintenance and with underlying economic causes. With rising labour costs, cotton no longer provides a worthwhile return and the farmer increasingly depends on food cash crops for income, but water supplies are often inadequate in this sector. The high cost of fertilizers has resulted in reduced inputs and lower yields. Poor maintenance through lack of incentives has caused an increase in waterborne disease and resulted in damaging floods in 1978. Poverty and malnutrition are reported to be general. In the Khashm-el-Girba scheme, the basis of a considerable resettlement of sedentarized nomads and agricultural labourers, the main problem is siltation from the Atbara River, and water storage capacity had fallen by 40% by 1980. Wheat production has been particularly affected by water shortages, and the incentive to grow cotton, as elsewhere has diminished. The area irrigated has now declined to 60% of the peak of the mid-1970s, and yields of cotton and wheat fluctuate at 50–75%

of their former levels. Some 25,000 settlers have moved away and the former nomads are tending to shift their interest back to livestock. Desertification associated with an increasing demand for fuelwood is most marked around the cities, and a secondary consequence is a reduction in the area of *Acacia senegal* and a drop in gum arabic production. Three major groundwater basins, the Sahara Nubian, Sahara Nile and Eastern Kordofan, have experienced falls in watertables and lowered yields, with adverse effects on drinking-water supplies.

Horn of Africa (Djibouti, Ethiopia, Somalia).

Salinization of irrigated lands is the critical problem for this region, with associated waterlogging in Ethiopia. A number of irrigated lands have been abandoned, while some farmers have switched to less valuable, more salt-tolerant crops. In Somalia, the enormous scale of resettlement of nomadic populations displaced from the northern regions is placing considerable environmental and operational stress on schemes along the Webi Shabelle and Juba Rivers. Deforestation is proceeding at an alarming rate for the whole sub-region. In Somalia particularly it is being carried out for the purpose of opening up land for irrigation. Forest once covered 40% of Ethiopia but now covers only 4–6%. Deterioration of rainfed croplands is serious in Somalia, which is experiencing problems in feeding its indigenous and refugee populations, in Djibouti and in the marginal zones of Ethiopia. Deterioration of rangelands, related to growing and locally displaced populations and associated over-stocking, is acute for Djibouti and the arid zone of Ethiopia, and serious in Somalia. Sand-dune encroachment is serious along the coast, but is elsewhere only a moderate problem.

East Africa (Kenya, Uganda).

The two major desertification problems in this sub-region are deterioration of rainfed croplands, a function of land pressures under a variable climate, and deforestation for fuelwood and charcoal productions. Both have contributed to large-scale accelerated water erosion. Deterioration of rangelands is also serious, due to increases in human and livestock populations and restrictions on movement of stock, with consequent overgrazing. Salinization of irrigated lands is important, and in Kenya the Bura Settlement Project on the lower Tana River shares the problem of budget overrun common to many schemes in the region.

Desertification Trends in the Sudano-Sahelian Region

From the forgoing assessment it is concluded that, although there have been local successes, the intensity and to a lesser degree the extent of desertification have generally increased in the region since 1977. This is particularly disturbing in view of the large investment in loans and grants from donor countries to assist the affected countries in their drought-recovery efforts and in campaigns to combat desertification. There is no country where the trend of desertification has slowed, whilst two groups of countries show a markedly accelerating trend: these are the countries of Sahelian West Africa (Chad, Mali, Mauritania and Niger), and those of the Horn of Africa (Djibouti, Ethiopia and Somalia). Sudan might also be included in this class. The survey indicates that this upward trend in desertification is general for all indicators, although in some countries certain indicators are downward. The processes continue to operate over the whole range of land uses, and climatic, economic and demographic factors contributing to this decline remain operative today.

Demographic indices promise a continuing high rate of population growth for the region. Despite increasing rates of urban growth, levels of urbanization remain relatively low by world standards, and crude birth rates, which are generally inversely linked with urbanization and higher incomes, are unlikely to fall in the next decade. The region is therefore destined to experience a further massive increase in rural population and corresponding increases in livestock numbers and in demand for fuelwood. This will impose increasing pressure on a fragile environment and, taken together with agricultural policies favouring mono-cropping and irrigation and with continuing sedentarization and likely political strife, will maintain a very high desertification hazard throughout the region. The pressures will be locally intensified around the growing towns and in localities receiving population from desertified areas or from areas of political unrest.

In the arid and semiarid rangelands, land-use pressures continue to increase locally through government sedentarization policies, extension of cultivation, political constraints on the movement of nomadic pastoralists, the voluntary growth of settlements and the provision of perennial water supplies. Livestock numbers will continue to increase in step with the human populations in these areas, and the effect of increased grazing pressure will be compounded around settlements by the removal of woody vegetation for fuel and other purposes, and by excessive burning off. There is evidence that natural regeneration of rangelands may occur in runs of good years on suitable soils where grazing pressures remain moderate and seasonally appropriate; the more critical areas in future are likely to be the more closely settled and heavily stocked rangelands of the semiarid margins and the grazing lands within the agro-pastoral zone.

Although rangeland deterioration remains the most widespread form of desertification, the more serious desertification hazard in terms of potentially permanent environmental damage, loss of production, and human impacts resides in the rainfed cropland and local grazing lands, where accelerated water and wind erosion under intense pressure of land use can create very severe and virtually irreversible desertification. In the subhumid zone (as around Kano), experience suggests that a stable intensified agriculture is compatible with close settlement under favourable conditions, but the situation is less favourable near the dry limits of cropping, where encroachment into grazing lands continues apparently unchecked. As with the rangelands, desertification and political strife in adjoining territories continue to aggravate the problem locally by causing influxes of population or by displacing farmers into agriculturally marginal areas. It seems unlikely that the slow improvement in yields and increases in the area cropped, that have sustained production in the last seven years, can keep pace with growing food needs over the next decade without further intensifying pressure on the environment.

Next to the deterioration of rainfed croplands, the destruction of woody vegetation poses the most severe continuing desertification hazard. Fuelwood scarcity is already acute over most of the region. Given the current level of consumption and projected population increases, 2 million m^3 of wood per year will be needed to meet demand by 1995. Denudation of woody vegetation is occurring around all the larger cities to distances of up to 50 km, resulting in increased dust storms and locally in dune encroachment. Rising charcoal consumption has been shifting the area of production southwards from Khartoum by an average of 15–20 km per year, and supplies now come from as far as 400 km. Expansion of agriculture also takes its toll of woodland and forest. For example, it claims 60,000 ha annually in Senegal. In the East African highlands cropping has extended into forested terrain which is unsuited to traditional agriculture, resulting in severe accelerated water erosion.

Irrigation promises major increases and greater stability in production of food and cash crops. A large number of irrigation projects are due for completion in the next five years and the pressure for investment in major schemes that has characterized the period since 1960 is likely to continue. On the evidence of the performance of many of the completed major schemes and of progress in those under construction, the outlook for such large-scale projects seems poor, particularly since there is little sign of learning by experience. Delays in construction combined with inflation have escalated costs far beyond planned budgets, while falling commodity prices relative to costs of labour and other inputs have lowered returns on investment below those originally estimated. The impacts of these schemes on traditional farming in the area, both rainfed and irrigated, have commonly been adverse and in some cases disastrous, provoking local opposition. The intended beneficiaries have commonly been the losers. There is little evidence that these large river basin schemes are supported by adequate catchment conservation, and operation and maintenance have fallen below the necessary standards. There is a growing recognition that smaller-scale projects better co-ordinated with existing land use may be more advantageous. These aspects and the question of protecting the economic interests of the irrigators are in this region more urgent than the environmental questions which tend to predominate in areas of longer-established controlled irrigation.

Africa South of the Sudano-Sahelian Region

Background

This region consists of countries in or bordering on the Kalahari Desert (Angola, Botswana, Namibia, South Africa, Zambia and Zimbabwe) and an outer area of territories through Central, East and West Africa south of the Sudano-Sahelian region (Burundi, Central African Republic, Ghana, Lesotho, Madagascar, Malawi, Mozambique, Swaziland and Zaire).

Climate and vegetation.

A belt of arid and hyperarid climate extends along the southwest African coast from southern Angola, reaching inland in southern Namibia and South Africa. Outside this is the broader semiarid zone of the Kalahari Desert in Botswana and southern Namibia, and of the lowveld of South Africa, southern Zimbabwe and southern Madagascar. Beyond this again, a belt of subhumid climate rings the Congo Basin, but with local contrasts due to relief.

With the exception of a winter-rainfall area in the southwest and an equatorial tract with two rainy seasons, the region has a monsoonal summer-rainfall regime. Outside the arid desert regions proper, the dry season ranges from 3 to 8 months. The whole region is prone to periodic drought and to unfavourable distribution of rain within the season. There has been widespread drought across the region since 1979, which in many areas set in before complete recovery from the droughts of the early 1970s.

Much of the arid zone bears thorn scrubland with a sparse ground cover. The semiarid zone is characterized by dry woodland savanna with short grasses. The subhumid areas have woodland, with tall grassland along the moister valleys. Scattered through the savanna zones are significant open tracts of short grassland, generally on heavier soils.

Land use.

Rainfed cropping is the backbone of the economy of the region, but the extent and productivity of arable land are limited. Of a total area of 943 million ha, only 219 million ha have no serious limitations for cropping, mainly in the subhumid zone. The area presently under rainfed crops is around 52 million ha and has increased only slightly since 1977. A growing rural population is putting great pressure on the available cultivable land, particularly where constraints on land tenure, commonly carried over from colonial times, have perpetuated an imbalance between the distribution of people and available land, as in parts of Zimbabwe and Swaziland. This has resulted in some areas in an extreme and inefficient subdivision of family holdings, with encroachment of houses on farmland, and extension of cropping into former grazing lands and into other unsuitable marginal areas. The area available to rainfed cropping is in any case less than might appear, since large areas of the savanna woodlands are subject to bush-fallow cropping or to shifting cultivation. In Zambia, for example, only 10–15% of the area classed as cropland is under cultivation at any one time. The cropping is largely subsistence farming, with sorghums, millets, maize, groundnuts and beans among the main food crops. However, cash cropping is extending into areas of traditional farming, applying further pressure in the struggle for self-sufficiency in foodstuffs. There are also significant areas of plantation agriculture with supplementary irrigation (as in Swaziland and Zimbabwe). In general, production of food in the region has failed to keep pace with increasing demand.

Livestock raising is second only to rainfed cropping in the economy of the region. Most farming households in the drylands keep livestock, the numbers of which relate closely with the human populations. However, in the arid and semiarid lands (as in Botswana, Namibia and much of South Africa, and also in Madagascar) extensive grazing of rangelands is the more important activity, both in terms of employment and in its contribution to the national economy, and in these areas it is the predominant cause of desertification. These rangelands include the thorn scrublands and grasslands of the Kalahari Desert proper, with extensions into Lesotho, Namibia and South Africa. Namibia and South Africa are exceptional in that sheep, for the production of wool or karakul fleeces, are more important than cattle. The rangelands are coming under increasing grazing pressure, particularly where new settlements and additional watering points have contributed to increased stocking. There is a tendency for livestock numbers to build up here during better rainfall periods, with adverse effects on the range in a subsequent drought. It is in the farming areas, however, that some of the highest concentrations of stock are found, with small livestock commonly exceeding cattle in numbers. Livestock numbers in these areas increased at about 3% annually through the 1970s paralleling the growth of human populations, and the prestige value of cattle as an index for wealth opposes any limitation of numbers. Swaziland, Rwanda and Burundi show particularly heavy concentration. Concentrations are further increased where tsetse infestation limits the extension of grazing. In the farming districts, as in the tribal lands of Botswana, grazing lands are generally communally owned, which hampers the introduction of improved management. Drought from 1979 onwards caused a sharp fall in cattle numbers in Botswana, and in sheep numbers in Namibia, where economic depression has also contributed to the decline of the karakul industry, and elsewhere to a check in the upward trend of livestock populations.

The area under irrigation in the region is 1.92 million ha, still small in relation to the extent of potentially irrigable land. Swaziland is exceptional in that 80% of the irrigable area was developed by 1977, and production of sugar cane under irrigation accounts for half the national export income; but lack of water will limit further extension here. Apart from South Africa, Madagascar is outstanding for the area irrigated (470,000 ha in 1980). Several countries have shown marked increases in the area irrigated since 1977, notably Zimbabwe and Tanzania. Many large schemes are now under construction or advanced planning, including the Rufiji River Basin scheme in Tanzania and the Kagera River Basin Project in Rwanda. A range of valuable commercial crops is produced under irrigation. Extension of irrigation has been matched by an increasing importation of agricultural fertilizers into the region.

Demographic trends.

In 1970 the population of the region was estimated to be 68 million and by 1980 it had increased to 90.2 million, representing an annual growth rate of just under 3%. Whilst the population remains mainly rural, there was a significant relative increase in the urban component over the period, from 15% to 20%. Zambia with its industrial sector is exceptional with an urban population in excess of 40%. The distribution of population is influenced by climate, the availability of agricultural land or other primary resources, by the incidence of disease vectors such as the tsetse fly and the malarial mosquito, and by the location of industrial and administrative centres. For this reason low average population densities are misleading and disguise the intense human pressures on the land in favoured areas. Exceptionally high rural populations (in excess of 100 per km) occur in Burundi and Rwanda, in Swaziland (up to 50 per km2) and in fertile sectors in a number of other countries. Significant population movements within the region have contributed to the threat of desertification. The exceptional growth of urban centres is supported by immigration from rural areas due to incentives of employment or, as in Botswana, under pressure of drought. Massive migration beyond national boundaries occurs in response to labour demands, notably in South Africa, where in Swaziland it involves up to 10% of the population at any time. Whilst bringing additional income, these movements can have adverse social impacts, and the selective out-movement of young males creates a local scarcity of agricultural labour. Other population movements have resulted from political conflict, notably from southern Angola, and from drought, with a recent northward migration of men and animals from southern Zimbabwe and a relatively large movement into Gaberone and other centres in Botswana. Nomadism is still locally important, as among the Masai of northern Tanzania and southern Kenya.

Economic conditions.

Five of the 16 least developed countries of Africa are found in this region: namely Botswana, Burundi, Lesotho, Rwanda and Tanzania. Lack of economic resources has drastically limited the implementation of development programmes. High transport costs arising from the land-locked position of many of the territories is a further handicap, and in the case of Lesotho and Swaziland increases economic dependence on South Africa. As a producer of agricultural commodities, the region has suffered deteriorating terms of trade throughout the 1970s. A number of countries earn significant income from minerals, including Botswana (37% of GDP) Zaire (37%), Zimbabwe (35%) and Swaziland (31%), but in this sector also there have been adverse price fluctuations. As yet, manufacturing is in its infancy. Other adverse economic factors in the period 1977–84 include shortages of technical skills, low literacy levels, and rising oil prices, almost all of the countries being oil importers.

Political development.

In the 1960s civil disturbances and ethnic rivalries led many people to flee from Burundi, Rwanda and Zaire and seek refuge in adjoining countries, particularly in western Tanzania, where settled immigrants now number more than 380,000. Wars of liberation in Angola, Mozambique and Namibia and the struggle for majority rule in Zimbabwe have continued this political strife, whilst Lesotho, Mozambique and Zimbabwe remain under strong political pressure from

South Africa. The adverse effects include lack of stability and continuity for progress with planned development of anti-desertification programmes, diversion of essential resources, community breakdown and abandonment of lands in affected border areas, and undue pressure on the environment in localities receiving refugees.

Current Status of Desertification

The World Map of Desertification (UNCOD 1977) shows high desertification hazard in the arid southwest, increasing to very high in Namibia (Ovamboland) due to dense rural settlement and over a larger area of southern Namibia due to pressure of livestock numbers. The processes threatened are deflation and sheet erosion with some gullying. This is extended northeastwards by areas of very high desertification hazard along the hilly eastern margin of the South African highveld, due to high grazing pressure and in the eastern Transvaal to dense rural population. These areas are threatened by accelerated water erosion, and in the eastern Transvaal by sand drifting. Had the subhumid zone been mapped, this belt of very high hazard would doubtless have been extended through the uplands of Lesotho and Swaziland. The semiarid and subhumid lands of south-central Africa were classed as of moderate hazard, with large areas subject to sand movement in the Kalahari Desert. Burundi and Rwanda were not classified. In this assessment, the main indicators of current desertification status are identified within sub-regions.

Kalahari Desert and environs (Angola, Botswana, Namibia, western South Africa, Zambia and Zimbabwe).

These territories contain the main areas of arid and semiarid climates and have prominent commercial livestock industries based on extensive grazing of rangelands. Sand-drifting and dune encroachment are locally significant, as in southwest Botswana and adjacent parts of Namibia, due to overgrazing of dunes, where they threaten roads and coastal and oasis settlements. Livestock numbers built up under commercial pressures during runs of good seasons have led to overgrazing during ensuing droughts. The problem is compounded by inequalities of grazing pressure due to imbalance of people and land, as in the Communal Lands of Zimbabwe where 3.5 million people and 2 million livestock exist on 16 million ha, by inadequate networks of watering points, and by displacements of people and livestock through drought and, as in southern Angola, through warfare. Communal ownership of grazing lands and the traditional view of cattle as wealth present obstacles to range development. Grazing pressure is evidenced by deterioration of vegetation, as in the eastward invasion of grasslands by woody shrubs across the southern African veld. More serious degradation has occurred around settlements and watering points. Deterioration of rainfed croplands is serious in areas of dense agricultural populations, as in Zimbabwe and Ovamboland (Namibia). Even in lightly-settled Botswana, land-pressure exists in the southeast, where cropping is confined by climate. Extensive accelerated water and wind erosion have followed further decline of naturally leached and infertile soils where land pressure has resulted in shortened fallows in systems of shifting agriculture. A closely linked and generally more critical problem is the destruction of woody vegetation in the dry savanna woodlands due to fuelwood gathering, clearing for agriculture, burning and overgrazing. Wood is the main available energy source, and in Zimbabwe for example the annual consumption is the equivalent of the destruction of 75,000 ha of woodland.

Eastern sub-region (Lesotho, Madagascar, Malawi, Mozambique, eastern South Africa, Swaziland and Tanzania).

These mainly subhumid lands include areas of very closely settled farming populations, resulting from limited arable land, restrictions of land tenure, population movements and settlement programs and the occurrence of vector diseases. They are mainly areas of mixed farming in which most households own livestock. The subregion contains the major continental watershed and includes much vulnerable hilly terrain. Deterioration of rainfed cropland results from pressure of growing rural populations on the land, from substitution of permanent cropping for shifting agriculture with the villagization of rural populations, as in Tanzania, from shortened fallows and continuous cultivation, and from the burning of crop residues. Yields have fluctuated markedly with rainfall and there have been serious shortfalls in food crops in recent drought years. Accelerated water erosion has already led to significant loss of good arable land in Tanzania and Lesotho. Deterioration of grazing lands has resulted from increased grazing pressure due to a steady rise in livestock numbers before the 1979 drought, and to increasing confinement of grazing to marginal lands, often communally owned. The main indications are pasture deterioration, with the invasion of woody shrubs, diminution of vegetation cover and accelerated water erosion. Destruction of woody vegetation for fuelwood supplies and in the process of clearing for agriculture is everywhere a serious problem which in most territories continues uncontrolled. The consequences of deforestation are increased soil loss and adverse effects on the hydrology and water-storage capacity of cleared areas, with increased flooding, seasonality of supplies and siltation in areas down-valley.

Central sub-region (Burundi, Rwanda and Zaire).

In this sub-region desertification is associated with mixed-farming systems in two situations: extremely closely-settled rural populations, in the uplands of Burundi and Rwanda, and areas with moderate densities of population practicing swidden agriculture, as in Zaire. Local concentrations of population are due to limitations of climate and availability of arable soils, and to restrictions on settlement due to tsetse infestation. The chief form of desertification is the deterioration of rainfed croplands due to continuous cropping or shortened fallows. Overall, crop yields are low due to nutrient-deficient leached tropical soils, but there is evidence of a continuing decline in fertility under use, quite apart from fluctuations due to drought. Increasing pressure due to growth of population has led to extension of cropping into marginal lowlands or into montane forests in Rwanda and Burundi, and to ever-shortening cycles in areas of swidden agriculture. These pressures are heightened by the impact of moderately high numbers of livestock. Closely linked with this degradation is deforestation due to clearing for cropping and for fuelwood.

Desertification Trends

Patterns and processes of desertification in the region generally confirm the prognostications of the 1977 Desertification Map of the World based on desertification hazard. Three main indicators of desertification—deterioration of rainfed cropland, destruction of woody vegetation and deterioration of rangelands—point to an increase in the extent and severity of desertification since 1977, accentuated by a current drought. This is not surprising in view of the fact that none of the pressures identified in the review of background trends has lessened since 1977, nor is likely to lessen in the immediate future. A predominantly rural population dependent on subsistence agriculture continues to increase at around 3% annually, whilst the area of arable land under cultivation remains almost unchanged. With the exception of Madagascar, the vulnerability of rainfed cropping has not been significantly reduced by the development of irrigation at this stage, although some countries have shown an appreciable development since 1977. The world economic recession brought low prices for agricultural commodities and for certain of the mineral products of the region. Political strife continues to affect a large number of territories and to divert resources that might otherwise have eased the threat of desertification. The few isolated measurements of the rate of desertification in the region confirm this unfavorable projection: an annual decrease in the cover of woodland of up to 3% in several dryland sectors; topsoil losses in excess of 200 tonnes per km^2 per annum from certain areas of rainfed cropping; a continuing decrease in available cropland of 0.25% annually in Lesotho; and a prediction that by the year 2050 the rangelands of Lesotho, approximately 80% of the territory, will have been engulfed by the eastward spread of low-value woody shrubs. Many such changes can have a positive feedback, and one can predict that the present onward desertification trend will accelerate further, unless major combative actions are initiated during runs of more favourable years.

Mediterranean Africa

Background

This region comprises the territories of Algeria, the Libyan Arab Jamahiriya, Morocco and Tunisia, with a total area of 4.75 million km^2, of which drylands comprise more than 95%. At least 80% is made up of the hyperarid Sahara, where settlement is confined to a few oasis and islands of higher ground. Rainfed cropping is confined to the narrow coastal plains, to the high intermontane plateau of the Maghrib and to the coastal plateau of Cyrenaica, and with minor exceptions the main settlements and economic activities are also restricted to these areas.

Climate and vegetation.

In the coastal tracts the drylands experience a southern Mediterranean subhumid to semiarid regime, with rainfalls of between 200 and 450 mm characterized by a single winter maximum. The high intermontane Maghrib plateau and Cyrenaica have a climate transitional between semiarid and arid, with between 100 and 250 mm rainfall showing a double peak in spring and autumn. Saharan conditions, from which northern Morocco is protected by the Atlas Ranges, reach progressively further north in Algeria and Tunisia and approach the coast in Libya, with a dry season of 10 months in Tripoli. The hyperarid Saharan regimes have less than 50 mm and generally less than 20 mm annual rainfall, with an increasingly irregular distribution southwards, where one or more years may pass without rain. In the north winters are cool, but in the Sahara proper they are warm, although with large diurnal temperature ranges; summers are everywhere hot in the lowlands, becoming very hot inland, and warm on the uplands.

Vegetation on the coastal plains and ranges was originally low evergreen woodland, but except at higher elevations this has been largely cleared or replaced by degraded evergreen shrubland. Inland, the semiarid plains are characterized by Artemisia shrubland or by low halophytic shrubland on saline soils, whilst the hyperarid sand deserts either lack perennial vegetation or have only sparse grasses, with shrubs and low trees along the wadis. The whole region is drought-prone, and in the period since 1970 serious drought has occurred in the seasons of 1972–73, 1976–77 and 1980–81, when rainfalls were between 50% and 60% of the long-term average. Rainfed crop yields were lowered, but the most serious impacts appear to have been on the pastoral industry. In Morocco alone livestock losses in the 1980–81 drought were 1.5 million, and production was lowered by 40%.

Land use.

Rangelands in the traditional sense cover about 65 million ha in the region, but extensive grazing also extends into a further 15 million ha of upland and forest, particularly in Morocco and Algeria, and the figure does not take into account occasionally-used desert rangelands in the south. Shrub steppes form the main perennial pastures, but uplands with degraded evergreen shrubland and the desert grasslands provide important seasonal grazing in summer and winter respectively. Nomadism and transhumance have declined in importance, however, in part through government policies of sedentarization begun in the colonial era, and are now of limited importance in Tunisia and Algeria. Livestock in 1981 number 56 million, of which sheep made up almost 70%. Morocco, where livestock-raising predominates in the national economy, has about 43% of the region's livestock, but numbers here have remained little changed in the past decade, whereas elsewhere there has been a steady overall increase. The number of goats has declined to 11.5 million, whereas cattle at 5.7 million have increased notably, particularly in Morocco. With the exception of Morocco, pastoralism has come to play a reduced relative part in total production in the region. Forest and woodland accounted for only 2.2% of the area, or about 10.5 million ha in 1980, much of it in the Atlas Mountains of Morocco, and to a lesser extent of Algeria.

There were 20.8 million ha of rainfed croplands in the region in 1980, forming 20–30% of the productive area in each of the four territories. The traditional crop-fallow system of dry farming prevails, and the area planted in any season falls well short of this figure. Yields are variable, particularly in the driest areas, where land is sown following early rains—often by pastoralists—on the chance of further rain. The main crops are wheat and barley. The area under rainfed cropping has increased in recent years with the growth of mechanization, particularly in Tunisia and Algeria, where cropping has extended into rangelands that are climatically marginal. In these countries cropping has become more commercialized, with increased use of fertilizers, and is no longer everywhere part of traditional mixed farming. Despite the changes, overall yields remain relatively low. Tree crops, including olives and fruit, form a significant part of production in this category, although the area under vines has diminished, notable in Algeria.

Irrigated lands cover 1.2 million ha, or a mere 5.5% of the cultivated area. In Morocco surface waters from rivers rising in the Middle Atlas provide the bulk of irrigation water, but there is an increasing dependence on the groundwater eastwards notably in the oases of eastern Algeria and in Libya, where the Kufra Project is based on the mining of groundwater over a fixed term. Irrigated crops include tree crops, particularly dates, vegetables, tobacco, cotton, and forage crops.

Demographic trends.

In 1981 the population of the region was estimated at 49.8 million. Average annual increase for the period 1975–81 was 3.1%, with Libya showing an exceptional 4.1% due to the immigration of foreign workers. The percentage of urban population is generally above 50%, save in Libya where it remains below 40%. The percentage of urban population in the region is growing at around 1% per year as a result of rural exodus, and there is also significant seasonal and permanent migration to Europe and the Middle East.

Economic background.

The contrast between the economy of Libya as a major oil-exporter and those of the remaining territories is shown in the 1977 GDP figures: $7422 in Libya, $954 in Algeria, $821 in Tunisia and $453 in Morocco. Agriculture accounts for only 2% of GDP in Libya, 8% in Algeria—later in its development of natural gas and oil reserves—and 17% in Tunisia, still newer in the field. These figures also reflect the importance of non-fuel minerals in the economies; even in Morocco, a non oil-exporter, the contribution of agriculture to GDP in 1977 was only 27%. Oil revenues have provided important sources of regional investment in the diversification of the economy, including the development of irrigation, afforestation and the mechanization of agriculture. However, agriculture has not shared significantly in recent economic growth, and low productivity and adverse differentials between urban and rural wages have fueled the rural exodus; in some parts of Tunisia up to 40% of rural households are involved, and everywhere it is the young males who predominate among those leaving. Wage remittances now provide an important element of rural income, but these do not generally enter into productive investment.

Current Status of Desertification

The Desertification Map of the World shows the region north of the-hyperarid Sahara as generally subject to high desertification hazard with certain closely settled coastal areas showing very high hazard, commonly with additional pressure of high livestock numbers. These include the Wadi Tennsift plains near Marrakech, the coastal plains and ranges of the Rif and Oran, the plains of central and southern Tunisia and their extensions via the Algerian chotts to the Oued Righ and into Tripolitania, and the coastal region of Cyrenaica. The main threat in most of these areas is accelerated water erosion, with salinization around the chott plains and in the Qued Righ. Moderate desertification hazard is confined to the interior steppe of Oran and northern Morocco.

Desertification and rangelands.

A general increase in livestock numbers and in some areas the encroachment of cropping and agriculture into rangelands have contributed to overstocking and overgrazing of rangelands in the region. Several factors have acted to give localized intense stocking pressures: for example, inadequate or irregularly sited watering points in some areas and in other the introduction of additional waters into already densely-stocked rangeland without restriction or any associated grazing strategy. Another general factor has been the sedentarization of pastoralists, resulting in livestock concentrations around settlements. This has also resulted in smaller individual flocks which no longer graze so extensively across the rangelands, again contributing to localized heavy grazing pressures. Among the settled population, pastoralism, because of its low returns, commonly becomes only a part-time occupation, and this has favoured shorter-term exploitive attitudes. The sequence of desertification has been well-recorded in the Tunisian Case Study (Mabbutt and Floret 1980). Despite protective legislation, desertification has already seriously effected 3 million ha of rangeland in Tunisia, and 400,000 ha very seriously. Deterioration of pastures through overgrazing has resulted in diminished vegetation cover, reduced above-ground biomass, and impoverished plant-species composition, particularly through loss of annuals. Soil compaction and diminished infiltration on sandy soils have resulted in a tenfold increase in water erosion (up to 300 tonnes per ha annually), and in the drier southern parts in widespread sand drifting which has threatened cultivated lands. Comparable problems are reported from Morocco where, however, it is the upland woodland pastures that are worst affected. In 1982 4 million ha were moderately desertified, 2.8 million ha seriously affected, and 1.5 million ha very seriously desertified. This situation is expressed in pasture deterioration and accelerated water erosion and has exacerbated the problems of flooding and siltation associated with deforestation in the area. An additional factor here is desertification associated with the passage of transhumant flocks. In the lowlands, overgrazing in adjacent study areas has contributed to sand encroachment on oases in the Draa Valley. Desertification of rangelands in Morocco has resulted in significant losses in livestock production. Closely associated with rangeland deterioration is the destruction of woody vegetation for fuel and constructions, particularly around settlements and camps. It is notably a problem of the shrub-steppe pastures.

Desertification of rainfed croplands.

Although no figures of the overall extent of this problem in the region are available, it is reported from Morocco, Algeria and Tunisia as being that of greatest concern and potential loss. Major factors mentioned include: the extension of cropping into climatically marginal areas and on to unsuitable terrain and soils; the inappropriate use of heavy machinery, notably disc ploughs, on predominantly light-textured calcareous soils; the entry into farming of settled pastoralists with little experience of local conditions or of the consequences of land degradation; shortage of manpower as a result of the rural exodus, with adverse effects on land maintenance; commercial pressures leading to an exploitive approach to land use; and increasing mechanization. The extension of cropping, commonly referred to in the regional literature, has been due in part to population increase, in part to sedentarization of former pastoralism, and has been made possible by the increasing use of tractors in the region. Consequences are described as accelerated water erosion of compacted and crusted, broken-down soils, deflation of light textured soils, and sand encroachment. No general figures on rates are available, but at Sbeitla in Tunisia for example, gullying is extending over an area of approximately 120 ha at the rate of 3 ha annually. Abandonment of rainfed croplands due to desertification has been reported from Morocco and Tunisia.

2. The Global Context of African Desertification

The scale of desertification in Africa as described in the foregoing assessments is best revealed by placing it in its global context, which moreover helps to identify the factors which Africa shares with other continents and those dimensions of the problem which are peculiarly African.

In Table I the extent of significantly desertified lands in the three African regions for which assessments have been presented is set against figures for the other continents and for the world as a whole. This table immediately separates North America, Europe and Australia from the remaining continental areas in terms of the relative extent of desertified lands, showing that—although a worldwide problem—desertification is significantly more widespread in the tropical drylands.

Table I. Extent of desertified lands areas in millions of ha. (1984)

Region	Total drylands	Rangelands			Rainfed croplands			Irrigated lands			Desertified lands	
		A	B	C	A	B	C	A	B	C	Area	D
Sudano-Sahelian	1080	320	288	90	90	67	75	2.8	1.4	50	356	87
Africa South of Sudano-Sahelian	620	250	200	80	52	39	75	0.2	0.6	30	240	79
Mediterranean Africa	450	80	64	80	20	14	70	1.2	0.8	65	79	78
TOTAL Africa	2150	650	552	85	162	120	75	4.2	2.8	65	675	83
Mediterranean Europe	119	30	10	33	40	12.5	31	6.4	1.3	20	24	31
Asia	2070	566	320	56	287.7	175	61	63.5	30.7	48	525.5	57
Australia	650	450	100	22	39	12	30	1.2	0.35	29	112	23
Latin America	628	250	180	72	30.5	21.75	71	11.65	4.6	39	206	71
North America	465	300	125	42	85	33	39	50	22.5	45	180	41
TOTAL	6082	2246	1287	57	644	374	58	137	62.25	45	1722.5	56

Key
A—Total Area
B—area of at least moderately desertified
C—percentage of desertified land in land-use category
D—all desertified land as a percentage of productive land

Part of the reason for this may reside in environmental differences. Tropical dry climates are more stressful and intense tropical rainfalls are more erosive in combination with vulnerable latosolic soils. More important, tropical drylands have experienced widespread severe and protracted drought over the past two decades, whilst rainfalls have been generally low and variable over the period as a whole.

What identifies these areas even more significantly is that they constitute the Third World drylands, where the undue pressure on land resources which has contributed to desertification is linked with poverty, lack of alternative livelihoods among rapidly growing rural populations, and inequitable access to means of economic and social improvement. Within these developing countries, the drylands tend to be the least favored sectors, remote from political influences and handicapped in respect of economic and social investment. The crisis of the 1970s in the drylands of the developing countries which led to recognition of desertification emerged from a convergence of environmental and economic pressures: on the one hand rainfall shortages and on the other worsening economic and social conditions in the Third World, where rising costs of oil and other imports and falling prices for their own agricultural products had contributed to an increasing financial burden of indebtedness. The PACD, recognizing the economic and social dimensions of desertification, stressed that programmes to combat desertification in these areas would need to form an integral part of the process of economic and social development.

What tends to set the African drylands apart from other Third World areas, however, is the extent of severely and very severely desertified lands. This is reflected in Table II, which presents statistics for the rainfed croplands, the chief support of African dryland populations, where the combined figures for these two categories in the African territories exceeds 60%. The extreme desertification in Africa may in part be explained by environmental factors, in particular the extent, severity and duration of droughts in the African drylands since the late 1960s, but these economic and related factors which identify the Third World drylands as the chief victim of desertification have acted with particular force in Africa.

The onset of adverse rainfall regimes in tropical Africa followed shortly on decolonisation. Most of the newly independent African national territories contain extensive dry lands and these countries have struggled for economic independence against a combination of poor

**Table II. Allocation of areas of rainfed cropland
to various categories of desertification (areas in million ha) (1984)**

Region	Extent of rainfed cropland	Category of desertification		
		Moderate	Severe	Very severe
Sudano-Sahelian	90	27	23	17
Africa South of Sudano-Sahelian	52	13	14	12
Mediterranean Africa	20	5.5	5.5	3
Mediterranean Europe	40	8	3	1.5
Asia	187.7	104	52.5	24.5
Australia	39	8	3.5	0.5
Latin America	30.5	9.8	7.8	4
North America	85	22	9.5	1.5
Total	544.2	197.3	118.8	64

agricultural seasons and increasingly adverse terms of trade. The need to reshape colonial economics geared towards the export of primary products rather than towards integrated development has been an added burden. Food production in these territories has commonly failed to met the needs of growing populations and rising levels of consumption and food imports have added to a trade imbalance. Economic instability has been linked with political instability and lack of security, which have militated against long-term measures required for development and for combating desertification, and the falling levels of per capita food production which distinguish the African drylands reflect the continuing degradation of resources. The critical conditions in West Africa that drew world attention to desertification in the early 1970s have subsequently recurred and persisted in Sudan and the Horn of Africa and continue to threaten wide areas of Africa to the south.

The drylands of the developed countries have sparse rural populations, and Table III shows that the human impacts of desertification, as measured by numbers dependent on the land in areas affected by desertification, are incomparably greater in the Third World countries. Table III indicates that these numbers are largest in the more populous Asian drylands, which include large areas of closely settled irrigated lands. It is also evident from Table III that these human impacts are greatest in the rainfed croplands and that it is these lands which must be regarded as most threatened by desertification, a conclusion which is particularly relevant to Africa.

When one considers population in areas subject to severe or very severe desertification, however, the focus shifts to the African drylands, where the populations likely to be suffering extreme hardship through desertification match or slightly exceed the Asian total, as indicated in Table IV. This has been an important consequence of including tropical sub-humid lands in the present assessments, for in Africa these include areas of considerable rural overcrowding, with

Table III. Populations affected by desertification under land-use categories (in millions) (1984)

egion	A	B	Rangelands C	D	Rainfed croplands C	D	Irrigated C	D	E	F
udano-Sahelian	80	65	15	13.5	45	35	5	2.5	52.5	80
frica south of Sudano-Sahelian	70	55	10	8	40	30	3.5	1	39	71
lediterranean Africa	47	22	5	4	14.5	10	2.5	1.5	15.5	70
OTAL Africa	197	142	30	25.5	99.5	75	11	5	107	75
lediterranean Europe	125	50	4	1.3	40	12.5	6	1.2	15	30
sia	367	254	21.5	13.7	92	64	152	72.5	144.2	57
ustralia	1.5	0.65	0.15	0.07	0.32	0.1	0.07	0.24	37	
atin America	93	43	5.5	2.7	29	21.5	6	2.5	28.8	67
orth America	67	15	4	1.7	6	2.4	4	1.8	5.9	40
OTAL	850.5	504.65	65.15	44.97	267	175	179	83	337.9	67

ey
—Total population of drylands
—Rural population of drylands desertified
—Population related to land-use category
—Population affected by desertification in land-use category
—Total rural population affected by desertification
—Rural population affected by desertification as percentage of total rural population

Table IV. Estimated rural populations in areas undergoing severe
or very severe desertification (millions)

Region	Rangelands	Rainfed croplands	Irrigated lands	Total
Sudano- Sahelian	6.25	20	0.6	26.85
Africa south of Sudano-Sahelian	4	15	0.15	19.15
Mediterranean Africa	2	6.2	0.4	8.6
Mediterranean Europe	0.65	4.5	0.3	5.45
West Asia	1.5	8	4	13.5
South Asia & China	5	22	12.5	39.5
USSR in Asia	0.5	1.5	2.25	2.75
Australia	0.035	0.03	0.035	0.1
South America	1.9	10	0.4	12.3
Mexico	0.5	1.5	0.2	2.2
North America	0.8	0.75	0.45	2
TOTAL	23.135	89.48	21.285	132.4

Including an urban increment (40%) of 53 million, a total population of 187 million is estimated
to be severely affected by desertification

population densities of up to 100 per sq km in Rwanda and the Kenyan Highlands for example. Such local pressures are in part a result of inequitable land distribution dating from colonial times, in part of a reflection of the localization of good farming land, and partly a result of the exclusion of settlement from large areas subject to animal or human diseases.

3. Future Trends

Current trends of desertification for the main dryland regions in the period since 1977 are indicated in Table V. As stated earlier, these are based in part on the assessments of current desertification status and in part on projections of the factors regarded as contributing to desertification. Generally, desertification has continued in all land-use

Table V. Desertification trends since 1977

Region	Rangelands	Rainfed croplands	Irrigated lands	Forest & woodland	Groundwater reserves
Sudano-Sahelian	+ #	#	+ o	#	
Africa south of Sudano-Sahelian region	#	#	+ o	#	
Mediterranean Africa	+	+	+	+	+
Mediterranean Europe	o +	o +	o +	−	
West Asia	+ #	+	+ o	#	#
South Asia & China	o # +	# +	# o −	#	+
USSR in Asia	+ −		− +	−	
Australia	+ o	o	o +	o	
Latin America	# +	# +	+ #	# +	+
North America	− o	o	o +	−	#

Key
+ continuing desertification
# accelerating desertification
o status unchanging
− status improving
Symbols placed above each other indicate opposing trends in the same region, with the upper symbol predominating. Symbols in two columns indicate contrasting areas within a single region, with the left-hand column predominating.

sectors, with local successful reversals in USSR and China and on a smaller scale in the developed countries. But it is the tropical drylands, including Africa south of the Sahara, which stand out as areas of accelerating desertification, above all in the deterioration of rangelands and rainfed croplands and in the destruction of woodland resources.

Causes of failure to combat desertification since the inception of the PACD have been many. Seasonal rainfalls in the tropical drylands, and above all in Africa, have been generally unfavourable; man and livestock populations have continued to increase and maintain pressure on land resources; economic conditions have worsened generally, especially for Third World countries; in many of the worst affected countries, and above all in Africa, political strife and warfare have not only disrupted programmes to combat desertification but have worsened the problem through the breakdown of livelihood systems and the displacement of populations. In face of these obstacles the political will to reverse desertification has been lacking.

Against the bleak and uncertain prospects for environmental improvement must be set the certainty of increased population pressure on the Third World drylands in the future. Table VI contains population projections for dryland regions for the year 2000, showing that the African drylands south of the Sahara, with their still predominantly rural populations must expect the highest increases (more than 30%). If present trends continue, it must be assumed that livestock numbers will also rise in proportion. In the African drylands, where irrigation presently supports only a small proportion of the crop-based population, it can be assumed that this increased demographic pressure will fall primarily on the rainfed cropping sector.

For the drylands as a whole an expected increase of 20% in the area under irrigation by the year 2000 might support 30 millions of this predicted additional rural population, but this amounts to only one third of the anticipated increase, little more than the increment from areas already under irrigation. Africa south of the Sahara, with its present relatively small area under irrigation, might be expected to experience above average development in areas such as West Africa where water and land area available. However the social and economic problems with recent irrigation schemes in the region, as in Nigeria, are a reminder that irrigation is not inevitable panacea for dryland problems. Elsewhere in the African drylands, for example in

Table VI. Projected dryland population in year 2000 (millions)

	Africa South of Sahara		Other Developing regions		Developed[+] regions		Total drylands	
	1981	2000	1981	2000	1981	2000	1981	2000
Total popn	150	247	360	508	340	427	850	1182
Urban popn	30	90	153	250	174	256	345	596
Rural	120	158	217	258	168	171	505	586
Increase in Rural popn (%)	31		23		Negligible		16	

+ includes China and USSR

much of east and southern Africa, the resources for large-scale development of irrigation are limited.

From present trends it seems likely that by the year 2000 the semitropical drylands will be even more clearly identified as the area of maximum impact of desertification with potentially critical conditions in the rainfed croplands, particularly in Africa. This trend will doubtless be accompanied by an increase in the present exodus of population from the desertified areas, but should present economic trends continue this option will no longer suffice, since it will be impossible to sustain the levels of food imports needed to support the increased urban populations. Faced with this prospect it will be essential to increase food production by combating the problem of desertification on the ground rather than avoiding it through migration.

Acknowledgment

The author gratefully acknowledges the support of the United Nations Environment Programme and its Executive Director, Dr. Mostafa Tolba, in assembling this information on desertification in Africa, and specifically the assistance of its Desertification Branch under Dr. Gaafar Kataar. The opinions expressed are, however, his own.

References

Adams, W.M. and A.T. Grove, eds. 1983. *Irrigation in Tropical Africa*. African Studies Centre: Cambridge.

Mabbutt, J.A. and C. Floret, eds. 1980. *Case Studies on Desertification*. Prepared by UNESCO/UNEP/UNDP, Natural Resources Research XVIII. UNESCO: Paris.

UNCOD. 1977. United Nations Conference on Desertification. World Map of Desertification. UNEP: Nairobi.

UNEP. 1984. General Assessment of Progress in the Implementation of the Plan of Action to Combat Desertification. UNEPGC, 12/9: Nairobi.

Desertification: The Historical Significance

On the association of desertification with drought, famine and poverty in Africa in the late twentieth century.

Brian Spooner

*University of Pennsylvania,
Department of Anthropology
Philadelphia, Pennsylvania 19104*

"When the scientist has a very serious message
to convey he faces a problem of disbelief"
—Mary Douglas, Environments at Risk

1. The Problem with the Campaign

Desertification is generally recognised to be a critical problem of international significance. It is currently causing annual reductions in the productivity of the renewable natural resources of the world's dry lands that constitute one third of the land surface of the world, and in the long term it may seriously reduce the habitability of the world as a whole. It is therefore considered a major threat to the future of humankind. In 1977 official delegations from 95 countries and 50 UN offices and bodies, eight intergovernmental organizations and 65 nongovernmental organisations accepted invitations to a United Nations Conference on Desertification in Nairobi (UNCOD 1977a), where they approved a Plan of Action to Combat Desertification (PACD) which was designed to halt and reverse the process by the year 2000. A progress report prepared in 1984 in accordance with the PACD showed continuing degradation in the Third World, and only slight amelioration in the industrialised countries (Mabbutt, this volume). Today, eleven years later, all reports continue to show only continuing deterioration. The worst news comes from Africa.

Although the objective data reported in the previous chapter depend on a high degree of extrapolation, they raise a number of obvious questions: why is desertification allowed to continue? Why does the International Campaign to Combat it not succeed? Why do the numerous individual efforts to reduce and reverse these processes of ecological degradation in dry lands not have more significant over-all impact?

Although these questions are sometimes asked in relation to specific projects, they are rarely if ever raised in these general terms. If, as I suspect, this is due to a general reluctance to address them, the reason most probably lies in a shared sense that the obvious answers are unwelcome—for two reasons: on the one hand they show the problem to be more complex than is presented in the literature, requiring more research and more careful planning; on the other, they imply a need for change in the related planning and decision-making processes, a change that would affect the distribution of bureaucratic power and political authority as it relates to available funds.

The intention here is to verbalise these answers. Stated in simple terms they may not be persuasive for the target audience, those who bear the major responsibility for the conduct of the campaign so far. Nevertheless, since a full exposition would require more space than a single chapter, it may be worthwhile to begin with a very simple summary of the answers to serve as a guide to the remainder of the chapter.

Desertification is a real problem, but there is something awry in the way it is understood, analysed and presented. This distortion inhibits both constructive debate and successful action. Specifically, the accepted definition is couched in terms of the loss of renewable natural resources, but the causation is attributed to human behaviour. The definition and the campaign are promoted by scientists, but if the threat is real it should not take the sophistication of science to grasp the significance of the desertification threat. The threat is presented in the cultural and ideological terms of a particular branch of science, and in the social terms of a particular sector of modern society, far removed from the experience of most of those who have so far been the victims. The reason desertification is presented as a global problem that potentially affects everyone is that our economy and our politics have become global. It can be resolved therefore only in similar global terms: terms, that is, that define responsibilities and costs and benefits globally.

The problem so far, then, lies in the partiality of the definition and presentation. But the perceived threat must be seen for what it really is—a product of the interaction of human activity and natural processes on a global scale—in more generally meaningful terms, meaningful especially to those most immediately concerned (as distinct from putative future generations). In fact desertification is not simply an ecological process resulting from particular human activities. The campaign to combat it is not in essence a campaign about how certain resources may be used. Desertification is a total social phenomenon, which is a byproduct of the total global society that we have become. Desertification is grasped as a crucial problem for humanity now, rather than earlier, because it is only recently that we have developed a global awareness of human experience. The anti-desertification campaign that began in the mid-1970s is part of the larger-scale struggle for resources that has also recently become global, the struggle about who (what individuals, what communities, what categories of people) can control and use what. Since global planning or coordination of projects is beyond our capability, and perhaps also politically unacceptable, a dilemma confronts us. Even if we can successfully reformulate the problem in its larger spatial and temporal context, we may find ourselves equally impotent to resolve it. But we should certainly benefit from an increased awareness of the related human activities. Assuming that as scientists we believe in the power of rationality, however, the more we can bring this debate out into the open the quicker and more efficiently we shall be able to work towards a resolution.

Desertification is obviously a dimension of the development debate. Like the development problem it cannot be resolved solely by the type of transfers of money, materials and technology that reinforce existing relationships. That would be too easy, and thirty years of development effort show that it does not work. The problem is to change the relationships. But relationships are of course notoriously resistant to change by planning or legislation.

This chapter does not, however, end pessimistically. Most of it is devoted to working through the complexity of the problem with special reference to the Campaign as it has evolved so far. This is done by progressively enlarging the context of the discussion in each section up to and including Section Five which considers other relevant factors that need to be integrated into the discussion. The concluding section brings the discussion back to Africa and the outlook for the future.

2. The Problem with the Debate

The international debate on desertification that has developed since the early to mid-1970s is confusing and unbalanced. What is desertification? Everyone, generally, knows; but objective scientific definition is elusive. It is most simply glossed as the development, spread or intensification of desert-like conditions (UNCOD 1977a:6). But what is a desert? The scientific definition of "desert" is similarly problematic. The range of criteria considered and the point on the continuum from lushness to infertility where steppe becomes desert or environmental change becomes desertification is essentially relative to the observer and the scientist. Accepted canons of diagnosis depend exclusively on physical and biological criteria. But it is generally understood that the desertification that is at issue does not occur except as the result of human activity. All human activities are loaded with meaning, and other people's activities tend to accumulate negative meanings. It is not surprising, therefore, that discussion of desertification tends to throw doubt on the legitimacy and the morality of any human activities that can be related to it. These issues have not been systematically addressed, still less integrated into the general debate.

There is an unconscious feeling that desertification carries or ought to carry, its own punishment. It is often assumed that it causes famine, and that it is therefore a root cause of the African famines of the past twenty years. We seem generally susceptible to arguments that make such direct connections between human experience and natural conditions or processes. Such arguments are often called "ecological." Since they are rarely based on convincing evidence they tend to be at best misleading oversimplifications. At worst they deflect our attention from the factors that may cause famine again in the future. But ecological arguments are pervasive and resilient, and attempts to argue against them are handicapped because they invite immediate censure.

That there should be some relationship between desertification and famine is common sense. But it does not take very much historical investigation to show that although desertification may be a factor in some famines, it has probably never been a sufficient cause. However, would the current African famine have developed in the absence of any desertification? Either answer to this question would be difficult to prove, but there is an argument on both sides. Some famines certainly have occurred in the absence of adverse ecological change, and even in the midst of relative plenty (cf. the examples given by Sen, 1981). The problem lay in distribution, not in availability, in social factors rather than geographical. Desertification may similarly be viewed as change in the distribution of people in relation to natural resources rather than simply local diminution of those resources. In fact this view is strongly suggested by the combination of our current global preoccupations and the fact that human activity has throughout history changed the productivity of natural resources. It would not seem to be difficult, therefore, to make a case for exploring the social dimension of both desertification and famine.

Africa is overall the world's poorest continent. Its population is the poorest in terms both of exploitable natural resources and of economic and technological activity and value added. It is relatively poor in both minerals and soils. Seventy five percent of its territory is characterised by seasonal or annual water deficit (periods, that is, in which evaporation exceeds precipitation), and is frequently afflicted by extended drought. Given the rising population growth rates of the present century it is not surprising that desertification has become a major problem. However, China and India also suffer from desertification. Moreover, they support three times the population of Africa in half the area. But paradoxically they succeed economically in living with their rate of desertification, whereas (although it is difficult to measure) it is probably true to say that the population of Africa suffers more from desertification than any other part of the world. It may be relevant to add that many Asian populations because of their different place in the history of the world have much longer experience of what might be called "creeping desertification." The onset in Africa has been relatively sudden, making the effects relatively more sensational and difficult to accommodate—emotionally, politically, and scientifically.

In Africa, as in other parts of the world, over the past hundred years dry lands have undergone conspicuous ecological change. The rate of change has accelerated since the middle of the century and may still be accelerating. It is this acceleration that has made desertification a global issue—with Africa as the most tragic case. In what follows there is no attempt to question the degree, the rate or the extent of ecological change in the African dry lands or the seriousness of that change. Rather, attention is directed to the implications of that seriousness for current and future human life and to the nature of the relationship between the natural processes of desertification and the human activities and experience that are involved, with special reference to the case of Africa.

Both before and since UNCOD there has been a tendency to take desertification at face value, to put all our faith in science, to upbraid politicians for not managing their constituencies to harness the resources available to combat it. It has been assumed we know everything we need to know about desertification in order to control it; if only we can put our knowledge into practice we shall gradually reverse that process everywhere (UNCOD 1977a: 61). For this reason the PACD provides for desertification to be diagnosed and monitored by trained observers of physical and biological criteria. Interpretation on the basis of comparison with similar physical and biological data serves as a basis for action, on the assumption that (1) this recording alone is sufficient to dictate urgency, and (2) the related human activities can easily be changed. But on the one hand human activity patterns have proven less than ideally malleable, and on the other hand we should know that no description of such a process as desertification can ever be fully comprehensive, if only because we have no explicit theoretical basis for it. The unconscious selection that shapes all scientific description operates here as elsewhere. It derives from the experience of the scientist, professional and personal. When it is not guided by theory, social and cultural bias inevitably takes its place. The data we have on desertification in Africa are the product not only of Western science and western education but of Western experience and values, and its significance continues to be evaluated publicly only in those terms. Given our overall objective of not only conserving renewable natural resources for future generations but of reducing the current suffering among the (presumptive) parents of those future generations, we may find it more realistic to attempt to describe desertification in Africa as elsewhere in terms of its total historical context, with particular attention to local social, economic and cultural factors.

Since the causation is obviously complex, it should not be simply assumed even on the basis of comparison with apparently similar cases elsewhere. In order to sort it out satisfactorily we must establish and analyse each component process in a comprehensive theoretical framework. Such a framework should include not only objective data on ecology, population, and food production, and economic and political development, but also less readily measurable social and cultural factors, such as motivation, intention, evaluation, social cohesion and differentiation and morale. It must not be forgotten that ecological processes that involve human behaviour occur in history as well as in nature. The history of Africa has been different from the history of other parts of the world in ways that are particularly significant in the present context. But that significance can only emerge from a reconstruction of the world-historical context of recent experience.

As it is, the suffering and starvation that occurred during the "Sahelian" drought of 1968–1973 were understood in the West mainly as a consequence of the cumulative effects of maladaptive non-industrial types of land use in communities undergoing accelerating population growth. The maladaptation was put down to the backwardness (scientific and social) of the communities concerned.

There has been criticism of this attribution. Unfortunately, it is not realistic to investigate it empirically. Such an investigation would require a research effort of a magnitude far beyond the means of those likely to support it. The few attempts to generate such an effort over the past fifteen years have been unsuccessful, and may anyway not have been feasible from the beginning. Social science does not have the experience or the equipment to deal with this type of problem in the field. Even if it could solve the funding problem, the large amounts of either quantitative data or case histories that might be produced would not test a hypothesis in a way comparable to natural-science research. We should finish up with a largely philosophical debate at the level of grand theory. Probably the best we can hope for, therefore, is some success in raising public awareness of the independence of social and cultural dynamics in what has now generally come to be known as "human ecology."

It may be possible to make a significant contribution to the campaign to combat desertification by rethinking the assumptions underlying its conceptualisation, which are implicit in the PACD. Although some attempts have already been made in this direction (Spooner and Mann 1982), a new attempt now may have a greater chance of success because of changes in the intellectual and political climate surrounding the campaign, and disillusionment with the lack of progress so far. I have chosen to do this here by asking questions about the larger framework in which we—not always consciously—discuss desertification. There has been a tendency to take for granted the fact that desertification, famine, drought and poverty should be found together, or more correctly that populations characterised by a high incidence of poverty in dry lands are particularly vulnerable to desertification when drought inevitably recurs, because they are easily led into over-exploiting their renewable natural resources. Although they can get away with a certain degree of over-exploitation in average to good years, when the bad years come their production plummets and famine strikes. This assumption does not rest on a firm basis of evidence, and there are several reasons why we should break ranks with those who rely on it. Some of these reasons have already been noted in the small but significant amount of critical literature that has developed over the past ten years. It is well known, for example, that many of the populations suffering from famine had received considerable amounts of aid in the form of projects that increased their productive capacity in good years but made them dependent on practices that could not be continued when the inevitable low-rainfall years came around again. But there is more to be said, and a comprehensive statement is needed that will contextualize the conventional arguments.

Over the past fifteen years, desertification, drought, famine, poverty and Africa have become inseparably linked in the media and the public mind, to the point where it is difficult to discuss any one of these topics without raising the others. However, scientists still discuss them separately, and each factor does occur without the others. Why then should they all coincide in Africa now? Even if they are not causally dependent, are they perhaps mutually reinforcing? More importantly, are they likely to reinforce each other in the foreseeable future? Why should desertification be particularly bad in Africa now (rather than, say, Asia)? What is the engine that drives desertification? Does it depend on decisions that could be foreseen and made differently, or changed? And to what extent are other factors, besides famine, associated with it and how?

The argument developed here may perhaps claim some originality in that it allows room for optimism about the future. It suggests that in Africa desertification and famine are related not in the manner of direct cause and effect, like parent and child, but as cousins. Like distant cousins they trace their relationship to a prior agency, but the details of the genealogy are vague. It can be difficult to establish exactly which common factors may have led to both desertification and famine at the present day, but much may be gained from reconstructing the combined human and natural context from which they were generated. By putting desertification in its place as a component factor in our general condition in the late twentieth century we can expect it to be resolved along with other problems, according to our general inclinations for optimism or pessimism.

Full reconstruction is of course too large a task for a single chapter. The intention in what follows has been to make a useful beginning, in a framework which will clarify what still needs to be investigated. The next two sections develop the larger context in which desertification works and the historical meanings of its component processes.

3. The Larger Context of the Campaign and the Debate

Desertification, drought and famine often coincide in poor areas. In Africa they seem to coincide with some regularity. A priori, however, there is obviously no necessary causal relationship between any two of these phenomena. Each occurs independently of the others. Desertification, insofar as it is the direct result of human activity, occurs not only in poor countries but also in wealthy areas of the United States, Canada and Australia. It is related not only to the survival needs of the poor but also to the consumption demands of the rich. Drought (in the simple sense of significantly lower than average annual rainfall) is a common occurrence over at least the third of the world's land surface that geographers classify as dry (technically sub-humid, arid and hyperarid). But although it is all by definition vulnerable, not all of this territory is affected by desertification. Again, famine occurs not only in association with drought, but also in areas that have never been categorised as desertified and for reasons that have nothing to do with the decline in primary productivity that desertification denotes. In fact, the worst famines in this century (before the current African famine) have been associated not with desertification but with economic or political deprivation; the most sensational examples occurred (as already cited) as a consequence of government policy in the Ukraine in the 1930s and largely as a result of war in Bengal in the 1940s. Not only were they not in dry lands, but the productivity of the land was not a factor. But if desertification and famine are independent variables, how should we explain their apparently persistent coincidence, and the recurrent association of each with drought, on such a scale particularly in Africa? It may assist us in our investigation of this question if we remember that the fourth variable, poverty, which is also independent, is a common factor.

To begin with, desertification is generally considered to be the consequence of overexploitation of renewable natural resources—soils, plant communities and water supplies—as the result of increased demand. In the poorest populations increased demand tends to be primarily a function of rising levels of population. In affluent countries rising population is not necessarily a major factor at all, and in much of the Third World rising economic demand irrespective of population growth is often also significant. The market, therefore, plays a role in the dynamics of desertification, as in famine. How can we determine the relative significance of this role? It is true that since desertification involves the reduction of primary productivity, at any given level of technology it inevitably reduces the ability to produce food. So, the statement that there is no necessary connection between desertification and famine requires more justification. The justification lies in the fact that on the one hand there has probably never been an exclusive one-to-one relationship between a set of natural resources and a population at a constant level of technology or intensity of resource use (other factors, such as the movement of population, commodities and ideas have complicated the situation). On the other hand, if we assess the significance of desertification on the global level, we must remember that technology has in the past made possible increased production per resource unit, and appears to continue to do so. The problems, therefore, lie more in social, legal, economic and political arrangements for ownership, access and distribution. In this regard one aspect of the significance of desertification that goes unnoticed because of the general reluctance to look at desertification as a social problem is that, since it changes the distribution of access to resources it inevitably causes political and economic change, and presumably change in the cultural perception and assessment of resources and landscapes. It changes our perception of our environment and of ourselves.

We shall look more closely at the concept of desertification in the next section, and at famine in the following section. For the time being we can state that the process does not automatically lead to famine, because no population depends exclusively on local food production, and there is no global shortage of food. People everywhere travel and trade. Those who happen (whether unconsciously or calculatingly) to reduce the primary productivity of their immediate resources can always, and in most cases do, modify their economy (either, as Boserup, 1965, argued, by intensifying their technology, or more simply by diversifying their activities), or move on.

It is true that the first victims in any famine tend to be found among the rural poor (cf. Grove 1986: 194), who are of course themselves food producers. But as Sen (1981) has ably shown they are victims not simply because their own food production has failed, but because this failure has rendered them unable to participate in the local market. Whether or not they would normally depend on the market for dietary staples, their plight is to be understood in terms of their relationship to the market: because they are also poor, they have lost their "food entitlement" in the local economy. Nonfoodproducers are less often afflicted, partly of course because the market affects them differently. Famine now rarely afflicts the urban poor directly, and almost never the affluent, although they may suffer indirectly from secondary effects, such as epidemics. Defined as local scarcity of food (whether in particular geographical areas or in particular sectors of a community), therefore, famine is more directly related to factors of distribution and power than to ecology and production. This part of the argument is easier because although the population of the world has increased at a steadily rising rate, most conspicuously since the beginning of this century, the global incidence of famine has decreased—while there is no doubt that at the same time the rate of desertification has been increasing. An important factor underlying all these phenomena is the combination of social, political and economic changes that have engulfed the world in the forty years since the general upheaval that followed on the Second World War. Perhaps, then, it is rather the nature and the effects of this upheaval that we need to understand in relation to all the problems discussed here.

If there is no a priori connection between desertification and famine, why do we tend to assume one? I think the answer to this question may be found in two conditions of modern life. The first may be general to Western culture, or even to human nature. It is the propensity to focus on the external material world at the expense of our awareness of the dynamics of our own social relations. The second, which is certainly specific to our modern technological and political condition, is our relatively new tendency to see all large questions in global terms. We see desertification as a threat to our global resource base. Global terms though large are limiting. They carry connotations of being non-expandable, and of competition within. Earlier we thought in local, national or regional terms, which suggested there was always room for expansion (though often at the expense of other people). Globalism is an essentially modern formulation, that would have made little impact before the middle of this century. We tend to treat desertification as a criminal act, carrying criminal responsibility. We point the finger at the communities that suffer from it, or we pin blame on governments whose policies we disapprove of, or whom we oppose ideologically. Assuming a relationship between desertification and famine allows us to see famine as the just desert (the pun is spontaneous and apt) of those who because they live in desertified areas and currently over-exploit their resources are considered to be tainted with responsibility. In some cases, especially in Southwest Asia, it is likely that the worst phase of desertification was before the middle of this century, but we still visit the sins of the fathers on the sons.

The correlation between desertification and famine is a typical expression of the general public (scientific and popular) assumption that there is a direct causal relationship of "adaptation" between material (physical and biological) processes and human activities (both thought and action). If human activity really were adapted to natural conditions we should have no occasion to blame people for causing ecological degradation. On the other hand, if ecological decline were inevitable for other—non-human—reasons, we should be obliged neither simply to sympathise with the victims, nor to persuade them to defy the "natural" process, by attempting to take command of it and reorganise it! In fact, however, the assumption that there should be a predictable relationship between natural conditions and human experience, and that where there is not the human beings in question are contravening the natural order, continues to vitiate most ecological discourse. The argument is reminiscent of the Physiocrats, who maintained that not only human survival but all wealth derived from basic agricultural production. But the Physiocrats were discredited at the dawn of modern economic thought. Furthermore, there is evidence that the desertification of agricultural land began with the Neolithic, but has been accompanied *pari passu* by increasing human technological capability and innovation that has neutralised any disadvantageous effects it might have had on production. This perspective stands the conventional concept of adaptation on its head.

The idea of adaptation has such explanatory power (however deceptive) that we continue to ignore the fact that a great deal of human activity in the industrialised world flies in the face of what many would call ecological common sense. (The same is of course true outside the industrialised world, but the implications are less awesome.) How does it become so powerful? It seems even to take on the multivocality of a symbol. It is both appealing and persuasive and at the same time vague and confusing. It is an assumption about how the world is and at the same time about how the world ought to be (a common confusion in Western science). For example, we assume comfortably that people adapt, as when pastoralists move nomadically in order to exploit seasonal or ephemeral pastures, and at the same time that people ought to adapt, as when we catch the same nomads grazing to the point where the regeneration of the range in subsequent seasons may be impaired. Actual adaptation can be assessed only in the light of all possible options. Evaluation of any choice made among those options, in terms of adaptation, will vary according to the interests of the observer.

The related assumption of maximisation entails similar problems (though they may be easier to resolve). It neither explains why people do what they actually do, nor why they do not do other things. Just as it is impossible to adapt to every external condition, opportunity or constraint, in the environment, it is also impossible to maximise every resource. We have no way of explaining why people adapt to or maximise one factor in their environment rather than another. It is true that people maximise, but they maximise different variables in different situations according to different criteria—which significantly reduces the value of the concept! Generally, it may be true that human beings tend to maximise their enjoyment of particular conditions in a particular community, or in a particular social environment. When it comes to resources and territory or living space, we are concerned with not only what we own or control, but (depending on our cultural views of the relationship between the individual and the community) either who we own or control it with, or who our neighbors are. In most human situations there is a tendency to adapt to or maximise social opportunities and minimise constraints. These social strategies are difficult to predict because they depend on personal as well as cultural evaluations. It is even more difficult to predict how they will translate into adaptation to the natural environment. Finally, we struggle not only for more and more (up to a point of lessening returns), but for monopoly and exclusiveness in particular company. Those who are not with us, we tend to consider to be against us. It is a short step then to fear they may overwhelm us in the future! These social preoccupations colour our conceptualization of desertification as well as our orientations to its victims.

"Carrying capacity" is another of the terms commonly used in this debate which entails similar problems. The carrying capacity of a piece of land varies according to the production technology applied to it. If agricultural technology had not increased carrying capacity continually from the Neolithic up to the present, population would not have grown to its present level. We do not know whether agricultural technology will continue to increase carrying capacity sufficiently to keep up with population growth. But we did not know this in the past either. The technology that generates the carrying capacity of our natural resources continues to change at an accelerating rate at the centres of human activity. Although it is only inadequately extended out into the margins, we have not yet begun to approach our global capability to produce food.

This discussion helps us to see how it is that we get left with a paradox (the first of many that will appear in the course of this discussion): on the one hand, the people who suffer from desertification are letting the side down by not adapting, and so reducing resources for all; on the other hand, little or no interest is shown in research to understand why they do not adapt, or what leads to the behaviour that is immediately or ultimately associated with desertification. At the same time, adequate resources are not made available to combat it. The paradox goes deeper, involving the manner in which funds are allocated. Resources are assessed in economic or financial terms. Funding is allocated to or through national governments whose priorities require quick and visible results. Allocations are made according to a number of criteria, including the capacity of the national economy to absorb. In practice there is little relationship between the assessment of need in relation to desertification, and the determination of levels of development aid. Few donors and few governments want to see their money spent on research, when it could be producing political or other capital. Furthermore, the careers of individual planners and programme officers depend on their record for moving money rather than later assessments of what the money achieved. All-in-all most donors are unenthusiastic about projects whose main justification is desertification-control.

Finally, although we have grown used to associating desertification, drought, famine, poverty and Africa, the only contributing factor (among those generally recognised) that is worse in Africa than in Asia is the current rate of population growth, and it is not the current rate but earlier rates that are most significant for present conditions. But what causes the current high population growth rate in many African countries? It is at least plausible that it results from the same underlying factors that cause the rate of desertification and the famine, rather than that one of these phenomena is the cause of the others, and that these are social pressures which derive from historical processes in particular contexts.

Ultimately, the difference in Africa can only be explained and resolved in social terms, terms which take account of the way African societies fit into our current global relations, networks and conceptions, whatever the contribution of environmental factors. In any case, it is not scientifically sufficient to study each of these problems in isolation, or even to compare two geographical contexts (e.g. Asia and Africa). Such approaches are essentially extensions of what is now well known as the Orientalist view of the world, which despite its obvious achievements numbers among its deficiencies the tendency to interpret the rest of the world in terms conditioned by our values and interests. Our ecological terms may often be the best available. But insofar as the interpretation of the relationship between ecology and the history of others is concerned it may be possible to improve on them. All these factors in both continental situations must be seen in a global-historical framework.

In order to pursue such an argument we must make two parallel investigations. First, we must explain in more detail what desertification is in historical as well as ecological terms. Secondly, we must discuss what human conditions or situations might possibly be construed as causally related to it. In what follows we shall trace in broad outline the story of the anti-desertification effort so far. We shall then develop the human dimension of the story and establish the relation to drought as a physical variable on the one hand, and famine and poverty as social variables on the other.

4. The Meaning of Desertification

Perhaps the biggest mistake of all has been to take the meaning of desertification for granted, devoting attention only to scientific detail. The obvious lesson to be learned from the difficulty we have experienced in formulating a generally acceptable scientific definition is that although like "adaptation" desertification has symbolic appeal, or even compulsion, like all symbols it is difficult to tie down. It will be easier to deal with if we can form a better idea of the range of variation of its meaning in space and time. For desertification as we know it today is largely a matter of comparison with other places, other times and other populations, other ecosystems, other successions and other technologies. In each case there is a point in a long-term process when we would say that desertification set in. Others might locate the point differently. The degree of human impact that is considered acceptable varies according to a range of factors that are only partly ecological. What tips the balance and alerts a constituency to see it as a problem for policy?

Although desertification has a long history, it has only recently been conceptualised as a serious problem. Evidence can be traced back into the nineteenth century with some ease, and intermittently from there back through the Mediaeval Period into the Ancient World. It has probably attended on all human activity in some degree since the Neolithic, or even before. Modern consciousness of what was happening to the natural environment, and of the implications, was slow to dawn.

In 1951 a number of scientists who had access to government and gained representation in intergovernmental bodies, initiated efforts that led in 1956 to the establishment in UNESCO of a Major Project on Scientific Research on Arid Lands. The theme of this project was the application of science to the problem of how to increase production in areas that were considered poorly utilised. UNESCO's Project on Arid Lands in the 1950s led into the geographically broader (but disciplinarily more focused) International Biological Programme (IBP) in the 1960s. The same movement in turn gave birth to UNESCO's Programme on Man and the Biosphere (MAB) in the 1970s, which still continues. As the research evolved first into the more systematic and quantitative methods of IBP, and then into the more human orientations of MAB, numerous publications on the special problems of dry lands were generated, many of which are among the best sources of information on desertification to have been produced before the idea came into its own in the mid-1970s. In 1975 the UNCOD Secretariat under UNEP assumed the responsibility for assembling and organising all available information relating to desertification and leading the campaign to get it applied. It was convenient to organise the information into four basic categories, according to the dominant types of resource use. For the sake of convenience I shall keep to these categories here, even though as I explain them it will become clear that while the categorisation is appropriate to the immediate objectives of the science that produced them it may oversimplify and distort the local meaning of the activities. Three of these categories are related to food production directly, the fourth indirectly. The three may be conveniently characterised as over-grazing, over-cultivation, and over-irrigation, in ascending order of the intensity of land use, investment and potential productivity per hectare, and decreasing order of total area at risk; the fourth is the use of vegetation for fuel. Of these, over-grazing and fuel use are probably the most significant for Africa as a whole.

Over-grazing is the least understood (outside pastoral populations) because to the Western mind, and perhaps to the modern mind generally, pastoralism is an exotic and alien technology. Its ecology can be grasped only in the context of areas too vast to map or monitor efficiently. The facts of desertification in relation to pastoralism are that natural rangelands sustain pastoral exploitation up to a certain threshold beyond which grazing and browsing are likely to eliminate not only individual plants but entire species. When this happens the composition of plant communities is modified and the percentage of plant cover throughout the range is reduced, leading to reduced absorption of precipitation, and increased run-off and erosion. Although less vulnerable species may take the place of those eliminated, they are inevitably less palatable or nutritious, and so less useful to pastoralism (or any other form of food production). Invariably also they provide less protection against soil erosion. The threshold of grazing intensity beyond which this process sets in is not absolute. In any particular area it varies seasonally and annually with the variation in precipitation that is typical of dry rangelands. Population growth (or in some cases loss of territory to farming) in many pastoral societies has led to increases in animal population per hectare to the point where the limit is often and even continuously exceeded. Like most populations, pastoralists seldom adapt simply and directly to changes in their ecological situation; they do not spontaneously reduce their herd size in tune with the reduced carrying capacity of the range (cf. Sandford 1982). Their technological adaptability to recurrent conditions of reduced carrying capacity has also in some cases been prejudiced or impaired by the effects of nationally and internationally sponsored projects to increase their productivity and integrate it into the larger economy, especially by making new watering points available which facilitate greater exploitation and herd growth in good years (cf. Bernus 1977). The conventional cure for an overgrazed range is reduction of the animal population to the point where the vegetation may recover. But apart from the problem of how to support the population without irretrievable social disruption during the period of recovery, this measure does not always produce a simple reversal of the process. Undesirable species may invade and take over the range before the earlier vegetation (which may have lost its seed base) can re-establish itself (cf. Conant 1982). Finally, there is a growing body of evidence that indigenous forms of pastoralism have more to offer in the African context than range scientists had credited (cf. Cossins 1986, Sandford 1986).

In the case of rainfed cultivation, the main hazard arises from its extension onto marginal soils that will not support it. Opportunistic ploughing of such soils, which may produce a few good harvests in the short term, in the longer term leads to erosion. The wild vegetation that grows on such soils often comprises the better rangeland of traditional pastoralists. As a result of erosion the land is soon lost to both agriculture and pastoralism, and the pastoralists are thereby pushed back in denser numbers onto less productive land which consequently becomes further impoverished. In addition to being extended, cultivation is sometimes intensified by the reduction of fallow periods, a process which similarly leads to the impoverishment and loss of soil and to long-term reduction in productivity. These forms of "over"-cultivation have been encouraged not only by population growth but by increased economic demand and opportunity resulting from integration into a larger, cash economy, and also by increasing availability of mechanical aids to labour such as tractors. These aids allow a much faster rate of growth in acreage than would be possible given simply the rate of population growth (cf. Schultz 1982).

An important factor in each of these desertification processes is a shift in the distribution of responsibility. Over-cultivation is often a function of the farmer's increased dependence on his land and therefore also his responsibility to it. This shift and its implications in the historical study of the relationship between natural processes and human activities have been appropriately termed "the ecological transition" (Bennett 1976). The economic opportunities of industry or urban life gradually provide viable social alternatives to rural life and individual farmers can afford to be less concerned about the possibility of decline in the productivity of their land. In this way the socioeconomic reorganisation that goes with development may bring in its train reduced ecological sensitivity in rural populations. In the case of Western societies it is worth noting that the social security of such populations has at the same time been increased.

Over-irrigation occurs in the land use system which is not only the most intensive and productive (though the smallest in actual and potential extent), but the most directly caused by industrialisation. Unlike most other desertification processes over-irrigation has little to do with local pressures of population: it is financed by the larger economy and depends on the large-scale engineering of irrigation, in which the local operators do not control their own operation, did not develop it themselves and therefore have only a folk understanding of their part of it, rather than a detailed understanding of the larger ecology (cf. Spooner 1984: 32–39).

Developers have always approached intensive irrigation as an enterprise in economics or engineering, and now that the ecology is understood it remains to work out ways to arrange for ecologically efficient operation of the system. In short, the limiting factor in agricultural production in many dry areas is water. Many dry areas can be transformed into agricultural miracles by the controlled application of water—which is possible, especially in large river basins, given large-scale organisation, engineering and above all industrial construction. But in order to be ecologically successful over a long period the flow of irrigation water must be engineered in such a way that it goes straight to the root zones in optimum quantities for the particular needs of the specific crops. Although this may sound simple, it is even now rarely achieved. All excess water accumulates and causes ecological problems. The most common problems start in seepage from the channels and below the root zones. However deep the original water table, the excess gradually builds up until it approaches close enough to the surface to cause first salinisation (since it invariably has a high mineral content) through capillary action, and finally waterlogging. The result is serious decline in yields and, in severe cases, total loss of productivity for indefinite periods. Since this type of land use system is basically modern and industrial, generated by national or international investment, and integrated into the larger economy, loss of its production due to desertification is of more obvious economic significance (given conventional econometric standards) than in the case of over-grazing or over-cultivation which are often unintegrated with the consequence that the potential value of their production in the larger economic context is less tangible and more difficult to determine. In the case of over-irrigation, therefore, figures are more available and more reliable, but should not necessarily be allowed to speak for themselves.

In many cases of desertification the production system may constitute a less significant pressure on the environment than the use of increasing amounts of vegetation for fuel and construction. In pastoral areas, apart from forage the vegetation often has to satisfy the need for fuel for heating, cooking and in some cases also for processing milk into other products, and for construction of animal pens and even dwellings. In an area of arid rangeland in northeastern Iran the average domestic consumption of firewood has been estimated at 5.3 metric tons per year per family plus as much as an additional 7–10 tons for milk processing (Horne 1982; available data for Africa is summarised in Brokensha 1986). Historically the same area has also produced charcoal for urban markets. In other Middle Eastern rangelands, where no ligneous vegetation survives to satisfy even local fuel demand, animal dung is collected for use as fuel. Perhaps the most surprising point is that wood still serves as a major fuel for heating in cities like Addis Ababa, and even some with cold winters such as Kabul.

Whatever the technology, the basic spiral of desertification leads along the following chain: impoverishment and reduction of vegetative cover, loss of biological productivity, exposure of the soil to accelerated water and wind erosion, reduction in nutrient content of the soil with crusting and compaction and deterioration of its hydrological properties, salinisation or alkalinisation or accumulation of other substances toxic to plants or animals. In many situations, especially in poor countries and especially in Africa, but by no means everywhere, these ecosystemic processes are associated with deterioration in human livelihood systems, including decline and abandonment of communities, disruption of social relations, decline in morale, deterioration in standards of nutrition, health and mortality, increased social and political strife, migration and further impoverishment and marginalisation. But the association is not simply causative; it is dialectical, which is to say that each effects the other but does not predictably determine it. In the case of pastoralism recent research has shown that the ecology of the range vegetation, the behavioral characteristics of the sheep and goats and the herding techniques of the pastoralists reinforce each other in a way that is likely to have taken hundreds if not thousands of years to evolve (Nyerges 1982). If this set of relationships is now disrupted in order to raise the level of primary productivity at the expense of current pastoral output, it would probably take just as long again to develop it. The animal behaviour and the human technology have co-adapted with the plant communities and become integral to the ecosystem. Actual disruption and decline is always of course a function of the organisation of the larger (usually now national) society which may provide alternative livelihood opportunities. Up to a point it can be stopped. However, what actually happens is more often due to incidental changes in the larger political economy than to any direct measures. Beyond a certain point a process of declining productivity becomes more and more difficult to stop, as it develops its own dynamic into a downward spiral of social and ecological impoverishment.

Poverty in Africa and Asia has been a matter for international concern since the 1950s. The current multi-billion dollar international network of development operations began to evolve then in response to that concern. The Sahelian drought appeared to threaten that whole edifice. The fact that it had become known as the Sahelian drought, even though it affected a much wider area of the developing world, is largely because parts of West Africa had received particularly heavy investment in the previous decade. The alarm was sounded by the agencies that financed the development effort. It was comparable to the earlier alarm about the population growth rate, and to the later alarms about the greenhouse effect and the ozone hole. In the series of United Nations conferences that began with Stockholm on the Environment in 1972, desertification followed on Population (Budapest 1974), Water (Buenos Aires 1975) and Habitat (Vancouver 1976), and was succeeded by Science and Technology in Vienna in 1988. The world-conference format was already well developed. Each topic was considered to be the major problem or issue confronting the world at the time. UNCOD drew attention to the fact that desertification may not only reduce the global patrimony of renewable natural resources, but also affect global climate patterns by increasing atmospheric dust and surface albedo.

In December 1974, following the worst drought year in the Sahel for over thirty years, the UN General Assembly called for a global conference to deal with desertification. To organise it and prepare background documentation it appointed a secretariat, headed by the man who had at that time just successfully completed the Population Conference. A number of other UN and international agencies played a role in research and development specifically concerned with the problem, and contributed to the preparations. At the Conference in August 1977 in Nairobi the Secretariat presented the governmental delegates with a comprehensive synthesis of existing knowledge in the form of an Overview and four component Reviews, on Climate, Ecological change, Population and Society, and Technology (UNCOD 1977a), Case Studies from each of twelve countries illustrating different records of experience in specific projects, Australia, Chile, China, India, Iran, Iraq, Israel, Niger, Pakistan, Tunisia, U.S.A., U.S.S.R. (Mabbutt and Floret 1980, Biswas and Biswas 1980), and six Feasibility Studies demonstrating practical ways to achieve transnational co-operation for combatting specific problems, cooperation at the level of ecological and regional rather than national units. These included two ecological monitoring projects in Southwest Asia and South America, two greenbelt projects (in the North African and Sahelian countries), and a livestock stratification project (in the Sahel) and a groundwater conservation project (in Northeast Africa and the Arabian Peninsula). In these documents the Conference was told that possibly as much as five million hectares of land were being lost to production annually. A Committee of the Whole, chaired by the most distinguished agricultural scientist of the most scientifically advanced developing country, M.S.Swaminathan, finalised an International Plan of Action to Combat Desertification (PACD) which was approved by the delegates at the final session, for the purpose of arresting the spread of desertification throughout the world (and especially in the developing countries) by the year 2000. Finally a Special Account was also established to receive funds to finance it.

What exactly was the conference actually about? According to the PACD the focus of the Conference, desertification, is:

> . . . The diminution or destruction of biological potential of the land [which] can lead ultimately to desert-like conditions. It is an aspect of the widespread deterioration of ecosystems and has diminished or destroyed the biological potential, i.e. plant and animal production, for multiple use purposes at a time when increased productivity is needed to support growing populations in quest of development (United Nations 1978: 7).

A second definition was used in the World Map of the Status of Desertification in the Hot Arid Regions produced for UNCOD (1977b):

> The intensification or extension of desert conditions is a process leading to reduced biological productivity, with consequent reduction in plant biomass, in the land's carrying capacity for livestock, in crop yields and human wellbeing.

One of the major American writers on desertification in the Third World gives the following definition:

> Desertification is the impoverishment of terrestrial ecosystems under the impact of man. It is the process of deterioration in those ecosystems that can be measured by reduced productivity of desirable plants, undesirable alteration in the biomass and diversity of the micro and macro fauna and flora, accelerated soil erosion, and increased hazards for human occupancy (Dregne 1985: 19).

Others could be cited (see, for example, Le Houerou 1977). They may differ slightly in approach, in disciplinary orientation (between, say geographers, soil scientists, wildlife ecologists). But they all fail to pinpoint specific factors that can be objectively and unequivocally diagnosed and documented on the ground, irrespective of the interests of the local population, of government policy and of the international scientific community. This is not to say that desertification is not a real problem, or that it is not, in many cases, obviously recognisable, but that it is extraordinarily difficult to define it in a way that will not either be completely arbitrary or include all the effects of human activity on dry lands since before the beginnings of food production! The tendency to move from topical to disciplinary formulations probably exacerbated the problem. Even at the level of simply linking reduction in primary productivity to human activity, it remains vague, because the relationship between natural processes and human activities is both unspecified and poorly understood. It might be better to throw out the term altogether and start afresh to define exactly what should be stopped, except that since it has now been in continuous use for over a decade, and large (though pitifully inadequate) sums of money have been spent on combatting it, "desertification" has a place in history as well as in ecology.

The first difficulty lies in the relationship between the physical and biological components on the one hand and the social and cultural on the other. Physical and biological scientists either ignore the social and cultural components or attempt to produce a definition that would make them irrelevant. Social scientists generally do not appreciate the significance of the natural processes involved. In fact the four dimensions of any particular situation (physical, biological, social, cultural) are inseparable, because the natural situation is the product of the local human history and its significance differs according to the social interests and cultural values of the observer.

A second difficulty lies in the distinction between desertification and general ecological degradation. Dregne (op. cit.) would like to extend the definition to cover extreme ecological degradation anywhere. But most interested scientists consider desertification to be a problem characteristic only of areas with either a continuous or a recurrent water deficit. Although this approach to the problem still basically stands, there were already at the conference moves to broaden it to include the effects of deforestation in the humid tropics. The reasons for this are interesting in the present context since the twenty five percent or so of Africa that is not covered under the standard definition would presumably be included in the category of humid tropics at risk of deforestation. These moves came mainly from the countries of Southeast Asia which saw the possibility of gaining attention and possibly financing for one of their own major ecological problems of development. UNEP was in a dilemma. The scientists, which provided its legitimacy, argued that since deforestation of the humid tropics was not drought related it was ecologically a distinct process and mixing it up with desertification would confuse the (scientific) issue. This position also made sense to the politicians of developed countries (of which some had desertification, but none had any humid tropics they were seriously worried about) whom UNEP looked to for financing of the PACD. The representatives of developing countries saw the development issue as central to the desertification debate, but were divided since while some were concerned to gain access to a potential new source of funding others did not want to see it spread more thinly. The UNCOD Secretariat, which with Dr. Mostafa Tolba as both Secretary-General of the Conference and Executive Director of UNEP, was for practical purposes synonymous with UNEP, and was after the conference converted into a branch of UNEP (currently called Desertification Control Programme Activity Centre or DesPAC) to stimulate and coordinate the PACD, had invited all United Nations member countries to the Conference. It could not then turn round and tell them that their concerns were excluded from the subject matter, especially when it needed the maximum support for the campaign. Any one who has seen the environmental problems including desert-type landscapes that have resulted from post-deforestation erosion in, for example, northeast Thailand and parts of Indonesia, in the presence of continuing high rainfall, would find it difficult to deny their case, except on somewhat purist grounds. The Southeast Asian countries continued to press their case in their own United Nations regional organisation, the Economic and Social Commission for Asia and the Pacific (ESCAP), and it has now been generally admitted.

A third problem lies in the relationship between present symptoms and future implications. Besides the physical factor of drought definitions commonly relate desertification to the social and human factors of population growth and occasionally also increase in economic demand (though there is rarely any attention to other social or cultural factors). But the focus of the major attempts to define it is always on its immediate significance for the future. It involves assumptions of our stewardship for all future generations.

All definitions ignore the problem of distinguishing between normal ecological change and desertification. Adjectives like proper and improper, wise, abusive are used liberally as though their meaning was obvious. Since change is after all the natural order of things, and is always evaluated differently from different perspectives we need to be more specific. Differentiating between good and bad ecological change can be like distinguishing between good and bad evolution! We are implicitly passing judgement on what we predict to lie in the future, on the basis of our evaluation of the past. Not surprisingly we do not all agree. Most significantly, most Western-trained scientists disagree with many local communities and governments. Much disagreement is stifled by the global authority of particular sciences. But we do not need scientific or political consensus to see that what is good for some living now may be bad for others ten generations hence, or vice versa. Two types of conflict of interest are involved: a straightforward political conflict between living communities; and a vicarious conflict between some living communities and the projected offspring of other living communities.

The problem of definition became explicit early on in the debate. It was partly for this reason that minimal working definitions such as those cited above were extended by a number of "understandings," such as the following which were cited at UNCOD and made implicit in the priorities of the PACD. Firstly, many processes contributing to desertification operate at global scales as part of a widespread ecological trend towards drier conditions under the pressure of human land use. However, the term "desertification" was applied by UNCOD only to such degradation within the world's dry lands, that is the zones of low and variable rainfall which are inherently subject to periodic water stress and droughts. Within the dry lands, attention was focused on the more extensive and settled warmer sectors in the tropics, sub-tropics and mid-latitudes. This same climatic basis was maintained in the 1984 assessment, according to the criteria of the UNESCO World Map of Dry Climates. Secondly, studies carried out in support of UNCOD established the position that desertification had everywhere resulted from a complex interaction of environmental stresses and human pressure. The significance of the human factor was clear in the 1974 UN resolution and is implicit throughout the PACD, both of which reflect the orientation of Third World governments. In fact, it is the extent of human involvement that determines the scope for combative measures.

The third "understanding" was that although desertification is commonly recognised and assessed in ecological or other environmental terms, the significance of the threat today rests primarily in its impact on human-use systems, on living conditions and on human well-being in the areas affected. It is especially important to note that the countries most severely affected by desertification include some of the least developed nations, with populations subject to poverty and to chronic malnutrition. Desertification is understood to be intimately related to such lack of development and to unequal access to resources. Campaigns to combat it should therefore be formulated as an integral part of national programmes aimed at promoting economic progress and social welfare, with broader public participation and the local definition of priorities. Fourthly, the causes of desertification do not reside necessarily with the areas directly affected. Exogenous factors operate from outside the dry lands within the country concerned, from outside the country within the region, and from beyond the region itself. Taxation and investment policies and the terms of trade, for example, at national and international levels, typically operate to the detriment of the dry lands as disadvantaged or marginalised sectors. Equally, the consequences of desertification, whether environmental, biological or human, are not confined to the affected dry lands but are nationally and globally shared. The lesson of desertification is interdependence (we might now add "as distinct from dependence") at national, regional and global scales, and the perspectives of combative actions must be geographically appropriate. However, these numerous moves to "globalise" the problem were accompanied by a reluctance to admit the political implications.

These understandings were worked out at UNCOD as part of a subtle process of negotiation between scientists and politicians, but they should not be seen merely as a sop to the political realities of intergovernmental meetings. It is obvious that desertification in combination with poverty was felt to be the real problem by the majority of the delegates. We might go further and suggest that the desertification-poverty axis was brought to the attention of the world as a subset of the desertification problem for political reasons. But there are other political reasons why desertification generally might be seen rather as a subset of the general poverty problem. These undercurrents in the Conference and in the larger debate will be explored more fully in the next section. They are introduced here to show that although desertification was presented as a global problem affecting industrial and non-industrial countries alike, it was clear that the political weight of numbers was with the poor countries who were looking for additional arguments for aid. Meanwhile the richer countries did not need a conference to solve their desertification problems for they monopolised the expertise anyway. However, the Conference was useful to them also insofar as it satisfied certain sectors of their scientific communities by providing them a stage from which to persuade the poor countries to do what was considered necessary, and to some extent also to advertise and sell their expertise.

Looking back now it seems that the excitement of UNCOD never climaxed. Every two years or so, in accordance with the PACD, UNEP has convened the Consultative Group for Desertification Control (DesCon) with representatives from likely donors and a few deserving countries, to consider and pledge towards the financing of ready-formulated projects and assist in mobilising resources for PACD activities. This has for the most part produced only grudging results. There have also been regular meetings of a UN Interagency Working Group to coordinate efforts among the various UN bodies, again convened by UNEP in its overall "coordinating and catalytic" role. Finally, UNEP's Desertification Control Bulletin which publicises and popularises the results of the campaign has reached its eighteenth issue. But there is no sense of progress or achievement.

The First General Assessment of progress in implementation of the Plan of Action reported to the UNEP Governing Council in 1984 as scheduled (summarised in Mabutt, this volume) confirmed the scale and urgency of the problem of desertification, but showed that the goal set by UNCOD, to arrest the advance of desertification by the year 2000, was no longer feasible. The report reckoned that in 1984 desertification threatened 35% of the earth's land surface (45 million km2) and 19% of world population, or some 850 million people). Sixty percent of the population were assessed as already affected. The total desertified area of 34,750,000 km2 in 1984 was assessed at 75% of the productive area in the world's dry lands and 40% of the entire world's productive area. The direct cost of desertification in the form of a loss in agricultural production was calculated at $26 billion annually, not counting the serious costs in social disruption. Summing up the situation, Tolba said that in 1977 everyone agreed what had to be done, but "here we are just where we were then!" An expert study group estimated that it would cost about $4.5 billion per year over a 20 year period, or $90 billion in all, to put into effect the main components of the PACD. But it must be noted that these components focus on the redirection of natural trends and pay little or no attention to the underlying human motivations, which are likely to reinforce those trends.

UNCOD told us that the technology to cure or prevent desertification is available. All that needs to be done is to find the money to put it into effect. Because of the speed with which desertification is progressing we must move fast. There is no time to check the facts, or do feasibility studies or research on actual processes. We knew enough to be sure that this is a crisis, with the implication that any cure was preferable to the disease. UNEP had calculated how much it would cost to beat it by the year 2000. However, in many cases where the cure may involve further disruption of social relations and distortion of values, it is easy to see that for the present generation the cure can easily be more painful than the disease.

Money alone of course would in fact not solve the problem. But money has not been forthcoming anyway. Less than $50,000 has been deposited to the Special Account. It is true that much more has been spent on projects "said to have a desertification component," as much as $10,000 million between 1977 and 1984 according to one estimate (Dregne 1985: 31). But most of these projects were not directly concerned with the rehabilitation of degraded land or with preventing degradation. They were mainly concerned with public works, such as the improvement of domestic water supply and the construction of feeder roads, or with measures to increase rural income, such as seed-multiplication and the control of animal diseases. The primary objective was to improve living conditions in areas suffering from desertification. Some projects listed under the anti-desertification heading may actually have accelerated desertification, insofar as they made it possible for people to increase pressure on the land. In no case did any of these projects address the causes of desertification (ibid.). The money was spent according to the priorities of donorship.

Desertification is now a term used by both scientists and politicians, mostly by scientists in the hope of motivating politicians. Because of the way it is used it acquires all the emotional and ideological ambiguity that ecology also entails. Like ecology it becomes both a science (a systematic intellectual endeavour to understand certain types of situation and process) and a movement (a social or political endeavor to change the way things are). It is diagnosed by ecologists, who then explain it by reference to human or social factors, but instead of applying to social scientists for explanation of these factors, they go directly to politicians and policy makers who are presumably part of the problem!

There are two reasons why ecologists thus bypass social scientists. These reasons have to do respectively with ecologists' perception of social science, and social scientists' perception of themselves and their role. Ecologists are quite clear about the fact that desertification is not just a scientific problem (i.e. a problem in science), but a human problem (a problem in everyday life). The future of the world, and therefore also their own future, is threatened. They must do something about it urgently. Since social scientists do not understand ecology, and social science is not exact science, they must go to politicians. Not being social scientists, ecologists do not consider the analysis of the human role in desertification problematic. Social scientists on the other hand are concerned with social problems rather than ecological problems, and mainly in Western societies, and to the extent that some have attempted to explain the relationship between human behaviour and natural processes in the Third World, most particularly with the concept of "adaptation," they have been unsuccessful. We have no understanding of this relationship that can be used predictively.

We are now in a position to sum up the paradoxes that suffuse the public uses of "desertification." It is both absolute and relative; natural and social; ecological and moral; to some degree the inevitable accompaniment of all human activity, but unpredictable; everyone's problem but no one's responsibility. Meanwhile it marches on; but loses its place in the headlines as other newer problems usurp our attention. It not only seems to defy the administrative and political measures that are taken with the aim of bringing it under control; it also frustrates our efforts to think clearly about it. As an objective problem it appears obvious but intractable. As a topic of debate and analysis it remains vague and emotive. A review of the record of discussions, projects and the now extensive literature suggests that there is less than total agreement about exactly what we are dealing with. If we state it in terms of factors, it is difficult to be more precise than simply listing for example) precipitation, soils, hydrology, vegetation, people, etc.; the precise relationship between the factors remains unclear. If it is expressed in terms of processes, such as drought, deforestation, population pressure, technological intensification, and erosion; certain relationships become implicit but remain undemonstrated. After all, each of these processes does occur without desertification. If we could achieve a greater measure of conceptual clarity that would comprehend the physical, biological, social and cultural dimensions of desertification, we might have a better chance of achieving our short- and long-term resource-management objectives. But we are mired in arguments about the priority of the various factors. The concept straddles two sectors of science, the "two cultures" of Western society. Since desertification is diagnosed from natural symptoms, the natural scientists extend their hegemony over the debate. There is so far no social-science definition of desertification. In fact, it is difficult to see how there could be, because it would seem to be a social definition of a natural process, which would be absurd. But natural scientists alone are unable to harness and operationalise the human resources necessary to deal with the problem.

We have known since early in the debate that an integrated (rather than a disciplinary or sectoral) approach is necessary, but we seem not to know how to produce one. We need to work out how to conceptualize desertification in such a way that we integrate the social and natural dimensions of the problem with the concept. The lack of an integrative concept or framework is the biggest problem in (human) ecological studies generally today. A resolution of the paradoxes of the desertification debate may help us on our way to developing one.

A clue to this resolution may lie in the fact that even though desertification is not new it has been conceptualised as a problem only now. The reason is obvious, but it will be enlightening to review it because the literature does not follow it through to its logical conclusion. It has to do with population growth and the relation of population to renewable natural resources—but not in the way that is most commonly stated, not in the simple and misleading terms of carrying capacity.

The rate of desertification has increased disturbingly since the middle of this century. But the reason for our recent panic about it lies not so much in its acceleration per se as in the interpretation that our vital interests are threatened. Until very recently there was always more land, and more resources. Since the beginning of food production (the Neolithic "Revolution") we have continually upgraded our productive technologies. We have produced larger and larger quantities per hectare, though generally (as Boserup 1965 has shown us) at the cost of increasing amounts of labour or other forms of energy. Until recently, it continued to be possible to expand into new lands if productivity declined. It was not necessary to think in terms of global limits to production, because most governments, and most communities, could still expand their own areas of production. For most this has now ceased to be possible. Whereas most individuals have always been constrained by the interests of their neighbours, it is only recently that most communities have become aware of the finiteness of the total of available resources.

Although needs are expressed terms of scarce material goods (economic or ecological), they reflect social differences, differences in the way the communities fit into a larger society. We must recognise that for human beings social needs are primary. We have to satisfy our immediate social needs (as individuals and members of a community) before we can (as scientists and members of a profession) worry about habitat (although the distinction between community and profession may sometimes be blurred), let alone long-term global ecological viability. The material and the social aspects of desertification—the damage to primary productivity and the harm to people—appear so obviously related, but they are difficult to describe satisfactorily because the natural is supposedly universal whereas the social is implicitly divisive. Because of their different interests desertification means different things to different people, and these meanings change over time. It is only a short step from this point to an acceptance of the equal validity of different people's rights in relation to a desertification process, irrespective of the interests of the global community. Once rights are allowed, they tend to be difficult to deny.

The social differentiation in the desertification debate reflects an underlying moral problem, the problem of the evaluation of self-interest and of its re-evaluation over time. The people who campaign against desertification implicitly make assumptions about the motivation of those that cause it. These assumptions are not scientific assumptions, because they are not systematically derived from scientific principles; they are made not by psychologists or social scientists, but by physical or biological scientists. People assume that all human beings are similarly motivated and that their motives have to do with short-term self-interest, and vary according to individual I.Q. and access to information. Desertification seems to be a material process, caused by (supposedly irrational) human activity. Efforts to solve the problem of desertification so far have attempted to reorganise the way people think about it, on the assumption that this reorganisation can be achieved by feeding information and controlling self-interest by force or incentive, or some combination of both. But the people who suffer from desertification are more concerned with the reorganisation and redistribution of resources (according to self-interest), and (by implication) of the economic and political order on a global scale.

In one sense the underlying problem is one of morality. But it is between groups that do not share a moral universe. In any case moral problems do not have scientific solutions. We can accept that other people have different values, but we often have difficulty in accepting that they may have legitimate interests that conflict with ours. This is especially true in situations where we (as scientists) have more awareness than they have (as marginalised populations). Morally, if we have more awareness, we have more responsibility. But we also have a greater temptation to make decisions on their behalf according to our interests. The importance of the modern concept of rights is that it should help us to think of other people's self-interest on a level with our own. But it is very difficult to balance the rights of the individual relative to the group, of the group relative to the species, or the species relative to the system. This discourse has now been further complicated by a vagueness in the distinction between human rights and civic rights.

The situation is in fact even more complex than at first appears. We know that desertification is caused by, for example, over-grazing that reduces primary productivity and the palatability of range vegetation, by cultivation that exposes fragile soils to erosion, and by irrigation that raises the level of sub-surface water tables. But these are not types of behaviour. They are the results in particular circumstances of a wide variety of different types of human behaviour for which we need to investigate much more carefully than has been done so far the occasion, the motivation and the intention. Not only is there no specific type of behaviour, or behaviour pattern, that can be categorically associated with desertification. In fact, very often, positive patterns of behaviour that we should wish to encourage for other reasons, such as entrepreneurship, are most obviously at fault! An approach that looks for types of behaviour, therefore, for example by means of social indicators, does not lead to any resolution of our problem.

Another common approach looks for differences in thinking or in cultural orientation, in the perception of nature and natural resources. Despite the difference in orientations towards nature and natural resources that have been remarked on by many—for example, between the idea that we are stewards responsible to God for conserving what He has provided, and the idea that the material world is there for us to use as we will without giving any account of our actions—there is no evidence that any of these orientations is peculiar to particular societies or cultures. It appears to be truer to say that in any society we might expect to find a variety of orientations over time towards the exploitability of renewable natural resources and ecological responsibility (cf. Passmore 1974: 1–30). It seems, therefore, that there may be no cultural indicators either.

Even if it is true that there are no cultural ways of thinking and no specific social formations that are in any way mechanically linked to desertification, there obviously is a relationship between human behaviour and desertification. It must, therefore, be possible to make systematic (that is, scientific) statements about that relationship. The fact that we are so far not able to does not mean that the situation is hopeless. It means rather that we must try to find another way of asking the question. This argument directs our attention towards the assessment of a much broader range of social and cultural criteria than have been used so far.

Instead of looking for types of behaviour, we should look for common factors in the human conditions where desertification occurs. But this also must be done with care. For example, "The Tragedy of the Commons" has been seen as such a common factor, and to be invariably associated (in dry lands) with some degree of desertification. The idea was introduced (by Hardin) in 1968 and has enjoyed considerable influence. It states that where rights of access to a resource are held in common, not only is there no incentive to conserve, but each individual will be led to over-exploit on the assumption that if he does not, others will do so at his expense. It is, therefore, in his interests to get in before the others. The argument had already been made somewhat more sophisticatedly for Western society (for which it is more useful) under the title "The Logic of Collective Action" (Olson 1965). It is an important and a persuasive argument, but does not necessarily hold for all societies, and in the case of desertification it can easily be shown that there are communities with common access that have not caused desertification, as well as communities with individualized rights that have caused desertification. It is therefore empirically unwarranted to introduce as a matter of principle individualised land use rights in order to minimise the risk of desertification. It becomes an excuse for saying that desertification is caused by people who are not like us. It may in fact be argued that individualisation of land rights in some cases disrupts community life, which could in itself lead to desertification. For disruption of community life leads to depopulation. Several of the cases of desertification that were studied in the Turan Programme of ecological research in Iran (see Spooner and Horne 1980, Spooner and Mann 1982: 138–292) provided examples of desertification as a result of depopulation, rather than (as is generally expected) depopulation resulting from desertification. Some village communities had disintegrated as a result of the economic pull of the towns with the result that there was no one to maintain the investment in agricultural land and irrigation engineering and it was invaded by (non-anthropogenic) sand.

The conclusion here appears to be that in any case of desertification we should look at the range of human interests that are involved both in the "desertification-population" itself and outside, and ask what is the total universe of motivation related to the human activities that are directly implicated, and what is the distribution of relative political and economic power. The answer is invariably outside the desertification-population. Most people in most countries neither suffer directly from desertification, nor are professionally concerned with it. It is there that the roots of desertification lie, but it is there also that its meaning has a different quality and is at its weakest.

5. The Other Agendas

Since UNCOD there have been few large public debates on desertification. Attention has been directed at potential projects, and we have come to rely more and more on the public record, the excellent documentation prepared and assembled by the Secretariat (much of which has been published in the works already cited), or, perhaps to an even greater extent now, on the meticulous re-documentation prepared for the review in 1984. However, there was much to learn from the day-to-day deliberations of UNCOD, both formal and informal, and of the related regional meetings before and after, that should not be forgotten. The other agendas which underlay the formal discussions must be talked out if we are to come to terms with desertification as a global issue.

UNCOD was a unique event, perhaps more so than the other UN conferences have been, even Stockholm. It was convened and conducted on the basis of an epistemology that was not fully shared by all the participants. The background documents and the draft plan of action, for all the liberalism that went into them, argued from the assumptions of the ecology of ecosystems (a paradigm that has since lost its dominant place in scientific ecology), in which human activity was a perhaps necessary but nevertheless intrusive element, defying explanation except insofar as it was adaptive. The documents called for ecosystem management. It was never explicit that solutions to problems of ecological management inevitably raised questions of management of the political economy and general human social organization. As often happens in such international forums, where the common syntax and vocabulary of an international language are imperfect vehicles for widely differing cultural intentions, the discussions were conducted on more than one level. While ostensibly the delegates were engaging the problem of how to organise programmes in which they would cooperate to mobilise resources for a campaign against desertification, many were implicitly bargaining about political relationships. Most delegates saw the solution to desertification in the mobilisation of resources, but many also blamed what they discerned as the incentives for exploitation of people and resources inherent in the current economic order of things, and saw the solution in the reorganisation of that order. All delegates publicly accepted the ecological explanations of desertification and the direct technical solutions that were offered, but many were more concerned with ultimate causes and ultimate solutions: the economic and political conditions that generate land use decisions at the level of ecological management. The "political will and determination" that they sought to stimulate for that purpose were more abundant at the latter level of political bargaining, though more difficult to harness! The Conference provided a classic case of a generally recognised form being used differently by different interests. Just as we have learned in the study of modern complex societies that efforts to manage society cannot be kept entirely separate from efforts to reorganize it, so the campaign to conserve resources can never entirely avoid stirring up a campaign to reorganise the distribution of resources. These subversive tendencies derive not from a fear of desertification, but from the awareness of inequality and especially of poverty.

Drought, famine and desertification describe three relationships between human communities and their natural resources. Each is associated with poverty. Desertification is the global issue because it has global implications. But drought, famine and poverty are more immediate factors for most desertification-populations. Since none is inevitably linked to any of the others it may be useful to pick up the discussion of them where we left it in section three above and explore the meaning of each in more detail.

Drought and famine may be dealt with summarily since drought is well studied by geographers and though it is a complex enough subject in itself its complexities do not bear on the present discussion, and famine is investigated in other chapters. Poverty, however, requires more attention since it fuels conflict in debates in national and international affairs and development economics, deriving from conflicting ideologies. The available analyses and interpretations have not yet been introduced into the desertification debate or related in any detail to any specific desertification problems. Since it is a concept that is generally debated in the context of the relationship between people and material resources, it may serve as a key to the integration of social and natural science approaches in the problem of desertification. Let us deal therefore with drought and famine first.

Drought is in fact not so straightforward a concept as is generally believed. Not only is it as relative as the other concepts we are dealing with, but it is implicitly relative to human activity patterns, to human dependence on a particular level of annual or seasonal precipitation. Like desertification, outside a particular human context it can have only arbitrary meaning according to the time scale chosen for diagnosis, and its human context is always liable to change. Any definition of drought, since it assumes a level of human dependence on precipitation, assumes a social context; and by attempting to define it according to objective measurements apart from such a context we run the risk of misleading ourselves about its significance. Scientific diagnoses are not usually derived from local needs.

To be more specific, drought signifies extended soil moisture deficiency. Almost every region of the world experiences a deficiency in soil moisture at some time during the year. In deserts it may be continuous and perennial. In semi-arid areas it is generally seasonal. In temperate and humid climates it may be occasional or even exceptional. In general the lower the annual average precipitation, the greater the range of annual variation, and the more frequent the incidence of extended (longer than average) periods of relative drought. In addition to annual variation there is also variation on a longer time scale. For example, there is evidence of periods of greater than "usual" drought in the Sahel at intervals of several decades, since systematic measurement was begun in the last century, e.g., 1911, 1940, 1973. The fact that we have made systematic objective measurements of precipitation, evaporation and water deficit with little or no reference to the water dependence of local production activities has encouraged us to think of drought in absolute terms, or in terms of Western agricultural science. Local production activities, which though they were by no means unchanging had in most cases undergone little escalation of technology or intensity before the introduction of Western technology and demand, had been generally extensive, flexible and mobile enough to accommodate these fluctuations without too much disruption. Whatever the medium or long-term trends that may be extrapolated by meteorologists as a basis for prediction for the future, the key to adaptive technology will always be flexibility. Drought often triggers famines and processes of desertification in situations that are beyond the current technological and social flexibility of local populations.

Famine is more complex, though the situation has been greatly clarified by Sen's (1981) analysis in terms of "food entitlement." Whatever the significant or efficient cause of particular famines, the immediate cause is failure in a network of distribution. Only in cases where a domestic group normally produces all the food it needs, as an autarkic unit, can famine be purely a question of the ecology of production. Even then, in the past the problem may have been solved by mobility or migration. We have come to think of famine as a problem primarily of insufficient production as distinct from inadequate or uneven distribution. This view is encouraged by the reduction in mobility and in opportunities for migration, and increased competition for productive land, that go with increased levels of population and new political forms in most poor countries in the Third World. Local autarky, if it ever existed, does not survive in the modern world. The hallmark of modernity is economic incorporation and interdependence. Why then should the incorporation of Africa into the global economy be marked by an increased incidence of famine, and why should such famine be explained as an automatic product of desertification? The answer may be in the balance of interdependent relations, that is in the degree of dependence.

If famine is due to failure of distribution, we need to know what causes that failure. What is the cause of the disentitlement that we gloss as poverty? Distribution may be disrupted or impaired by either natural (ecological) or human (social) factors. The ability to repair disruptions has increased with modern progress in the technology of communications and transportation. Famine may potentially be caused by any factor that changes the distribution of food access, which could be change in natural conditions which in turn could be embedded in a longer term process of desertification. Ecological access problems may lead to economic problems. Change in the terms of trade—a factor in all famines—is invariably to the disadvantage of the poor, because they are excluded from any influence on prices.

Since it is economic and by implication also political, Sen's argument against the conventional explanation (which he formulates as "Food Availability Decline") as a general explanation of famines provides support for the present argument against desertification as a cause in Africa or elsewhere. He applies systematic analysis of the Ethiopian and Sahelian famines of the 1970s to demonstrate that

> "A person's ability to avoid starvation will depend both on his ownership and on the exchange entitlement mapping that he faces. A general decline in food supply may indeed cause him to be exposed to hunger through a rise in food prices with an unfavourable impact on his exchange entitlement. Even when his starvation is caused by food shortage in this way, his immediate reason for starvation will be the decline in his exchange entitlement" (Sen 1981: 4).

and clarifies his approach further by emphasising that we should escape "the hold of the tradition of thinking in terms of what exists" and think rather "in terms of who can command what" (ibid.: 8). "The mesmerizing simplicity of focusing on the ratio of food to population has persistently played an obscuring role over centuries, and continues to plague policy discussions today much as it has deranged anti-famine policies in the past" (ibid.). We can add that the conventional explanations of desertification have suffered from an equally mesmerising simplicity.

The complementary political concept of "enfranchisement," suggested in a review of Sen's book by Appadurai (1984: 481), adds an important dimension to this approach. Those who suffer from famine are those who have lost their food entitlement. The process that led to this loss may have been triggered by a combination of drought and desertification, but the loss would be less likely to have occurred if they were not both poor and disenfranchised in the economic universe into which they had become incorporated. Amplified in this way, Sen has in effect considerably enhanced our understanding of the dynamics of famines by discussing their political economy (ibid.: 482), rather than simply what might be called their ecological economy.

People who cause desertification (insofar as they are aware of it) do so in pursuit of what seem to them at the time to be reasonable objectives. They may be acting in desperation, or they may simply have their eyes on other socio-economic objectives in the larger society. In the latter case, the type of desertification that occurs in the industrialised countries might be called affluence-desertification. The process is probably best managed by manipulation of the costs and benefits, the terms of trade, at the level of the national government. In the former case, which we might call poverty-desertification, the same strategy is possible but more difficult because in the developing countries where it occurs there is a lower level of integration of local communities into the national unit: often barriers of tribal solidarity reinforced by generations of conflict complicate economic relations, and even in a desperate situation pride of identity may militate against any form of compromise between neighbouring groups. In either case the reason is to be sought in the relationship with the outside. These are the complex problems of marginalisation, exclusion from more productive resources and from the political processes that control them, along with exclusion from information networks, leading to cultural isolation, which leads in turn to different perception of interests, and conception of time and nature (cf. Douglas and Isherwood 1979: 71–95). What is new in the modern world is our ability to marginalise on a greater scale than ever before.

Marginalisation in the competition for social and economic resources can easily lead to over-exploitation of natural resources, often (especially in the Third World) in desperation, though sometimes (especially in industrialised countries) as a way of producing goods in order to trade back into the social centre. Desertification is therefore related to drought in an indirect way, but it is directly related to the inequalities associated with social and economic marginalisation. This argument suggests a conclusion that entails yet another paradox, the last in our series: that the fight against desertification will be won not with increasing awareness of ecology, but with increasing political awareness. It appears to be generally true that political awareness has been increasing throughout the world with the technological development of communications and the information industry. Redclift (1984) and Bauer (1988) also argue (from different points of view) that aid has led to politicisation.

The explanation of poverty has evolved in a similar way. Poverty became an issue in the West in the 18th century. To begin with, the most common explanation was laziness and lack of discipline. Gradually, an increasing number of writers began to suggest structural explanations. The debate between structural and psychological approaches continues. Our new global consciousness has applied it to nations. The structural approach essentially maintains that economic theories based on self-interest and psychological theories based on individual capacity or intention are unsatisfactory because they fail to go to the heart of the problem. Poverty has to do with relationships and identity, integration and autonomy. It is a part of the discourse of class, and the discontinuities of class are not apparent to the economist, who sees only a gradation of income and other statistical distributions across all classes (cf. Douglas and Isherwood 1979: 204). People who have feel safer with other people who have, rather than with people who have not, and exclude them. This is a normal dynamic of self-interest. Advanced technology increases inequality and the exclusionary capacity. Poverty therefore often occurs in resource-poor environments, but not as a consequence of them. All current environmentalism is a product of the prosperity of our particular stage of historical development. It is used in the political negotiation between groups in conflict over resources. In this conflict the poor are at a disadvantage. Our relationship to the poor and the desertified has changed as we have become part of a global society. We are now all part of one "total political unit," as Simmel understood already at the beginning of the century ([1908] 1971: 157).

Desertification processes can be mapped onto the distribution of marginalised populations. This mapping works in America and Australia as well as in Africa and Asia (though the implications of the marginalisation are different). At UNCOD the delegates representing marginalised countries, or countries with significant marginalised populations, were making exactly this argument, though it did not come through clearly in the public record. But even if some of us may be ready to hear the message now, what can we do about it? Look at America, Europe, the Soviet Union, China. They all have significant marginalised populations and appear to make little progress in their attempts to relieve their situation. Even where these populations are not indigent, they are often associated with desertification or other forms of what ecologists have come to call "resource abuse."

Desertification in the Third World is different from desertification in the relatively affluent countries with Western or Western-style political systems, because of the difference in opportunity for afflicted populations to make their own choice. There is an argument that this situation is not helped by aid. Aid is in general government-to-government subsidy and tends to lead to further marginalisation. The tendency to blame all these ills on colonialism should be resisted, however, since it is doubtful whether the rate of various forms of man's inhumanity to man has changed significantly in terms of percentages since early historical times. What has changed is the total numbers of people, and our global awareness and technological capabilities. Without aid now there is no such collectivity as the Third World or the South (cf. Bauer 1988: 66). Just as aid has produced the Third World, it has also produced our condemnation of the populations that do not make aid work in the way we mean it to work. The fact that it is politically unacceptable to question aid leads us to make other accommodations. So desertification (as the concept is used in practice) is a function of the international politics of aid. There is another minority argument that aid ensures and maintains "underdevelopment." The same argument can be applied to desertification: the International Campaign to Combat Desertification, as it is conceived and practised, serves to maintain and even promote desertification processes. The reason for this is straightforward: it attacks the ecological symptoms, while reinforcing the social causes. The Campaign and the PACD are based on a purely ecological conceptualisation (whatever the effective working definition) of desertification and ignores completely the fact that it is caused by human activities. That it is in fact caused by human activities is a major point in the ideology of the ecological desertification lobby, but the implication—that the campaign should therefore be directed at social dynamics rather than resource management—is not followed, and probably cannot be followed given the current structure and interests of our institutions.

Anti-desertification projects are invariably a form of aid, approved and implemented according to a combination of economic and political criteria. There are basically two possible arguments about what is wrong with this strategy. Either the amounts given have been grossly insufficient; or there is something fundamentally wrong with the strategy, with the implication that any aid is too much. Bauer has recently made a strong case for the latter. He concludes:

> "The contemporary Third World is not short of natural resources. Most of Africa and Latin America and much of Asia is sparsely populated. Many millions of extremely poor people have abundant cultivable land—witness among others the tribes-folk of Black Africa and the Amazonian Indians, who live in areas where land is a free good. Conversely, many of the most prosperous areas of the Third World (Taiwan, Hong Kong, Singapore, and parts of Malaysia) are very densely populated, even where the land is not inherently fertile . . . Poverty and riches depend on man, his culture, his motivations, and his political arrangements. Herein lies the wealth and poverty of nations" (1988: 75).

We finish up with a kind of equation between poverty and desertification. Marginalisation is the product of a social process. The impact of human activity on the environment is also a social process. Marginalisation impoverishes both people and land. Desertification is first a social and only secondarily an ecological process. The solution is to reintegrate the marginalised populations into the larger social process, and of marginalised nations into the international community. The environment as we perceive it and evaluate it is an extension or projection of society as we live it. Reintegration of the people will at the same time reintegrate the land, and change the way people relate to it. Reintegration is not achieved through aid, which institutionalises dependence and reinforces marginalisation, but through re-entitlement and re-enfranchisement (cf. Redclift 1984: 130). This is, however, politically difficult. Direct efforts to re-entitle and re-enfranchise may not work. But at least we can desist from measures that reinforce the current relationships.

6. Africa and the Long Term

In an important sense, desertification is the special problem of Africa. It was the recent experience in Africa, as interpreted by the international partnership of science and technology working in economic development, that led to the initial coinage and definition of the term, inspired the efforts to convene a world conference on it, and consequently raised awareness of the general danger in most of the rest of the world. The major UNCOD documents (such as UNCOD 1977 and United Nations 1978), all introduce their case with a summary of the African experience.

As is shown by the figures in the preceding chapter, desertification in Africa is at a different order of magnitude than in any other part of the world. It has transformed wider areas and disrupted more communities. It still seems to progress there at a faster rate than anywhere else. The economic and logistical difficulties involved in organising relief and remedial work are also greater than in most other vulnerable areas. The problem is significant for seventy five percent of the continent. Only a small number of African countries escape being affected by virtue of being located entirely within the humid tropical areas in the central western part of the continent. Desertification might be said to be the African issue par excellence of the second half of the century.

It is not surprising, therefore, that Africa which dominates little else in the world is geographically dominant in the arena of desertification-control. Specialised agencies have proliferated. Interested UN-related agencies alone include the United Nations Sahelian Office (UNSO), the Club du Sahel, which was established in 1976 to support the work of the Comité Permanent Inter-états de Lutte contre la Sècheresse dans le Sahel (CILSS or Permanent Inter-State Committee to Combat Drought in the Sahel, which includes Burkina Faso, Cape Verde, Chad, Gambia, Mali, Mauritania, Niger, and Senegal, and has its headquarters in Paris), the Economic Commission for Africa (ECA), the International Livestock Centre for Africa (ILCA), and the African branches of the International Crop Research Institute for the Semiarid Tropics (ICRISAT) and the International Institute for Tropical Agriculture (IITA). These activities reflect the intensity of the larger international enterprise, which includes numerous non-governmental organisations as well as the World Bank, UNDP and all the major bilateral donors. There has been a more determined effort to arrest the process of desertification in Africa than anywhere else.

But just as desertification is not a single problem, it is not the only African issue. The same populations that are plagued by desertification, suffer also from other problems, such as poverty and various forms of economic and political instability. Environmental problems and social problems have a habit of coinciding. But in Africa the environmental problems have been more difficult to overcome or to live with and the social problems are more general.

The nature of Africa's natural endowment is well known. The northern third of the continent is desert, except for the narrow Mediterranean littoral which historically has been much more closely related to the Middle East and Europe than to the rest of Africa. The larger portion south of the Sahara is isolated not only by the desert to the north and the surrounding ocean but by the nature of the coasts which provide few good harbours and only poor access to the interior plateau. The vast expanses of the interior are poor in the type of resources that would encourage integration into a larger economy. Unreliable rainfall patterns and poor soils have inhibited investment in agriculture. The climate and ecology support a consistently heavy burden of disease, which acts as a brake on demographic growth and on the organisation of labor. Disease in Africa has resisted the spread of modern health care because of social conditions which are characterised by sparse populations, and inherently low levels of social integration along with political and economic instability (cf. Kopytoff 1987). When Africa was subsumed into the political economy of Europe in the last century it fell inevitably into a condition of dependence and marginalisation. The nation-state governments that the Europeans left behind on decolonisation in the 1960s are inadequate mediators between vernacular African conceptions of authority and Western economic power.

From this perspective the outlook is not bright. Africa fits into the inhabited world in a way that is special both geographically and socially, and presents problems that the modern world has not been good at solving—outside a laboratory. Results of efforts so far have been unencouraging. The agencies responsible are all extensions of Western bilateral aid and development interests. Progress is evaluated in terms of amounts of money expended and visible short-term material results, with an emphasis on investment and the transfer of technology. There is little long-term monitoring of the effects. Recent work, however, has begun finally to demonstrate that other factors may be more important. At the Second International Rangelands Congress in Adelaide in 1984 tables were presented (based on work carried out by ILCA) demonstrating that traditional pastoral systems in Africa can be more efficient in terms of productivity per hectare than ranching systems in either developing or developed countries (Cossins 1986). Other studies have begun to elucidate in significant detail the mechanics of the relationship between African pastoralists and their resources (Sandford 1986). The African situation is not hopeless and African history has its examples of empire and other larger forms of social, political and economic achievement, as well as locally viable technologies of food and other production. Indigenous cultural dynamics have met the challenge of local conditions in the past. What is new in the modern world is our ability to marginalise on a greater scale than ever before. Desertification is most serious in Africa because Africa is the most marginalised area in the world today.

What can be done about it? In one important sense this situation like history, is irreversible. Africa cannot be detached from the modern world. The solution, if there is one, must come from reworking its incorporation into the larger political economy. Over the past few years there have been signs of a sea change in orientations and objectives, as larger institutions catch up with the implications of the general increase in political awareness, that might possibly move us in that direction. The World Bank has concluded that "the full explanation of why Africa is in such straits has to be sought in the political economy of the region" (World Bank 1986), and has announced a major reorganisation of its policies, including "much more attention to resource conservation and the environmental aspects of development projects" (Science 236: 769, 1987). This reorganisation does not of course signal a change in the direction that is being suggested here—the purpose of the World Bank is still aid for development—but it is obviously influenced by the same currents. The following is another example of a response that while differently inspired can lead to parallel results:

" . . . the greatest hope for stopping and reversing desertification lies in making more intensive use of the best lands. Pressures on marginal lands must be reduced. Given the growing population, the only feasible way to do so is to increase productivity on favorable lands. Traditional agriculture is a low-risk, low-yield food production system capable of functioning indefinitely at the subsistence level if the dependent population is small and has modest needs. Such a system, however, usually cannot cope with rapid population increases and with restrictions on freedom of movement within and between countries. Intensification of production through improved technology seems to be imperative to meet growing urban requirements" (Dregne 1985: 30). "The solution to desertification in arid regions is to increase productivity on the better endowed lands by targeting technical and financial resources there. The much maligned 'trickle down' theory of economic development is the effective approach in desertification control. There is no future to expending scarce resources on the least productive areas" (ibid.: 33).

This approach may have the expected results, but probably for rather different reasons: it will not increase the dependency of the desertification-populations. But once again it may not be feasible politically. Aid fills political vacuums; redistributing or concentrating it has political implications and can create vacuums. It would seem, therefore, that only the increasing political awareness of the populations themselves can lead to a resolution. The wave of increasing political awareness that has been accelerating as a result of the politicisation of modern, literate complex societies since the middle of this century continues to spread (cf. Gellner 1983: 126–127). Although its effects are by no means all appealing, since it also generates conflict, it militates against marginalisation and it may repair some of the damage caused by the marginalisation of recent times.

The marginalisation that is at issue here is largely a consequence of the consolidation of European and American power over the past hundred years. De-colonisation could have been a first step towards reversing it, but retreating powers were naturally reluctant to leave behind either vacuums or opportunities. Wherever there has been politicisation, there has been some reduction in marginalisation, and either the rate of desertification, or the suffering it causes, has diminished. But in most cases, and especially in Africa, perhaps for the reasons suggested in the previous section, there has so far been relatively little politicisation, compared to most other parts of the world, and desertification continues unabated. Discussion of environmental problems continues to be conducted in isolation from discussion of global economic relations. The ecological lobby has tried desperately to get environmental questions included in development planning, and with the Bank's recent decision has finally made some headway. But their objective is to subordinate development to environmental concerns, which in the long term is not politically feasible.

It is interesting that Marxist approaches to the problems of the Third World have failed to explore this debate. The ultimate problem with an ecological approach is that it can analyze only in terms of approximation to equilibrium (despite the sophistication of some concepts such as "succession"; cf. Douglas 1970). But the complementary argument that would make the environment part of the political dialogue about development and the analysis of underdevelopment has barely been begun (cf. Redclift 1984: 1). In fact, Marxists have scarcely even challenged the general tendency to depoliticize environmental issues. This neglect may partly be explained by the fact that natural resources were never important in Marxist thinking, which paradoxically has seen the environment as a given rather than as a distributive issue, and natural resources as capital to be exploited, as much or even more so than other Western orientations (ibid.). It is possible now to read new significance into Marx's statement in his Preface to a Contribution to the Critique of Political Economy, which was not evident when it was written:

"In the social production of their life, men enter into definite relations that are indispensable and independent of their will, relations of production which correspond to a definite stage of development of their material productive forces . . . At a certain stage of their development the material productive forces of society come into conflict with the existing relations of production" (see Marx apud Redclift 1984: 6).

This text provides a Marxian insight into both the Green Movement inside Western societies and the desertification problem in their extra-territorial economies. There are other indications of this type of link between problems in the West and in the developing world, and the World Conservation Strategy (1980) though from an environmentalist point of view seeks to establish similar objectives. So the scene may be set for a rapprochement or at least some sort of compromise or accommodation between the environmentalist and the structuralist orientations.

If we are to make any progress in the resolution of environmental problems such as desertification, it is essential that we begin to see them as political issues in a larger context, but this change of orientation will require broadening the disciplinary basis of research and interpretation beyond the ecological monopoly to include the study of the political and moral economy of resources and of the environment at the national and international levels. It is necessary both to make the environmental crisis a central concern of political economy and to make its structural causes a central concern of environmentalism (cf. Redclift 1984: 2).

Desertification cannot be combatted by measures that increase the cost to the populations already afflicted. We cannot expect them to accept calls to save the future. The best we can feasibly do politically is to make things better for ourselves and everyone else today. Otherwise it is possible that conservation could leave posterity worse off (see Passmore 1974: 80–100). Despite the overwhelming impact of descriptions of suffering in the desertified parts of Africa there is still room for doubt about whether the quality of life generally, or the standard of living, is declining specifically as a result of desertification, because people often shift from their dependence on local natural resources to a dependence on socio-economic resources outside their community. But if it is declining, our first duty is to living generations. The PACD, as it exists under UNEP's authority since 1977, is of little or no relevance for current famine in Africa since it is concerned more with the productivity of renewable natural resources for future generations, rather than the inclusion of marginalised African populations into social networks that will give them equal political and economic status.

We have learned that the direct attack on desertification does not work. The reason is simple: it ignores the causes. Direct measures to change the land use of associated populations also does not work. Except perhaps in the short term we are unable to organise or control the disentitled and disenfranchised. We also know from experience that direct attack on poverty does not work either, for similar reasons. Marginalisation is double-edged: it puts people beyond our control. Therefore, de-marginalization by re-entitlement and re-enfranchisement will reduce both poverty and desertification. What needs to be done is to organise society so that people living in the least productive areas have a fully enfranchised place in it. Depopulating the least productive areas will not work beyond the short term for two reasons: (1) enforced movement of population is always disruptive both in the community of origin and in the community of destination; (2) the best way to prevent marginalisation, and the attendant disentitlement and disenfranchisement, is to prevent communities from becoming geographically isolated and depopulated. There is a relationship between spatial distribution and social differentiation. The more homogeneous the settlement pattern, the more homogeneous the society is likely to be.

Although the increase in political awareness that is a byproduct of the politicisation of the Third World will help, our own experience in Western societies is sufficient to show that reducing marginalisation will not be easy. The process can be assisted further by efforts to increase awareness specifically of environmental factors. Is it possible that desertification seen in historical context could in this way have a significance completely different from that predicted by the ecological scientists who have played the major role in generating the campaign so far? That it could evolve into a major factor in the larger campaign for social justice both within and between nations? In any case, whatever the future significance of desertification may be, the primary current significance in Africa is that it disrupts communities and the distributive networks with and among them. This disruption is leading to new social problems that are likely to bring in their train increasing political awareness that will finally go to the heart of the marginalisation that causes desertification, and have much more lasting effects on the ecology of the continent than the direct efforts of conventional land use management projects, that must of course anyway be continued.[1]

---

[1] Portions of sections 3 and 4 have been adapted from Spooner 1982, 1984 and 1987.

References

Appadurai, A. 1984. How moral is South Asia's economy? *Journal of Asian Studies* 43(3): 481–497.

Bauer, P. 1988. Creating the Third World. *Encounter* 80(4): 66–75.

Bennett, J.W. 1976. *The Ecological Transition.* London: Pergamon Press.

Bernus, E. 1977. Case Study on Desertification: The Eghazer and Azawak Region, Niger, prepared for UNCOD and published in *Case Studies on Desertification.* UNESCO: Paris (1980)

Biswas, M.R. and A.K. Biswas, eds. 1980. *Desertification*. Pergamon Press: Oxford.

Boserup, E. 1965. *The Conditions of Agricultural Growth*. Aldine: Chicago.

Brokensha, D. 1986. Deforestation. Paper prepared for the Workshop on Conservation and Survival, University of Pennsylvania, Philadelphia. (May 1986).

Conant, F.P. 1982. Thorns paired, sharply recurved: Cultural controls and rangeland quality in East Africa. In *Desertification and Development*, ed. by B. Spooner and H.S. Mann. Academic Press: London. pp. 111–122.

Cossins, N.J. 1986. The productivity and potential of pastoral systems. In *The Developing World: Challenges and Opportunities*, ed. by B. Spooner. CSIRO: Deniliquin, New South Wales.

Douglas, M. 1970. Environments at Risk. Lecture at ICA, reprinted in *Implicit Meanings*, Routledge and Kegan Paul: London. 1975 pp. 230–248.

Douglas, M. and B. Isherwood. 1979. *The World of Goods*. W.W. Norton and Co: New York.

Dregne, H.E. 1983. *Desertification of Arid Lands*. Harwood Academic Publishers: Chur, Switzerland.

_____ 1985. Aridity and land degradation. *Environment* 27(8): 16–20, 28–33.

Gellner, E. 1983. *Nations and Nationalism*. Cornell University Press: Ithaca.

Glantz, M.H., ed. 1977. *Desertification. Environmental Degradation in and around Arid Lands*. Westview Press: Boulder, CO.

Grove, A.T. 1986. Desertification in Africa. *Georgraphic Journal*.

Hardin, G. 1968. The tragedy of the commons. *Science* 162: 1243–1248.

Horne, L. 1982. The demand for fuel: Ecological implications of socio-economic change. In *Desertification and Development*, ed. by B. Spooner and H.S. Mann. Academic Press: London. pp. 201–216.

Kopytoff, I., ed. 1987. *The African Frontier: The Reproduction of Traditional African Societies*. Indiana University Press: Bloomington, IN.

Le Houerou, H.N. 1977. The nature and causes of desertification. In *Desertification*. ed. by M.H. Glantz. Westview: Boulder, CO. pp. 17–38.

Mabbutt, J.A. and C. Floret, eds. 1980. *Case Studies on Desertification*. Prepared by UNESCO/UNEP/UNDP, Natural Resources Research XVIII. UNESCO: Paris.

Marx, K. 1859. Zur Kritik der politischen Oekonomie. Translated in K. Marx and F. Engels 1970. *Selected Works*. Lawrence and Wishart: London.

Nyerges, A.E. 1982. Pastoralists, flocks and vegetation: Processes of co-adaptation. In *Desertification and Development*, ed. by B. Spooner and H.S. Mann. Academic Press: London. pp. 217–247.

Olson, M. 1965. *The Logic of Collective Action*. Harvard University Press: Cambridge, MA.

Passmore, J. 1974. *Man's Responsibility for Nature, Ecological Problems and Western Traditions*. Charles Scribner and Sons: New York.

Redclift, M. 1984. *Development and the Environmental Crisis.* Methuen: London.

Sandford, S. 1982. Opportunism and conservatism. In *Desertification and Development*, ed. by B. Spooner and H.S. Mann. Academic Press: London. pp. 61–80.

_____ 1986. Traditional African range management systems. In *The Developing World: Challenges and Opportunities*, ed. by B. Spooner. CSIRO: Deniliquin, New South Wales.

Schulz, A. 1982. Reorganizing deserts: Mechanization and marginal lands in Southwest Asia. In *Desertification and Development*, ed. by B. Spooner and H.S. Mann. Academic Press: London. pp. 27–41.

Science 1987. 236: 769.

Sen, A. 1981. *Poverty and Famines.* Clarendon Press: Oxford.

Simmel, G. 1908. The poor. *Soziologie.* Duncker and Humboldt: Munich and Leipzig.

Spooner, B. 1982. Rethinking desertification, the social dimension. In *Desertification and Development*, ed. by B. Spooner and H.S. Mann. Academic Press: London. pp. 1–25.

_____ 1984. *Ecology in Development.* United Nations University: Tokyo.

_____ 1986a. Human Ecology in the MAB Programme. Report to the MAB Scientific Advisory Committee, UNESCO: Paris.

_____, ed. 1986b. *The Developing World: Challenges and Opportunities.* Proceedings of the second International Rangelands Congress. CSIRO: Deniliquin, New South Wales.

_____ 1987. The paradoxes of desertification. *Desertification Bulletin* 15: 40–45.

Spooner, B. and L. Horne, eds. 1980. Cultural and Ecological Perspectives from the Turan Programme, Iran. *Expedition* 22(4).

Spooner, B. and H.S. Mann, eds. 1982. *Desertification and Development. Dryland Ecology in Social Perspective.* Academic Press: London.

United Nations. 1978. United Nations Conference on Desertification. 29th August-9 September, 1977. Round-up, Plan of Action and Resolutions. United Nations: New York.

UNCOD. 1977a. *Desertification: Its Causes and Consequences.* Compiled and edited by the Secretariat of the United Nations Conference on Desertification, Nairobi. Pergamon Press: Oxford.

UNCOD. 1977b. United Nations Conference on Desertification. World Map of Desertification. UNEP: Nairobi.

World Bank. 1986. *Research News* 6(4).

World Conservation Strategy. 1980. IUCN, UNEP, UNESCO: Paris.

The Persistence of Nutritional Stress in Northeastern African (Sudanese Nubian) Populations

Debra L. Martin

School of Natural Science
Hampshire College
Amherst, Massachusetts 01002

George J. Armelagos

Department of Anthropology
University of Massachusetts
Amherst, Massachusetts 01003

Kay A. Henderson

School of Natural Science
Hampshire College
Amherst, Massachusetts 01002

Introduction

Recent interest in the long-term effects of malnutrition on the growing child, as well as on the adult segments of populations, has generated a wide variety of approaches to studying nutrition, morbidity and mortality. Data from experimentally-induced malnourished animals, and clinical data from humans experiencing nutritional deprivation and protein-energy malnutrition are available for this purpose. Epidemiological studies provide information on spatial and ecological factors affecting malnourished human groups. While these studies are important, they are often missing an historical or temporal perspective. This chapter provides a temporal dimension to the study of malnutrition in one region of Africa.

Anthropologists interested in the biological past have explored patterns of dietary stress and malnutrition which span thousands of years, and these studies provide an important temporal dimension to the documentation of nutritional deficiencies (Wells 1964, Brothwell 1972, Steinbock 1976). A more recent approach documents the impact of the shift to an agricultural subsistence pattern on the health of human populations globally (Cohen and Armelagos 1984).

Theoretical and methodological developments in skeletal biology have moved beyond the descriptive phase into processual analyses. These processual approaches integrate elements of paleopathology, epidemiology, nutrition and cultural anthropology to elucidate nutritional diseases that affect bone and teeth (e.g., Wing and Brown 1980, Cohen and Armelagos 1984,Mielke and Gilbert 1985). Dietary and health data provide time depth and geographic variability to the understanding of the short- and long-term consequences of nutritional stress.

We can now document the occurrence and persistence of nutritional stress for a number of prehistoric Northeastern African populations found in Egypt and the Sudan. Iron deficiency anemia, retarded bone growth, and premature osteoporosis (bone loss) in prehistoric Sudanese Nubian populations suggest that nutritional inadequacies have been a chronic problem in the area for the past two thousand years and possibly for 5000 years. Skeletal analysis of these populations reveals that children of weaning age and young adult females in a subsistence base dominated by intensive cereal grain agricultural production suffer from severe problems in development and maintenance of the skeletal system.

While an agricultural subsistence pattern has persisted for at least 10,000 years into modern times, indicating successful cultural adaptation, there have been significant biological costs. We argue that endemic and chronic undernutrition is the biological cost to subgroups such as pregnant and lactating women, infants, and weaning children. Furthermore, many of these problems are associated with, and further exacerbated by, the reduction of birth-spacing. Certain subgroups are at particularly high risk because a cycle involving the mother and infant becomes difficult to break: when maternal nutrition is poor, both maternal and infant health can be compromised (Allen 1984: 171–172). The combined effects of high infant mortality, reduced birth spacing, and chronic nutritional shortages on the health of both mother and child is deleterious and has implications for understanding the health of successive generations (Population Reports 1975, Villar and Belizan 1981, Popkin et al. 1982, Labbok 1985).

Methods for analysis of sketetal remains have advanced tremendously in the last ten years. These advances are the result of new technologies and a systematic application of existing technologies. Researchers now have the capacity to obtain health and dietary data from skeletal populations themselves. Archaeological reconstruction further yields information on paleoclimates, landscape, and resources through floral and faunal analyses. It is now possible to obtain a fairly complete picture of the eco-system and population adaptation of groups living thousands of years ago.

The use of archaeological skeletal populations provides a unique opportunity for assessing dietary deficiencies. For example, Nubian skeletal series are available which span a 10,000 year period from the Mesolithic to the present. The later Nubian archaeological skeletal populations are well preserved and many of the burials have mummified tissue. Hair, skin, and some muscle is present and in about 20% of the individuals the sex of the adults can be determined from the mummified genitalia.

The Sudanese Nubian population represents one of the most intensively studied skeletal populations in the world (Strouhal 1981). Growth and development (Armelagos et al. 1972), general pathologies (Armelagos 1968, 1969), specific pathological conditions such as osteoporosis (Dewey et al. 1969, Mielke et al. 1972, Martin and Armelagos 1979, 1985) and iron deficiency anemia (Carlson et al. 1974), and demographic studies of mortality (Swedlund and Armelagos 1969, Green et al. 1974) are among those reported. These studies use a biocultural approach (Van Gerven et al. 1973) to document adaptation. Features of health and disease are used to measure the biological success of the population adapation.

The subsistence shift to food production in the Neolithic period has long been thought to herald an era of improved nutrition and health. The increased food production of agriculturalists is considered one of the most important factors in the adaptation of human populations. In fact, the dramatic increase of population size following the development of food production is frequently cited as evidence of improved health following the Neolithic period. However, theoretical and empirical evidence suggests that improved health and nutrition is not a necessary consequence of agriculture (see for examples, Clark and Brandt 1984, Cohen and Armelagos 1984).

The development of primary food production often leads to changes in the environment which can increase the potential for nutritional and infectious disease. The potential of drought and plant blight may be a factor which increases the possibility of food shortages. The reliance on single crops of cereal grains may dispose the population to inadequate dietary protein and other serious deficiencies. Sedentism, degradation of the environment, increased population size and density, and the accumulation of human waste increases the possibility of infectious disease (Armelagos et al. 1984).

We show that during the last 2000 years and possibly for the past 5000, Nubian and Egyptian diets have been low in usable iron and calcium. Along with increased energy expenditures during growth, pregnancy and lacation, these factors significantly compromised the dietary adequacy and the health of subgroups within the population.

Food Production, Nutrition, and Skeletal Biology

Populations used in this study are primarily from the C-Group (2400–1000 B.C.), Meroitic (350 B.C.-A.D. 350), X-Group or Ballana (A.D. 350–550), and Christian (A.D. 550–1300) periods. This material was excavated from sites in Lower Nubia (described as the portion of the Nile River Valley that extends from the First Cataract at Aswan, Egypt, to the Second Cataract at Wadi Halfa, Sudan) (Figure 1). Prehistorically, the region represents a major line of communication between sub-Saharan Africa and the Mediterranean. The sample consists of both subadults and adults of varying ages and both sexes. Today the local peasantry continues to eat a diet comprised of the same cereal grains prepared in much the same way as did their ancestors.

The C-Group (2400–1000 B.C.) in Lower Nubia represents a mixed subsistence pattern using gathered, hunted and agricultural products (Adams 1970). The Meroitic, X-Group and Christian groups subsisted fully on agricultural products. During the Meroitic period, the development of the saqia (waterwheel) in upper Nubia allowed the intensification of agriculture thus increasing the productive potential of the region, and permitting the support of a larger population (Adams

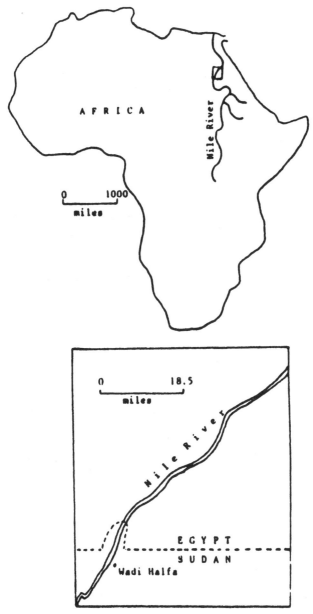

Figure 1. Map showing the study area of Lower Nubia which extends from the First Cataract at Aswan, Egypt, to the Second cataract at Wadi Halfa, Sudan.

1970). Farmers from this period to the present could now grow several crops a year, and were able to irrigate farther from the Nile (as well as the banks higher than those next to the river) (Trigger 1965). Crops grown on these lands required a much greater energy investment per acre than did single annual crops grown on the alluvial flood plains.

The archaeological record shows a strategy that involved three growing seasons. Crops harvested included millet, wheat, barley, beans, tobacco, lentils, peas and watermelon (Trigger 1965). Dates, mangoes, and cirtus trees could also be kept watered during dry seasons to produce more fruit. Cattle, sheep and goats probably were herded; however cattle were used to run the waterwheel and were most likely not eaten (Adams 1970). Milk and butter may have been used in trade (Trigger 1965).

In the classic volume *Growing Up In An Egyptian Village*, Ammar (1966) documents the day-to-day life in a modern peasant community living along the banks of the Nile. The village, Silwa, is approximately 350 km north of the archaeological site used in this study. This descriptive account confirms the archaeological reconstruction provided by Adams (1970) and Trigger (1965) for the prehistoric Sudanese Nubians. Intensive farming activities consume the largest portion of adult activity. Millet, wheat and barley form the basis of the subsistence base, and other crops are grown for cash or trading. Some livestock such as cattle are kept as resources for milk and butter, which is also sometimes traded. Ammar convincingly suggests that Silwa largely represents traditional agriculturally based communities in the region, and his accounts lend credence to our interpretation of the prehistoric Sudanese Nubian lifeways.

Skeletal Analyses and Nutritional Health

Linking health to subsistence can be accomplished indirectly with the use of a number of skeletal indicators of disease stress. Bone is a part of the living human system and is intimately linked to metabolic, nutritional, physiological and biomechanical processes. With bone as the focus of this study, our objective is (1) to understand any deviations in patterns of growth and development of bone, and (2) to relate the pathophysiological changes of bone to biological and nutritional variables.

Patterns of skeletal growth, development and maintenance were assessed from a microradiographic analysis of femoral cross-sections taken from an area directly below the lesser trochanter. The balance between the processes of bone formation and bone resorption determines the amount and quality of bone present at any given time. During growth, formation normally exceeds resorption with a resulting gain in bone mass. In the young adult, the processes are in equilibrium and bone mass is maintained or increases at a relatively constant state. Beginning in middle age, resorption slightly exceeds formation and some bone mass may decrease.

Once bone has been shaped by growth, it is maintained, and can be altered, by the continual process of bone formation and bone resorption. Analysis of histological units of bone (osteons) in various stages of development is a good source of information on bone health. Since osteons respond constantly to changing physiological and nutritional conditions, they provide a history of stress and strains.

Using quantification of osteonal remodeling, four features of bone histology for the prehistoric Nubians were measured: percent cortical area (the area of the cortex which is osteonal bone versus medullary cavity), bone formation (the number of newly forming osteons), bone resorption (the number of areas where bone is actively being resorbed), and growth disruption (osteons which show disrupted patterns of mineralization, called Type II osteons) (see Martin and Armelagos 1985, for a detailed description of the methodology).

Nutritional Stress and Subadult Bone Growth

In the Sudanese Nubian population, the occurrence of iron deficiency anemia provides indisputable evidence of a significant dietary problem. Porotic hyperostosis (Figure. 2) is a physiological response to anemia which results in an increase in the production of red blood cells causing an expansion of marrow cavities of the thin bones of the skeleton. The thin bones of the crania, which are a primary area for the production of red blood cells, are particularly vulnerable to these changes. The marrow portion of the skull expands and the outer layer becomes very thin and may actually disappear exposing the middle

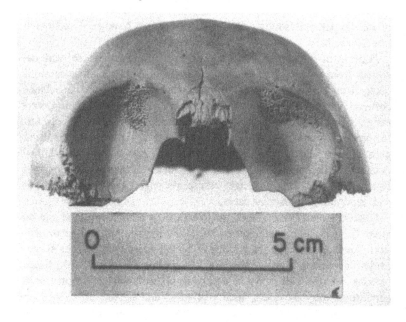

Figure 2. Photograph of a Nubian subadult cranial portion showing the cribrotic lesions in the orbits as a result of iron deficiency anemia.

(diploe) layer of bone (Steinbock 1976). Differential diagnosis of non-nutritional and nutritional anemias can be difficult; however Moseley (1965) and Hengen (1971) have shown that nutritional anemias are less severe and more limited in distribution on the body.

The location and severity of the lesions, the incidence of lesions by age, and the reconstruction of the subsistence patterns for the Nubians strongly suggests that these lesions are the result of iron deficiency anemia. Carlson et al. (1974) noted that 20% of the subadults from the Sudanese Nubian skeletal population used in this study show evidence of iron deficiency anemia, and the highest frequency (32%) was noted among children aged 6 years and younger. Diet, parasitic involvement, and poor hygenic practices are suggested as factors that increase the potential for anemia. Furthermore, the problem of iron deficiency anemia in children living along the Nile persists into the present. Patwardhan and Darby (1972) have documented its prevalence, suggesting that a diet deficient in usable iron and infestation with parasites such as hookworms and bilharzias is the underlying cause.

An association is often made between nutritional deficiencies and infections, with either condition increasing the likelihood for the other (Scrimshaw et al. 1968. This does not appear to be the case for Nubian children since there is a very low frequency of infectious reactions on the skeletal remains. The absence of infections has been explained by the presence of tetracycline in the prehistoric Nubian's skeletal tissue (Bassett et al. 1980). Tetracycline is a broad spectrum antibiotic which was most likely present in the grain stores and became ingested as the grain was used (Keith and Armelagos 1983).

With the documentation of nutritional problems such as iron deficiency anemia in the prehistoric Nubian skeletal remains, other indications of poor health emerged. Since growth is one of the most widely used indicators of nutritional status in children, analyses of bone growth and development were initiated. Armelagos and co-workers (1972) analyzed cross-sectional growth data from the Meroitic, X-Group and Christian populations. They found that the Nubians, when compared to an American standard, were smaller. The relative percentage increase was similar to the American data, but there was some evidence that suggests that younger individuals (under the age of 6) may have been experiencing growth retardation.

In order to identify periods of probable stress, Huss-Ashmore (1978) and co-workers (1982) integrated growth in long bone length with patterns of cortical maintenance for a subset of 75 Nubian subadults from the X-Group series. Long bone growth (femoral length plotted against dental age) was characterized by a generalized growth curve approximating the normal curve for modern populations. For Nubians, increase in length is rapid from the first through the second years, and slows down thereafter. Growth is maintained at a slow but fairly constant rate up to about age nine, after which there is a second marked increase in length.

While the pattern of growth is within the normal range, the amount of growth appears to be reduced between the developmental ages of two and six. When cortical thickness is plotted by age, the Nubian subadult bones do not appear to maintain comparable growth in cortical thickness. Not only does the cortex fail to grow, it actually declines after the age of ten. This decrease in cortical thickness corresponds in timing to the rapid increase in length (Huss-Ashmore et al. 1982).

These data suggest strongly that for Nubian children, overall bone growth is being maintained at the expense of an increase in cortical thickness. Since the process of growth requires high inputs of energy and protein, any factor that interferes with these requirements can affect growth. Growth retardation could be a result of either decreased nutrient intake or increased nutrient requirements, as in the case of disease.

Evidence exists from other archaeological populations from similar regions that show similar patterns of growth reduction. Van Gerven and co-workers (1985) examined the growth and development of subadults living at Kulubnarti along the Nile River (approximately 100 km south of the site used in this study). These individuals are from the late Christian period (c. 1400 A.D.). Periods of relative cortical bone loss (expressed in percent cortical area) were documented for the period from birth through age three, as well as for individuals older than 12. Evidence for dietary stress on the Kulubnarti children is abundant, with iron deficiency anemia and delays in skeletal maturation reported.

Huss-Ashmore made the observation that percent cortical area (the percentage of the total cross-section occupied by cortical bone) drops sharply after age two, and despite periods of apparent recovery, remains low throughout childhood. A comparison of the Nubian data with those reported by Garn (1970) for a well nourished group shows that while the slopes of the lines for the first two years are identical, it is after that point that the Nubian sample departs from the expected trend.

The generalized pattern of femoral growth and cortical thickness for Nubian children approximates that of humans undergoing nutritional stress (Garn et al. 1966, Garn, 1970, Sutphen 1985). Despite continued growth in length, cortices are thin. Normal subadult long bone has a histological pattern which shows resorption at the inner bone surfaces balanced by areas of well formed bone as the cortex expands in size and increases in mineral density. Comparing this with an osteoporotic juvenile (Figure. 3), the histological profile includes excessive resorption throughout the cortex, few well mineralized osteons, and many forming osteons.

Huss-Ashmore (1981) and Martin (1983) analyzed the histological patterns of osteonal development for the Nubian subadults. Analysis of forming osteons and resorption spaces showed that the histological profile for 2–6 year olds was particularly deviant from expected patterns. Percent cortical area is lower and the frequency per millimeter

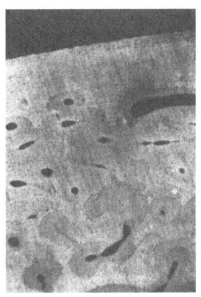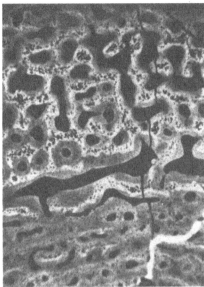

Figure 3. Photomicroradiograph of Nubian subadults comparing a normal cortex (left) with one that is osteoporotic (right) (age 2–6).

of bone for forming osteons and resorption spaces is high. Thus, in addition to a possible failure to develop cortical bone of normal thickness in most of the Nubian children, children at the weaning age (2–6) were also in the process of actively losing bone mass through rapid resorption and a retardation of the mineralization process.

While a relative decrease in bone mass is a normal feature of the adult aging process, its occurrence at younger ages is an important indicator of biological stress. Juvenile osteoporosis (bone mass decrease) has been observed to result from protein-energy malnutrition in contemporary populations (Himes 1978, Garn and Kangas 1981). The picture which emerges for the majority of Nubian children is that their long bones are thin and porous with excessive resorption throughout the cortex.

Adult Premature Osteoporosis

Turning to the adult Nubians, an analysis of male and female cortical bone for the combined Meroitic, X-Group and Christian remains suggests that there are significant differences in almost all age categories (Martin and Armelagos 1986). There is an early age of onset and a distinctive pattern of bone loss for females which suggests that some individuals were undergoing both loss of bone and a slowing of bone mineralization (Martin 1983).

A pilot study quantified numbers of resorption spaces and forming osteons and showed that at the inner bone surface (endosteum) females and males had similar trends in the numbers of forming osteons (Martin and Armelagos 1979). Females in the younger age category had significantly higher frequencies of resorption spaces signifying a problem with maintaining existing bone. While bone was being actively resorbed at the inner surface, it was being deposited on the outer periosteal surface. However, as reflected by higher frequencies of forming osteons, the newly deposited bone was not properly mineralized.

Two separate processes at the histological level appear to be the determinants of the total amount of bone present. First, young females exhibit bones that are extremely porous due to the increase in resorptive activity, and second, the bone that is present is not well minerized suggesting a slower rate of formation than normal. While these data are indicative of problems in bone formation and maintenance, the micromorphology was analyzed to determine the rate of bone resorption and formation (turnover).

Assessment of bone turnover involves the quantification of several parameters of bone microstructure. Since bone formation occurs in discrete units, and osteons contain a constant amount of bone, each completed osteon remains visible for many years and can be extrapolated by quantifying various components of the visible bone (Wu et al. 1970, Stout and Teitelbaum 1976).

In the calculation of rates of bone turnover for Nubian adult males and females, the rates of bone remodeled per 2.45 square millimeter of bone annually in females is greater ($p<.01$) than males. This pattern is illuminated when turnover is analyzed by region, that is, turnover as calculated for the outer, middle, and inner bone surfaces (Figure. 4). The patterns of turnover reveal that the most significant difference between males and females occurs at the inner endosteal surface, with females exhibiting rapid turnover at the younger and older age categories. Thus, females are rapidly remodeling bone at the inner endosteal surface, but maintaining a fixed rate at the

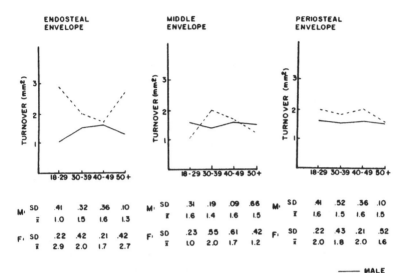

Figure 4. Rates of bone turnover calculated for age groups for the inner endosteal, middle, and outer periosteal envelopes. The mean (x) and standard deviation (SD) is given for both males (M) and females (F).

middle and outer surface of the bone cortex. In looking at differences in remodeling between young and old females with osteoporosis, Martin and Armelagos (1986) found a distinctive pattern for the young osteoporotics. Not only was remodeling rapid, but there was a definite failure to mineralize existing bone. For elderly Nubian females, while there was rapid remodeling and bone loss, the existing bone was well mineralized.

Bone cannot maintain itself when the stimulus for turnover is high and the incoming nutrient status is low. Both clinical studies and experimental animal data have shown that during times of dietary stress, bone responds by remodeling at a more rapid rate, but may fail to mineralize (Stewart 1975).

The extent of the mineralization problems was analyzed further by examining one type of osteon deviation. Type II osteons, or osteons which show a reversal line and different levels of mineralization within the osteon border, were counted for adult Nubian males and females (refer to Martin and Armelagos 1985 and Richman et al. 1979 for a detailed description of Type II osteons). At each region of bone surface, males and females show similar patterns of Type II osteons, but females show increased numbers, particularly at the inner endosteal envelope (Figure. 5.)

Type II osteons are best understood as osteons which are sites of localized skeletal remodeling where complete (mature) osteons are partially resorbed to maintain mineral homeostasis in the face of increased mineral demands. The resorption event does not go beyond the boundaries of the osteon. Increased numbers suggest an inability to meet calcium requirements through dietary means.

The cumulative result of a variety of mechanisms which resorb bone have resulted in Nubian females showing bone loss and poorly mineralized bone. A normal well maintained cortex for a young adult female should show numerous well mineralized osteons and a cortex which is relatively robust (Figure. 6). An osteoporotic young adult female shows a cortex which is resorbing bone at the inner zone, with a net loss of cortical bone. In summary, the following observation for young adult Nubian females is supported: they have thinner cortices,

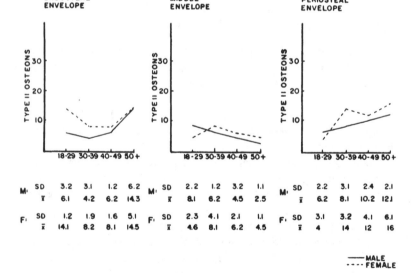

Figure 5. Frequency of Type II osteons per square millimeter of bone for age groups for the inner endosteal, middle and outer periosteal envelopes. The mean (x) and standard deviation (SD) is given for males (M) and females (F).

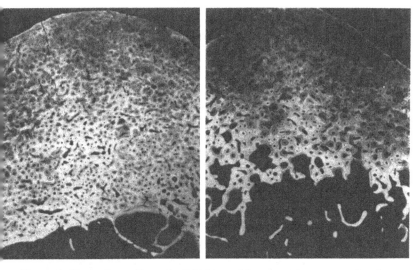

Figure 6. Photomicroradiograph of Nubian adults comparing a normal male on the left (age 30–35) with an osteoporotic female on the right (age 30–35).

higher rates of bone resorption, slower rates of bone minerization, and loss of bone is greatest at the inner endosteal region.

Pregnancy, Lactation and Mother-Infant Health

The pattern of skeletal disorders for subadults and young adult females provides strong evidence of chronic nutritional problems. Given the dominance of cereal grains in the Nubian diet, various dietary and behavioral practices must have combined to create subgroups within the larger population that could not adapt during periods of increased nutrient demands which occur during growth in infancy and childhood, and during pregnancy and lactation. In deprived environments, reproductively active women become part of a vicious cycle of high fertility and high infant mortality, combined with maternal poor health and morbid, growth-retarded infants and children.

For reproductive aged women, pregnancy and lactation have extremely high physiological costs in energy, protein, calcium, and iron. Well nourished women in Western cultures sustain a negative energy and calcium balance, and often become anemic during the course of pregnancy and lactation (Dallman et al. 1984). These conditions are exacerbated for women on diets which lack variety, women who become pregnant before they are physiologically mature, and women with short between-birth intervals (Finch and Cook 1984).

The additional daily energy requirement for pregnancy is estimated to be 350 kcals (World Health Organization 1973). Women who do not consume this additional energy are at risk of producing abnormally small and less viable infants. Worthington et al. (1977) recommend a 300 kcal/day increase in energy for an average daily intake of 2400 kcal/day. When energy requirements are not met, weight gain accompanying pregnancy may not be sufficient. Weight gain by pregnant women in developing countries rarely meets minimum requirements. Villar and Belizan (1981) cite data from a rural Guatemalan study whereby mothers gained only a total of 5–7 kg (instead of 9.3 kg, the estimated normal combined weight of the fetus, amniotic fluid, uterus, breast tissue, interstitial fluid and blood volume). This represents a one-quarter deficit during gestation which indicates that supporting structures for the mother and fetus must be created at the expense of other maternal tissues. Lawrence and co-workers (1985) report that women living in rural Gambia, eating their "customary poor diet", showed very little fat gain especially during seasonal food shortages. This in turn affects the weight and viability of the infant at birth.

The energy requirement for pregnant adolescents is even greater than that of mature pregnant women (Frisancho et al. 1983). Worthington-Roberts and Rees (1985) report that in developed nations, pregnant adolescents gain more weight (up to 16.6 kg). The recommended energy intake for pregnant adolescents probably underestimate the requirements of growing young women in less developed countries who have much higher activity levels than the American teenagers studied.

Adolescent women grow at a de-accelerating rate, and usually complete their linear growth at four years post-menarche. Thus, the greatest physiological stress is on those adolescents who become pregnant within the first two years after menarche. Data from Ghana (Lamptey 1981), Guatemala (Chavez and Martinez 1982), and Egypt (Ammar 1973) suggest that first pregnancies often occur during adolescence. Early adolescents are also at greater risk for physical complications during pregnancy. Moerman (1982) has shown that the pelvic inlet does not reach its mature size until late adolescence, and may contribute to birthing difficulties in teenagers.

During gestation, there is a progressive net retention of approximately 30g of calcium, primarily by the fetus. In well nourished women, a calcium intake of 1.2g/day meets the demands of pregnancy (RDA 1974) and prevents the depletion of bone calcium (Rosso and Cramoy 1979). For growing adolescents, the need for calcium is even greater (1.6g/day) (Ohlson and Stearns 1958). Fattah and co-workers (1978) have shown for pregnant women in Egypt, described as "low socioeconomic status poor", that many have biochemical abnormalities in calcium metabolism and riboflavin deficiency resulting in osteomalacia. This condition is brought on by a failure of bone to mineralize, resulting in very porous and weak bones.

Anemia is one of the most prevalent complications of pregnancy, even though the efficiency of iron absorption increases during gestation (Apte and Iyenger 1970). For a singleton pregnancy with iron readily available in the bone marrow, 0.5 mg/day of iron is used for increased maternal erythropoiesis and 0.2 - 0.3 mg for fetal and fetal placental hemoglobin. The need for iron in the last half of pregnancy increases to 6 mg/day (Hillman and Goodhart 1973). Patwardhan and Darby (1972) have documented iron deficiency anemia in modern rural Egyptian women. Over 90% of pregnant women had hemoglobin levels below 10 g/100 ml, and were diagnosed as anemic, and increasing parity was found to have a negative effect on hemoglobin status.

Lactating women in the United States are also often reported to be iron deficient (Finch and Cook 1984). Patwardhan and Darby (1972) report that over 80% of the nursing women had hemoglobin levels under 10 g/100 ml. In many ways, lactation is an even greater physiological stress than pregnancy. An estimate of the energy requirement for lactation by the FAO/WHO Ad Hoc Expert Committee on protein and energy requirements is 550 kcal/day. This is a caloric increase of 25% for a total intake of 2200 kcal/day. This assumes a daily production of 850 ml of milk containing 600 kcal.

Lactating women are continuously in a negative calcium balance. The pilot study of Atkinson and West (1970) suggests that well nourished British women with adequate calcium intake lose 2.2% of their bone mineral per 100 days of lactation. Dietary calcium deficiency promotes increased calcium mobilization from bones while maintaining the calcium levels in the milk (Worthington-Roberts 1985). There is some evidence that suggests that bone demineralization occurs in lactating adolescents (Chan et al. 1982). Changes in bone mineral content during pregnancy have been documented (Lamke et al. 1977), and there is beginning to be a growing literature on osteoporosis associated with pregnancy and lactation (Gruber et al. 1984, Smith et al. 1985, Wardlaw and Pike 1986). While the mechanisms of bone loss are poorly understood, evidence for a nutritional stress component in osteoporosis is mounting (Schaafsma et al. 1987).

In summary, there is an important connection between the nutritional and health status of the mother and the health and viability of her offspring. What we are proposing here is that the many and complex nutritional factors underpinning pregnancy and lactation in turn effect both the overall health of the mother and potentially the health of the infant. In the face of chronic undernutrition, both mother and child will certainly suffer. What the data from the prehistoric Sudanese Nubians show is that the skeletons afford a means for establishing the extent of involvement, and the importance of calcium and iron in the diet of these groups.

Conclusion

We propose that the data presented here support nutritional stress effects for Nubian children and women living in Northeastern Africa more than a thousand years ago and possibly even for 5000 years ago. In this analysis, the underlying process of increased bone resorption, decreased mineralization, and net loss in cortical bone for children and young adult female Sudanese Nubians supports an interpretation of dietary stress. Snyder (1983), in a study of 155 skeletons from Kerma (25 km from the Dongoli Region of the Nile and dated at 1780–1580 B.C.), uncovered a pattern of bone loss in young adult females similar to that of individuals in this study. He argues that the bone loss in these females is related to childbearing and lactation, a conclusion supported by research discussed here.

Reproductive aged Nubian females appear to be collectively experiencing the most deleterious effects of nutritional stress. While pregnant females are placed under additional biological stress, both the mother and the fetus become an integrated system which physiologically and metabolically compromises to meet both maternal and fetal needs (Rosso 1984). While it has been suggested that pregnancy increases the efficiency with which mothers absorb nutrients from the gut, chronic and moderate malnutrition will negate this adaptation.

As a dynamic system, bone can be resorbed at any time in order to release stored calcium for maternal or fetal needs. However, the fact that Nubian females not only lose bone, but also fail to mineralize existing bone signifies that dietary inadequacies in addition to increased biological demands are amplifying the effect.

The dietary and cultural practices in prehistoric Nubia are probably similar to those of peasants on subsistence diets worldwide today. In Africa, breast-feeding is still almost universal for the first year of life (Maletnlema 1986). Popkin et al. (1982) found 91.8% of Egyptian children partially breast-fed and 23.8% fully breast-fed at 6 to 11 months. By 12–23 months, only 3.3% were fully breast-fed, but 65% were partially still breast-fed. Maternal diet has direct bearing on lactational performance, and poorly nourished women often produce less milk (Butte et al. 1984), and milk that is lower in fatty acids (Borshel et al. 1986).

For rapidly growing infants and children, calcium and other nutrients are critical components of normal growth and development. Underwood (1985) has documented patterns of serious malnutrition prevalent in weaning aged children in "deprived" modern settings. She suggests that quality and quantity of the weaning foods are critical variables during the transition from breastmilk to solid foods. For Nubian children, it is likely that the weaning foods included millet and sorghum gruels which are poor sources of iron, calcium and protein. Ammar (1966) has documented for Egyptian rural children a pattern of limited access to food and preferential treatment of boys over girls in the quality and quantity of food. Underwood (1985) and Whitehead (1985) have shown that variety is critical in the weaning child's diet and the onset of malnutrition is often linked with weaning diets which rely on a single monotonous food source.

Hassouna (1975) has documented dietary practices affecting the health of contemporary young Egyptian children from two locales approximately 300 kilometers north of the Sudanese Nubian archaeological site. In general, there is a high mortality rate for children up to 24 months of age. Diarrheal disease is a significant cause of infant death. After weaning, the child eats family meals, and milk is not considered essential to the child's diet. More than half of the children studied exhibited signs of protein-calorie malnutrition. These data suggest that cultural practices combined with limited natural resources can create serious long-term health problems.

Archaeological remains offer an unusual opportunity to investigate the impact of malnutrition on the skeletal system. Archaeological populations represent a relatively complete sample of individuals of both sexes and varying ages, providing the possibility of assessing the risks to various segments of the population. From what we know of the prehistoric and modern peasant diet in Sudan and Egypt, it would appear that multiple pregnancies coupled with long lactation periods have been major contributing factors in the rates of morbidity and mortality associated with reproductive-aged women. In a variety of ways, infants, weaning-aged children and adolescent girls are likewise at risk for mineral depletion, higher rates of morbidity and earlier mortality than older children and adolescent boys.

The findings of bone loss observed in prehistoric Nubians are likely present in their modern counterparts. Future studies which include sub-clinical measures of nutritional stress such as calcium balance studies and bone density measures may prove important for establishing earlier recognition of subgroups at risk.

References

Adams, W.Y. 1970 *Nubia: Corridor to Africa*. Princeton: Princeton U.

Allen, L.H. 1984 Functional indicators of nutritional status of the whole individual or the community. *Am. J. Clin. Nutr.* 3:169–173.

Ammar, H. 1966 *Growing up in an Egyptian Village. Silwa, Province of Aswan*. New York: Octagon.

Apte, S.V. and L. Iyengar, 1970 Absorption of dietary iron in pregnancy. *Am. J. Clin. Nutr.* 23: 73–77.

Armelagos, G.J. 1968 *Paleopathology of Three Archaeological Populations from Sudanese Nubia*. PhD Dissertation, U. of Colorado.

Armelagos, G.J. 1969 Disease in ancient Nubia. *Science* 163: 255–259.

Armelagos, G.J., J.H. Mielke, K.H. Owen, D.P. Van Gerven, J.R. Dewey, and P.E. Mahler, 1972 Bone growth and development in prehistoric populations from Sudanese Nubia. *J. Hum. Evol.* 1:89–119.

Armelagos, G.J., D.P. Van Gerven, D.L. Martin, and R. Huss-Ashmore, 1984 Effects of nutritional change on the skeletal biology of Northeastern African (Sudanese Nubian) populations. In J.D. Clark and S.A. Brandt (eds): *From Hunters to Farmers:*

The Causes and Consequences of Food Production in Africa. Berkeley: U. of California, pp. 132–146.

Atkinson, P.J. and R.R. West, 1970 Loss of skeletal calcium in lactating women. *J. Obs. Gyn.* 77: 555–560.

Bassett, E.J., M.S. Keith, G.J. Armelagos, D.L. Martin, and A.R. Villanueva, 1980 Tetracycline-labeled human bone from Ancient Sudanese Nubia (A.D. 350). *Science* 209: 1532–1534.

Borschel, M.W., R.G. Elkin, A. Kirksey, J.A. Story, O. Galal, G.G. Harrison, and N.W. Jerome, 1986 Fatty acid composition of mature human milk of Egyptian and American women. *Am. J. Clin. Nutr.* 44: 330–335.

Brothwell, D.R. 1972 *Digging Up Bones*. Ithaca, New York: Cornell University.

Butte, N.F., C. Garza, J. Stuff, E. O'Brian, and B. Nichols, 1984 Effect of maternal diet and body composition on lactational performance. *Am. J. Clin. Nutr.* 39: 296–306.

Carlson, D.S., G.J. Armelagos, and D.P. Van Gerven, 1974 Factors influencing the etiology of cribra orbitalia in prehistoric Nubia. *J. Hum. Evol.* 3: 405–410.

Chan, G.M., N. Ronald, P. Slater, J. Hollis, and M.R. Thomas, 1982 Decreased bone mineral status in lactating adolescent mothers. *J. Pediatrics* 10: 767–770.

Chavez, A. and C. Martinez, 1982 *Growing Up in A Developing Community*. Mexico City: Instituto Nacional de la Nutricion.

Clark, J.D. and S.A. Brandt, eds. 1984 *From Hunters to Farmers: The Causes and Consequences of Food Production in Africa*. Berkeley: U. of California.

Cohen, M., and G.J. Armelagos, eds. 1984 *Paleopathology at the Origins of Agriculture*. New York: Academic.

Dallman, P.R., R. Yip, and C. Johnson, 1984 Prevalence and causes of anemia in the United States, 1976–1980. *Am.J. Clin. Nutr.* 39: 437–445.

Dewey, J.R., G.J. Armelagos, and M.H. Bartley, 1969 Femoral cortical involution in three Nubian archaeological populations. *Hum. Biol.* 41: 13–28.

Fattah, M.A., G. Gabrial, S. Shalby, and S. Moreas, 1978 An epidemiological and biochemical study of osteomalacia among pregnant women in Egypt. *Z. Ernahrungswiss* 17: 140–148.

Finch, C.A. and J.D. Cook, 1984 Iron deficiency. *Am. J. Clin. Nutr.* 39: 471–477.

Frisancho, A.R., J. Matos, and P. Flegel, 1983 Maternal nutritional status and adolescent pregnancy outcome. *Am. J. Clin. Nutr.* 38: 739–746.

Garn, S.M. 1970 *The Earlier Gain and Later Loss of Cortical Bone in Nutritional Perspective*. Springfield, Illinois: C.C. Thomas.

Garn, S.M., C.G. Rohmann, M., Behar, F. Vittri, and M.A. Guzman, 1966 Compact bone deficiency in protein-calorie malnutrition. *Science* 145: 1444–1445.

Garn, S.M. and J. Kangas, 1981 Protein intake, bone mass and bone loss. In H.F. De Luca, H.M. Frost, W.S.S. Jee, C.C. Johnson and A.M. Parfitt (eds): *Osteoporosis*. Baltimore: U. Park. pp. 258–263.

Green, Sheryl, S. Green, and G.J. Armelagos, 1974 Settlement and mortality of the Christian site (1050 AD- 1300 AD) of Meinarti (Sudan). *J. Hum. Evol.* 3:297–316.

Gruber, H.E., D.M. Gutteridge, and D.J. Baylink, 1984 Osteoporosis associated with pregnancy and lacation: bone biopsy and skeletal features in three patients. *Metab. Bone Dis. Rel. Res.* 5: 159–165.

Hassouna, W.A. 1975 *Beliefs, practices, environment and services affecting the survival, growth and development of young Egyptian children: a comparative study in two Egyptian governates.* Cairo: Institute of National Planning, Document #1115.

Hengen, O.P., 1971 Cribra orbitalia: pathogenesis and probable etiology. *Homo* 22: 57–75.

Hillman, R.W. and R.S. Goodhart, 1973 Nutrition in pregnancy. In R.S. Goodhart and M.E. Schils (eds): *Modern Nutrition in Health and Disease Dietotherapy.* Philadelphia: Lea and Fabiger, pp. 647–658.

Himes, J.H. 1978 Bone growth and development in protein-calorie malnutrition. *Wor. Rev. Nutr. Diet.* 28: 143–184.

Huss-Ashmore, R. 1978 Nutritional determination in a Nubian skeletal population (Abstract). *Am. J. Phys. Anthrop.* 48: 407.

Huss-Ashmore, R. 1981 Bone growth and remodeling as a measure of nutritional stress. In D.L. Martin and M.P. Bumsted (eds): *Biocultural Adaptation: Comparative Approaches to Skeletal Adaptation.* Research Report No. 20, Dept. of Anthropology. Amherst, Mass. pp. 84–95.

Huss-Ashmore, R., A.H. Goodman, G.J. Armelagos, 1982 Nutritional inference from paleopathology. In M.B. Schiffer (ed): *Advances in Archaeological Method and Theory* Vol. 5, New York: Academic Press. pp. 436–474.

Keith, M. and G.J. Armelagos, 1983 Naturally occurring dietary antibiotics and human health. In L. Romanucci-Ross, D.E. Moerman and L.R. Tancredi (eds): *The Anthropology of Medicine: From Culture to Method.* Hadley, Massachusetts: Praeger Scientific. pp. 221–230.

Labbok, M.H. 1985 Consequences of breastfeeding for mother and child. *J. Bio. Sci. Suppl.* 9: 43–54.

Lamke, B., J. Brunden, and P. Moberg, 1977 Changes of bone mineral content during pregnancy and lactation. *Acta Obstet. Gynecol. Scand.* 56: 217–219.

Lamptey, P.R. 1981 How much energy do poor women need? In P.W. Blair (ed): *Health Needs of the World's Poor Women.* Washington, D.C.: Equity Policy Center. pp. 33–38.

Lawrence, M., J. Singh, F. Lawrence, and R.G. Whitehead, 1985 The energy cost of common daily activities in African women: increased expenditure in pregnancy? *Am. J. Clin. Nutr.* 42: 753–763.

Maletnlema, T.N. 1986 The problem of food and nutrition in Africa. *Wld. Rev. Nutr. Diet.* 47: 30-79.

Martin, D.L. 1983 *Paleophysiological Aspects of Bone Remodeling in the Meroitic, X-Group and Christian Populations from Sudanese Nubia.* PhD Dissertation, U. of Massachusetts, Amherst.

Martin, D.L. and G.J. Armelagos, 1979 Morphometrics of compact bone: an example from Sudanese Nubia. *Am. J. PHys. Anthrop.* 51: 571–578.

Martin, D.L. and G.J. Armelagos, 1985 Skeletal remodeling and mineralization as indicators of health: an example from prehistoric Sudanese Nubia. *J. Hum. Evol.* 14: 527– 537.

Martin, D.L. and G.J. Armelagos, 1986 Histological analysis of bone remodeling in prehistoric Sudanese Nubian specimens (350 BC - AD 1100). In R.A. David (ed): *Science and Egyptology.* Manchester, England: Manchester University Press. pp. 389–398.

Mielke, J.H. G.J. Armelagos, and D.P. Van Gerven, 1972 Trabecular involution in femoral heads of a prehistoric (X-group) population from Sudanese Nubia. *Am. J. Phys. Anthrop* 36: 39–44.

Mielke, J.H. and R. Gilbert, (eds) 1985 *The Analysis of Prehistoric Diets.* New York: Academic Press.

Moerman, M.L. 1982 Growth of the birth canal in adoloscent girls. *Am. J. Obs. Gyn.* 143: 528–532.

Moseley, J. 1965 The paleopathologic riddle of ''symmetrical osteoporosis''. *Am. J. Roent.* 95: 135–142.

Ohlson, M.A. and G. Stearns, 1958 Calcium intake of children and adults. *Fed. Proc.* 18: 1076–1080.

Patwardhan, V.H. and W.J. Darby, 1972 *The State of Nutrition in the Arab Middle East.* Nashville: Vanderbilt University Press.

Popkin, B.R., R.E. Bilsborrow, and J.S. Atkin, 1982 *Breast-feeding patterns in low income countries.* Science 218: 1088–1093.

Population Reports 1975 Effects of childbearing on maternal health. *Pop. Rep Ser. J.* No. 8 pp. 125–139.

RDA 1974 *Handbook on Human Nutritional Requirements.* Geneva: World Health Organization.

Richman, G.A., D.J. Ortner, and F.P. Schulter-Ellis, 1979 Differences in intracortical bone remodeling in three aboriginal American populations: possible dietary factors. *Calc. Tis. Res.* 28: 209–214.

Rosso, P. 1984 Nutrition during pregnancy: myths and realities. In M. Winick (ed): *Nutrition in the Twentieth Century.* New York: John Wiley. pp 47–70.

Rosso, P. and C. Cramoy, 1979 Nutrition in pregnancy. In M. Winick (ed): *Nutrition, Pre- and Post-Natal Development.* New York: Plenum. pp. 133–228.

Schaafsma, G., E.C. Van Beresteyn, J.A. Raymaker, and S.A. Duursma, 1987 Nutritional aspects of osteoporosis. *Wld. Rev. Nut. Diet.* 49: 121–159.

Scrimshaw, N.S., C.E. Taylor, and J.E. Gordan, 1968 *Interactions of Nutrition and Infection*. Geneva: World Health Organization.

Smith, R., J.C. Stevenson, C.G. Winearls, C.G. Woods, and B.P. Wordsworth, 1985 Osteoporosis of pregnancy. *Lancet* May 25: 1178-1180.

Snyder, P. 1983 *Bone Mass Variation in Earlier British and Nubian Populations*. PhD Dissertation, University of Cambridge, England.

Steinbock, R.T. 1976 *Paleopathological Diagnosis and Interpretation. Bone Diseases in Ancient Human Populations*. Springfield, Illinois: C.C. Thomas.

Stewart, R.J.C. 1975 Bone pathology in experimental malnutrition. *Wld. Rev. Nutr. Diet*. 21: 1-74.

Stout, S.D. and S.L. Teitlebaum, 1976 Histological analysis of undecalcified thin sections of archaelogical bone. *Calc. Tis. Res*. 21: 163-169.

Strouhal, E. 1981 Current state of anthropological studies on ancient Egypt and Nubia. *Bull. et Mem. de la Soc. d' Anthrop. de Paris* t. 8, serie XIII: 231-249.

Sutphen, J.L. 1985 Growth as a measure of nutritional status. *J. Ped. Gastr. Nutr*. 4: 169-181.

Swedlund, A. and G.J. Armelagos, 1969 Une recherche en paleo-demographie: la Nubie Soudanaise. *Annales: Economies, Sociétés, Civilisations* 24: 1287-1298.

Trigger, B. 1965 *History and Settlement in Lower Nubia*. New Haven: Yale U. Press.

Underwood, B.A. 1985 Weaning practices in deprived environments: the weaning dilemma. *Am. J. Clin. Nutr*. 41: 447-458.

Van Gerven, D.P., D.S. Carlson, and G.J. Armelagos, 1973 Racial history and biocultural adaptation of Nubian Archaeological populations. *J. Afr. Hist*. 14: 555-564.

Van Gerven, D.P., J.R. Hummert, and D.B. Burr, 1985 Cortical bone maintenance and geometry of the tibia in prehistoric children from Nubia's Batn el Hajar. *Am. J. Phys. Anthrop*. 66: 275-280.

Villar, J. and J.M. Belizan, 1981 Women's poor health in developing countries: a vicious cycle. In P.W. Blair (ed): *Health Needs of the World's Poor Women*. Washington, D.C.: Equity Policy Center Publ. pp. 39-44.

Wardlaw, G.M. and A.M. Pike, 1986 The effect of lactation on peak adult shaft and ultra-distal forearm bone mass in women. *Am. J. Clin. Nutr*. 44: 283-286.

Whitehead, R.G. 1985 Infant physiology, nutritional requirements and lactational adequacy. *Am. J. Clin. Nutr*. 41: 447-458.

World Health Organization 1973 *Energy and Protein Requirements. Report of a Joint FAO/WHO Ad-Hoc Expert Committee*. WHO Technical Report Series 522. Geneva.

Wing, E.S. and A.B. Brown, 1980 *Paleonutrition: Method and Theory in Prehistoric Food Ways*. New York: Academic Press.

Wells, C. 1964 *Bones, Bodies, and Disease*. London: Thames and Hudson.

Worthington, B.S., J. Vermeersch, and S.R. Williams, 1977 *Nutrition in Pregnancy and Lactation*. St. Louis: Mosby.

Worthington-Roberts, B.S. 1985 Lactation and human milk: nutritional consequences. In B.S. Worthington-Roberts, J. Vermeersch and S.R. Williams (eds): *Nutrition in Pregnancy and Lactation, Third Edition*. St. Louis: Mosby. pp 236–303.

Worthington-Roberts, B.S. and J.M. Rees, 1985 Nutritional needs of the pregnant adolescent. In B.S. Worthington-Roberts, J. Vermeersch and S.R. Williams (eds): *Nutrition in Pregnancy and Lactation, Third Edition*. St. Louis: Mosby. pp. 207–235.

Wu, K., H.M. Frost, and A.R. Villanueva, 1970 Haversian bone formation rates determined by a new method on a mastodon, and in human diabetes mellitis and osteoporosis. *Calc. Tis.* Res. 6: 204–219.

Ecology and Politics of Food Availability

Ellen Messer

Alan Shawn Feinstein World Hunger Program
Brown University
Providence, Rhode Island 02912

Introduction

This paper presents basic facts and ideas about the political ecology
of famine. It provides examples of how politics affects ecology and
how, in interaction, they both cause famine. It offers a simple historical perspective on the "political versus ecological" factors in famine
and a food systems model to describe political influences on the ecology of famine to analyze specific recent famines. In closing, it dis-
cusses some of the contemporary scholarly "solutions" to famines
and suggests what the ordinary citizen can do about famine problems.

Some Historical Background

Since recorded history, both ecological and sociopolitical factors have
been implicated in the etiology of famine. In Western tradition, the
Bible, for example, cites drought, but also sociopolitical actions like
siege and warfare as sources of starvation (Genesis 12:10; Genesis
41ff; Deut. 28:52-57; see also, Cahill 1982; Dando 1983). Food shortages are interpreted to be acts of God, but humans are empowered
to blunt their impact through planning, storage, and food distribution.
In Eastern tradition, Classical Chinese texts viewed famines as due
to natural causes, to poor administration by governments, or both;
and siege and starvation were taught as military tactics. As in Western tradition, famine was interpreted to be the Will of Heaven—as
expressed through acts of nature—but humans might control it
(Perdue 1986).

The interdependence of political, socioeconomic, and environmental factors in the production and amelioration of hunger is evident throughout history in all parts of the world. Historians suggest that, even in view of climatic fluctuations, European nations had the capacity to remain free of famine after about 1700:

> "With the evidence available, we can claim that the weather was crucial only where economic, social, and governmental protections were lacking" (Appleby 1980).

Confusion or carelessness of governments plus insurrections and wars, however, periodically kept thousands hungry. Political-economic policies favoring the well-to-do over the poor further contributed to hunger at local, national, and global levels (de Castro 1952). While in recent years weather has not been unimplicated in food shortages, other factors—such as national and international development projects deleterious to social equity and to sustainable agriculture, pastoralism, and to traditional mechanisms of adaptation to scarcity—have been considered more responsible.

In Africa, the roots of contemporary hunger can be found in colonial policies which resulted in highly specialized and vulnerable economies, which favored commercial over local subsistence production. National governments then failed to invest sufficiently in rural areas to improve production and food self-sufficiency. International and national development projects which worsened the local relationships of people to land and incurred huge national debts were all disastrous precursors to the current crises of low rainfall and inadequate relief and development efforts (Independent Commission on International and Humanitarian Issues 1985). Disheartening spectres have been drawn of poor land management, soil erosion, and mounting food production crises (e.g., Brown 1970; Brown and Wolf 1984). UNICEF's consideration of famine and the "quiet crisis" of hunger and nutrition-related illness among the world's poor children also implicates local land mismanagement and poor food production processes in the context of global recession, Cold War politics, and almost constant civil strife (e.g., Grant 1985).

United States involvement in connecting international, national, and lower level politics with ongoing nutrition problems in the developing world has been emphasized by activists like Frances Moore Lappé and colleagues, whose three editions of *Diet for a Small Planet*

(Lappé 1971; 1975; 1981) and *Food First* (Lappé and Collins 1977), along with other writings have focused on the interdependencies between energy-wasteful dietary practices in the United States, United States Food Aid, and counterproductive United States development policies in the Third World.

More dramatically, war has continued to use hunger as a weapon: in the United States decimation of croplands in Vietnam (Mayer 1967); in Nigeria's war against Biafran insurgents (Mayer 1969); as well as in the most recent examples of the Ethiopian government's efforts to starve insurgents into submission, by controlling production, movement of people, and finally, blocking emergency food aid relief.

In brief, historians provide ample lessons about the interdependencies among political, socioeconomic, and environmental factors in the genesis of famine.

Food Systems

A related approach to hunger and famine, characteristic of anthropologists, geographers, and ecologists, is "food systems research" which considers the interrelated aspects of:

- the ecology of food production and economics of market food availability;
- the cultural classifications of food and rules for social distribution;
- and the nutritional consumption patterns of food.

Food systems research also considers how traditional societies coped with periodic disasters in food supply, and under what circumstances such mechanisms fail to provide food security under contemporary conditions of "economic development" (e.g., Colson 1979; Hoben 1985). Both the food systems model and a consideration of why food security measures no longer work are useful approaches for investigating the ecology and politics of famine.

The Ecology and Economy of Food Supply

Human ecology considers the interrelationships between a human population, other biological populations, and physical characteristics

of their environment. Climate (sunlight, temperature, moisture regimes), soils, and additional sources of water are physical features of-
fering constraints and opportunities to humans in their land-use/food
production strategies. The plant and animal populations coexisting
and interacting in a locality of given climate, soils, and moisture are
additional dimensions of the environment potentially managed by humans, the ecological dominants directing environmental use.

Studies of traditional agriculture and herding investigate what
plants and animals are managed, what labor they entail, and under
what conditions of tillage and husbandry such ecosystems are self-
sustaining. In Africa, most traditional cultivation systems were long
or short fallow. Forest (bush) would be cleared and burned, introducing nutrient-rich ash into the soils. Crops then were laid in for one to
three years or more, during which time fertility was maintained by
green manuring (composting), animal manuring, mixed cropping, and
crop rotation. After this, fields were allowed to rest for 7–20 years to
restore vegetative cover and fertility. A simple lesson in ecology is
that over the years, excess clearing of bush, insufficient fallow time
to allow nutrient recycling and plant cover to regenerate, in some
cases accelerated by ploughing, has set in motion of process of declining soil fertility and erosion in many areas (see e.g., Ehrlich,
Ehrlich, and Holdren 1973, Chapter x). The causes of these environmental destabilizing processes, however, can be analyzed as political.
Colonial policies which froze former shifting cultivators on limited
reserves was a first factor (Allan 1965). Migration of men to work in
mines and other cash labor pursuits meant alternatively that bush
clearance did not take place as often, and people overtaxed existing
land, failed to produce sufficient food, and became enmeshed in a
cycle of ongoing undernutrition (Richards 1939). Emphasis on cash
crops has further exhausted land and reduced the capacity of people to
feed themselves by ruining traditional food, fodder, and fertilizer exchange between pastoralists and farmers (Franke and Chasin 1980).
Thus, not only drought, but other internal and external processes
cesses associated with population growth and integration into the cash
economy have affected the ecology of food production, food distribution, and food self-sufficiency.

Pastoral societies offer a second lesson in ecology and short-
sighted political and ecological policies. Ecological devastation and

hunger in the Sahel, though triggered by drought, were largely created by human animal and land mismanagement. Traditionally, pastoralists moved in the dry season to let animals graze on the field stubble of sorghum and millet fields; farmers exchanged grain for manure. Cash cropping, as already mentioned, upset this symbiotic arrangement. Moreover, short-sighted donors, who dug boreholes in the 1960s, encouraged herders to keep more and more cattle, with the result that pasture rather than water, became the limiting factor. In a short time, animals out-ate their ranges, erosion ensued, and populations of animals and humans were decimated by hunger. Although overpopulation of humans and animals were part of the problem in this drought area, land mismanagement exacerbated the disastrous consequences (Franke and Chasin 1980; Wade 1974).

Political Factors In Food Ecology

Alternatively, famine can be examined as more a problem of food distribution than of food supply. Food may be produced in an area, but shipped out. (Historical examples include the 19th century Irish famine, triggered by potato blight, during the height of which the British were taking cereal grains out of Ireland; and the 1930s Ukrainian famine, an artifact of Stalin's political agenda to extract the Ukraine's grain to feed the rest of the Soviet Union and to bolster Soviet trade on foreign exchange markets. See Conquest 1986 and Woodham-Smith 1962). Political factors such as taxation, hostile confiscations, and adverse terms of trade mean that even if farmers and pastoralists are potentially self-sufficient, their efforts have insufficient monetary value, or they cannot hold onto enough of their value to ensure these producers of subsistence. Hostile land tenure and land use policies also destroy incentives of people to work and their access to the means of production. All are aspects of the total range of ecological relationships between people, plants, animals, and land which affect whether or not the land yields subsistence.

Market Factors in Food Supply

Under ecological and political circumstances where people find it impossible to be self-sufficient in food, one must consider to what extent the market supplies both adequate income and adequate food. In many African societies, peoples—lacking adequate land, labor, or both have been underproductive and seasonally short of food. They compensated for such shortfalls by occupational diversification through crafts, trade, and migrant labor. It is important to understand why such food strategies are now yielding insufficient returns.

One reason is the loss of local occupations which traditionally compensated subsistence agriculture. When men began to work in the colonial cash economy, they brought back commercial goods, purchased for cash, and undermined local crafts production in clothing and tools. Therefore, seasonal crafts specialization, which traditionally helped people secure income in their home localities, is in most cases no longer an option.

Daily wage labor in food production or public works is possible in some localities, but in most of the areas affected by drought, which lack agricultural wherewithal and other commercial developments, this is not an option. Under such circumstances, the main recourse of those unable to secure a living from agriculture has been wage labor outside of the community.

Wage labor has had the dual advantages that it supplies some outside income to the laborer's household while at the same time removing that laborer as a household consumer. Its disadvantage for the household and community, as mentioned above, is that wage labor may remove vital agricultural labor during the planting and thus set limits on future household food production. To secure food, there must also be sufficient wage income, adequate income must be sent home, and there must also be food in the home locality that consumers can afford to buy.

The failure of the market mechanism to supply isolated village with food, coupled with the people's lack of purchasing power, have been major problems in contemporary famine situations. When land fails to provide a living, and there is insufficient wage or crafts employment to cover sufficient food purchases, particularly as the prices of basic staple foods tend to rise under conditions of food shortages, people must either rely on temporary sources of aid through traditional kinship, marriage, or trading networks, or turn to external sources of food aid. Along with these mechanisms, they also turn to famine foods.

Food Classification and Social Distribution of Food

Traditional societies have definite cultural rules for classifying and preferentially ranking potential comestibles as food, and for sharing resources around a community when they are inequitably distributed. Knowledge of wild food resources and how to extend existing foods are critical during food shortages. At the sign of a bad season, people shift from three to two or fewer meals per day, change from preferred to less preferred foods, and demonstrate increased reliance on foraging. Coarser grains may be more coarsely ground to give a sensation of fillingness, even in the absence of more food value, and more meals are derived from fibrous leaves and barks of trees and herbs. Anthropologists, geographers, and biologists working with foraging, agricultural, pastoral, and urban populations (the last, usually under siege), have noted the extensive knowledge people have about potentially edible fauna and flora, and the nutritional value such items contribute in times of food stress (e.g., Grivetti 1978; Brokensha, Warren, and Werner 1980). As long as climatic conditions and rules of land usage which caused shortfalls in the desirable foodstuffs do not affect the production of these supplementary and emergency foods, people may be able to tide themselves over limited periods of hunger by exploiting them. The same climatic conditions of drought or plague which decimate staple crops, however, often affect the yields of these emergency foods also. Similarly, political factors which made insufficient land available to poor households for subsistence food production usually limit lands available for gathering emergency foods as well. Moreover, "efficient" cultivation factors which favor monocropping and elimination of weeds with herbicides, and cutting down of bush for pasture lands, further eliminate terrain and species of emergency foods. Even where available, however, such emergency foods cannot provide long term food security to the households and populations experiencing multiple years of famine.

Social Networks

In addition to alternative sources of food, people also turn to social mechanisms, which, in times of scarcity, pass food from those with surplus to those suffering dearth. Ordinary rules of hospitality dictate that one should offer food to guests, so that those with sufficient stores are bound by social convention to share them. In times of plenty, households build up credit by liberally sharing grain with beneficiaries whom they can then call on for loans or food during periods of hunger. Ritual feasts, usually sponsored by community leaders, have also been analyzed as food management practices meant to tide residents over during episodes of crop failure.

Unfortunately, during times of extreme food shortage, such food sharing mechanisms also shrink. Hospitality, for example, may be restricted to members of one's immediate household, instead of extending to a wider network of relatives who ordinarily enjoy such rights and obligations surrounding food. Although it is the usual practice that cooperative efforts increase under an initial environmental stress, as stress peaks, such cooperative efforts dissolve, as each household and individual finally seek to preserve their own lives (Laughlin and Brady 1978). Under disaster conditions, local groups begin to experience breakdown in social as well as ecological resources. As this happens, individuals, households, or whole social groups will try to exploit social relationships with other groups who have not suffered similar disaster, by moving temporarily to areas which still have food and with which they have social ties, or by borrowing to tide them over with food until they can produce another crop. Famine is a sign, however, that all such mechanisms have failed. To the extent that people see the land under its existing socioeconomic organization as unable to provide them with food, and no external sources of aid forthcoming, they begin to move, either to other agricultural areas, to town, or to anywhere there appears to be a possibility of gaining subsistence.

Before movement of whole households and groups out of an affected area, households and communities may also try to adjust the numbers of consumers left at home. As mentioned above, adults of either sex may seek wage work through migrant labor. Elderly nonproducers may be left to fend for themselves. Children may be left in the fosterage care of grandparents or other relatives and receive the benefits of remittances of such external wage sources. Alternatively, children may be sent away to be fostered among relatives in villages where there is still food. The households who receive them receive the benefits of their labor; they, in turn, receive food and care. A less attractive option, still practiced among groups suffering food shortage, is pawning (sale) of children from food-short areas to areas of greater food abundance.

Nutritional Consequences

Principles and mechanisms of food selection and distribution, given food availability, have their nutritional consequences. Usually, the first to suffer nutritional deficit will be women of reproductive age, young children, and the elderly. This is because feeding rules may dictate that working males are fed first, which means that they get first choice of what foods are available, at the nutritional expense of women and children. Unless a society has specific rules mandating that children feed their parents, the elderly may also find themselves without a source of livelihood and without food.

Signs of nutritional deficit include slowdown in activities, weight loss, and eventually clinical signs of malnutrition. Across a population, malnutrition rises, mortality rates increase, particularly among the very young and the very old, and all who are food-short suffer increased incidence and severity of illness. Despite doing the best they can by falling back on traditional starvation foods, social mechanisms, and physiological adaptations to hunger, lack of food may still result in nutritional distress and social unrest.

Famine policy analysts emphasize that it is important to intervene before this point occurs. It is instructive to consider how political and ecological factors enter into the policies which have been proposed to redress and, in the future, avoid famines.

Famine and Relief Policy

Africa's current food crisis is usually linked to insufficient or declining per capita food production and, particularly in recent years, uncertain or sparse rainfall. It has been argued that the occurrence of famine where production is low and climate precarious might have been avoided had intervention come early enough in the drought cycle. McAlpin (1987) argues that the affected countries failed to gather sufficient local information to intervene promptly and effectively, and that they still lack capability to recognize and address impending food disasters in incipient stages. Moreover, in the African case, when relief was offered, it was of the wrong kind: it was not used to create projects that would contribute to the development of the affected area. Agricultural and pastoral populations found themselves without working capital or credit at the end of a food crisis, and, equally important, government and other efforts to alleviate hunger were not coordinated to build food producing capacity in the region.

Recommendations for famine relief policy by academics generally have been prescriptions along the lines of "the government ought to do the following . . ." type (e.g., McAlpin 1987). Yet, watching for early warning signs of famine in isolated regions—careful monitoring of weather, pastoral movements, food prices, and epidemiological information in most of the areas of Africa affected by famine—demands the training and coordination of a team of civil servants at various levels, an infrastructure to systematically review such reports, a reactive famine relief team to plan and implement employment and economic development programs, and mechanisms to provide credit to the famine-stricken to rebuild working capital. Relief programs also necessitate substantial funds for public works, wages, capital and credit. Moreover, such efforts, if not coordinated and carried out by national governments of the affected lands will have to be carried out by foreigners.

By contrast, others (Independent Commission of International Humanitarian Issues 1985) have suggested that what famine-affected areas need are non-governmental private voluntary organizations to stimulate development at the village level, which villagers can then take over themselves. These formulas tend to be of the "communities need . . ." type. Some of the "needs" which communities should undertake, according to this view, are grain storage and self-reliant agriculture; they should take such measures under the auspices of non-governmental groups because they cannot rely on governments to put people's freedom from hunger above their other political interests.

This view (ibid.) does not expect governments to amend their political priorities, end their wars, or mend their ways by helping their rural poor toward self-sufficient food production. As in McAlpin's scenario, there is ample attention to finding out from the victims or potential victims of famine, their perceived needs and creative solutions to their problems. In the Humanitarian Commission's tract, there is also substantial commitment to restoring "traditional" farming systems, which will "fit within environmental limits" to reverse the debacle of misguided agricultural development policies. They envision demand-led rural credit schemes as prime movers for development aid, to build a peasant-led farming system. Noting that in the past, people knew how to farm and store food for bad years, they downplay peasant involvement in the cash economy, land and market conditions, and population dynamics as possible deterrents to their rural credit scheme, and feel that peasant initiative can overcome the mistaken political and ecological policies and "inefficient management" of the past. At the same time, they prescribe that special agricultural research be applied to such areas, along with health, forestation, storage, and marketing schemes.

According to one view (McAlpin 1987), then, famine is an environmentally triggered problem, which can only be dealt with politically, from the state (top) down. According to the other (Ind. Comm. 1985), it is a politically triggered problem which can only be dealt with ecologically, by bypassing national politics from the bottom up. Yet essentially both agree that solutions must be political and deal seriously within an ecological framework of increasing food production. More generally, solutions which propose renegotiating the African national debts, alongside integrated agricultural and health development, also take a joint political and ecological approach to a problem which encompasses both ecological and political dimensions. As academics and international organizations struggle with planning such ecological and political programs to make more food available, several actions for individuals are also recommended.

What Can We Do?

Most of the actions which can be suggested in relation to famine are political. As historical and recent analyses of famine suggest, famine is not simply the result of sudden or extreme food shortages, but occur in contexts where there is sufficient food—or potential to produce it. One way people can act against famine is through financial support for organizations that are both providing emergency relief and building ongoing economic capacity. They can also support political lobbies for policies which will promote development for affected countries in the future, and political (some would say, moral) education about the interdependencies national politics, international economics, and world hunger. Only by public pressure can national and international development efforts be swayed toward policies which will promote health and end malnutrition.

Along the lines of the earlier efforts by Frances Moore Lappé, it has also been suggested that people in any country can also promote international understanding of health and nutrition problems by setting good examples in their own health habits through a healthful life style and non-wasteful nutritional habits. They can also avoid patronizing companies known to exploit and endanger the health of Third World populations.

Conclusions

Political as well as ecological factors have always been implicated in famine's etiology, and in hunger at national, community, and household levels. Government rules affect food availability through control of land, occupations, and population mobility. They affect nutrition and health through control of food and also relief policies. Although most populations which traditionally have been food-short developed emergency food strategies, including eating less preferred food, and adjusting household numbers, in the current African food crises, these mechanisms are being exhausted rapidly by multiple years of drought and hostile government interventions.

We all participate in an as-yet imperfect world system, in which activities in one part of the world affect survival in other parts of the world. The moral imperative to end human hunger is also a political necessity if we hope to achieve peace. The ecology of famine areas involves the interaction of the local human populations with climate, edaphic features, plant and animal populations, but also other human populations both within and beyond their immediate areas. Through political and ecological manipulations, both the local people and outsiders intent on "developing" the region are seeking to dominate, or at worst, not be dominated by, the forces of nature or Acts of God. Tracing non-local influences on the ecology of food production, rules of food classification and social distribution, and nutritional consequences of such interactions can help define political-ecological interactions in famine's etiology and in famine's potential solutions.

References

Allan, 1965, *The African Husbandman*. Edinburgh: Oliver & Boyd

Appleby, A.B. 1980, Epidemics and Famine in the Little Ice Age. *Journal of Interdisciplinary History* X,4: 643–63

Brokensha, D. D.M. Warren, and D. Werner, Eds. 1980, *Indigenous Knowledge Systems and Development*. Wash. D.C.: University Press of America

Brown, L. 1970, *Seeds of Change*. NY: Praeger

Brown, L. and E. Wolf 1984, Food Crisis in Africa. *Natural History* 93/6:16–21

Cahill, Ed. 1982, *Famine*. Maryknoll: Orbis

Castro, J. de 1952, *The Geography of Hunger*. Boston: Little Brown

Colson, E. 1979. In Good Years and Bad; Food Strategies of Self-Reliant Societies. *J. Anthrop. Res.* 35: 18–28

Conquest, R. 1986. *The Harvest of Sorrow: Soviet Collectivization and the Terror-Famine*. New York: Oxford University Press.

Dando, W.A. 1983. Biblical Famine, 1850B.C.–A.D. 46: Insights for Modern Mankind. *Ecol. Food Nutr.* 13:231–49

Ehrlich, P.R., A.H. Ehrlich, and J.P. Holdren 1973. *Human Ecology: Problems and Solutions*. San Francisco: W.H. Freeman. Ch.x. "Disruption of Ecological Systems"

Franke, R. and B. Chasin 1980. *Seeds of Famine. Ecological Destruction and the Dilemma of Development in the Western Sahel*. Totowa, NJ: Alanheld Osmun

Grant, J. 1985. Famine Today, Hope for Tomorrow. Working Paper No. 1. The Alan Shawn Feinstein World Hunger Program. Working Papers on Food Crises and Economic Development. Providence, Rhode Island: Brown University

Grivetti, L.E. 1978. Nutritional Success in a Semi-Arid Land; Examination of Tswana Agro-Pastoralists of the Eastern Kalahari, Botswana. *Am. J. Clin. Nutr.* 31:1204–20

Hoben, A. 1985. The Origins of Famine. *The New Republic* (Jan. 21, 1985): 17–19

Independent Commission of International Humanitarian Issues 1985. *Famine: A Man-Made Disaster?* NY: Vintage

Lappé, F.M. 1971. *Diet for a Small Planet*. NY: Ballantine

_____ 1975. *Diet for a Small Planet. Second Ed*. NY: Ballantine.

_____ 1981. *Diet for a Small Planet. Third Ed*. NY: Ballantine

Lappé, F.M. and J. Collins 1977. *Food First: Beyond the Myth of Scarcity*. Boston: Houghton Mifflin

Laughlin, C.D. and I.A. Brady 1978. Introduction, In *Extinction and Survival*. C.D. Laughlin and I.A. Brady, Eds. NY: Columbia University Press

McAlpin, M.B. 1987. Famine relief policy in India: Six lessons for Africa. In *Drought and Hunger in Africa*, ed. by M.H. Glantz. Cambridge: Cambridge University Press, pp. 391–414.

Mayer, J. 1967. Starvation as a weapon: Herbicides in Vietnam. *Scientist and Citizen* 9:15–28.

Mayer, J. 1969. Famine in Biafra. *Postgraduate Medicine* 45:236–40

Perdue, P. 1986. Personal Communication. MIT

Richard, A. 1939. *Land, Labour, and Diet in Northern Rhodesia: An Economic Study of the Bembi Tribe*. London: Routledge.

Wade, N. 1974. Sahelian Drought: No Victory for Western Aid. *Science* 185:234–38

Woodham-Smith 1962. *The Great Hunger. Ireland 1845–49*. London: Hamish Hamilton, Ltd.

The Prevention of Famine

John R.K. Robson

330 Middle Street,
Mount Pleasant,
South Carolina 29464

Introduction

During 1984 and 1985, the tragedies of famine in Ethiopia were brought into the homes of the more fortunate inhabitants of the Western World by the technological achievements of electronic communications. Although drawing public attention to the existence of such disasters is most desirable, television programming usually focuses on the relief of the problem. Little, if any, time is devoted to the question of famine prevention. In addition, past experience indicates that the attention span of the West is short, and the devastating effects of food shortages are soon forgotten. For most observers, the conscience is salved by the knowledge that millions of dollars and tons of food have been funneled *toward* the affected area.

However, a review of the history of famines does not confirm the effectiveness of human concern. Even scholars concerned with studying food crises have often emphasized the catastrophic nature of these events, setting them apart as unusual, unpredictable, and uncontrollable. Despite evidence to the contrary, there is a continuing tendency to assign the blame for famine to climatological problems, which are clearly beyond the control (and therefore the responsibility) of human agents. Similarly, famines in India have been associated with excess population growth. If this relationship were valid, even the vast resources of the West could not be expected to relieve the problem by direct means. Further, the high *frequency* of famines in history is usually overlooked, such that it may come as a surprise to many to learn that 100 years of hunger have occurred in the last thousand years (Robson 1981:3). Far from being a rare event, the prevalence of famine appears to be increasing with the passage of time, a poor reflection on the efforts of scientists to improve world food resources.

However, the last fifteen years have seen an unprecedented scrutiny of the factors involved in the ecology of famine (see, for example, Messer, this volume, and Robson 1981). One positive conclusion reached during that time has been the recognition that numerous factors are involved in the evolution of famine. It is now known that many famines are not only man-made, but may also be perpetuated by ill-conceived efforts to improve food supplies. Although these interventions may be short term, as in disaster relief, they may completely—and to all intents and purposes, permanently—disturb market economy. Well intentioned long-term efforts to increase agricultural production by modern farming techniques may also lead inexorably to catastrophe, as will be described later. Above all is the disconcerting fact that at present there is no organized international effort for preventing famine. In many countries at risk of famine, there may not even be a government organization with the competence to define famine risk or monitor food supplies in areas at risk. The following article offers suggestions on the establishment of global and national famine prevention programs. Such programs will require, first, integrated multidisciplinary data collection, and second, effective administration at the national and international levels.

The Nature of Famine

In attempting to develop a plan for the prevention of famine, it is necessary to understand not only the effects of famine, but also its causation. As a first step to that understanding, famine must be clearly and indisputably defined. It is surprising therefore to find that after hundreds of years of experience, there is still a divergence of opinion on what constitutes a famine. For example, the Swedish Famine Symposium (Blix, et al. 1971) concluded that famine is "widespread food shortage leading to a significant rise in the regional death rates." This concept can be criticized as being too simplistic to further causal understanding. It appears to suggest that famine is basically an epidemiological problem, focusing on only two aspects of the complex situation, namely food shortages and the consequences of these shortages measured as mortality. Alamgir (1981) has reviewed encyclopedia definitions, as well as those of international agencies. Although these expand the definition to include the notion of severe, prolonged, or widespread shortage, they are also incomplete. For his own study, Alamgir defines famine as:

> ". . . a general state of prolonged food grain intake decline per capita giving rise to a number of sub-states (symptoms) involving individuals and the community as a whole which ultimately lead . . . to excess deaths in the country or region (Alamgir 1981:20)."

Currey (1981:123) also reminds us that the community is a key to understanding the context of famine. He further emphasizes that famine has numerous causes and suggests:

> "Famine might be more effectively defined as the community syndrome which results when social, economic, and administrative structures are already under stress, and (is) further triggered by one, or several, discrete disruptions . . . ."

This is important because it describes famine as having remote (ecological) as well as immediate (etiological) causations.

Even when famine is operationally defined, any plans to relieve or prevent famine must involve a knowledge of local conditions. This knowledge may require gathering data from diverse sources of information including agriculture, economic sources, and health administration. Paradoxically, much of the data gathering may have to take place when food supplies are adequate and public interest in food shortages is low. There is a need to study not only the disaster which triggers the disruptions which result in famine, but also to examine and evaluate the many other influences which may need to be controlled. Governmental policy is one such background factor. Many famines can be attributed to carefully thought-out, well-meaning governmental interventions which subsequently exerted an unforseen negative effect on food supplies. In Africa, the promotion of cash crops for export and food price subsidies for urban consumers are two such factors which have been implicated in food shortages.

In attempting famine prediction and prevention, priority for data gathering should be given to those areas with ecological characteristics that put them at risk. Cox (1981) asserts that famine-prone areas have two basic ecological characteristics. First, the climate is inevitably characterized by seasons which tend to be variable in the timing and amount of resource availability. Second, there is a major reliance by human populations on subsistence food production and local markets. Thus, not only does the supply of local resources fluctuate, but there are few alternatives to that supply.

Widely variable year-to-year weather patterns have a major influence on subsistence systems, and the fluctuations require the community to store excess food produced during favorable circumstances. Unusually prolonged rain or drought can decimate these stores, such that the human population is forced to migrate and resettle in more predictable environments. Areas with increasingly arid or unpredictable climate are therefore prime targets for increased data gathering and intervention in the attempt to prevent famine.

Most climatologists agree that there have been significant shifts in average conditions of temperature and precipitation in the tropics (Bryson 1974). Some of these shifts, such as the increasing aridity in Africa, have persisted for decades or centuries. There are major differences of opinion on the extent to which these changes reflect the impact of human activities on atmospheric carbon dioxide concentrations and particulate matter. If there is a foundation to the assertions that humans are primary agents in climatic change, famine prevention will need to provide for the control of any human activity with the potential to influence climate adversely. This will need to be done regardless of the need for economic (i.e., industrial) development.

Measures to control climatic influences must recognize the systemic nature of global climate and food supply. This means recognizing the possibility that future food shortages may not occur in the same location as atmospheric changes. In the past, when rains have failed, some communities exposed to food shortages have had the ability to purchase food elsewhere. These purchases have had profound secondary effects, such as the disruption of markets in areas with marginal food supplies. For example, the 35% shortfall in Soviet grain production in 1975 led worldwide purchases of wheat that effectively exhausted food reserves in rich grain-producing countries. In more normal circumstances, these reserves would have been available to help avert disasters occurring in other impoverished and famine-threatened parts of the world.

The far-reaching effects of human activity are not confined to climate and the marketing of food. Cultural change introduced in the name of progress may induce second-and third-order changes which affect food supply. Thus, the introduction of medical services to isolated populations may quickly lead to reductions in death rates, while the prevailing high birth rates may be unaffected. The resultant overall population growth can easily outstrip the supply of food, which continues to be limited because of agricultural or economic constraints. Similarly, it may seem inconceivable that water resource development projects designed to help produce food in the arid parts of the world may eventually pose a threat to food supplies. Yet it is easy to recognize with hindsight that increased water availability will usually increase grazing capacity (Benefice, et al. 1984), and if overgrazing around the new-found water is allowed, the total productive capacity of the land will be reduced. Such was the experience in the the Sahel, which saw a rapid buildup of animal herds as a result of several years of good weather. The coincidental construction of wells and control of livestock diseases increased cattle production, which was believed to be beneficial to the inhabitants. Over the short term, this may have been true. Yet the devastating famine which followed twenty years later was aggravated and possibly initiated by these development projects. It is obvious, then, that measures designed to prevent famine must recognize the intricate relationships between the environment and culture.

The Theory of Famine

In order to prevent food shortages effectively, it is necessary to have not only a definition of famine and information on the context in which it occurs, but also an understanding of how famines evolve. That is, it is necessary to construct a *theory* of famine. Such a theory facilitates the identification of potential problem areas, the collection of pertinent data, and the assignment of priorities. It may also facilitate the integration and coordination of preventive and remedial action.

A causal theory of famine recognizes that such disasters have multi-factorial origins. They result from the cumulative action of (1) background factors in the ecosystem, (2) precursors such as climatic, social, and cultural factors, and (3) precipitating factors such as earthquakes, storms, or war (Table 1). Parrack (1981:41) refers to this cumulative sequence as the "Ontogeny of Famine." In the 1974 Bangladesh famine, the Brahmaputra River was identified as the eco-

Table 1. Ontogeny of famine; some suggestions on background factors, precursors to famine, and precipitating factors.

Ontogeny of Famine		
Background factors	Pathological factors (precursors)	Precipitating factors
basic biotic and ecological factors (ecosystems)	meteorological	floods
	biotic	storms
	economic	drought
	social (including political)	war
		blight

(Source: Parrack 1981:41.)

logical background factor, with the consequent flooding being due to a number of pathological precursors, including adverse weather. Other factors which precipitated the famine included excessive growth of water hyacinth which interrupted agricultural activities. Increased underemployment and unemployment followed as a result of decreased agricultural activity, and this lowered the purchasing capacity of the landless (Currey 1981).

Probably the most comprehensive theory of famine to date is that proposed by Alamgir (1981). This theory attempts to describe the complete chain of events leading to famine and to show how this differs with different types of food crises. Examination of this causal chain can then be used to indicate which type of famine will result. Causal sequences are expected to be different for general famines (those affecting all classes of people in all regions of a country) than for local, regional, or class famines (those affecting only one area or class of people).

While the proximate cause of famine is a decline in the intake and availability of food grains (or other staples), a complex web of factors may lead to that point (Alamgir 1981). Ultimate causes may be a combination of natural, economic,and political factors, such as natural disasters, war, insufficient imports, low crop yields, inefficient government management, and changes in agrarian structure. Figure 1 presents factors and some possible sequences of events leading to lowered food availability.

Of all the factors listed, crop yield is one of the most critical. Crop yield is not only a major influence on food supply, it is one of the

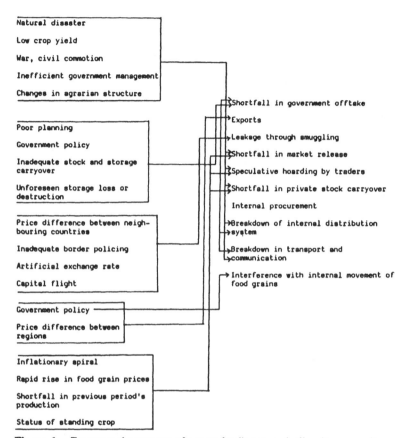

Figure 1. Factors and sequence of events leading to a decline in per capita food grain availability. (Source: Alamgir 1981:35).

factors most amenable to change. Total agricultural productivity depends on adequate and timely rainfall, but also on technological inputs, such as irrigation and fertilizer, proper labor supervision, and the availability of draft power. If the adverse effects of a lack of any of these components is to be alleviated, a number of government departments will need to provide, and be supplied with, data. This implies the need for continuous surveillance of local economic and ecological conditions. That surveillance effort and the resulting actions of government agencies must be coordinated. If a clearly defined and new agricultural policy aimed at preventing food shortages is to be developed, existing government food production policies need to be evaluated and the impact of new proposals studied.

While it is difficult to predict the future impact of new policy, such policies should be subjected to cost-benefit analysis. Potential advantages and disadvantages of agrarian reform need to be defined to provide assurance that such reform will not have long-term negative effects on crop yield. The impact of new technologies in agriculture, veterinary science, and plant husbandry should be carefully studied, not only for their effect on staple crops, but also for their impact on sources of wild or supplementary foods. *Carte blanche* acceptance of technological advances should be avoided and more attention given to simple, well-proven forms of traditional agriculture with which the population is familiar. On the other hand, there is a risk that new policies and technologies which do not appear to have *immediate* positive effects on crop yield may be disregarded by government, despite the fact that they may prove to be strong anti-famine measures over the course of a decade or more.

Despite the attention given to crop yields, Figure 1 demonstrates that there are many other factors which finally determine food grain availability. In preventing famine, the effect of imports and tariff controls and the manipulation of foreign exchange needs to be anticipated. Imported foods play a vital role in famine and its prevention, but food imports often depend on export performance, the flow of foreign capital into the country, the production capacity of other countries (which may be experiencing economic or food problems of their own), and the ever-present effects of inflation.

Inadequate per capita food grain availability is merely the final insult in the genesis of famine. The complexity of inter-related factors affecting this availability emphasizes the magnitude of the task of prevention. One of the components that lends itself to prevention is the attempt to keep food distribution networks operating. This requires measures to prevent breakdowns in transport and communication. For example, delays in the rebuilding of bridges and roads after a particularly heavy or prolonged rainy season may result in lost markets for crops. In addition, depletion of grain stores may occur as the isolated population is deprived of food from other areas. Civil disturbances and banditry may also interfere with internal movements of grain, as observers in Ethiopia and Mozambique have reported. Preventing these disruptions in food distribution should be within the capabilities of responsible governments.

An Administrative Approach To Prevention

It may be concluded that the development of measures designed to prevent famine will require the intensive study of existing data—on climate, on food supplies, on productive capacity, and on the impacts of changing technology. For these data to be used effectively, it will be necessary to secure intergovernmental and interdepartmental cooperation. This might be achieved by administrative reorganization or by coordinating an administrative approach.

Some possible strategies for preventing famine are suggested in Table 2 and Figure 2. For example, it should be possible to study current government policies with a view to ascertaining whether these are contributing to famine risk. The Department of Agriculture and other departments involved in economic and social development are obvious targets for review. Such a review will require not only tactful, objective, and critical appraisal, but it will also require measures to insure that the government departments affected *accept* the findings of the review. In addition, their continued collaboration must be assured. Collaboration is unlikely unless there is persuasive direction from the top levels of government. At the same time, definitive cabinet-level decisions may not be reached unless the architects of government policy are assured that the data have been validated and

Table 2. Suggested approaches for famine prevention.

IDENTIFY WHERE INTERVENTION MAY BE APPROPRIATE (Agricultural policies etc.)

ESTABLISH AN INTERNATIONAL FAMINE PREVENTION ORGANIZATION

COLLECT DATA (Cultural, health, agricultural, economic, climate)

DEVELOP EARLY WARNINGS

IDENTIFY NEEDS FOR CHANGES IN POLICY (Governmental and International)

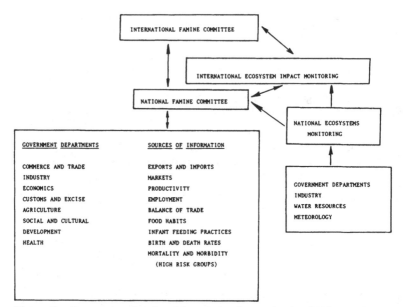

Figure 2. Proposed national and international organization for famine prevention.

approved by all departments concerned. There is therefore a covert, vicious circle that must be identified and broken.

Despite the usual criticism leveled at international agencies, it may be possible to use the weight of an International Famine Prevention Committee to encourage inter-departmental collaboration within individual famine-prone countries. Such a body would have as its primary role the charge of securing collaboration between countries. While no such organization currently exists, an International Famine Prevention Group would be indispensible for the achievement of success.

The 1984 and 1985 famines have brought to public notice the plethora of interested parties who presumably have entered the field of famine relief (and hopefully famine prevention) on purely humanitarian grounds. However, political overtones to aid are inevitable. For example, Cuny (1981) points out that food aid donors are often rewarded, either politically or economically, in proportion to the amount of aid that they distribute. For small non-profit agencies, this arrangement may be the only way in which they can continue to exist. However, it encourages them to continue to provide donated foods, even when this activity may not be in the best interest of the recipient country. Famine prevention programs need to recognize the inevitability of such phenomena, and to even exploit them when the opportunity arises.

The Functional Model

In addition to the proposed administrative model for famine prevention, a functional approach may prove useful. This approach assumes that the routine functions and activities of governments can be organized to monitor events related to famine. For example, if one of the etiological factors in famine is believed to be population pressure, then famine prevention should involve monitoring and eventually changing those factors which demographic theory has shown to be related to population growth. This might involve measures to promote birth control, optimize labor migration, correct economic impoverishment, improve education (especially for women), reduce unemployment, increase infant survival, and improve food distribution, transport, and communications. If drought is implicated, it may be useful to integrate the collection of data on rainfall, crop production, food storage, soil moisture levels, pasture conditions, and the condition and size of livestock herds. These data and policy domains are areas in which governments normally function. The functional approach would provide a focus for these normal activities, coordinating them for the prevention of food crises.

In order to prepare appropriate recommendations for government action, it would be necessary to use a number of different disciplines and sciences to collect the information needed. Using the functional approach, it is possible to visualize specific roles for each participating group. For example, anthropologists may be able to predict the effect of proposed social, industrial, or economic development plans on food availability. One area for study could well be the impact of emancipation of women on food availability in the household. Workers in the health sciences and nutritionists could evaluate the effects of improved health care on per capita food availability.

It is also essential to study the impact of technological change on the environment. Increased fertilizer use and the use of pesticides have the potential for groundwater pollution, in developing countries as in industrialized areas. Hydroelectric schemes and the diversion of water supplies for irrigation, pisciculture, etc., are often seen as answers to the needs for greater energy and agricultural production. However, these too may result in long-term environmental degradation. In view of the evidence that technological innovations such as these may eventually be harmful to food supplies, there is a need for community warnings of impending disaster, which would allow early remedial measures to be taken.

Early warning systems for food crises depend on monitoring not only environmental changes, but also economic or cultural changes (Benefice, et al. 1984). The USAID famine early warning system, put into effect in 1985, has attempted to do just that (Walsh 1986, 1988). Using satellite images, crop assessments, and social data, this system has predicted a new crisis in Ethiopia. Ironically, data on the physical environment have proven easier to gather and interpret than data on the local community.

Community warnings might be based on changes in dietary habits or in marketing practices. The shift to one meal a day or to wild or toxic foods is often a signal of worsening food supplies. Selling of valuables or livestock may also signal impending shortages. Watts (1983:436) provides a series of such responses for the Hausa of Northern Nigeria. These responses range from short-term reversible actions to irreversible actions such as outmigration during prolonged food crises. Famine prevention plans must try to intervene before social and economic changes become irreversible.

Conclusions

At the present time, the concept of famine prevention is largely confined to small groups of enthusiasts often lacking any sustained support for their efforts. Yet the recent Ethiopian famine has stimulated the formation of an international body, the Office for Emergency Operations in Africa (OEOA), which coordinates famine relief. The proponents of famine prevention may criticize this apparent preoccupation with famine relief measures, since the damage has already been done, and the ecology and etiology established for the next catastrophe. Despite this, there is now recognition, at least, of the international nature of famine. This should be exploited, and the opportunities that the Ethiopian famine provided are timely. Attracting support will require a clear definition of objectives and strategies. Nutritionists, anthropologists, and the numerous other disciplines involved need to define in detail how they can contribute, and how their work might be integrated with that of the others. As a basis for discussion, the following ideas are offered.

First, there should be established an international group whose task would be to identify geographical areas, populations or groups of populations who are at risk of famine. Such a group would require an information collection network within countries at risk. Because countries at risk of famine tend to be impecunious, international funding would be required. The collectors of information might need to be arranged in functional or topical groups and be exempt from interdepartmental politics, intrigues, and jealousies. For example, one group might concentrate on social milieu, another on agriculture, another on health. Each group in itself might be interdisciplinary, and each would be answerable to a central coordinator.

Certain key areas might be given special priority, as these are already known to have potential in famine prevention. Indigenous foods have been suggested as an answer to some of the problems of food production. Subsistence farmers who abandon traditional farming and who move into the market economy are particularly prone to famine. An objective study of the potential of indigenous foods and traditional farming practices is needed. Perhaps subsistence farmers should exploit the best features of so-called primitive methods. Scientists need to produce data supporting or refuting the hypothesis that energy and nutrient output per unit area is greater when traditional agriculture is used compared with modern intensive farming. This project would require the coordinated efforts of behavioral scientists, agronomists, and development specialists who would need to compare energy yields (and costs) with nutrient yields per unit area. Such teams are already employed in Farming Systems Research projects in many parts of Africa, identifying constraints to technological change in agriculture. Their coordinated efforts might be used to shed some light on the feasibility and advantages of promoting better subsistence farming, and discourage farmers in vulnerable areas from becoming involved in more advanced farming techniques (at least until their area is seen to be free from famine risk).

In many ways, the present situation does not seem to be too different from that which prevailed in East Africa thirty years ago, when lessons were being learned the hard way on how to prevent protein-calorie malnutrition. At that time, only the etiology of kwashiorkor was considered, and the ineffectiveness of international food programs that provided tons of powdered milk without any real impact on the problem was a great disappointment. It was only when the ecological factors leading to kwashiorkor were identified that a more effective approach to the prevention and control of malnutrition emerged (Robson, et al., 1962). Thus, changing inappropriate tribal law and land tenure systems which inhibited food production was found to be helpful. Discouragement of harmful traditional child-rearing practices was similarly effective. It was also obvious that no one discipline could be responsible for the work and that there had to be a leader with sufficient administrative power to override interdepartmental lack of cooperation. Julius Nyerere in Tanzania was particularly effective in ensuring collaboration among the various government departments involved in food production.

Like prevention of malnutrition, prevention of famine will need collaboration between the sciences and politicians. It will require the definition of clear, realistic, and attainable goals, and the use of reliable methods of evaluation. Above all, famine prevention requires support at high levels of government, and it requires direction and leadership by an international body.

References

Alamgir, M. 1981. An approach toward a theory of famine. In *Famine: Its Causes, Effects, and Management*, ed. by J.R.K. Robson. New York: Gordon and Breach, pp. 19–40.

Benefice, E., S. Chevassus-Agnes, and H. Barral. 1984 Nutritional and seasonal variations for pastoralist populations of the Sahel (Senegalese Ferlo). *Ecology of Food and Nutrition* 14:229–247.

Bindon, J.R. 1984. An evaluation of the diet of three groups of Samoan adults: modernization and dietary adequacy. *Ecology of Food and Nutrition* 14:105–115.

Blix, G., Y. Hofvander, and M.D. Vahlquist, eds. 1971. *Famine: A Symposium Dealing with Nutrition and Relief Operations in Times of Disaster*. Stockholm: Alqvist and Wiksell.

Bryson, R. 1974. A perspective on climatic change. *Science* 184:753.

Cox, C.W. 1981. The ecology of famine: an overview. In *Famine: Its Causes, Effects, and Management*, ed. by J.R.K. Robson. New York: Gordon and Breach. pp. 5–18.

Cuny, F.C. 1981. Issues in the provision of food aid following disasters. In *Famine: Its Causes, Effects, and Management*, ed. by J.R.K. Robson. New York: Gordon and Breach. pp. 89–94.

Currey, B. 1981. The famine syndrome: its definition for relief and rehabilitation in Bangladesh. In *Famine: Its Causes, Effects, and Management*, ed. by J.R.K. Robson. New York: Gordon and Breach. pp. 123–134.

Parrack, D.W. 1981. Ecosystems and famine. In *Famine: Causes, Effects, and Management*, ed. by J.R.K. Robson. New York: Gordon and Breach. pp. 41–48.

Robson, J.R.K., ed. 1981. *Famine: Its Causes, Effects, and Management*. New York: Gordon and Breach.

Robson, J.R.K., G.A. Carpente, MC. Latham, R. Wise, and P.G. Lewis. 1962. The district team approach to malnutrition. *Journal of Tropical Pediatrics* 8:60.

Walsh, J. 1986. Famine early warning closer to reality. *Science* 233(4769):1145-6.

——— 1988. Famine early warning system earns its spurs. *Science* 239(4837):249-50.

Watts, M. 1983. *Silent Violence*. Berkely: University of California Press.

STRATEGIES FOR COPING WITH DROUGHT, HUNGER, AND FAMINE

Indigenous Taita Responses to Drought

Anne Fleuret

Senior Research Fellow
Institute of African Studies
University of Nairobi
P.O. Box 30197
Nairobi, Kenya

Introduction

Drought and famine are not unusual in sub-Saharan Africa. Most of us in the West were not well-acquainted with African drought until the 1970s, and tended to regard the Sahel drought disaster of that decade as something that would be "over" and could be "fixed," after which life would return to "normal." However, history tells us that drought and consequent food shortage are regularly recurring events which have stimulated adaptive responses. These responses do not remain static and unchanged, but affect and are affected by other events and changes occurring in society.

These points will be illustrated by examining drought historically with reference to the Taita of southeastern Kenya. I will describe how, where, and why Taita have experienced drought and will also show how they have dealt with food shortages that have occurred as a consequence of drought. This will be done by comparing food acquisition strategies employed in the same group of households during a season of adequate rainfall (1981) and one of widespread rainfall deficiency and crop failure (1984). The analysis demonstrates that while strategies classified as "traditional" (e.g., consumption of wild foods and other changes in dietary patterns) are an important category of response, the roles of modern-sector employment and cash-based market exchange are much more significant. I conclude by outlining some of the policy implications of these findings.

The Setting

The Taita live in a compact and highly dissected hill area totally surrounded by arid, scrub-covered plains. Average annual rainfall varies from 540 mm in the plains to 1300 mm in the mid-altitude levels of the hills. Most Taita are smallholder farmers growing combinations of food and cash crops on holdings of 2 ha or less. The single most significant variable in Taita agriculture is rainfall. The use of irrigation and soil conservation or improvement measures is not widespread, so successful farming depends on the amount and the distribution of rainfall within seasons, from season to season, and from year to year. A look at historical accounts and rainfall records shows that no year is the same, nor is rainfall reliable for any given month over a sequence of years. Month-by-month records show that the amount of rain that falls in the mid-level high potential zones during the month of March, the first month of the long rains and the single most important planting month, can vary from less than 50 to more than 200 mm. Taita farmers generally expect two rainy seasons, the long rains from March through June and short rains from October through December. The bulk of the rain falls during those months and determines the timing of planting the principal crops of maize and legumes. But government reports record "failure" (however that is defined) of one or both rainy seasons in at least some parts of Taita for 30 of the 65 years between 1919 and 1984.

Taita farming must thus deal with both "risk" and "uncertainty" as defined by Wharton (1971). Traditional Taita agriculture was well-adapted to coping with both (cf. Harris 1972, Nazzaro 1974, P. Fleuret 1985). Farmers attempted to control rain-fed land at different elevations and in different rainfall zones, as well as waterlogged land for perennials such as bananas and taro, and land served by indigenous irrigation canals. Male landowners might control 10 or more dispersed plots in various agro-ecological zones. These plots were planted in different crops and/or different combinations of crops at different seasons of the year; sequential and staggered plantings permitted exploitation of particular fields at optimum times as well as the efficient deployment of labor. Even under the worst rainfall conditions this system was able to produce some foodstuff(s) every month of the year. Hence, while the surrounding Taveta, Kamba, and Mijikenda peoples who were not protected by such an agricultural system or whose habitat was more vulnerable to rainfall variability suffered devastating droughts followed by food shortages and famines between the 1880s and 1920s, the hill-dwelling Taita did not experience the mass migrations, epidemics, inter-tribal strife, subsistence on wild foods, and famine relief of neighboring tribes during this time. An agricultural system such as that of the Taita is not unusual in areas of vertical zonation. Taita share this risk-managing agricultural system with other East African hill populations who similarly use plot dispersal, staggered plantings, indigenous irrigation, planting of perennials, cultivation techniques promoting soil moisture retention, and complex, integrated systems of food exchange to insulate themselves against drought-induced food shortage (cf. von Clemm 1964, Feierman 1972, P. Fleuret 1979, P. and A. Fleuret 1980). Travellers in the Taita area between 1848 and 1910 commented on the abundance of food available for sale in Taita communities and markets even at the height of cycles of drought, and deplored the Taita willingness to exchange foodstuffs for "frivolous goods" such as cloth, beads and ornaments (Merritt 1975). While government and mission sources do record the occurrence of drought and crop failure in Taita during these early years, such incidents were generally confined to the plains and very lowest hill zones, at elevations of 1000 m or less; farmers were usually not resident in these drier zones, but exploited plains land seasonally for agricultural and pastoral purposes.

The First World War seems to mark a turning point with respect to the capacity of the Taita agricultural system to sustain the population through drought, for it is in 1919 that District records first note poor rains and food shortages such that ". . . in every Location some of the inhabitants have been compelled to buy food." Subsequently, famine-relief efforts, including distribution of subsidized food and mobilization of labor for public works compensated in food, have been required four years of every ten. The ability of the individual Taita household to control land in a number of different microniches has gradually been reduced under the onslaughts of rapid population growth, tax and labor demands, and land tenure reform. Tenure reform has the objective of consolidating fragmented holdings into one single "viable" or "economic" holding which cannot be subdivided below a minimum size (which varies between 2 and 6 hectares in Taita, depending on soil quality and rainfall potential). Now, instead of possessing dispersed holdings of plains, pasture, hillside, waterlogged, and irrigated land, the overwhelmingly male titleowners have one piece of land approximately equal in size to the sum total of their former dispersed holdings. This makes it impossible to take advantage of local ecological variation, although some farmers whose holdings have been consolidated in this way cultivate additional plots in areas where tenure has not yet been reformed (cf. A. Fleuret 1988).

As a consequence of escalating need for cash to meet tax obligations, to pay school fees, and to purchase modern consumer goods, ever-increasing numbers of Taita, particularly men, have sought paid employment in distant urban centers. The long-term absence of these men has further reduced the efficiency of the food production system by making their labor unavailable. Colonial policy favored the development of Taita agricultural production in the direction of high-value, intensively cultivated cash crops, especially exotic vegetables, rather than self-sufficiency in food production. Multiple forces thus converged, resulting in the loss of Taita's capacity to be self-provisioning. While many contemporary Taita farmers produce most of the cereals and all of the tubers and legumes that they consume, the combination of land and labor shortages, low yields, and drought forces virtually every household to purchase supplementary maize meal during one or more months of the year. The cash-equivalent value of production for home consumption is substantial, but is equalled or exceeded by income generated from agricultural sales and from off- and non-farm employment. A viable household strategy for most rural Taita today must combine food production with other income-generating activity. Householders readily agree that salaried work without farming or farming without supplementary cash income would not sustain the unit over the long term.

Continued population growth, in addition to reducing opportunities to control land in a variety of ecological zones, has forced some Taita farmers to become permanent squatters on the semi-arid plains surrounding the hills, rather than temporary visitors exploiting the bush for seasonal extensive cultivation, herding, hunting, or collecting such products as honey, gum arabic, and fuel. Permanent plains dwellers also have a tendency to be socially marginal. Often they have opted for plains settlement because of involvement in witchcraft cases as victim or witch, abandonment of a spouse, excessive drinking, loss of pawned land or other resources, pregnancy outside of marriage, or extensive investment in livestock. A number of plains-dwellers are non-Taita who have been forced by economic or other circumstances into permanent migration. A few are retired long-term sisal estate workers who no longer possess land ownership or use rights in the hills. Since permanent plains residence is a recent development (post-1950), and the original homes of these people so diverse, there has been little opportunity for the formation of ties of consanguinity and affinity in the area which would bind the inhabitants into networks of co-operation and exchange. The settlement pattern is one of dispersed nuclear or 3-generation extended household units. The houses are masked by the scrub, isolated from one another. Marginality, lack of access to social and economic resources, and the demise of risk-controlling agriculture combine to reduce the ability of plains settlers to survive in this new environment.

Drought Management Strategies

While hill-dwelling Taita have been protected from the more serious consequences of drought by their farming system, plains migrants, in a new setting and lacking social cohesion, have not been so fortunate. One must therefore ask what strategies plains-dwellers are now using to cope with a drought which results in drastic reduction in food availability. Such a situation occurred in 1984. The long rains of March-June, which is the principal planting season for the plains, failed totally. Most of the farmers attempted to plant the usual crops of maize and beans, but the rains diminished prematurely and the maize did not even set cobs before it was withered by the hot sun and lack of moisture. The beans did not flower. Even the hardy pigeon-pea, so widely planted in semi-arid areas of Kenya, did not mature.

In order to investigate food related drought responses, 91 plains households with one or more children under six years of age were randomly selected for observation during the months June-August 1984. Households with young children were explicitly selected to obtain anthropometric indicators of nutritional status and physiological response to food stress among the most vulnerable segment of the population. Data on household size and composition, farming activity, food consumption patterns, durable assets and investment, and income-generating activity were collected. Anthropometric and health assessment of young children was also carried out.

Some aspects of farming outcome for the first farming season of 1984 in these 91 households are summarized in Table 1.

All but three of these 91 households attempt to produce their own food and claim that farming is their principal economic activity. 59 of them cultivated farmplots located in the plains only. All such plots are effectively controlled by men, none of whom had legal title or security of tenure to the land. Most often the right to cultivate particular pieces of ground had been obtained by providing gifts of local beer to any previous cultivators of the plot and to those who worked plots adjacent to or in the vicinity of the desired parcel. Once use-rights are established by such a transaction they endure for as long as the individual and/or his heirs (exclusively male) and assigns (primarily female, especially wives) continue to exercise them. Such rights may be temporarily or permanently transferred in exchange for cash, beer or produce. None of these 59 households totally dependent on plains plots had anything to harvest from the 1984 long rains cropping season. 22 more households experienced a partial crop failure when their plains plots dried up but were also fortunate enough to possess small riverine or highland parcels from which they obtained some food, especially tubers and bananas, and often some vegetables to sell. Seven household were protected from crop failure because they cultivated only riverine or highland plots which they owned, borrowed or rented.

Of the 88 farming households, then, over 90% were exposed to a greater or lesser degree of food stress because their lowland plots did not produce the basic subsistence food crops of maize, beans and tubers, whose cash-equivalent value at current retail prices is over Kshs 400 (U.S. $25) per month. To compensate for this loss, the households had to employ other income-generating strategies, which are

Table I. Results of farming activity, 91 plains households, 1984

Outcome	N
Total crop failure and/or	
failure to plant	59
Partial crop failure	22
No crop failure	7
Non-farmer	3
Total	91

summarized in Table II. These figures show that household members utilized a wide range of opportunities both in the local economy and at a distance. Over half of the households had one or more members working as a labor migrant. The majority of Taita labor migrants work in the coastal city of Mombasa, 120 miles away. Many have regular and stable skilled, white-collar and/or civil service employment. Only a small minority do not have a regular job and work as casual laborers. Taita have been much in demand as employees since the early colonial period; their employment tends to be secure and their salaries high. They are thus able to send substantial remittances to their kinsfolk in the rural areas. The usual pattern is for adult males to seek employment while their families remain in the rural areas. The amount of money sent to support these families is sufficiently large that migrants' wives and children are in the aggregate better clothed, housed, and fed than those in households without migrants. Remittances also permit migrant families to replace the labor of absent members by employing local casual labor for such tasks as weeding, harvesting, hoeing, carrying fuel and water, and looking after livestock. Such casual employment, usually compensated on a daily basis, provided income to almost 42% of all households. The

Table II. Income-generating strategies, 91 plains households, 1984

Source of income		% of households
Local permanent salaried employment		13.2
Local casual labor		41.8
Migratory wage labor		52.7
Shopkeeping		6.6
Skill or craft (local)		9.9
Sales of:	crops	14.3
	firewood/charcoal	24.2
	beer	9.9
	poultry/eggs	11.0
	cattle	8.8
	goats	28.6
	sheep	4.4
	hides	8.8
	honey	13.2
	milk	6.6
	handicrafts	7.7

incomes of migratory workers and those in local permanent salaried employment (principally schoolteachers) were thus supporting the rest of the community to a significant degree.

These households sold not only labor, but goods as well. As might be expected, crop sales in this year of drought did not benefit many households. Livestock, poultry, and their products were a significant source of income for those who kept animals. Sixty-four of the 91 households owned some animals, and 45% of those actually in a position to do so sold some of their animals off in order to obtain cash. About ¼ of all the households sold firewood or charcoal. Ostensibly there is a ban on charcoal production and sales in the area because its manufacture is believed responsible for rapid and rampant forest and watershed destruction. The authorities tend to turn a blind eye to charcoal production, however, because it is the principal fuel of the urban population as well as being one of the few income-generating options for the very poorest rural folk (cf. Brokensha and Riley 1977, A. and P. Fleuret 1977, O'Leary 1980). Manufacture of beer, generally using honey, or sugar cane grown in riverine plots, is also illegal and is prosecuted more vigorously, but is easier to hide. Wild honey is another widely-available and often-sold commodity, although theft and/or destruction of hives is reportedly on the increase. Handicrafts include baskets and implements made from forest products; they are sold in local markets.

During the period covered by this survey—the first seven months of 1984—plains households each employed an average of two to three income-generating strategies and derived 70% of their income from off- and non-farm sources.

To what extent do these activities represent an adaptive response to drought-induced food shortage? This question may be addressed by examining similar data collected from 59 of the same households during the non-drought year of 1981. Farming was a much more profitable enterprise during the long-rains season of 1981, when none of the households suffered even a partial crop failure and one-third of them rented or borrowed extra farmland in order to maximize production; none chose deliberately not to cultivate. Other income activities of those households are shown in Table III. In 1981 the households had fewer members out as migrants, but the same proportion working as local casual labor. Sales of crops and of stock, poultry and their products were much greater. Households in 1981 used over three

Table III. Income-generating strategies, 59 plains households, 1981

Source of income		% of households
Local permanent salaried employment		11.9
Local casual labor		39.0
Migratory wage labor		39.0
Shopkeeping		5.1
Skill or craft (local)		20.4
Sales of:	crops	52.5
	firewood/charcoal	11.9
	beer	3.4
	poultry/eggs	28.8
	cattle	18.6
	goats	39.0
	sheep	5.1
	hides	1.7
	honey	13.6
	milk	16.9
	handicrafts	5.1
	wild produce	3.4

income-generating strategies each, and derived less than half—47%—of their income from off- and non-farm sources. The areas of significant difference in income generation between 1981 and 1984 are presented in Table IV. Most of the differences seen here can be explained by the drought. As O'Leary has noted, drought ". . . diminishes the capacity of the households of labor migrants to save" (1980:325) and, I would add, also reduces their scale of capital investment. Labor migrants are the principal employers of local skilled craftsmen; when migrant cash is channelled into increased food purchases, and the employment of local casual labor is maintained in order to ensure future food production capability, local carpenters and masons suffer. Likewise, so far as sales are concerned, drought seriously affects poultry, causing high mortality and reducing their yield of eggs; drought also reduces the availability of milk. Many beasts died during the drought, so that sales of hides increased dramatically. The decline in cattle sales is largely offset by sales of hides. Although several other studies (Campbell 1984, Turton 1977) have shown sales of stock to rise significantly during drought, or to be a preferred means of acquiring cash for food purchases, affluent Taita prefer to invest in improved dairy cattle rather than unimproved plains animals.

Table IV. Comparison of income generating strategies, plains households, 1981 and 1984

Source of income		1981	1984	% change
Migratory wage labor		39.0	52.7	+35
Skill/craft (local)		20.4	9.9	−51
Sales of:	crops	52.5	14.3	−72
	firewood/charcoal	11.9	24.2	+103
	beer	3.4	9.9	+191
	poultry/eggs	28.8	11.0	−62
	cattle	18.6	8.8	−53
	hides	1.7	8.8	+418
	milk	16.9	6.6	−61

So many animals had become emaciated by lack of pasture that even local butchers were refusing to purchase them. When an animal dies, then, the meat is consumed by family and friends and the hide is sold. The increase in sales of firewood and charcoal, as already noted, is a sign of households in extremis. Despite the greater risks—manufacturers of beer are vigorously pursued and prosecuted—brewing too was much more often used to generate income during the drought of 1984 than during 1981.

Comparison of food consumption patterns during the months of August 1981 and August 1984 shows that dietary changes are also a conscious response to food shortage and drought stress. Food consumption data were collected for each household twice a day for one week and do not include information on most snacks or foods consumed outside the home by individual members. The figures are expressed as percentages of the two principal meals, which are taken at midday and in the evening. The mainstay of the diet is maize, which is the staple item in 80% of all meals during both surveys. Maize meal, which is used to prepare the popular stiff porridge (mswara), is sold at controlled and subsidized prices in all the local shops. However, during the drought year when proportionately more food had to be purchased, it was much more common to find the mswara served with a garnish of cultivated green leafy vegetables, at a cost of shs 1.66 per meal, than beans, at a cost of 5.36. The consumption of kimanga, tubers and legumes pounded together, was down, and that of ungarnished tubers up. Pure, pounded soft maize cooked with beans, was altogether absent during 1984, because the whole maize required for its preparation was unavailable. Meat consumption was up slightly during the drought, as mortality among livestock probably made meat more widely available than at other times, and consumption of uji, a thin gruel prepared by boiling maize meal in water and flavoring it with sugar, salt or lemon juice, increased substantially. And, significantly, households deliberately fasted at almost 10% of the midday and evening meals during the drought, preparing and eating no food at all.

The comparison in Tables IV and V of the same households in drought and non-drought years shows that plains-dwelling Taita have successfully coped with drought-induced food shortage principally by an expansion in their involvement with cash markets. Although the average number of strategies employed by individual households was reduced, significant increases in certain categories of activity can be noted. An important strategy that is, in large measure, not a function of market-based activity is change in dietary patterns. These changes took the part of reduced expenditure and/or reduced intake, although such reductions were not sufficiently great to affect the nutritional status of young children. More significant than dietary shifts are the increased reliance of the household and the community on transfers of cash from labor migrants and sales of non-agricultural commodities, particularly cattle hides, charcoal, and beer, manufacture of the latter two commodities being illegal.

Table V. Consumption patterns in plains households, 1981 and 1984

Meal	1981	1984	% change
Mswara, cult veg	27.0	36.8	+ 36
Mswara, wild veg	14.9	14.8	nil
Mswara, beans	19.5	7.2	− 63
Mswara, meat	4.7	6.0	+ 28
Uji	9.6	15.1	+ 57
Tubers (plain)	1.6	3.2	+ 100
Kimanga	9.3	2.3	− 75
Chapati	2.9	3.2	+ 10
Pure	4.5	—	n/a
Rice	0.6	—	n/a
Other	1.7	1.7	nil
Nothing	3.9	9.8	+ 151

Taita Strategies in Comparative Perspective

To what extent do the responses to drought and drought-induced food shortage found among both hill-dwelling and plains-dwelling Taita over the years resemble those used by other societies to cope with similar circumstances? Highland Taita were fortunate that during those years prior to the First World War, when other East African populations were suffering the violent and distressing dislocations described by, among others, Herlehy (1984), and analyzed by Dirks (1980), the indigenous food production system was still capable of satisfying local consumption needs. As noted, this system was similar to that employed by highland populations who are exposed both to risk and to uncertainty in their agricultural enterprises, both in eastern Africa and in other parts of the world (cf. Brush 1973, Guillet 1983). By the time the agricultural system began to break down after 1920 or so, remittances and investment income from migratory wage labor had become widespread, and profitable enough to satisfy local needs even in times of food shortage.

Highland and lowland Taita reliance on market relations to bridge drought-induced production shortfalls is not an isolated response. O'Leary too emphasizes the importance of migrant income and/or local off- and non-farm employment to household food security in nearby Kitui District (1980). Holy (1980) notes of the Berti of Darfur, Western Sudan, that willingness to engage in local casual labor increased after the drought of the 1970s, and that wealthy households subsidize the poor through such employment, in the same way that Kamba and Taita labor migrants provide support in the form of wages to casual workers in their home communities. The Mursi pastoralists of southern Ethiopia described by Turton claim that sales of cattle for grain sustained them through the drought of the mid-1970s (1977:185). More recently, some Mursi have spontaneously resettled in Mago, a higher-altitude area close to a periodic market where livestock and other products can be sold; ". . . the first serious food shortage in the Mago settlement demonstrates the importance to the Mursi of market exchange as a means of coping with famine. . . ." (1984:183). Kikuyu and Kamba farmers recently settled in traditionally pastoral areas of south-central Kenya also responded to drought-induced food shortages of the mid-1970s by using cash generated by off-farm employment, remittances, and local wage labor to purchase food. Like the Taita plains-dwellers, their recent movement to the area and isolation from kinsfolk meant that social networks were poorly developed, so that they were much more reliant on their own resources than the Maasai pastoralists utilizing the same area (cf. Campbell 1984).

On the basis of observations in Ethiopia, Cutler (1984) has posited that survival by farming households over long periods of food shortage is made possible by income which supplements the food production system. This process proceeds in five stages:

1. sales of stock: small stock initially, cattle later
2. wage labor (which may lead to a collapse of the labor market if supply overwhelms demand and depresses wages)
3. borrowing of cash and food
4. sale of valuables, jewellery, firearms
5. migration, after total crop failure, sale of capital assets, or loss of capital.

Each of these stages signals greater distress, the last culminating in the virtual collapse of the productive system despite that fact that some migrants may have left capital assets in the guardianship of less-severely affected kinsfolk, permitting a return to food production if conditions improve in the future. Cutler's observations, and those of the other authors cited above, show that the market-based Taita drought-response strategies are neither unique nor novel, but are widely employed in a number of diverse settings (cf. A. Fleuret 1986). These societies are no longer self-sufficient isolates, but rather integrated to a greater or lesser degree into complex regional and international systems involving the buying and selling of labor, services and commodities.

Conclusion

The data presented in this paper provide a basis for making the following generalizations about indigenous Taita drought response and strategies employed in the face of drought-induced food stress:

1. Communities and households both display a high degree of ingenuity and resilience when exposed to drought and food stress;

2. A wide range of management strategies has been and is employed under circumstances of drought-induced food shortage;
3. In pre-colonial times and prior to agrarian reform and population increase, the most effective strategies were based on risk management through the exploitation of ecological variability;
4. In the present day limitations on the viability of ecologically-based risk management have led to its replacement by economic alternatives, most particularly migratory wage labor, which in turn subsidizes local non-skilled labor, and sales of farm produce and non-agricultural commodities.

Highland Taita risk-management strategies have been seriously compromised as a consequence of social and economic change, but as Hogg notes for the Boran, their patterned response to drought and food shortage ". . . is open to change and adjustment as conditions permit, and new resources are introduced into their environment" (1980:303). Individuals, households, and communities are sufficiently flexible and resourceful both to adapt traditional responses to modern circumstances and to devise new strategies when old alternatives prove unworkable. Cultivation of squatter parcels by registered land-owners from other localities is such a response, as is the subsidization of farming with income generated by non-agricultural activity.

The diversity of strategies employed is also noteworthy. Rural-dwelling Taita maintain access to multiple and diverse streams of income, which may be jointly or individually managed. Even farmers with large holdings do not depend entirely on their farms for support. In fact the most successful farmers tend to be those who have added to their landholdings through purchase; the cash necessary for land purchases is commonly generated by urban employment (cf. A. Fleuret 1988). A given household may have an adult male member in permanent employment, an adult woman producing food as well as vegetables and baskets for local sale, and a teenage school-leaver in local casual employment. More such channels are available in good times than in bad, but even during the drought in 1984 households were able to exploit multiple opportunities.

The significance of ecologically-based management strategies has declined as land reform has proceeded and population has increased, but in communities as yet unaffected by the consolidation program the exploitation of multiple plots in differing micro-environments continues to be the basis of the farming system, and a remarkable diversity and quantity of food is produced using this system by farmers whose land is sufficient. The historical evidence from Taita also demonstrates the effectiveness of plot dispersal and the attendant risk-management strategies throughout the pre-colonial and early colonial periods.

As the capacity to utilize the existing farming system for the management of drought-induced food gaps has been compromised, the most important new alternative has been an increased reliance on market relations to bridge such food production shortfalls. It is important to emphasize that access to cash and consequent ability to withstand short-term gaps in the food supply is by no means equitably distributed among the Taita; Hogg (1980, 1985), Tobert (1985), O'Leary (1980), and others have also pointed to increasing socioeconomic differentiation in rural communities. This can become an additional consequence of even short-term drought, as those without access to cash through employment are forced to sell productive assets such as land and cattle to wealthier villagers in order to obtain money for food purchases.

These findings have substantial implications for food and development policies. Despite the diversity and resilience of traditional drought-response mechanisms, the integration of smallholder farming and pastoral households in the contemporary world into the market economy is a critical component of their ability to withstand food shortages precipitated by drought. Such findings for Taita as well as for other societies demonstrate the importance of an integrated approach to African development, such as that advocated by P. Fleuret (these volumes). Food production systems are not isolated from other social and economic events and institutions in the society, but must be considered in their total context. For Taita, as well as for others, access to cash through employment or through exchange is the principal means by which the rural household survives times of crisis and achieves food security even in the face of production shortfalls.

This is not to say that non-market-based drought response mechanisms are no longer viable. Many of these institutions function to permit the continuation of the usual social and economic routine without much modification. Highland Taita agricuturalists not yet subjected to land reform are a case in point. Further, many traditional management institutions, such as communal granaries, can be incorporated into development planning (as, indeed, they have been in Rwanda). A number of these institutions have been identified and described in the available literature; they continue to function at household and community level.

The consistency of the responses described in a number of different societies points also to the utility of monitoring local patterns of behavior in order to calculate the degree of stress being experienced. Such information can be utilized in the development of famine early warning systems. While it can be argued that changes in nutritional status occur so late in the cycle of food stress that they do not constitute an effective warning of a situation to come but an indicator of deprivation well-advanced, other social and economic indicators occur at an earlier stage of the drought-food stress cycle. In the Taita case, escalating sales of fuelwood and beer are one such indicator, as sales of goat, sheep and cattle are in societies more reliant on livestock for their subsistence.

Planners, policy-makers, social scientists, government officials, and others who are working to develop long-term solutions to questions of drought and food shortage in Africa have much to learn from villagers. In particular, we must all recognize the contributions of indigenous responses, both traditional and modern, to the resolution of such problems.

References

Brokensha, D., and B. Riley. 1977. Forest, foraging, fences and fuel in a marginal area of Kenya. Paper prepared for USAID social forestry seminar.

Brush, S. 1973. *Mountain, Field and Family.* Madison: University of Wisconsin Press.

Campbell, D. 1984. Response to drought among farmers and herders in southern Kajiado District, Kenya. *Human Ecology* 12:35–64.

Cutler, P. 1984. Famine forecasting: prices and peasant behavior in northern Ethiopia. *Disasters* 8:48–56.

Dirks, R. 1980. Social responses during severe food shortages and famine. *Current Anthropology* 21:21–44.

Feierman, S. 1972. *The Shambaa Kingdom.* Madison: University of Wisconsin Press.

Fleuret, A. 1986. Indigenous responses to drought in sub-Saharan Africa. *Disasters* 10:224–229.

———— 1988. Some Consequences of tenure and agrarian reform among the Taita of Kenya. In *Land and Society in Contemporary Africa,* ed. by R.E. Downs and S.P. Reyna. Hanover, NH: University Press of New England. Pp. 136–158.

Fleuret, A., and P. Fleuret. 1977. Sex roles and peasant economics in the Usambara Mountains. Paper presented at the annual meeting of the Southwestern Anthropological Association, San Diego.

Fleuret, P. 1979. *Farm and Market: Society and Agriculture in Northeastern Tanzania.* Unpublished Ph.D. dissertation, University of California, Santa Barbara.

—— 1985. The social organization of water control in the Taita Hills, Kenya. *American Ethnologist* 12:103–118.

Fleuret, P., and A. Fleuret. 1980. Nutritional implications of staple food crop successions in Usambara, Tanzania. *Human Ecology* 8:311–327.

Guillet, D. 1983. Towards a cultural ecology of mountains: the central Andes and the Himalayas compared. *Current Anthropology* 24:561–574.

Harris, A. 1972. Some aspects of Taita agriculture. In *Population Growth: Anthropological Implications,* ed. by B. Spooner. Cambridge, MA: MIT Press.

Herlehy, T. 1984. Historical dimensions of the food crisis in Africa: surviving famines along the Kenya coast, 1880–1980. Working Paper No. 87, African Studies Center, Boston U.

Hogg, R. 1980. Pastoralism and impoverishment: the case of the Isiolo Boran of northern Kenya. *Disasters* 4:299–310.

—— 1985. The politics of drought: the pauperization of Isiolo Boran. *Disasters* 9:39–45.

Holy, L. 1980. Drought and change in a tribal economy. *Disasters* 4:65–71.

Merritt, H. 1975. *A History of the Taita of Kenya to 1900.* Unpublished Ph.D. dissertation, Indiana U, Bloomington.

Nazzaro, A. 1974. *Changing Use of the Resource Base among the Taita of Kenya.* Unpublished Ph.D. dissertation, Michigan State Univ., East Lansing.

O'Leary, M. 1980. Responses to drought in Kitui District, Kenya. *Disasters* 4:315–327.

Tobert, N. 1985. The effect of drought among the Zaghawa in northern Darfur. *Disasters* 9:213–223.

Turton, D. 1977. Response to drought: the Mursi of southwestern Ethiopia. In *Human Ecology in the Tropics,* ed. by J. Garlick and R. Keay. London: Taylor and Francis. Pp. 165–192.

—— 1984. Spontaneous resettlement after drought: an Ethiopian example. *Disasters* 8:178–189.

von Clemm, M. 1964. Agriculture and sentiment on Kilimanjaro. *Economic Botany* 18(2):99–121.

Wharton, C. 1971. Risk, uncertainty and the subsistence farmer. In *Economic Development and Social Change,* ed. by G. Dalton. New York: Natural History Press.

Occupation and Drought Vulnerability: Case Studies from a Village in Niger[1]

John J. Curry

*Swaziland Cropping Systems
Research and Extension Training Project
Malkerns, Swaziland*

Introduction

Since 1969, the sedentary and nomadic populations of the West African Sahel have experienced two major droughts and famines. The interval between these two droughts has been sufficiently short to remind those concerned with short-term humanitarian aid and with long-term development for the region that:

> . . . drought and consequent food shortages are regularly recurring events which
> have stimulated adaptive responses (from local populations).
>
> (Fleuret 1986:224)

In cataloguing a wide range of indigenous responses to drought, Fleuret has noted that rural populations are relying increasingly upon participation in the larger market economy through wage labor and commerce as one of these adaptive responses. She asserts that:

> . . . despite the diversity of traditional drought response mechanisms, the integra-
> tion of smallholder farming and pastoral households in the contemporary world
> into the market economy is an essential component of their ability to withstand
> food shortages precipitated by drought (Fleuret 1986:228).

It is access to cash through employment or through exchange, she continues, that permits rural households to survive times of crisis and

[1]The field research from which the examples are drawn was conducted by the author as a member of the Niger Range and Livestock Project, 683–0202, under USAID contract no. 683-A-10003, through research permission granted by the Institute Recherches en Sciences Humaines, Universite de Niamey. The author gratefully acknowledges their support. All statements in this paper are the sole responsibility of the author.

achieve food security even in the face of production shortfalls (loc. cit.). Occupation, then, becomes an important factor in determining the capacity of individuals and domestic units to withstand drought.

This paper uses case material drawn from nine households pursuing different occupations in a village in Central Niger to illustrate the interrelationships between occupation and persistence in a drought-prone environment. The village of Shadawanka, located at the northern limit of rainfed cereal cultivation, is an important livestock marketing center for the pastoral, agropastoral and agrarian populations of the region. Data for these case studies were collected during two wet seasons and one dry season in 1981 and 1982, as climatic and agronomic conditions worsened. An examination of resource endowments and activity patterns for these households, then, should provide an indication of the numerous ways in which people and households combine occupation with agricultural production to cope with conditions of increasing aridity, and potential food shortage.

The discussion begins with a presentation of a framework devised by Fleuret (1986) for categorizing indigenous responses to drought. Examples drawn from other studies illustrate these responses. This is followed by an introduction to the village of Shadawanka and to the regional economy in which its residents ply their trades. The analysis concludes with a description of the occupational and activity patterns for the nine households and a discussion of the implications of these patterns for understanding occupational response to drought.

Indigenous Strategies for Coping with Drought

In a recent review of the literature, Fleuret (1986) has listed a number of indigenous responses to conditions of drought and famine by local populations in Sub-Saharan Africa. These include: flexibility of local production strategy, exchange and market networks, risk insurance (principally food sharing), dietary diversity, food preservation, dietary change (i.e., modification of customary dietary practices), agricultural innovation, social organization (use of social networks for sharing), supernatural means (i.e., prayer) and increased participation in the market economy (from Fleuret 1986:227).

Scholars interested in these adaptive responses have, during the last two decades, produced a number of studies which document the strategies that local populations employ to cope with periodic drought and the famines which often accompany them. The strategies most frequently identified in these studies relate to the use of locally available resources by bands of hunter-gatherers, camps of pastoral nomads, or villages of sedentary farmers.

For example, Hitchcock reports that the foraging groups of Basarwa[2] in the Kalahari Desert of Botswana respond to drought and the declining food base by regulating group size through aggregation and dispersal in order to minimize pressure on local resources. These groups are:

> . . . dispersed over the landscape . . . well-adapted to local conditions . . . are highly mobile and tend to aggregate and disperse, depending on the availability of surface water or moisture-bearing plants (Hitchcock 1979:93).

When surface water sources become dry, the Basarwa rely on melons, and, ultimately, roots, as water sources. They also utilize fire to promote the growth of melons and other wild foodstuffs. These groups depend upon an array of risk-reducing strategies which include utilization and preservation of a wide range of wild food resources (Campbell 1986), food sharing (Cashden 1985) and exchange networks (Wiessner 1977).

Similar diversity in coping strategies can be found among pastoralists and agriculturalists in Sub-Saharan Africa. Pastoralists, like the Wo'daa'be Fulani of Niger, will loan some of their livestock to kinsmen in other locales to minimize loss to their herds in the event of drought in their own grazing areas (Maliki 1982). The Wo'daa'be also use a variety of types of mobility including intra- and interlocal movements, migration and migratory drift (Stenning 1957) to exploit pastoral resources. Hausa farmers in Northern Nigeria use a variety of cultivation techniques to maximize moisture capture in areas of low rainfall, and intensively cultivate bottomlands (*fadama*) during droughts (Watts 1979).

---

[2]Referring to foragers in Botswana by the Setswana term, Basarwa, is far less restrictive than "San," used by Lee (1979) and others, to refer to groups of San-speakers who inhabit the Central Kalahari. It is certainly preferable to the commonly-used and often pejorative term, "Bushman" (Hitchcock-personal communication). Here, the term Basarwa will be applied to a variety of groups who speak any of a number of San, Khoi, and even Bantu languages, yet depend to a large extent on foraging for their survival.

In addition to what could be seen as traditional responses to drought, Fleuret includes cash income-generating activities as "modern" drought responses. Households in the Taita District of Kenya responded to the 1984 drought-induced food shortage with:

> . . . a number of market oriented strategies including migratory wage labor . . . local cash-compensated casual labor . . . and sales of livestock, poultry and their products, firewood and charcoal, illegal beer, honey and handicrafts (Fleuret 1986:277).

These cash-producing activities accounted for 70% of household income during the drought year of 1984. However, in 1981, a non-drought year, these activities accounted for less than 50% of the total.

Cash-oriented responses to food shortage are by no means limited to the Taita. Fleuret provides numerous examples drawn from pastoralists and agriculturalists in East and Southern Africa to support her observation that integration into the market economy is rapidly becoming an important mechanism for coping with drought and food shortage in Sub-Saharan Africa.

Several issues emerge from Fleuret's analysis of "modern" responses to drought. She notes that many of the localized drought responses, such as use of wild foods, dispersal and mobility by foragers and pastoralists, and food and labor-sharing networks, have been rendered ineffective in many instances by government policies and the development of cash markets. If this reduction of effectiveness of local strategies becomes an irreversible condition, then the array of possible defenses against food shortage would be reduced. This would further increase dependence upon the market in times of crisis.

Equity of risk sharing during drought is another potential problem. The ability to withstand food shortage via access to cash is, Fleuret points out, not equally distributed among rural households. This inequity can be ascribed to an " . . . increasing socio-economic differentiation in rural communities," (Fleuret 1986:277). Differences in vulnerability to food shortages should become more acute in instances where increased dependence on cash has undermined the effectiveness of food and labor-sharing networks.

Indeed, the occurrence of drought may accelerate socioeconomic differentiation in rural communities. Fleuret notes that even short-term drought may promote inequity when those without access to cash are forced to sell productive assets (e.g., land and livestock) to wealthier villagers to obtain money for food purchases (Fleuret 1986:277). This appears to have been the case in Northern Nigeria during the 1969–1973 drought. Watts (1979) reports that already-existing wealth differences were increased as local elites profited from speculation on the local grain market and from purchases of farmland.

The use of money to obtain food during times of drought and food shortage implies an economy in which cash transactions have already become the dominant mode of exchange. Thus, the socioeconomic differentiation which contributes to variations in drought vulnerability can be said to be occurring in the context of local economies which are becoming monetized. As rural households rely increasingly upon cash for protection against famine, the problem of socioeconomic differentiation as a consequence of monetization becomes central to our understanding of variation of response to drought.

Monetization and Vulnerability in Central Niger

Research conducted in Niger since the 1969–1973 drought clearly shows that the relationship between access to cash and survival in semi-arid areas is becoming increasingly important. Raynaut's work (Raynaut 1976, 1977) in the Maradi region indicates that local exchanges of goods and services in kind are rapidly being replaced with cash transactions. This process is termed *monetization*. The result is, according to Raynaut:

> . . . intense monetary pressure; this is . . . a concrete reality, sadly experienced by the vast majority of the rural populace. The "search for money" (*neman ku' di*) is for them a daily necessity. It is particularly urgent for household heads. These people, in effect, find themselves placed under a multiciplicity of responsibilities with respect to those who work with them on the common field. They are only able to discharge the majority of these burdens with money . . . (Raynaut 1977:160, translation mine).

Reyna (1979) has identified monetization as one of two cyclical processes that promote rural poverty. Monetary burdens, e.g., taxes and the need to procure agricultural inputs, are often accompanied by an increase in imported consumer goods in local markets. In this case, cash needs increase significantly. This heightened need for cash prompts farmers to sell grain from their domestic stocks. Such grain sales reduce the self-sufficiency of farmers—a self-sufficiency already diminished by participation in cash crop production.

This cycle of increasing dependency through monetization is concurrent and symbiotic with a cycle of increasing debt. Sutter (1979) has pointed out that the volume of grain sales in villages in the Zinder region of Niger increases at harvest time when prices are low. Many farmers sell grain at this time to repay loans of seed and agricultural inputs. They incur these debts as a consequence of having depleted their household grain stocks prior to planting time. These farmers often must purchase grain later in the year, when prices are high. To obtain grain during the pre-harvest period, they will work in the fields of other, more successful, farmers, to the detriment of their own farming operation.

Thus, the monetization cycle creates for rural producers an increase in cash needs while simultaneously reducing their ability to be self-sufficient. This lack of self-sufficiency in staple foods promotes indebtedness through borrowing the means of agricultural production and, ultimately, through sales of grain to repay these debts. The combination of the two cycles creates two groups of farmers: debtor farmers, who must borrow to obtain food and the means of production, and creditor farmers who provide loans of inputs, sources of wage labor, and, perhaps, a market for debtor farmers' grain.

In highly monetized local economies such as have been described by Raynaut, Reyna, and Sutter, access to cash is the principal means through which people acquire sustenance and the means of production and by which they discharge their social responsibilities on a daily basis. For many, off-farm sources of cash become essential components in their survival strategies. This is particularly true during drought, as agricultural conditions worsen. The village of Shadawanka in Central Niger provides us with examples of how differences in off-farm occupation can translate into differences in vulnerability to drought and food shortage.

Shadawanka in Local and Regional Context

Shadawanka is one of approximately 957 villages which house the sedentary population of the Tahoua *department* in the center of the Niger Republic (Figure 1). It is located approximately 90 km. to the

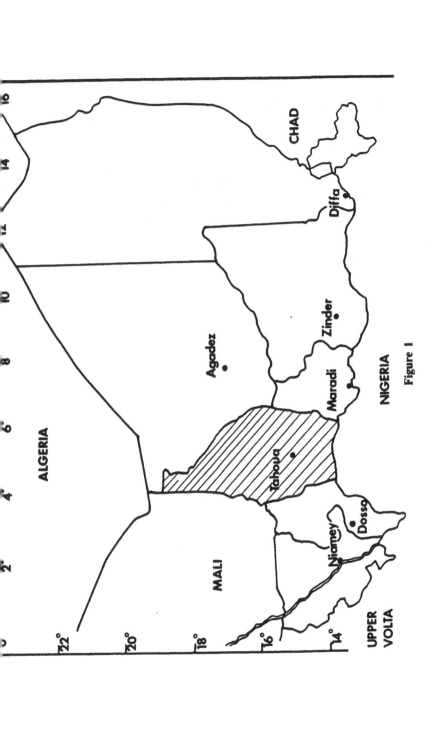

Figure 1

northeast of the town of Tahoua (Figure 2), at the northern edge of the Ader Doutchi Plateau. To the south of the village lies an area formed of valleys and plateaux. This area receives, on average, between 500–600mm of rain annually and is the site of intensive cultivation of staple, grains and cotton by Hausa sedentary farmers. To the north, beyond the town of Abalak, is a series of broad plains. These receive 150–300mm rainfall per annum, and are covered by annual grassland and thorn thicket vegetational communities.

The area immediately surrounding Shadawanka is composed of stabilized sand dunes and bottomland areas, formed by the runoff of water during the rainy season. Climate in this area is Sahelian. It is characterized by a single, short rainy season from June or July to September, followed by a long dry season lasting from October to May. Annual rainfall averages between 300 and 400mm per annum, with considerable local and interannual variability. Soils range from light brown or reddish sands in the dune formations to heavy clays in the bottomlands. These soils vary greatly in their capacities to absorb and retain moisture, their general level of fertility, and their potential for agricultural and pastoral production. Moreover, these soils are highly susceptible to wind and water erosion (Curry 1986:197).

Situated as it is between two major landforms, the landscape in which Shadawanka is found has been designated by planners as a "transitional" zone (Ministere du Plan 1980) between the pastoral grasslands to the north and the agricultural plateau/valley areas to the south. However, the location of the village at this northern limit of cultivation implies that the sedentary population of the village has, to some extent, encroached upon pastoral grazing lands in establishing their farming systems.

In addition, the area, like other Sahelian locales, is seriously subject to risk of drought and food shortage. As Wetherall, Holt and Richards note:

> Extreme variation in annual rainfall undoubtedly represents the most important threat to Sahelian pastoral and agricultural communities. Variation of more than thirty percent from the long-term mean can result in serious food and fodder shortages and localized variation is a common feature whereby, in the same season, fields only a few kilometers apart show marked differences in the amount of grain harvested (Wetherall, Holt and Richards 1979:131).

The resources of Shadawanka and its environs are used by a number of ethnic groups, each having a distinctive subsistence pattern.

The Village of Shadawanka and the Research Area

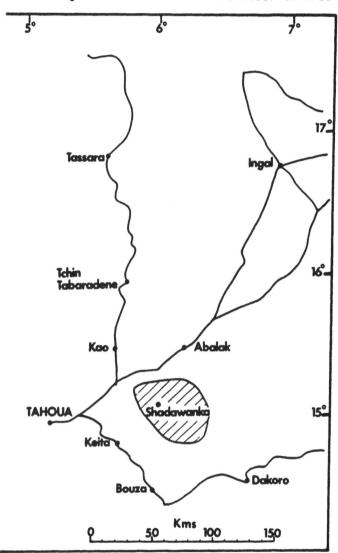

Figure 2. Location of Shadawanka—Central Niger. (Source: Curry 1986:208)

Hausa residents live in sedentary villages and subsist via cultivation of millet and sorghum, keeping of livestock, and trade. Tamasheq and Fulfulde-speaking agropastoralists,[3] who both farm and keep livestock, live in nearby camps and trade at the village's market. During the rainy season, some members of these groups take the herds to the northern pastures, returning to the Shadawanka area after the rains have ceased. The rest of the group stays behind to cultivate the family grain fields. Transhumant and nomadic pastoralists from other Kel-Tamasheq and Ful'be groups pasture their herds of cattle, camels, sheep and goats on the annual grasslands in the vicinity as part of their annual migrations agricultural and pastoral areas, or in times of drought. In so doing, they often come into conflict with the sedentary and agropastoral residents of the area.

Agricultural and Occupational Strategies

The village of Shadawanka is, in reality, two villages—each with its own headman. The villages are located on either side of the market which is situated on an island in the seasonal water course. The residents of the western side of Shadawanka are predominantly Hausa from the Ader Doutchi Plateau, in the vicinity of the town of Keita (Figure 2), where they are censused. The composition of the eastern village is more heterogeneous. While most of the residents are Hausa from either the Ader or Gobir regions, there are a few Ful'be or Kel-Tamasheq families, as well. This eastern village is under the jurisdiction of the authorities in Abalak. All future references to Shadawanka will pertain to this eastern half of Shadawanka.

The population of 429 lives in 66 residential units, whose structures exhibit a wide range of variation (Curry 1984:218–225). Local pro-

---

[3]This paper will use the terms Ful'be or (the less accurate, but widely-known) Fulani to refer in general to speakers of Fulfulde. Specific groups will be referred to by their commonly-known name (e.g., Wo'daa'be or Farfaru). Similarly, Tamasheq speakers will be referred to as Kel-Tamasheq ("the people of Tamasheq") or the more widely-known, but less accurate term of Twareg. The latter should, in fact, refer only to members of the noble class (*imagheran*) of the numerous Kel-Tamasheq confederacies.

duction consists of dryland cultivation of millet, sorghum, and cow-peas, livestock raising, and traditional crafts, such as tanning. "The farming system of Shadawanka is best considered as an abbreviated, and arid, variant of the general Hausa farming pattern . . ." (Curry 1986:209–210). Nearly all of the work is done by hand: fields are cleared from April to June with bush knife; crops are planted at the beginning of the rains in June or July and weeded during July-August with a variety of hoes; the heads of millet and sorghum are harvested in September-October with a small knife and carried in bundles to household granaries on the heads of the workers. The use of oxen to clear land, to plant and to cultivate the crop—a practice found in some of the more intensive Hausa farming systems to the south—is totally lacking in Shadawanka. In addition, farmers use neither organic nor inorganic fertilizers on their fields, claiming that it would burn up the crop due to the "hot" soils they cultivate (Curry 1986:211).[4]

Labor is drawn primarily from the household. Unlike Hausa communities in Northern Nigeria, where women are kept in seclusion, Shadawanka women participate in planting, harvesting and, sometimes, the first weeding of crops.

The practice of this type of extensive dryland agricultural system in a marginal climatic regime should be expected to produce poor results. Yields of millet and sorghum for a sample of 20 households were estimated to have averaged about 287 and 208 kilograms per hectare for 1981 and 1982, respectively.[5] Such yields fall far short of supplying households with sufficient grain to sustain them for even a single, annual cycle.[6] Table 1 reports the estimated average number of days

---

[4] The "hot/cold" system of soil classification used in Shadawanka and elsewhere in Tahoua appears from informants' statements to refer to the soil's capacity to absorb and retain moisture, rather than to soil type and structure.

[5] The estimate of 1981 mean yields was calculated by dividing the kilograms harvested per household reported in Table 1 by the mean hectares of millet and sorghum cultivated per household of the village (2.99) as reported by Curry (1984: 236 Table 22). This average has already been reported in Curry (1986:211). The divisor used for the 1982 figure, however, was derived from the mean hectares cultivated per (sample) household, given by Curry (1984:271 Table 31.)

[6] This yearly shortfall is severely at odds with the Hausa traditional strategy of keeping a three years' supply of grain in the household granaries as a

Table I. Grain consumption by sample households—Shadawanka

Year	1980	1981	1982
Kg. of grain harvested per household.	676	817	690
Average daily consumption (kg)	—	5.36	—
Number of days of grain consumption from harvest	118	140	114

Source: Curry 1986:213.

that grain yields would support households after the harvest. The data suggest that, during the years preceding the most recent drought, households in Shadawanka were capable of producing, on average, between 114 and 140 days of their cereal requirements per year. Moreover, there was considerable variation not only from year to year, but also among households *within* any given year (Curry 1984:217).

Consequently, even in non-drought years, the people of Shadawanka must rely heavily on purchases of staple grains to sustain themselves throughout the year (Curry 1986:211–212). Table 2 presents data on purchases of grain by a sample of households for a period of 22 weeks both before and after the 1981 harvest. Households spent on average about $US 6.80 for grain throughout the period, and continued to purchase grain after the harvest in October. One can conclude, therefore, that the local agricultural system in Shadawanka is incapable of providing even the minimum food needs required by the populace.

In order to obtain the cash necessary for purchases of food and other necessities, the inhabitants of Shadawanka pursue a variety of income-generating activities. Table 3 lists the principal non-agricultural occupations reported by villagers to be their primary source of cash. There is considerable specialization by sex. Food processing and sales, and certain traditional crafts and services are sources of income available to women. Males derive income from both traditional and "modern" traders (e.g., tanning, smithing, radio repair), commerce (especially livestock), transport and migratory wage labor. There is considerable variation in the amount of income these occupations can provide.

About 58% of the adults in the village derive income from occupations involving sales, rather than crafts or wages. Eight men list oc-

---

subsistence hedge—a strategy related by the villagers of "Tudu" in the southern part of the Tahoua *department* to Faulkingham (1977).

Table II. Grain purchases by sample households—Shadawanka

		Millet	Sorghum	Total
Number of households	21			
Number of weeks	22			
Total kilograms purchased		5,210.77	3,061.54	8,272.31
Average kilograms per week per household		11.28	6.63	17.9
Total value purchased (In FCFA)		809,975	345,800	115,775
Average purchase per week per household		1,753.19	727.54	2,480.73
Average price paid per kilogram		155.44	112.97	134.21

Source: Curry 1984:277.

cupations which are directly associated with commerce in livestock. Livestock intermediaries (Hausa: *dillaalai*) assist buyers and sellers in negotiating sales at the periodic livestock markets. They display for sale animals tethered at their station, providing water and fodder for the duration of the market. During the bargaining, they convey offers and counter offers between the negotiating parties. Their reputations for honesty and good character (*kirki*) provide assurances to both parties that the transaction is a fair one. For these services, they receive a commission on the sale. It is not uncommon for a *dillaali* to engage in livestock sales as a buyer or seller.

Livestock trading need not necessarily be pursued as a full-time occupation. Some people sell their own animals to obtain cash in emergencies, or engage in speculation on the market on a seasonal basis. For example, during the 1981–1982 dry season, several villagers not listed as livestock sellers bought sheep and goats in the Shadawanka market with loans obtained from neighbors. They then drove the animals on foot (or by truck) south to the Nigerian border for sale to other Hausa buyers, who transported the animals to Lagos for slaughter.

Both individuals and households may combine agriculture with one or more occupations to obtain sustenance. Examples taken from the households studied in 1981–1982 provide illustration.

Household 1.

Ibro is a tanner who heads a large, polygynous family of seventeen persons. The family of his eldest son, who migrates frequently to Nigeria seeking wage employment, also lives with him. The family cul-

Table III. Non-agricultural occupations—Shadawanka

Occupation	Male	Female	Total
Basic Production			
Herder	4	—	4
Sub-total	4	—	4
Craft Production			
Tanner	11	—	11
Smith	5	—	5
Potter	—	2	2
Mat Weaver	—	2	2
Sub-total	16	4	20
Traditional Services (receive fee)			
Marabout	3	—	3
Koranic Student	2	—	2
Griot	6	—	6
Sorcerer	1	—	1
Tailor	3	—	3
Butcher	1	—	1
Water Carrier	—	1	1
Hair Braider	—	2	2
Sub-total	16	3	19
Food Processing and Sales			
Fried Cake Maker and Seller	—	34	34
Tuuwoo Maker and Seller	—	2	2
Groundnut Oil Seller	—	2	2
Milk Seller	—	1	1
Meat Seller	3	—	3
Sub-total	3	39	42
Commerce Sales			
General Commerce	15	—	15
Livestock intermediary (Dillaali)	7	—	7
Livestock Sales	1	—	1
Rope Seller	1	—	1
Mat Seller	1	—	1
Sub-total	25	—	25
Other			
Radio Repair	1	—	1
Migrant Wage Laborer	1	—	1
Transporter	1	—	1
Sub-total	3	—	3
TOTAL	67	46	113

Source: Curry 1984:249.

tivates nearly 5 hectares of millet and sorghum, four of which is a single, common field.

During the rainy season, all resident household members over the age of six work on the fields at least some of the time. The adult women work their own fields and assist with the planting and harvesting of the large common field. Ibro, however, divides his time between the large field and his tanning trade. During this time, a boy, aged six, gathers grass to feed the animals—cattle, sheep, goats and a horse (Curry 1984:296–297).

By harvest time, the household members are engaged in a variety of non-agricultural activities. Ibro devotes full time to tanning and marketing hides. The co-wives intermittently prepare and sell in the village and at the weekly market fried cakes made of millet flour. Two of the older boys leave the household on short trips "searching for money" (*neman ku'di*). Two of the younger boys are in school. The young boy charged with tending the animals will occasionally gather grass to sell in the village.

In 1982, the rains began early in June, but stopped shortly afterwards. This required two reseedings. One of the older boys left for Nigeria in mid-August, and was unavailable to help out with the second weeding of the crop. Despite these problems, Ibro's household harvested about 1160 kg of grain, an improvement over the approximately 895 kg harvested the previous year.

Household 2.

Another tanner in the village is Iliya. He lives in a household consisting of his current wife and his children by the current, and a previous, marriage. Although they cultivate about seven hectares, they obtain only about 564 and 658 kg of grain during 1981 and 1982. This will last the household about 92 to 107 days.

With such a meagre output, family members must turn to other pursuits to supplement their grain supply. Iliya tans and sells hides throughout the year. This income, lower than Ibro's, is supplemented by loans and gifts, and by a remittance from one of his two sons who left for Nigeria during the dry season. When they are home in the village, these young men work occasionally as porters at the weekly markets in Shadawanka and Abalak (Curry 1984:304). With no co-wife or adolescent girl to help her, Iliya's wife has no income-generating activity.

Household 3.

Lawali, a livestock intermediary, is the head of a household consisting of five persons. The children, two boys and a girl, are 17, 15 and 13, respectively. Lawali's farm totals about 2.5 hectares. The farm yielded about 528 and 514 kg. of millet for 1981 and 1982.

Nearly everyone in the household pursues at least one income-generating activity. Lawali works as an intermediary in the Shadawanka and Abalak livestock markets throughout the year. The older boy migrates to Nigeria during the dry season to seek wage employment. While in the village, he works at repairing radios, and as an occasional wage worker on neighbors' fields. The younger son assists Lawali with the family livestock business, tending animals, and gathering fodder. The woman of the house (*uwar gida*) and the daughter prepare and sell fried cakes and milk.

Household 4.

Another household which derives substantial off-farm income from livestock is that of Hassan. He is head of a large household (18 persons) which consists of his two wives, their children, and 10 of his siblings, who came to live with him upon the death of his father. Only six members of the household are 14 years of age or older: consequently, the dependency ratio in this household is quite high.

Hassan's farm consists of two fields totalling about 3.7 hectares. In 1981, he harvested about 1155 kg and in 1982 about 894 kg of millet and sorghum.

Hassan spends much of his time throughout the year buying and selling livestock, and acting as an intermediary. He will occasionally buy animals and trek them to Nigeria for sale. Other times, he works as a wage laborer in the village, or is absent from the village "searching for money." In the latter pursuit, he is occasionally joined by a younger brother. The other younger brother migrates to Nigeria, where he would "eat the dry season" (Curry 1984:319). One of his wives, and his oldest daughter, prepares and sells fried cakes.

Household 5.

Unlike the heads of household previously mentioned, Usman's income source comes from a source other than livestock. He is a used clothing merchant in the periodic markets in and around Shadawanka. By his trade, he supports his household in Shadawanka, which consists of two wives and five children, and another wife who lives in another market town. From his 5 hectare farm, he harvested 1424 kg of millet in 1981 and about 1373 kg in 1982.

Throughout the year, Usman regularly sells clothes at the regional markets. He occasionally joins the rest of the family in work on the farm. When the weeding labor is too great to be accomplished in a timely manner, he hires some of his neighbors to assist his wives and son, using cash he earns from the clothing sales. His son gathers straw and animal fodder from the bush to sell, and also works as a porter in the market and at house construction in the village for cash. The women of the household make and sell fried cakes.

Household 6.

Garba is a wage worker who migrates to Nigeria during the dry season. During 1982, however, he did not return to Shadawanka for even the rainy season. Instead, he sent back remittances to support his wife, their three young children, and his aged mother. This household harvested only 282 and 148 kg of grain during 1981 and 1982. A portion of the money Garba sent back to the household went for hired labor to weed the fields in 1982. The cash value of the grain would barely cover the cost of the hired labor. Garba's wife, Amina, pursued no income-generating activities.

During this period, the family survived through curtailing purchases of both food and non-food items. As a consequence of having a very restricted income, Amina limited her expenditures on food and other household items to about $US 6.85 to 8.00 per week, according to the budgets she reported for that period (Curry 1984:335). Income from remittances was supplemented by gifts from unknown sources, and by sales of their two sheep at the Islamic feast of Tabaski in September of 1982.

Household 7.

Mai Wa'ka combines wage work with a traditional occupation— praise singing—to generate cash. He and his wife, A'isha, have no dependents. At weeding time they will sometimes supplement their own farm labor with hired laborers.

To earn money for this and other expenses, Mai Wa'ka will work as a barber, house builder, agricultural wage worker, or praise singer at marriages and festivals. All of these occupations may require him to be absent from home occasionally during both the rainy and dry seasons. A'isha is responsible for domestic chores, weeding the farm, and tending the small stock. She might supplement her income by braiding hair for a fee.

Household 8.

Amu is an elderly widow who lives with her 15 year old son. They cultivate a field of 2 hectares, which yields 211 kg in 1981 and 141 kg in 1982. The son, who attends school, is sometimes absent during planting and harvest. Amu must then ask the help of neighbors' children, whom she repays with food she has prepared for them.

To earn cash, Amu spends about two hours per day carrying water. For this effort, she receives about $US 4 per month. In addition, she prepared fried cakes each week to sell at the village market on Mondays, and will occasionally gather grass and straw in the bush to feed to her animals.

Like Amina of Garba's household, Amu survives by restricting her expenditures. This is especially true when her son is at school. For most of 1982, she existed primarily on gifts of food from neighbors. These gifts often equalled or exceeded in value the money she earned from water carrying.

Household 9.

Another female water carrier is Talle. She lives with her daughter, who occasionally assists her with the farm work, and the preparation and sale of fried cakes. Talle will occasionally gather straw in the bush for sale.

The amount of grain that Talle derives from her quarter-hectare field of millet is inconsequential: between 30–40 kg. To a lesser extent than either Amu or Amina, Talle relies upon donations of food and other items to supplement her meagre harvests and earnings from food and water sales.

Conclusions

The nine examples presented in the previous section show the considerable variability that exists in Shadawanka in the size and composition of households, the success of these households in agricultural production, and the various income-generating strategies employed by members of these households to compensate for shortfalls in that production. Cash-producing occupations range from locally-based activities, such as tanning, food sales, water-carrying and petty commerce, to economic endeavors that pertain to the regional economy; e.g., livestock brokerage and sales, regional merchandising, and migratory wage labor. Table 4 provides a summary of the household demographic, agricultural, and economic characteristics of the nine examples.

Given the generally low and variable agricultural yields, and the failure of these yields to meet household subsistence requirements, household agriculture leaves most households in the village vulnerable to food shortage *vis à vis* household agriculture. Consequently, sources of cash become extremely important for maintaining the well-being of Shadawanka's population. Households usually combine several of these non-agricultural cash sources, depending on the size and composition of the domestic unit. In some cases, these cash sources determine the household's very survival.

Households whose head (most often male) participate in the regional economy, via the livestock trade or some other form of commerce, enjoy the highest per capita revenues (Curry 1984:361). Another livestock-related occupation, tanning, appears to offer the best, locally-based employment opportunity. Those households whose head must sell his or her labor appear to be the poorest in the village. Households most at risk and with poor access to cash appear to have as a major strategy the curtailment of purchases of food and other necessities, often to seemingly dangerous levels.

Regardless of the size or composition of the household to which they belong, younger adult males often combine casual wage labor in

Table IV. Summary of household characteristics: case studies—Shadawanka

Case #	Name of head of household Occupation and primary source of revenue	% of Persons	% of Fields	Total Hectares	Harvest (kg) 1981	Harvest (kg) 1982	Yields (kg/ha) 1981	Yields (kg/ha) 1982	Monthly per capita income (In FCFA)
1	Ibro 'dan Isu Tanner	15	3	5.24	895.35	1163.25	170.87	221.99	2,476
2	Iliya 'dan Shaibu Tanner	3	2	7.05	564	658.98	80.0	93.47	2,735
3	Lawali 'dan Mai Birni Dillai	5	2	2.43	528.75	514.65	217.59	211.79	23,307
4	Hassan 'dan Mohamadu Dillai	18	2	3.60	1156.2	888.60	321.27	246.83	4,200
5	Usman 'dan Abubakar Clothing Merchant	3	2	4.99	1412.1	1373.25	285.39	275.20	13,188
6	Garba 'dan Musall Migratory Wage Laborer	6	2	2.61	282	148.05	108.05	56.72	unavailable
7	Mai Wa'ka 'dan Umaru Wage Worker/Praise Singer	2	1	3.68	403	705	109.51	191.58	9,458
8	Amu 'diar Huseini Water Carrier	2	1	2.03	211.50	141	104.29	69.46	7,562
9	Talle 'diar Mai Nassara Water Carrier	2	1	.28	42.3	28.2	151.07	100.7	3,339

($1 US = approximately 360 FCFA)

Source: Curry 1984:358.

the village with periodic (sometimes seasonal) migratory wage employment as income sources. While migration may serve to generate off-farm income and relieve pressure on household grain stocks, the absence of young migrants at critical points in the agricultural cycle can produce labor shortages at the household level, further weakening the capacity of the household farm to sustain its members in times of both adequate and inadequate rainfall.

Female-generated income often contributes substantially to food-shortage coping strategies. This is particularly true of food preparation and sales activities. The significance of the contribution will vary greatly, however, depending upon whether the women engaged in the activity are members of a polygynous household with other sources of cash, or are female heads of households who must depend almost exclusively on this particular source.

Finally, the characterization of off-farm employment activities as "indigenous responses" to drought and food shortage should be undertaken with extreme caution. It is certainly true that rural agricultural populations in Africa are becoming increasingly dependent upon cash sources to buffer themselves against the consequences of drought-induced food shortage. However, this increased dependence may not derive solely from conditions of drought, but, as Fleuret has pointed out, from other processes of social and economic change. Moreover, the nature and efficacy of such "responses" to drought as migratory wage labor, food sales, and entrepreneurial activities are highly context-dependent, and subject to a wide range of variation. The examples taken from the highly-commercialized, highly-monetized regional economy in which the villagers of Shadawanka find themselves offer us a clear and often poignant reminder of how fragile a buffer against the threat of starvation such responses provide.

References

Campbell, A. 1986. The Use of Wild Food Plants and Drought in Botswana. *Journal of Arid Environments* 11:81–91.

Cashden, E. 1985. Coping with Risk: Reciprocity among the Basarwa of Northern Botswana. *Man (NS)* 20:454–474.

Curry, J., Jr. 1984. *Local Production, Regional Commerce, and Social Differentiation in a Hausa Village in Niger.* Unpublished Ph.D. Dissertation, Department of Anthropology, University of Massachusetts, Amherst.

260   John J. Curry

Curry, J.J., Jr., 1986. Adaptations of Farming Systems Research to the Study of Pastoral Systems: The Niger Range and Livestock Project. In *Social Sciences and Farming Systems Research: Methodological Perspectives on Agricultural Development*, ed. by Jeffrey R. Jones and Benjamin J. Wallace, Boulder: Westview Press. pp. 195–220.

Faulkingham, R.H. 1977. Ecologic Constraints and Subsistence Strategies: The Impact of Drought on a Hausa Village, A Case Study from Niger. In *Drougth in Africa*, ed. by David Dalby, R.J. Harrison-Church and Fatima Bezzas. London: IAI Oxford University Press. pp. 148–157.

Fleuret, A. 1986. Indigenous Responses to Drought in Sub-Saharan Africa. *Disasters* 10(3):224–229.

Hitchcock, R.K. 1979. The Traditional Response to Drought in Botswana. In *Proceedings of the Symposium on Drought in Botswana*, ed. by Madalon T. Hinchey. Worcester, Ma.: the Botswana Society in Collaboration with Clark University. pp. 91–97.

Lee, R.B. 1979. *The !Kung San. Men, Women, and Work in a Foraging Society*. Cambridge: Cambridge University Press.

Maliki, A. 1982. *Nganyaka*. Niamey: USAID Niger Range and Livestock Project Discussion Paper.

Ministere du Plan. 1980. *Plan Quinquennal de Developpement Economique et Sociale 1979–1983*. Niamey: L'Imprimerie Nationale du Niger.

Raynaut, C. 1976. Transformation du Systeme de Production et Inegalite Economique: le Cas d'un Village Haoussa (Niger). *Canadian Journal of African Studies* X(2):279–306.

——— 1977. Circulation Monetaire et Evolution des Structures Socio-economique chez les Haoussas du Niger. *Africa* 47(2):160–171.

Reyna, S. 1979. Equity in Niger: Cycles, Evidence and Options. Draft Report REDSO/WA Mimeograph. Abidjan: USAID.

Stenning, D. 1957. Transhumance, Migratory Drift, Migration: Patterns of Pastoral Fulani Nomadism. *Journal of the Royal Anthropological Institute* 87:57–73.

Sutter, J.W. 1979. Social analysis of the Nigerian Rural Producer. In *Niger Agricultural Sector Assessment*. 2 vols., ed. by Warren J. Enger and Melinda Smale. Niamey: USAID.

Watts, M.J. 1979. *A Silent Revolution: The Nature of Famine and the Changing Character of Food Production in Nigerian Hausaland*. 2 Vols. Unpublished Ph.D. Dissertation, Department of Geography, University of Michigan, Ann Arbor.

Wiessner, P. 1977. *Hxaro: a Regional System of reciprocity for Reducing Risk among the !Kung San*. Unpublished Ph.D. Dissertation, Department of Anthropology, University of Michigan, Ann Arbor.

Wetherall, H.I., J. Holt and P. Richards 1979. Drought in the Sahel: A Broader Interpretation with Regard to West Africa and Ethiopia. In *Proceedings of the Symposium on Drought in Botswana*, ed. by Madalon T. Hinchey. Worcester, Ma.: the Botswana Society in Collaboration with Clark University. pp. 131–141.

Adaptation, Drought and Development: Boran and Gabra Pastoralists of Northern Kenya

Asmarom Legesse

Department of Anthropology
Swarthmore College
Swarthmore, PA 19081

This paper examines the patterns of pastoral adaptation to arid environments, how the adaptive processes are affected by extended periods of drought, and what types of development might be appropriate under those conditions. The paper is a summary of several years of research among two closely related and interdependent pastoral populations in Northern Kenya: the Boran and the Gabra. Boran are cattle herders who live on the upland pastures of Marsabit mountain in Kenya and in Sidamo Province in Southern Ethiopia. Gabra herd camels and live in the semi-arid plains to the north and west of Marsabit mountain in Kenya. Both groups also raise sheep and goats in proportions that vary according to ecological constraints and economic opportunities.

Camels are highly desert-adapted; cattle are not. Sheep and goats occupy an intermediate position. As a result, the Gabra camel herders may raise some cattle when they are in the vicinity of the mountain or on it, and the Boran cattle herders often keep some camels among Gabra relatives and stock associates in the semi-desert. Sheep and goats serve as a fallback resource for both populations in times of extreme drought partly because they are desert-adapted and can survive the lesser droughts, and in part because they breed faster than camels and cattle and allow the nomads to restock their depleted herds more effectively.

The Boran-Gabra pastoral ecosystem is basically stable in spite of the fact that it is periodically exposed to deep perturbations. In anthropological studies of preliterate societies, subsistence economies are sometimes said to be "stable" or "stagnant" because they show no evidence of undergoing any change and seem to have remained at the same level of development for a major part of their history. My concept of stability is quite different from this. I understand stability not as the result of the absence of development, but as a dynamic process that requires important institutional inputs. Boran-Gabra society reached this stable relationship with its ecosystem as a result of having developed, over the centuries, many self-regulating properties. I refer to these properties as *adaptive strategies* when they are a conscious element of culture which the nomads can articulate, and as *adaptive responses* when they are part of the behavioral repertoire of the population which is not conscious (i.e., they exist just below the level of awareness or are actually denied.) I use the phrase *adaptive process* as a generic concept that refers to both patterns.

When I began my fieldwork, in 1963, I identified a number of customary prescriptions which my more ecologically minded colleagues had no difficulty recognizing as an unconscious "population policy." Boran require that marriage be delayed until a very advanced stage in the life course. The requirement applies to a major part of the generation-set system. After marriage, Boran require that these young families abandon their newborn children for another eight years, and their newborn daughters for yet another eight. At the time that I conducted field surveys among the affected age groups, the rules of infanticide were fully in force. Hardly any of the families who were required to abandon children had any children, and none of the families required to abandon daughters had any daughters. I observed only two exceptions in these surveys, children who were supposed to have been abandoned but were not. People were acutely aware of them and were embarrassed when I raised any questions about them.

The institution that required these practices is called the "*gada* system" and is a generation-set system somewhat similar to the age-set systems that are common throughout Eastern Africa. In my analysis of this institution, I conducted a computer simulation of hypothetical populations with average demographic properties in order to show what would happen to them under the rules of the *gada* system. The results showed that such a population would decline by about 50 percent during the first 80 years. Thereafter, it would remain steady for about two centuries and would then begin to rise at a very slow rate of growth. The rules remain the same, but their impact on the population becomes less and less over time. The important point for this discussion is that the *gada* system contained two processual features that make it especially interesting to a human ecologist. One is a demographic control mechanism that initially has a sizeable impact on population and subsequently sets a limit on the rate of population growth. The second is the built-in feedback mechanism that gradually weakens the population checks and thus permits the system to reach steady state, or something close to it. The rules of the *gada* system were developed at a time, in the seventeenth century, when the parent society, the Oromo, were undergoing a vast population expansion. The population could therefore sustain the rigorous constraints that are the basis of the institution (Legesse 1973).

In the investigation, I also discovered another feature that is of interest to human ecology. The Boran came together on annual and octennial cycles to perform very large ceremonies connected with the generation sets. Hundreds of families congregated around the shrines and, when they did, they would bring along more animals than the local habitat could support, especially when the ceremonies required a long period of preparation at the shrine. The customary rules required the pastoralists to bring only a few milch cows to the ceremonial grounds, thus limiting the potentially harmful effect on the pastures. The elders, who arrived at the site early, delimited a perimeter around the shrine within which grazing was not allowed. The few milch cows that were permitted were let into the inner perimeter only a week or so before the start of the ceremony.

When I recorded these observations in 1963, I had little understanding of their full ecological implications. Nor did I know then that I would devote the next decade of my research to the field of human ecology. Now, with the benefit of hindsight, I can see that I had stumbled upon two key components of a complex ecosystem. My recent research, from 1976 to the present, was conducted not among the Ethiopian Boran but among the Boran and Gabra of Northern Kenya. Its explicit purpose was to examine the nature of self-regulating institutions and practices in the area of demography, subsistence economy, and general ecological relationships, especially those between humans and domestic animals. I also investigated some plant populations that share the same habitat and are of critical importance to people and their livestock. This investigation of the pastoral ecosystem has produced the following results.

A. *Demographically*, many new factors have come up in the survey. To begin with, infanticide does not seem to be a significant factor among the Boran or Gabra of Kenya, as it is among the Boran of Ethiopia. However, late marriage has emerged as a major factor among both populations; approximately 50 percent of the women remain unmarried well into their thirties. For several years after the birth of a child the woman is subject to a postpartum sex taboo that bars her from having sexual intercourse. Nursing continues for about three years, sometimes much longer. This has the effect of spacing the births of children. These rules operate without reference to the *gada* system. They are in force in the nomadic populations of Northern Kenya where the *gada* system is not as dominant an institution as it is among the Ethiopian Boran. Thus, even in the areas where the *gada* system no longer has any meaning, demographic checks continue to exert an influence on the population.

B. *Ecologically,* the nomads maintain a balanced relationship with populations of other species that share the same habitat. They do this by setting limits on the degree and the manner of use of the grasses, shrubs, and trees in their territory. For example, they have taboos against killing some trees. These are mostly trees that are ritually protected or trees that demarcate ceremonial grounds and shrines. Other trees are protected not for specifically ritual reasons, but because they are seen as valuable resources and they make a conscious effort to limit the manner of their exploitation. Thus *Acacia tortilis,* which produces fruits that are consumed by sheep and goats, cannot be cut if it is a full grown tree and if there are other trees of the same species in the area. The full grown tree is called *korma* (bull) and is protected. The term reveals the implicit analogy between Gabra ideas of animal husbandry and range management. Bulls are needed for breeding purposes and are therefore left intact. By contrast, superfluous males are castrated and are, in due course, slaughtered or sold. Similarly, the "bull" of the trees is not cut down, but is protected as a breeding specimen from which future generations will come. This cultural provision obviously aids the regenerative potential of the protected species, ensuring that in each area there will be some well established specimens from which a population which is always vulnerable to overexploitation can continue to develop. *Acacia tortilis* is used extensively for fences and firewood; the trees that are most often used for this purpose are those that have been dwarfed by previous cutting. These will be kept in a dwarfed state for many years and are not protected from further cutting.

Similar taboos are in force with regard to many other species that are much more vulnerable than *Acacia tortilis*. For example, the tree which Boran call *Haroressa* (identification pending, probably *Grewia trichocarpa* A. Rich.), which grows in mountain areas and furnishes the most important supple branches used in the construction of the portable huts of camel nomads, is protected by taboos against over-exploitation. It is never cut down to the point where it loses all its foliage and is in danger of dying. In another instance, I was told that a tree located inside an area that was being cleared for human habitation was severely pruned to make room for huts and livestock. However, the apex was left intact with its foliage to let the tree grow vertically, but not laterally, and continue to live after the nomads left the camp site.

Other aspects of Boran culture reveal similar concerns. Pastoralists are often berated by range ecologists because they cut trees to build their fences (Lusigi 1981, Hugh Lamprey, personal communication 1979). These critics often do not pay attention to the way the fences are built, but focus only on the fact that fence building steadily depletes the vegetation. Boran have living stake fences that contribute to the sensible relationship that they maintain with the vegetation. When they build a fence, they plant many of the cuttings in such a way that they can reproduce vegetatively. They prepare the ground by digging a hole and filling it with wet dung. As a result, at least half of the trees and shrubs that make up the Boran fence are alive. Far from being a destructive practice, the building of fences among the upland pastoralists contributes to the natural regenerative capacity of the vegetation. The range ecologists' criticism may, however, have some validity in the case of the semi-desert dwellers. I saw no evidence of living stake fences among the Gabra. The fact that they cut trees to build fences whenever they migrate may be a wasteful practice. However, the range ecologists should measure the rate of destruction of the vegetation before they conclude that the practice is a major factor in ecological degradation. That has not been done, and as a result, the criticism has remained well-intentioned but somewhat gratuitous (Lusigi 1981).

Boran also plant trees at grave sites. The burial occurs soon after the death, but the final funerary rite cannot be performed until the sons of the deceased household head have gathered and each has planted a tree around the grave. For every Boran household head who dies, there are a few trees that come to life. Symbolically, the continuity of human life after death is tied to the coming to life of some species of trees. The trees that grow around the graves are ritually protected and cannot be cut or otherwise destroyed.

Boran wells reveal another feature of their symbiotic relationship with trees. Boran believe that they can locate underground aquifiers by digging along the roots of certain species of trees such as the *Podocarpus*. They believe that these large trees can survive in their territory only if the roots reach down to an underground reservoir. Surprisingly, when they dig along the roots, they do not kill the tree. Some of the root structure is exposed, but enough of it is left intact even when they dig to a depth of several meters. As a result, the well often has a large tree in it, sometimes directly on top of it and sometimes to one side. The roots that gird the well protect the sides from caving in and stabilize the whole structure. In due course, so much water is spilled at ground level that the tree develops an extensive shallow root system that is fed and fertilized by humans and their livestock. The tree offers excellent shade to the workers who draw water all day on the days when they bring their livestock to the wells. In observing these magnificent Boran wells, we become acutely aware of the degree of interdependence of trees, humans, and their livestock.

Trees such as the *Podocarpus*, the sycamore, and even some acacias, are often recognized as sacred trees and are treated as shrines where important rituals are performed. The trees may be sacralized because they are exceptionally large or because they happen to grow on sacred ground. The trunks of these trees are often anointed with butter on the occasion of rituals. These trees are not only protected, but the whole area around them and the paths leading up to them are also guarded. Farmers who cultivate land inside Boran territory often find themselves at odds with the nomads when they begin to chop down the trees indiscriminately and provoke the ire of the nomadic population.

Boran and Gabra also attempt to regulate bush encroachment on their pastures by maintaining a carefully regulated firing regime. The main purpose is to control or reverse the progressive degradation of their pastures because their livestock tend to over-graze the grass species which they find most palatable and neglect everything else. Uncontrolled, the upland pastures are often overrun by such useless shrubs as *Triumfetta flavescens* ("Icchinni") and *Solanum incanum*

("Hiddi"). These bushes are sometimes called "increasers," imply-ing that they are like pests and will expand to fill all open niches in their habitat when the opportunity offers itself.

When the pastures are set on fire, the increasers are set back or partially destroyed and the most desirable grasses such as *Chrysopo-gon aucheri* and *Themeda trianda* have a chance to establish them-selves. The procedure is highly effective as a range management tool. Its effectiveness derives from the fact that many of the trees that occur in the pastoral areas and nearly all the grasses are fire-resistant. The overgrazed and the ungrazed species are both set back and thus the original balance that existed prior to the overgrazing is reestablished. If anything, the ungrazed species may be affected more deeply be-cause the standing biomass is greater and the fire temperatures are commensurately higher. Observations made during the weeks after the firing reveal that the acacias were slightly scorched but not dam-aged, while the increasers such as *Triumfetta* and *Solanum* were very badly burnt. The grass was also burnt down to the ground, but the roots remained intact and the plants were able to regenerate quickly.

There is some evidence to suggest that many of the species of trees that dominate the pastoral ecosystem probably co-evolved under the influence of natural fires and that humans and their livestock entered the community and began using deliberate firing regimes to keep the system in a sub-climax state for their own benefit. In so doing, they also preserved the system for the wild species that share the same habitat. Fire, in its natural and artificial forms, is one of the key de-mographic regulators of the pastoral ecosystem.

Finally, a specialized type of nomadism has evolved in Boran and Gabra country that allows the pastoralist to regulate the density of human population in relation to the other populations that make up the pastoral ecosystem. This feature of nomadic adaptation, called the *fora* system, deserves special attention. In both societies, the herd is divided into two sections. A very small milch herd is kept at the camp site and grazed in the vicinity of the camp. The larger dry herd is taken far away from the camp site on a vast nomadic cycle that covers up to a 50 mile radius in normal times and may extend far beyond that in time of severe drought. The dry herd is cared for by adoles-cents and young adults who are, in most cases, unmarried. They have no huts or tents and carry only the most rudimentary equipment. With that minimal gear, they are free to migrate very frequently and over great distances. This is an extreme form of adaptation in which humans sacrifice all the comforts of home and family life so as to give their livestock the best that their harsh environment has to offer. This pattern of adaptation allows the nomads to maintain a high level of mobility, one that is appropriate for livestock in arid lands, but is intolerable for families and communities containing very young and very old members. In short, the significance of the *fora* system is that it allows the societies who practice it at one and the same time a more nomadic and a more sedentary way of life compared with societies that keep the entire herd as a unit and attempt to take the whole domestic establishment with them as they follow their herds.

The processes of adaptation described here are of critical importance in regulating the pastoral ecosystem and preventing the excesses that can disrupt the nomadic subsistence economy. Range ecologists must pay some attention to these features if they are to understand when human activity contributes to the process of desertification and when it tends to inhibit that process. The ecologists at IPAL (Integrated Project in Arid Lands) who are conducting research on desertification in Northern Kenya, under the auspices of UNESCO, have generally assumed that the nomads are contributing to a rapid process of desertification and must be taught to better manage their resources. However, the question of desertification is an empirical question which must be answered empirically, not assumed. The Rendille present us with fairly gross examples of ecological mismangement and some of the worst cases of ecological degradation to be found in the semi-arid regions of Kenya (Dolan 1980:129, Herlocker 1981:276, Lusigi 1981:28). Gabra, by contrast, are much better range managers. It would be highly misleading if the management proposals that IPAL has put forth on the basis of research on the Rendille were to be applied to other pastoralists who are very different from them (IPAL 1983). As yet we do not know which of the two is the commoner pattern among pastoral nomads generally. It would be most surprising if the Rendille disaster area were typical of rangelands elsewhere in Kenya.

Response to Drought and Famine

How did the Boran and Gabra respond to the great droughts of the 1970's and 1980's and what can we learn from these responses? The two societies are fundamentally different in terms of the degree of desert adaptation. Gabra are desert adapted and Boran are not. Gabra maintain extensive nomadic cycles; Boran practice a restricted type of nomadism. Gabra live in a harsh semi-desert environment north of the Chalbi desert; Boran live on the relatively wet habitats of Marsabit mountain and on the Moyale-Sololo escarpment. The Boran venture out into the semi-desert only during that part of the year when rain has transformed the area into lush pastures. The two societies are highly interdependent; each is free to try out the strategies of the other when their own patterns of adaptation fail.

During the great droughts of the 1970's and early 1980's we were able to observe how nomadic and semi-nomadic societies fared in the face of the greatest ecological disaster in living memory. One fact that became obvious as the drought progressed was that the Boran were hit much harder than the Gabra, in spite of the fact that their land normally has much more water and more pasture than Gabraland.

At the height of the drought of 1973, Boran embarked on long-distance migrations on a more extensive and more massive scale than anything I had seen during the preceding decade. They sent their herds across into Ethiopia and very far south into the Tana River valley. This was a very arduous migration that took weeks of trekking and they lost between 60 and 70 percent of their livestock on the trip. Gabra, by contrast, did not resort to mass migration. They migrated a few families at a time as they normally do, and they inched away from the drought-affected regions to areas they believed to be in better condition. The main difference in the two patterns of adaptation to extreme drought is that the Boran experienced a *critical threshold;* the Gabra did not. In other words, the Boran waited on the mountain too long. They reached a point of no return and they had to drive their emaciated cattle across vast territories before they could reach pastures that were appropriate for cattle. On the northern route, most of the semi-arid area they had to cross was occupied by Gabra and they did not face much threat from raiders. On the souther trek, however, they had to cross nearly the whole of Rendille territory and they were therefore very fearful of raiders. As a result, they drove their weakened cattle so hard that many collapsed and died on the way. They lost more cattle on the southern trek than they did travelling north into Ethiopia.

These observations clearly suggest that in times of drought a high degree of desert adaptation is an advantage. However, it is important to realize that Boran—who are not desert-adapted—made ample use of the skills and resources of their desert-adapted allies. The Gabra lent them pack camels to facilitate their migration. More importantly, some of the Boran sold their cattle and bought sheep and goats and moved into Gabra territory for the duration of the drought. They were also given milch camels by their Gabra stock associates. Some of those stock associates were families that had borrowed animals from their Boran allies and were now reciprocating by giving the Boran some of their own animals. The Boran who abandoned their mountain habitat and moved into the Chalbi desert had drastically altered their pattern of adaptation. In most cases this transformation was temporary. Some of the families who became desert nomads are now back on Marsabit mountain herding cattle and living in the environs of the mist forest. It is significant, however, that they did not get rid of the camels and the small stock they acquired during the drought. These animals were left with Gabra stock associates in the Chalbi desert. They are an insurance.

The network of stock associates is extensive, and the number of animals that are loaned out over a large territory ensures that a family will not lose all its stock in drought, epidemic, or raid. Boran and Gabra who have lost their herds often go on a begging tour over the whole of Boran-Gabra territory, receiving gifts from families who had in previous years or generations benefited from their stock gifts.

This institution, called *dabare* in Boran and Gabra, serves as an important insurance mechanism. Whenever the educated Africans in Marsabit, including myself, try to persuade Boran to start making use of savings banks to store their wealth and conserve it through the drought periods, the Boran remind us that they have their own bank in the form of the great network of stock associates. The analogy they are making is not trivial.

Dislocation and Sedentarization

The single most important, and apparently permanent, change that has occurred in the pastoral ecosystem is the departure of some families from the rangelands and their entry into the urban and peri-urban economies. Although sedentarization and urbanization continue at a slow pace in normal times, it was greatly accelerated because of the drought and famine. A significant part of the population, perhaps two to three thousand people, have been permanently dislocated from pastoral life and have been incorporated into the squatter settlements and farming communities on Marsabit mountain and elsewhere. Some have joined the permanent urban underclass, dependent on handouts from the state and from church organizations.

There are important lessons to be learned from the manner in which this process of dislocation came about and the role that the famine relief programs played in the rehabilitation of the new communities of squatters. One settlement scheme that was created during the drought of 1973 continued to receive small quantities of food from the Catholic mission for about ten years after the initial disaster. The clue that leads us to realize that there is something very odd about this community is that it has no name for itself except the derogatory name that it acquired from the outset; it was called "Olla Hiyyessa" by the neighboring villages and the name stuck. It means "village of the poor." In spite of all the aid that it received, or perhaps because of it, the community remained demoralized throughout the decade of the 1970's. It is the closest thing to an Ik type of non-community that I ever observed in Boran country (Turnbull 1980, 1982). The normal mutual aid networks that operate in all Boran-Gabra communities were non-existent here. Olla Hiyyessa is, in fact, the only place in Boran or Gabra country where I found a person starving, whom the neighbors felt that they had no obligation to help. They said, "How can we? We are all poor." The strange fact is that, at the time, some families had already started to make a good living out of their farms, but the stigma of poverty endured and had a disintegrative effect on social relationships.

Other communities that came into being spontaneously around Marsabit town, such as Olla Duba, lacked the stigma of being tagged "poor," although they were just as destitute as the people living in Olla Hiyyessa, and migrated into the peri-urban area at the same time and for the same reasons. The spontaneous communities were always named after the most senior residents and had an obvious pattern of neighborhood organization. Neighbors helped each other even under situations of extreme poverty. The spontaneously established squatter community turns out to be much healthier sociologically than the planned and managed settlement scheme. We have adequate data on the two type of communities which, when fully analyzed, will reveal the nature of the processes of social transformation associated with drought and famine relief and the kinds of communities that are created in the process. This is an area of research that deserves much greater attention than it has received so far.

The two types of communities look very different in terms of their physical structure. The settlement scheme was a straight row of rectangular houses about 30 yards apart, made out of corrugated iron sheets. These structures proved to be poorly suited to the needs of the settlers and to the particular habitat in which they lived. The normal wind velocity on Marsabit mountain varies between 10 and 30 miles per hour and very often gusts to much higher speeds. As the wind blows against the sharp edges of the buildings it makes a howling sound that makes the houses unlivable. The roofs were frequently blown off and had to be put back on by the helpful gentlemen at the workshop of the Catholic mission school. The men and women of the scheme could not do that for themselves because they knew nothing about corrugated iron sheets and did not have the tools or the skills required to work with them. Rather than trying to master the new technology, they used their own technology to build a new set of structures. Each family built a hut next to the mission-built house. Both calves and humans lived in the huts and the iron-sheet houses were used for storage. It took many years for some of the families to begin living in the iron-sheet houses. Urban visitors were received in the iron-sheet houses while rural visitors were received in the huts. This dual arrangement was their way of making a difficult situation work.

The naturally evolved design of the spontaneous squatter community was strikingly different. The physical layout of the living space was such that it brought families together around nodal personalities and landmarks, rather than stringing them out in some meaningless geometric array. It had a seemingly urban look about it because it had a "Main Street" in which the village water supply, the shops, and the two churches were located. Dramatically, the Catholics and Protestants had built churches at the two ends of "Main Street." The houses were arranged in clusters and each cluster was a collaborating unit, a neighborhood, or a *mogga* as Boran called it. As urban anthropology has revealed in many other situations, proxemics can make or break a community, but the famine relief programs in Africa do not seem to have discovered these fundamental verities. As they nurse starving families back to life, they neglect the communal needs of the settlements they create and sometimes produce new kinds of sociological problems.

Nomadic Adaptation to Extended Drought

The plight of these communities represents the most extreme form of dislocation experienced by the Boran and Gabra pastoral populations. Most of the nomads remained within the pastoral ecosystem and were therefore able to fall back on naturally evolved adaptive strategies with very little assistance from outside. Between 1970 and 1983 there were several years of adequate rain in which the drought-affected populations and their habitats were observed. The remarkable fact is that a few weeks after the rains, it was very difficult to realize that the habitat had gone through the worst ecological disaster of the century. The mountain pastures and the semi-arid grasslands appeared to rebound with such vigor that one had the impression of total and immediate rehabilitation. Of course, livestock densities were reduced, as was the human population pressure. The former occurred because of livestock deaths, the latter because of out-migration and sedentarization, as well as a limited increase in human death rates.

However, first impressions are misleading. For a few years after the long drought, many nomadic families continued to live a marginal existence depending on very small herds, on livestock loans, and on daily gifts of food from friends and kinsmen. They experienced seasonal hunger and sometimes had to supplement their nomadic income with income obtained by herding the stock of wealthier families and urban merchants. In short, there is a form of rural poverty among the nomads which is far less visible than the poverty of the peri-urban squatters. The two forms of poverty, however, are sharply different because the stigma that is associated with the latter is absent in the former. The nomads do not view poverty as a state of being but as an acquired trait. One does not *become* poor, one *catches* poverty, like a cold. Everybody has, at one time or another, caught this particular ailment.

Diet and Deficiencies

The most recent data that we gathered in the field concern nutrition. We measured daily food intake for about 80 Gabra and 30 Boran families. These data indicate that the content of Boran and Gabra diet went through major changes from season to season, from year to year. The seasonal variation was fairly simple; during the rainy seasons they reverted back to the classic nomadic milk and meat diet, and as the dry season advanced they relied more heavily on maize meal, sugar, and other energy-rich supplements to their basic diet.

The most important problem that the nomads faced during the long drought was calorie deficiency. They countered this problem by selling milk in the urban markets and buying maize meal and great quantities of sugar which they consumed with tea. During the drought, the supply of milk they have is an excellent source of most nutrients, but is not by itself an adequate supply of energy. Part of their milk supply must be exchanged for calorie-rich foods to sustain them through the period of shortages.

Next to calorie deficiency, the most important problem that Boran faced was iron deficiency. Boran women are generally in danger of developing anemia caused by shortages of iron in their diet. The traditional society has many customary prescriptions that ensure that women receive special iron-rich diets particularly in those stages of the life course when they are most vulnerable. During the course of sedentarization, however, these customary prescriptions are not followed, and as a result, nutritional anemia becomes a very widespread problem among the impoverished peri-urban Boran. Furthermore, the switch from the milk and meat diet of the nomad to the starchy diet of the squatters can have very unfortunate consequences.

A disruption of diet is one of the unexpected consequences of sedentarization associated with famine relief programs. The programs do not only feed people and save lives, they also introduce new food habits and significant imbalances in dietary systems.

Concluding Remarks

The greatest impact of famine relief is not on the nomads but on the small segment of the nomadic population that became sedentary and dependent on external assistance. Whether or not there is a way of reintegrating these dislocated communities into the self-sustaining subsistence economy remains to be seen. It is much more likely that they will become part of the urban-oriented cash-crop economy in which land, labor, and agricultural produce are treated as marketable commodities. There is an important lesson in development to be learned from the many false starts made by famine relief programs as they shifted their focus from relief to rehabilitation, and in the process, created non-communities such as Olla Hiyyessa. Analysis of these sociological disasters can help relief workers to establish the new communities in such a way that the homes are built with locally available materials and skills, construction materials are selected that are suited to the local habitat, neighborhoods are arranged in such a way as to enhance a sense of community and collaboration, relief is given in ways that are least demoralizing, and the community is weaned from relief as soon as food production is under way. The lesson that Olla Hiyyessa teaches us is that a collection of people who have nothing in common except the fact of their destitution cannot form a community. The stigma of poverty is as bad as the poverty itself.

The main impact of the extended drought on the nomads was felt in the third and fourth years of the drought. It is clear that Gabra nomads were able to withstand one or two years of drought without any major disruptions in their mode of adaptation. By the third year of drought they began to resort to more drastic action such as long-distance migration. But the transition from one to the other was an incremental process. The desert-adapted animals such as camels survived better than sheep and goats, while cattle herds were decimated. The desert-adapted human populations and their livestock moved away from the drought-affected region gradually, and suffered only limited losses in livestock. Only the Boran upland pastoralists experienced what I refer to as the threshold phenomenon—a point of no return. At that stage, their society underwent a drastic metamorphosis; nearly all the herds were taken away on long distance treks at great cost to the livestock population.

In spite of these effects, the nomadic and semi-nomadic populations had good regenerative capabilities that allowed them to return to their normal patterns of subsistence. The self-regulated ecosystem proved to be quite resilient and the doomsday messages about desertification have so far proved to be somewhat unrealistic. Careful studies of exclosures made by IPAL in Northern Kenya comparing heavily grazed and ungrazed areas during the drought years have yielded no evidence of permanent change in desertification resulting from overgrazing. It is worth remembering that these were controlled experiments in which the standing crop biomass was measured and the stocking densities were controlled in each of several fenced paddocks. Not only did the experiments not yield any evidence of desertification, they did not even demonstrate that there was an enduring change in the species composition of the grasses and herbs in the paddocks (Herlocker, personal communication, Nov. 8–16, 1979).

The impact of the extended drought on demography is significant but generally temporary and reversible. Population densities are of course reduced after a long drought, but the system does not seem to return to its normal stable or slow-growth pattern after a year or two of adequate rainfall.

The net effect of the drought and famine relief on diet is that it introduced serious imbalances into the diet of the sedentarized population and that it expanded the dietary base of the nomadic populations, making them more dependent on the market for a supply of energy-rich foods. These foods then became a necessary part of their diet during the normal periods of seasonal hunger, not merely during the long periods of drought and famine. Aside from this one important change, the nomad's diet remained largely undisturbed. In both situations, the impact on diet seems to be permanent. The squatters are in serious trouble in this regard and need help to develop food habits that add up to a reasonably balanced diet. For nomads, the change is incremental and minimally disruptive, so long as the newly introduced foods are a supplement to the traditional diet.

Boran and Gabra range management strategies continue to function well in areas that are somewhat removed from modern influences. Pastures quickly give way to bush encroachment in the vicinity of Marsabit town where farming and officialdom have come together to preclude the use of the firing regime. On the whole, however, Boran continue to use fire, sometimes illegally, to control bush encroachment on the grasslands. They continue to regulate the manner of exploitation of the shrubs and trees and to maintain a sensible relationship with the vegetation on which they depend. Only in the vicinity of the bore holes do we see new and damaging processes of desertification. These situations are comparable to the settlement schemes—they are the product of external inputs, a reckless and unintelligent kind of development that yields results only at the expense of the adaptive processes that have served the nomads well for centuries.

Development Potentials

Some preliminary conclusions can be made concerning development possibilities and processes at this stage of our research. First, Boran and Gabra must be taken as a unit. They are so dependent on each other that any development introduced into one society will have repercussions on the other. Similar patterns of interdependence between nomadic and semi-nomadic or agricultural populations occur throughout Africa, and I believe these relationships are very relevant to development planning. Spencer's study of Samburu and Rendille provides similar information to what we have obtained on the Boran and Gabra (Spencer 1973). In such situations, development planning should be done on a regional basis to encompass all the societies that have developed symbiotic relationships with each other. Sudden and massive development inputs in one area can become a magnet that draws people into that area and defeats the very purpose of development by depressing the standard of living of the developing communities. This type of influx occurs, for instance, when new water resources are introduced. However, regional planning does not mean incorporating any and all adjoining populations into the same development program. There are natural breaks in populations that can serve to delimit the boundaries of the region. For instance, the no man's land that separates Boran and Somali to the east of Marsabit mountain is such a break. An endemic state of hostility between Boran-Gabra and the Somali populations of North East Kenya keeps the no man's land uninhabited and unexploited. Similarly, the Chalbi desert is a natural ecological break between Samburu-Rendille on the one side and Boran-Gabra on the other side. Regardless of the development opportunities that are made available, there is very little flow of population across these boundaries.

The relevance of these ideas has become patently clear in the Hurri Hills, where an IPAL sponsored project has been engaged in development work aimed only at Gabra pastoral nomads to the exclusion of the Boran pastoralists. As the work advanced, there was an influx of Boran into the Hurri Hills, attracted by the development opportunities and encouraged by a Konso charismatic figure who became a major threat to the project. The response of the project director was to become a Gabra "nationalist," forever bemoaning the Boran "invasion" with little understanding of the cultural and demographic dynamic that historically bound the two peoples to each other. Boran cannot be separated from the Gabra, any more than Samburu can be separated from the Rendille.

The more important set of conclusions concerns the relationship of the development programs to the adaptive strategies and responses. I believe it is possible to design development in such a way that it supports the existing adaptive processes. By way of illustration, we might consider the population control mechanisms of the Boran and the Gabra. These are obviously important for the persistence of the pastoral ecosystem. If the modern government of Kenya decides to introduce family planning programs with a view to conserving natural resources and raising the standard of living of the population, the program should be offered not as an alien system of thought but as an idea for which there is already a precedent in the traditional culture. The ideal of limiting the numbers of children born to a family is repugnant to the Boran and Gabra, particularly if it involves the use of contraceptives. At the same time, however, they have developed techniques of postponing the age of marriage which I believe could very easily be incorporated into a modern program of population regulation. The Boran's and the Gabra's reasons for postponing marriage may be quite different from those of the national demographers— nonetheless they are mutually supportive ideas.

The single most important conclusion of this body of research is that development must build on existing adaptive processes. Failing that, the development program should be so designed that it does not undermine those processes.

References

Dolan, R. 1980. *Migration Patterns in the Rendille, 1923–1978.* UNESCO-IPAL Technical Report Number A-3. Paris: UNESCO.

Herlocker, D.J. 1981. *Range Ecology Programme: Past and Present Activities.* UNESCO-IPAL Technical Report Number A-5. Paris: UNESCO.

IPAL 1983. *Integrated Resource Assessment and Management Plan for Western Marsabit District, Northern Kenya*. UNESCO-IPAL Technical Report Number A-6. Paris: UNESCO.

Legesse, A. 1973. *Gada: Three Approaches to the Study of African Society*. New York: Free Press.

―――― 1983. A pastoral ecosystem: Field studies of the Boran and Gabra of Northern Kenya. Unpublished ms.

―――― 1983. Adaptive responses to ecological stress. Paper presented to the Ecostress Project Symposium, Nairobi, Kenya.

Lusigi, W. 1981. *Combatting Desertification and Rehabilitating Degraded Productive Systems in Northern Kenya*. UNESCO-UNEP Integrated Project in Arid Lands, Technical Report Number A-4. Paris: UNESCO.

Spencer, P. 1973. *Nomads in Alliance: Symbiosis and Growth among the Rendille and Samburu of Kenya*. London: Oxford University Press.

Turnbull, C. 1980. The mountain people. In *Anthropology: Comparative Perspectives*, ed. by D.E. Hunter, et. al. Boston: Little. pp. 225–232.

―――― 1982. Rethinking the Ik: A functional non-social system. In *Extinction and Survival in Human Populations*, ed. by C.D. Laughlin. New York: Columbia University Press. pp. 49–75.

Indigenous Institutions and Adaptation to Famine

The Case of Western Sudan

Soheir Sukkary-Stolba

American River College
4700 College Oak Drive
Sacramento, Calif. 95841

During the last two years, there has been an increased interest among both social scientists and the general public on the topic of famine relief efforts in Sub-Saharan Africa. However, a great deal of the available literature focuses on the Western response to the African crisis, and the efficacy of macro-level political organizations in dealing with the famine. The role of local level indigenous social, economic and political organizations has been mostly neglected. This paper describes the dynamic processes that were adopted by individuals vis-à-vis indigenous institutions as they were faced with food scarcity and famine in Western Sudan, Kordofan and Darfur. Moreover, an analysis of the field data collected in Sudan in the fall of 1985 is included in the paper. A conceptual framework that portrays the evolving food crisis with its temporal dimensions as it impacted individuals and communities is proposed as an analytical tool for studying food shortages.[1] An emphasis is placed on the variables which individuals had to consider in making decisions about migration, collection of famine food, and other adaptive strategies that Western Sudanese farmers and nomadic populations experienced during the years 1981–1985. This paper posits that during the early

[1]Research for this paper was funded by the Agency for International Development. During the month of November, 1985, the author was part of a four-person team that evaluated the U.S. response to famine in Sudan. The author is solely responsible for all views expressed in the paper. This paper has benefited from the efforts of many people especially the help extended to me in the field by Craig Noran and Judy Gilmore of U.S. AID.

stages of a drought, indigenous institutions played a crucial role in providing assistance to individuals living in their communities. However, as the drought continued, the role of indigenous institutions diminished, necessitating the use of new adaptive strategies by individuals.

Research Methodology

A total of 18 days were spent in Sudan[1]. Fieldwork was carried out in 11 villages utilizing a short interview schedule. Included in this random sample were villages from Northern and Southern Darfur and Kordofan. Five towns were visited and interviews with urban poor were conducted. The use of a helicopter to visit distant villages greatly facilitated the task of fieldwork, especially to many of the inaccessible rural areas of Northern Darfur. A hundred and thirty respondents were interviewed. The majority of respondents were farmers, therefore, the paper deals primarily with farming communities and to a lesser extent with pastoralists. Moreover interviews were conducted with village chiefs, *sheiks*, health representatives of the Sudanese Ministry of Health and various private voluntary organizations, truckers, grain merchants, midwives, nutritional surveyors, and Sudanese women. Three feeding centers were visited in both Darfur and Kordofan.

Because of the short duration of research, this paper draws heavily on secondary sources of data. Nutritional surveys done by Oxfam/UNICEF, League of Red Cross, Care, etc. are utilized. Moreover, it should be noted that this paper only presents preliminary findings. There is a need for further research on the topic.

Introduction: The Setting in Western Sudan

Sudan is the largest country in Africa. Geographically, it consists of various types of ecological zones that include savanna land, semi-tropical, scrub lands, sandy hills, and arid hills. Most cultivation is dependent on irrigation from the Nile. However, for Western Sudanese farmers, their subsistence, agriculture, relies mainly on rain. It should be noted that Sudan was a grain exporting country prior to the 1981 drought.

The 1983 census shows a population of 23 million people for the whole country and about 7 million people for Western Sudan. However, this census does not reflect the recent events of the massive population displacement associated with the drought, or the flood of refugees into Sudan. In fact, baseline data on population size, food intake for various groups, mortality and morbidity figures, etc., is all speculative. The country's vast territories, fluid nature of population movements, and lack of infrastructure make the task of collecting accurate demographic data impossible.

Sudan is divided into 12 provinces. The 1974 decentralization laws led to the emergence of semi-autonomous regional government structures in Western Sudan. At the micro level, village leaders, *sheiks*, are part of the regional government structure. The traditional role of sheiks is to allocate land to farmers and settle disputes among village groups. *Umdahs*, are the leaders of central villages, large villages of 4,000 people. Regional councils operate in towns and cities. Because of the fact that decentralization is a new experiment in Sudan's political life, the lines of responsibilities between central authorities and regional governments are not yet clearly delineated. This has often led to confusion at the village level, and it has certainly caused unnecessary complications in dealing with drought relief efforts.

During the last four years, Western Sudan has experienced a general noticeable decrease in the amounts of rainfall. The mean rainfall at Nyala, in Darfur, for 1954–1984 was 377 mm; this represents a decrease of 21 percent from the long-term average of 477 mm between 1920–1980 (Save the Children 1985:2). Northern areas of Darfur and Kordofan (Figure 1) received 60 percent to 80 percent of normal rains during the last four years. The decline in rainfall, coupled with the drying up of shallow wells, left most of the 7,000,000 people of the northern semi-arid areas and southern regions of the west in poor economic conditions. Massive migrations from the Northwestern to the Southwestern areas occurred. Many spontaneous camps of displaced people were formed. People migrated long distances to search for food and jobs.

The decline in precipitation brought about major changes in the lives of the farmers and nomadic groups. Nomads, who normally engage in traditional transhumance (seasonal migration movements) in

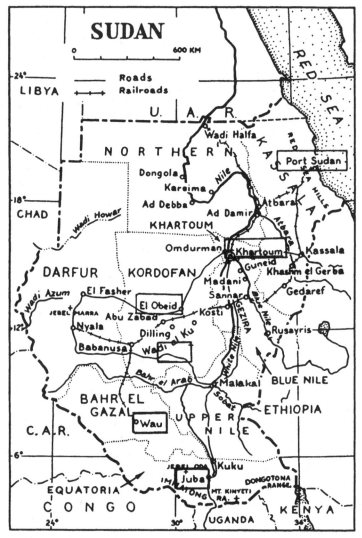

Figure 1. Map of Sudan, showing research sites.

search of good grazing conditions, suffered heavy losses. Under drought conditions, transhumant patterns of migration which are generally predictable were replaced by individuals' desperate attempts to reach urban centers or any areas where water was available.

Pastoralists in Western Sudan herd cattle, goats, sheep and camels. Among the known tribal groups of the west are the Kababish (camel-raising people), Baqqara, and the Beja (cattle herders). Herding is an occupation mostly restricted to males. These nomads are patriarchal, patrilineal, and patrilocal. Pastoralists inhabit the vast semi-arid regions of Northern Darfur and Kordofan. During the summer rainy season, nomads migrate southward. Very little horticulture is done by nomadic women; hence, millet is grown only for family consumption. Goats and sheep are sold to buy sugar, tea and coffee.

Despite heavy livestock losses, estimated to be 50 to 70 percent in cattle herds, nomadic groups tended to migrate as groups and seldom as individuals. Goat and camel herds were not as severely impacted as cattle. Nomads that owned goats continued to have milk in their diet. In an interview with a nomadic man from Darfur, he stated,

> "I took the few living cows in my herd to the city market. I was willing to sell them at any price so I do not have to feed them. In fact, I tried to give them away—the very weak ones. I did not want to see them die, and could not take them back to the camp."

As for farming communities, male migration was followed by massive migration of females and children. Women tended to join ethnic and village groups who migrated together. Older people and the sick preferred to stay in their villages. Individuals' responses to the drought varied, but the primary goal behind all decisions was to maximize survival. Urban areas attracted many displaced groups because food was always available in large urban markets. Population movements from the north to the south increased because water sources were more available in the south. Both farmers and nomads traveled southward.

1. A Conceptual Framework and the Dynamic Nature of a Drought

A drought is a natural phenomenon caused by an unexpected decline in rainfall. For both nomadic and sedentary populations who are

mainly dependent on rain for their livelihood, a drought has catastrophic effects on people, crops and livestock. The data from Western Sudan suggests the presence of two distinct stages that influenced
people's lives. During the first two years of the drought, 1981–1983,
people relied heavily on indigenous institutions for coping with food
shortages. Families, neighbors, and friends shared food and economic
and political leaders contributed significantly to elevate the suffering
of their community members. But as the drought continued, savings
were depleted and individuals migrated in search of food and work.
Dependence on foreign aid became a must for survival. Individuals
changed their strategies, from living close to their homes and villages, to migration to southern regions—where the drought was not
as severe as in the north.

A crucial concept that underlies such a perspective of change in
strategies is adaptation; that is, how individuals manage to deal with
the contingencies of daily life under conditions of scarcity. This process of adaptation establishes a moving balance between the needs of
a population and the potential of its environment. A drought threatens
this balance, and presents individuals and social systems with many
challenges. In the case of Sudan, during the first two years of the
drought, the strength of the Sudanese social fabric, and normative
rules of hospitality and sharing, operated efficiently to combat shortages of food. But as people sold their assets, spent their savings, and
became heavily indebted, social organizations were weakened, necessitating massive and large scale migration. For Western Sudan, Darfur and Kordofan, the past four years of the drought meant less
grain (sorghum and millet) and a dramatic 70 to 80 percent loss in
livestock in some areas (Oxfam/UNICEF 1985:ii).

In examining the nature of the dynamic relationship between people
and the environment, and the various adaptive strategies individuals
have utilized in Sudan to survive the various stages of the drought,
one finds that during the drought, certain variables became important
to individuals as they continually made decisions about whether to
remain in their villages or migrate to other regions. Some of the variables were identified as follows:

• The availability of sources of water other than rain in the village,
  e.g., deep wells, etc.;

- Distance to closest road, and availability of a means of transportation;
- The strength of the social organization;
- The degree to which the social values of sharing, reciprocity and hospitality are practiced; and
- Resources available to individuals, e.g., savings, jewelry, etc.

Generally speaking, the stronger the social organization, and the more access to resources a person had, the better were his chances for survival in the "first stages" of a drought—in the Sudanese case, the first and second year. Normally, Sudanese farmers dig shallow wells, and *hafirs* to procure water. But during the second year of the drought, many people complained that these wells silted up, and migration became the only viable solution to the continued drought conditions.

Moreover, when the drought persisted past a two-year period, resources diminished. Even under the best cultural conditions, where sharing is the norm, the "second stage" brought famine to the majority of the poor segments of a population. In western Sudan the year 1984–1985 represented the "second stage" of the drought. Only after the heavy April rains of this year, were most of the farmers in the southern parts of Darfur and Kordofan able to resume their agricultural activities. But for the northern sections of the west, the scarcity of the amounts of rainfall led to cases of zero to 40 percent harvest expectation for 1985.

During the first two years of the drought, farmers used their grain reserves, and sold jewelry and household belongings to procure cash or food. Farming, which is predominantly a female activity, was heavily curtailed because of the scarcity of rainfall. Traditionally, women in Darfur and Kordofan, grow millet, sorghum, groundnuts, and melons. Many of the women farmers mentioned that small vegetable gardens were grown around wells and sources of ground water. Children roamed the deserts to collect wild melons that grow in that part of the world.

Moreover, male migration increased in the "second stage" of the drought. Many men left their families and travelled to urban areas to look for work. For rural male dwellers in Sudan, there is a normal dry-season migration to the cities to search for jobs. During the-drought, jobs for unskilled laborers were scarce. Interviews with females indicated that many husbands who left their homes to try to find jobs in cities a year ago never returned to their families. Whether these men died, or failed to find work, or decided to stay in cities, is unknown.

Polygyny is practiced in Sudan. Moslem males are allowed to marry up to four wives at a time. Although the women tend to be economically self-sufficient, and many were largely responsible for providing for their children, women dreaded the low social status of a single woman. In an interview, a woman said "My husband left three years ago. Now I am the only person responsible to feed my six children. I am treated like a woman with no man."

Political Institutions at the Village Level

Small satellite villages are ruled by a *sheik*, a chief, and large central villages are ruled by *Umdahs*. Normatively, *sheiks* and *umdahs* allocate land for farming, settle disputes, help the needy and work to further the welfare of their community. With the drought, the role of political leaders was redefined, especially in the "second stage" of the drought. A village sheik said:

> I used to tell the women where to farm; and to give money or food to the poor. Early when the rains stopped I tried to get the merchants to contribute to the poor. I also gave from my personal moneys to the needy. But, within a short period of time, I had nothing to give. I now visit the sick and dying. I check on the women that lost their husbands and pray a lot for the rains.

The role of the chief had changed during the crisis. With scarcity, the role became more of a social/ceremonial one. Another chief summarized his role as follows: "We console people, arrange for quick burials, and try to reach higher authorities . . . but of course it is difficult."

Village *sheiks* (leaders) reported that they made every effort possible to inform regional councils of the plight of their communities. At the time of research, *sheiks* were actively involved in the distribution of foods donated by U.S. in their communities. They were observed to distribute the sorghum equally among households in the village. Equality is expected from chiefs, and many of them took pride in being "fair" to all. Few cases of discrimination were reported. These were often against single women.

Sudanese Cultural Values and Traditional Food Distribution Patterns in Sudan.

Understanding the cultural context in which a drought occurs is crucial in studying the impact of a drought on people. Societies where the values of sharing, reciprocity, and hospitality are deeply rooted in the culture, provide examples of traditional mechanisms for the redistribution of resources to the needy. In the case of Sudan, hospitality to guests and outsiders is the norm. In actuality, it is seen as the "duty" of an individual to share the best of one's resources with a guest. Under normal conditions, Sudanese hospitality amazes outsiders. Fortunately, these values of sharing, providing for the needy, and hospitality, did not all together disappear with the drought. But as the drought entered its third year, there was less to share, and migration became the only strategy for survival.

In an interview with a village leader sheik, he said "As long as we have some food in the village, we would share it equally." Equality of shares in distribution is a strong value that is deeply embedded in rural Sudanese social organizations. A leader's role is locally perceived emically as a person who ensures the equity of distribution in the village. Observation of the general distribution of sorghum in villages verified this role. A *sheik* distributes equal shares to families with the same number of children.

Islamic Charity, Zakah, and the Economic Elites

In a Moslem society, *Zakah*, distributing 10 percent of one's annual income to the poor, is one of the five pillars of Islam. *Zakah* is normally given to poor relatives, neighbors, or the needy in this descending order. There are Moslem countries like Saudi Arabia that institutionalize *Zakah* in the form of taxes collected from individuals and spent on welfare projects benefiting the poor. But there are other Moslem countries that leave it up to the individual to choose the recipients of *Zakah*. Under the *Sharia* law, Islamic laws, the former

Sudanese government wanted to collect the *Zakah* tax from individuals. However, many people preferred to be in full charge of selecting the beneficiaries of *Zakah* from among their families or communities.

In Sudan, during the drought, it was reported that many wealthy individuals fed and gave money to the needy as part of the *Zakah* custom. However, it should be noted that some merchants hoarded goods and raised the prices to increase their profits. Theft, hoarding, and incidents of social disorder were more common in towns than in villages. Traditionally, merchants give *Zakah* once a year at inventory time. The needy generally know the "inventory day" and wait outside the shops for a share of the *Zakah*. *Zakah* could be in the form of food, clothing or cash. Moslem feasts are generally the proper times for the distribution of *Zakah*. Also during Ramadan, the fasting month, a great deal of sharing of these foods occurs. Migration to urban centers occurred at times of scarcity because people knew that in the market place, the fortunate ones who were able to buy would give some of their purchases or give money to the needy.

However, as the drought continued over a number of years, *Zakah* decreased. Personal resources were depleted and the poverty base increased. Many of the respondents mentioned that in the first two years of the drought, people gave generously to the needy. But in the third and fourth years, less sharing occurred. A village leader explained, "There was nothing to share in some areas. This hurts us very much because we learn as children to share and give to others."

Karama and *Rahma* are customs related to giving the relatives of a deceased child a gift of food to ensure the survival of other children. A woman whom I visited showed me a small bag of grain given to her when her son died. This ability to give and share helped many Sudanese survive the drought.

High Absorption Capability of Sudanese Communities

Because of the Sudanese people's sense of hospitality, outsiders generally have a better chance of being absorbed in Sudanese communities. However, the tremendous increase in the number of Chadian and Ethiopian refugees, estimated to be above a million and a half people, and the deteriorating economic conditions in the country, has proved to be a challenge to this value system. Evidence of intolerance to

Ethiopian refugees surfaced in several incidents of hostility in the eastern regions of Sudan. The same intolerance is experienced by new Sudanese immigrants. A Sudanese woman said, "Two years ago when we moved, people always welcomed new guests—lately, everyone has many problems and people are afraid there would be no more water or food."

Other adaptive strategies of migrants included the sale of jewelry, household items, and cooking utensils. Livestock was sold for cash to buy grain. Families split in different city locations to maximize chances of begging for food. Despite the devastating impact of the drought on the family as a unit and the social organization in general, the Sudanese capacity to absorb outsiders remained relatively high. Sudanese hospitality and a deeply rooted sense of equality enabled many families to survive the hardships of the drought. Sharing of resources, no matter how small, continued to operate as a survival value in small communities. However, as expected, sharing was decreased in urban situations.

Traditional Diets and the Drought

Traditionally, the populations of Western Sudan eat *asida*, a porridge made of sorghum, *dura*, a millet, *dukhan* and *kisra*, a thin flat bread. Both are eaten with onions and dried okra called *mulah*. Milk is normally used in making the porridge. Watermelons and desert melons (melons devoid of sweetness) figure importantly in the diets of the people. Coffee and tea are usually served several times a day with large amounts of sugar. Meat is only eaten on festive occasions, but milk is particularly important to the nomadic populations. Vegetables are eaten by sedentary populations; and radishes, onions and tomatoes are consumed in large quantities.

During the drought, sorghum and millet yields drastically decreased, and market prices skyrocketed to 278 percent of normal prices. Cash decreased as jobs became scarce, and savings were depleted. Milk continued to be an important part of the diets of nomads, but it normally disappeared from the diets of rural populations who could not afford its high prices. Thus, the drought eliminated milk, a major source of vitamin A from the diet. Also, fresh leafy vegetables also became scarce. "Famine foods" replaced the traditional diets.

Western Sudanese food depends heavily on dried meat, seeds and vegetables. Also, leaves of local trees, *tabaldi*, are often eaten in the dry seasons. The staple is a sorghum of millet porridge served with one of the following relishes:

* *Mulah lubia*—beans, oil, onions, and dried okra;
* *Mulah roab*—onion, oil, ground nuts, dried okra and
* Grain stored by termites;
* *Um baz*—peanut shells eaten as flour paste;
* *Mukheit*—seeds of the poisonous plant (*Boscia senegule*) soaked in water for three days and boiled for several hours;
* *Lalob*—desert dates of *Balanites Aegyptiaca;*
* *Nubuk*—the fruit of *Zizypho spinachristi.* The flesh consumed directly and seeds ground;
* Dried watermelon seeds and shells;
* Dry grass, roots and tree bark;
* *Deleib*—palm seeds (*Borassus aethiopum*); and
* *Tebeldi*—leaves of the tebeldi tree (*Adansonia digitata*).

Individuals mentioned that they ate once a day instead of three times. Ten percent of the people interviewed said that during March and April 1985, they ate every other day. Displaced families concentrated their efforts in urban market areas, *souks*, begging individually for food.

Small vegetable gardens around wells were planted whenever possible, and small desert melons were observed in the fields of all villages of Northern Darfur. Desert melons, which are normally fed to animals, were eaten by humans during the drought.

"Famine foods" are foods that generally grow wild, and under normal circumstances are seldom consumed by humans except in very dry seasons. With food scarcity, people collected and consumed these food items. The following is a list of "famine foods":

* Grain stored by termites.
* *Um baz*—peanut shells eaten as flour paste
* *Mukheit*—seeds of the poisonous plant
              (Boscia sensgule) soaked in water for 3 days and boiled
              for several hours.

* *Lalob*—desert dates of *Balanites Aegyptiaca;*
* *Nubuk*—the fruit of *Zizypho spinachristi.* The flesh is consumed directly and seeds ground;
* Dried watermelon seeds and shells;
* Dry grass, roots and tree bark;
* *Deleib*—palm seeds (*Borassus aethiopum*); and
* *Tebeldi*—leaves of the tebeldi tree (*Adansonia digitata*).

A quick check on the caloric value of the above mentioned foods indicates that "famine foods" are rich in both calories and fibers. The overlap with normal relishes is striking. People collect famine foods individually and sharing occurs only with young children. It was reported by women that numerous incidence of child mortality were observed after a meal of *Mukheit.*

Conclusion

The preliminary findings of this study suggest that, faced with a major crisis of food and water shortages for a period of four years, rural populations in Western Sudan used numerous strategies to survive. Indigenous institutions and leaders played a crucial role in providing money, support, and food in the early stages of the crisis. However, with depleted resources, local leaders redefined their roles from that of provision of financial support to provision of emotional support, and advice to people migrating in search of food. Moreover, the traditional values of hospitality and sharing were tested because of the continuation of the drought. The decrease in rainfall forced farmers to change their traditional diets and utilize their knowledge of the edibles in their habitat. Roots, wild berries, and tree bark played a more significant role in individuals' daily food intake. Further research is needed to assess the extent to which indigenous institutions could overcome the negative impacts of a drought and resume their normal activities.

References

Eldridge, C. 1985. *SCF Dura Distribution in Darfour.* SCF Report. Save the Children Fund.

OXFAM/UNICEF. 1985. Field Report, May/June (unpublished).

Famine, Hunger Seasons and Relief-Induced Agonism

Robert Dirks

Anthropology Program
Illinois State University
Normal, IL 61761

Jean Mayer (1974) once complained that we communicate so ineffectually about the physiological, psychological, and sociological problems arising from famine that each new group of relief workers called upon to deal with a fresh catastrophe finds itself ill-prepared and prone to re-commit classic errors. Journalistic accounts filed from the drought-stricken regions of Africa suggest little improvement since Mayer made this allegation.

My intent in this paper is to communicate some observations of which relief specialists ought to be aware. These observations, collected as part of an effort to understand the cultural effects of famine, point to a problem recognized by those who have had to cope with specific instances of it. But, the sorry fact is that the observations themselves are problematic. Like pieces of a puzzle, they are difficult to fit together, and, what is more, certain pieces required for a solution are missing. My hope in setting out this partially described, ill-understood configuration of facts is that scientists and practitioners concerned with Africa's recurrent food crises, either by virtue of fieldnotes already recorded or by observations yet to be made, will contribute data that will assist in the solution of this puzzle.

Definitions

In studying descriptions of the behaviors of famished peoples, I and others have noticed a certain regularity. It is a phenomenon I believe deserves a label, and some years ago I gave it one—namely, "relief-induced agonism" (Dirks 1979). Relief-induced agonism includes a varied pattern of aggressive, exigent, and quarrelsome behaviors, both verbal and non-verbal. As the very name implies, this pattern is seen, not in the midst of famine, but during the course of its mitigation—that is, after food supplies intended for relief arrive on the scene and are being distributed to victims. The behavior at issue, then, appears to be a response to relief. Its expression, however, appears non-specific in the sense that it does not seem to be directed at any particular target. The agonism expresses itself more as a general irritability and a remonstrative or contestive attitude toward anyone at hand, including relief personnel. Definitionally, then, relief-induced agonism is distinguished by its timing and by the startling prospect of seeing a heretofore wasted, very much inactive, and emotionally apathetic people suddenly become quite animated, clamorous, and contentious.

My African examples are typical. Take for instance an account (M. Murray *et. al.* 1976) from an Ogaden relief camp. The authors found themselves faced with an unexpected epidemic of what they took as psychosomatic disease. As they described it,

> At least half of our clinic visitors had no physical disease to account for their complaints of headache, backache, muscle pains, abdominal stress, weakness, or fatigue. Further, they were persistent and vociferous in demands for treatment virtually any type of which, except refeeding, relieved their complaints (M. Murray *et. al.* 1976:1284).

To provide another, somewhat different example, in 1974 apparently frustrated relief workers reported that the Ethiopians they were assisting in Tigre Province ". . . have become belligerent, making distribution (of food) difficult, sometimes impossible (Shepard 1975:57)." The information presented in both of these cases is fragmentary (most accounts of relief-induced agonism known to me have been recorded merely in passing) but in each of these two instances we see what I take to be the key diagnostics, the occurrence of the phenomenon during refeeding and the fact that the distribution of relief does not bring unqualified relief. Instead it seems to produce signs of mental distress and behavioral agitation.

Africa is not the only place where this has been seen. What I take to be cases of relief-induced agonism were observed repeatedly near the end of World War II in Europe. Relief administrators at Belsen, for example, noticed that not long after their arrival the pattern of complaints changed among the camp's former prisoners. While starving, the inmates expressed their displeasure in a weary, helpless way. When nourishing rations were distributed, their manner turned fierce, bitter, and resentful (Mollison 1946). The mission to Sanbostel found prisoners' behavior characterized by the classic symptoms of starvation: vacant stares, virtually no emotional expression, little interaction. With renourishment they soon became noisy and complaining, *especially at mealtime* (R. Murray 1947). Among rescued P.O.W.'s, who previously had been in a badly undernourished state, Helweg-Larsen (1952:311) noted "The tone of voice became querulous and irritable. . . ."

The same basic pattern has been produced experimentally, though by accident. Ancel Keys and his co-workers (1950) found the subjects of their famous Minnesota starvation experiments remarkably docile during the starvation phase of the program. This changed shortly after the rehabilitation phase began. The men became difficult to manage. Their irritability increased, and the atmosphere of aggressive hostility reached such intensity that "At times the experimenters felt as though they were watching an overheated boiler, the capacity of the safety valves remaining an unknown variable . . ." (Keys *et. al.* 1950 II:917). Recognizing the importance of this from the point of view of relief administrators, the Minnesota investigators not only reported their own observations but also drew attention to those made by relief teams sent into the Western Netherlands in 1945. In the report on their operations, one finds a clear grasp of the general, practical significance of the difficulties emergency personnel came up against in dealing with victim hostility:

> The psychological condition of the underfed populations constitutes one of the greatest difficulties the (relief) teams encountered. The peculiar psychological state of individuals suffering from severe and prolonged calorie-shortage makes it necessary to pay the utmost to methods of approach, imparting of information and understanding of mental states. Apathy and irritability are the outstanding features in such a situation, which calls for special attention not only in regard to relations between doctors and patients, but to difficulties in dealing with civilian authorities. Good understanding will avoid delay of action and therefore be of life-saving importance. In any organization dealing with a similar emergency in the future,

attention should be given from the earliest day of planning to this important aspect
of undernourishment and starvation (Burger *et. al.* 1948:166)

Unfortunately, there is little evidence that this advice was ever
heeded.

Physical Cause

Physically, what accounts for relief-induced agonism? The Murrays
(1976) speculated that the abnormal behavior they saw among Soma-
lis was produced by sociocultural disturbance. Residence in a crowded
relief facility, in the Murrays' opinion, had a disconcerting effect on
people accustomed to a nomadic way of life. The cross-cultural pro-
venience of relief-induced agonism and its appearance at the end of
the Minnesota experiment render this explanation improbable. The
Minnesota group tried to explain the unrest of their subjects in cogni-
tive terms. The experimenters saw irritability as resulting from a frus-
trating disjunction between their subjects' expectations of a rapid
return to a normal physical condition following refeeding and the slow
progress that was actually made (Keys *et. al.* 1950 II:918). This
seems plausible but there is some evidence that relief-induced agonism also occurs following the end of hunger seasons (see below), and
in such cases individuals do not experience the degree of inanition
and disability induced at Minnesota.

A neurophysiological explanation might be more powerful. Zimmerman and his colleagues (1979:299), working with immature,
protein-starved monkeys, found highly emotional, neophobic responses to novel stimuli. The animals were ". . . fearful, yet aggressive in the social situation." The question is, do humans experience a
similar neophobia when starved? There also exists the possibility of a
hypoglycemic response. Ralph Bolton (personal communication) sus-
pects among relief recipients who have sustained major caloric deficits the intake of food high in carbohydrates will lead to a rapid
increase in blood sugar levels, followed by a quick uptake and con-
comitant drop in the free glucose. From this point on, Bolton hypoth-
esizes several alternative scenarios leading to subsequent agonism.
For example, hypoglycemia itself may produce irritability, lowering
the threshold of aggressive reaction to various stimuli. Or, low blood
sugar or rapid fluctuations in levels could affect neural circuits or

hormonal releases in ways that excite unrest and aggressive action (see Dirks 1979). The question of internal processes is wide open to research.

Seasonal Hunger and Ritualized Relief-Induced Agonism

Let me now turn from famine to seasonal hunger, a period of semi-starvation generally lasting several months. Seasonal hunger is not uncommon in Africa. It begins with the near depletion of stores set aside from one harvest and ends with the advent of the next crop. I propose that relief-induced agonism occurs at the end of hunger seasons and, further, that it can become ritualized, taking on a symbolic structure and definite social direction rather than appearing as a raw, unchanneled behavioral response.

One of my original inspirations for this hypothesis was a re-reading of Max Gluckman's (1954) famous Frazer Lecture, *Rituals of Rebellion in South-East Africa*. In that lecture Gluckman professed the kingship rites of Southeast Africa represented rebellion and that they did so because rebellion was structured into the political systems of that region. In short, Gluckman perceived a functional relationship between conflict expressed in ritual and tension existing between rulers and their subjects. This hypothesis has been discussed thoroughly among ethnologists, but what often gets forgotten is Gluckman's stress on biological considerations. As he carefully explained, the Swazi, Zulu, and their neighbors all experienced hunger months which depleted them physically and imposed a kind of moratorium on their social lives. Their rituals of rebellion came at the end of this trying period. Newly available food and the return to an energy-rich diet re-animated communities and all the reciprocities their order entailed. This re-invigoration extended to negative reciprocities, for the end of the hunger period was also the season for wars and the renewal of quarrels. Thus, Gluckman tied rituals of rebellion to an upsurge in agonistic activity across the board and placed the rites into the context of a massive ecological energy pulse. He explained that the superimposition of heavy ceremonial demands, including those associated with the kingship celebration, at the point of transition from want to plenty functioned to release a surge of human energy and emotion in a socially controlled and culturally meaningful manner.

Could it be that an infusion of food energy following a period of semi-starvation stimulates agonistic activity universally? Does this activity tend to become cultural and receive controlled expression through ritual in societies beyond the sphere of Southeast Africa?

I am exploring these questions cross-culturally by means of the Human Relations Area Files and its worldwide Probability Sample of 60 societies. I will report the outcome of this study in detail in the near future (Dirks n.d.). However, by way of preview, let me now say that of the 60 societies in the sample 33 have been adjudged subject to some degree of seasonal hunger. Of these, 23 disclose evidence of annual, ritualized conflict. In most cases wherein a determination can be made, the ritualized conflict in question falls right where expected—that is, at the end of the hunger season. One can say statistically with a rather high degree of confidence that a quite strong, positive correlation exists between the presence of seasonal epidemics of starvation and the annual celebration of rituals of conflict (n = 60, tau-b = +.314, p <.005).

The same can be said for the intensity of agonistic expression. This is shown by arranging annual rituals of conflict across a spectrum, placing those that merely contain verbal expressions of hostility at one end and those involving actual physical violence at the other. The relationship between the presence of a hunger period and the strength with which agonism is expressed is again strong and statistically significant (see Table I).

The Probability Sample contains two societies for which reports disclose post-hunger season violence occurring amidst celebration,

Table I. Distribution of agonistic activity against hunger season among probability sample societies

| | Hunger Season | | | |
	(1) Denied	(2) Not evident	(3) Occasional	(4) Annual
(A) None	10	8	6	4
(B) Verbal	2	1	1	2
Agonism				
(C) Contestive action	4	2	8	7
(D) Actual fighting	0	0	1	4

N = 60, Tau-b = +.349, p<.001

but without the fighting itself showing any ritual restraint. One of these societies is Bemba. As to why the Bemba, unlike the Swazi or Zulu, incline toward overt conflict rather than a more subdued expression there is no telling. However, one might hazard to put the entire matter of annual rituals of conflict into a trait-specific evolutionary context. If so, the seasonal quarrels that took place among the Bemba would have to be placed near the "primitive" extreme. One might hypothesize that the Bemba's propensity to fight at the end of the hunger months represents a relief-induced agonism culturally informed only to a limited extent. Aggressions occur within a framework of calendric festivities and are thus constrained with respect to timing, but still they have not been rendered essentially harmless as in those cases where agonism is expressed only in sham battles or verbal aggressions.

A case that could possibly represent an even less culturally constrained instance of relief-induced agonism comes to mind. I am thinking of some observations reported by nutritionist John Robson (1972 I:39–40). He witnessed among sisal workers on East African plantations annual social unrest toward the end of that period of the year when the laborers' diet was at its worst. Robson himself speculated the unrest that occurred at this time might be attributed to an outbreak of sub-clinical pellagra. However, in the absence of firm evidence in support of this diagnosis, and given the timing and the clock-like occurrence of the disturbance among these workers, I cannot help but think that we have here another instance of relief-induced agonism, its incidence a product of endemic, recurrent starvation. If so, we have an example apparently little elaborated by culture, possibly because of high population turnover or some other disequilibriating feature characteristic of plantation communities.

Robson advised others to be on the lookout for signs of uneasiness and tumult in similar nutritional circumstances. I can do no better than repeat his advice. I hope those who might find themselves on the scene of a relief mission attend carefully to the medical condition, social behavior, and mental attitude of the recipients and that those who do fieldwork in areas still bothered by seasonal hunger do the same, particularly at the point that the newly harvested crops usher in relief. Something very puzzling goes on at these junctures. There is a problem here with both practical and scientific significance, and Africa in its present unhappy condition could provide much of the data needed to figure out what this phenomenon is and what can be done about it.

Acknowledgments

Much of the information in this paper relating to famine has been reported previously in the journal *Disasters* (Dirks 1979). Deborah Dirks assisted in coding the data on hunger seasons and annual rituals of conflict. I wish to thank her and also the College of Arts and Sciences, Illinois State University, and the Illinois State Board of Regents for research support.

References

Burger, G.C.E. *et. al.* 1984. *Malnutrition and Starvation in Western Netherlands, September 1944–July 1945*, 2 parts, The Hague: General State Printing Office.

Dirks, R. 1979. Relief Induced Agonism, *Disasters* 3(2):195–198.

Dirks, R. (n.d.) "Annual Rituals of Conflict", *American Anthropologist*, in press.

Gluckman, M. 1954. *Rituals of Rebellion in South-East Africa*, Manchester: University Manchester Press.

Helweg-Larsen, P. 1952. *Famine Disease in German Concentration Camps, Complications and Sequels*, Copenhagen: Enjar Munksgaard.

Keys, A. *et. al.* 1950. *The Biology of Human Starvation*, 2 vols., Minneapolis: University of Minnesota Press.

Mayer, J. 1974. Coping with Famine, *Foreign Affairs* 53:98–120.

Mollison, P.L. 1946. Observations on Cases of Starvation at Belsen, *British Medical Journal* 1:4–8.

Murray, M.J. *et. al.* 1976. Somali Food Shelters in the Ogaden Famine and their Impact on Health, *Lancet* 1:1283–1285.

Murray, R.O. 1947. Recovery from Starvation, *Lancet* 1:507–511.

Robson, J. 1972. *Malnutrition: Its Causation and Control*, 2 vols., New York: Gordon and Breach.

Shepard, J. 1975. *The Politics of Starvation*, New York: Carnegie Endowment for International Peace.

Zimmerman, R.R. *et. al.* 1975. Behavior and Malnutrition in the Rhesus Monkey, *Primate Behavior: Developments in Field and Laboratory Research*, Vol. 4, ed. by L.A. Rosenblum, New York: Academic Press. pp. 241–306.

Drought, Drought Relief, and Dependency Among the Basarwa of Botswana

Robert K. Hitchcock

Department of Anthropology
University of Nebraska
Lincoln, Nebraska 68588

James I. Ebert

Ebert and Associates
Albuquerque, New Mexico 87107

Richard G. Morgan

Emergency Program Office
UNICEF
Maputo, Mozambique

Introduction

A hallmark of most anthropological and economic analyses of drought responses and problems in developing countries is the structuring of such discussions in terms of a rigidly-applied subsistence taxonomy which implies that agriculture, pastoralism and foraging are separate and, for the most part, exclusive pursuits. It must be realised that taxonomies are problem-specific, however, and different classifications are appropriate to different avenues of inquiry. In many developing countries, particularly those with relatively low population densities, the separation of agriculture, pastoralism, and wild food use may be inappropriate. In this paper, an analysis of responses to drought in Botswana illustrates this contention. It is necessary to examine the dynamics of shifts among adaptive strategies over relatively short time periods, as well as complex interactions between changes

Figure 1: Republic of Botswana in Southern Africa

in climatic, social, and economic factors in order to properly understand cultural responses to natural stresses.

As is the case in many semiarid parts of Africa, the Republic of Botswana (Figure 1) is affected by drought on a recurrent but irregular basis. Resident populations in the Kalahari Desert and adjacent areas in Botswana have devised a variety of indigenous strategies to cope with environmentally-induced rainfall shortages (Devitt 1977, 1979; Silberbauer 1979; Hitchcock 1979; Vierich 1977, 1979; Vierich and Hitchcock 1979). These strategies range from exploiting a wider variety of wild foods to increasing mobility and migrating to new areas. There are indications, however, that many of the traditional responses to drought are no longer as effective as they once were, in part because of environmental change and greater competition resulting from increased population. There is a trend among rural populations, particularly those which are poor, toward becoming increasingly dependent upon outside assistance to survive drought periods.

Often there is a lack of clear government action in response to drought problems. Even in cases where the political will to respond does exist, it has often become necessary for governments to seek donor aid in order to feed and care for their people. Seeking such aid can often delay the implementation of relief and recovery measures. There is a danger that rural populations may become overly dependent upon famine relief and that levels of employment and food production may decline as a result.

Botswana is one of the few countries in Africa with a coherent program for dealing with drought and its effects (Sandford 1977, 1979; Campbell 1979; Hinchey 1979; McGowan and Associates 1979; Gooch and MacDonald 1981; UNICEF 1983; Tabor 1983; Morgan 1985a-c, 1986; Holm and Morgan 1985). Hunger is not common in the rural areas, partly because of Botswana's drought surveillance system and the existence of efficient mechanisms for moving food, redistributing incomes, and making available other resources to drought-stricken areas. Botswana is a good example of a country that is concerned not only with short-term relief but also with longer-term development. Post-drought recovery measures are emphasized in the Botswana government's current development program (Ministry of Finance and Development Planning 1985; Morgan 1986). In many ways, Botswana can be argued to be a socio-economic success story when it comes to coping with at least immediate effects of drought, although the effectiveness of its past drought recovery strategy remains to be tested.

In spite of the successful drought strategies of both individuals and the government in Botswana, it appears as though there are certain segments of the population which are becoming increasingly vulnerable to drought-induced stresses. Botswana has a significant proportion of the world's last remaining hunter-gatherers, known as the Basarwa (Bushmen, San). It is often said that these people cope extremely well with arid conditions, and they have developed ingenious survival strategies in the harsh Kalahari Desert. Partly for this reason, as well as their foraging adaptation, the Basarwa have received considerable anthropological attention (Marshall 1960, 1976; Marshall Thomas 1958; Tobias 1957, 1964; Silberbauer 1965, 1972, 1973, 1981a, 1981b; Lee 1965, 1968, 1969, 1972a, 1972b, 1979; Lee and DeVore 1976; Tanaka 1976, 1980; Draper 1972; Yellen 1976, 1977a, 1977b).

The Basarwa, numbering at least 40,000 in Botswana (see Table 1), make up less than four percent of the total population of the country.

Like many indigenous minorities, the Basarwa are undergoing major socioeconomic transformations. Many of them have entered the wage labor market and are involved in a variety of occupations, ranging from herding livestock to working in the gold mines of South Africa. Large numbers of Basarwa have settled on the peripheries of cattle posts and villages, where they can get access to water, trade goods, and employment opportunities. Jobs are often casual and insecure, and there are relatively few positions available for unskilled workers in the rural areas of Botswana. In some cases, the economic and nutritional status of Basarwa has declined. This is due to the loss of access to adequate foraging resources, which in turn is a result of overgrazing and increased population pressure. Political changes, such as the imposition of hunting laws, have also had effects on the Basarwa.

Anthropologists have begun to pay increasing attention to socioeconomic change among Basarwa populations in Botswana (Tobias 1962; Geunther 1979, 1986; Childers 1976, 1981; Ebert 1978; Heinz 1967;

Table I. Population size and distribution of major Basarwa groups in Botswana

Group name(s)	Location	Population Size
!Kung (Zũ/wasi)	NW Kalahari	2,800
//Au//ei (Auen)	W & NW Kalahari	1,850
Nharo and other Ghanzi groups	W Kalahari	7,500
G/wi, G//ana	Central Kalahari	3,500
!Xõ	SW Kalahari	3,100
S. Kũa, Tshasi, E. /Hũa	SE Kalahari	2,500
N. Ǩua	E Kalahari	3,150
Tyua (/Taise, Ganade, Danisan)	NE Kalahari	5,800
Hiechware, Tati, Tuli Block, and Motloutse groups	E Botswana	3,300
River Basarwa (Bugakwe, /Tannekwe, Deti, etc.)	Okavango Delta, Botletle River	2,550
Kwengo	N Botswana	850
Balala (Ngwaketse groups)	S Kalahari	1,450
Balala (Kgalagadi District groups)	SW Kalahari	550
Urban groups (e.g. Gaborone, Mochudi)	SE Botswana	450
		39,350 (Total)

Hitchcock 1978, 1982a, 1982b; Lawry and Thoma 1978; Sheller 1977; Tanaka, Sugawara, and Osaki 1984; Draper 1975a, 1975b, 1976; Wilmsen 1978; Vierich 1977, 1978, 1981, 1982, n.d.; Government of Botswana 1985). It has been found that many of the changes which Basarwa are undergoing, including reduced mobility and dietary shifts, are having negative effects. A significant effect of the resource stress Basarwa are facing is that many of them have become more dependent upon other groups for their subsistence and income. An objective of this paper is to delineate some of the impacts of drought and drought relief measures on the Basarwa of Botswana.

Drought and Basarwa Populations

One definition of drought pertinent to Botswana is given by Sandford (1979:34): "a rainfall-induced shortage of some economic good brought about by inadequate or badly timed rainfall." Sandford (1979:34) also notes that the frequency and severity of drought not only on rainfall but also on trends in requirements (demand) and on factors other than weather which influence supply. As applied to the indigenous populations of the Kalahari Desert of Botswana, the "good" in question can be taken to be access to resources necessary for meeting subsistence and income requirements at levels at least sufficient to meet basic nutritional needs.

The specific resources sought for these purposes have changed in nature and quantity in recent years. There are a number of factors which have brought about these changes, drought being but one of them. The commercialization of the livestock industry and the spread of water sources has resulted in an increase in livestock numbers in areas that once could be used only seasonally by cattle. Overgrazing and trampling is a major problem in the vicinity of boreholes and wells. Foragers can no longer find wild plant foods as easily, and many wild animal species have moved further into the desert in order to avoid contacts with human and domestic animal populations. Overgrazing has resulted in bush encroachment, an increased rate of soil erosion, and localized rainfall changes through bringing about an increase in surface albedo (reflectivity).

Technological changes include the use of deep borehole drilling technology, which has enabled Tswana populations to tap underground aquifers for livestock watering purposes. One result of the exploitation of sub-surface water has apparently been a decline in the water table, which has made traditional methods of water procurement, such as sip-wells, obsolete. Basarwa groups are settling in increasing numbers around boreholes since they can no longer exist in the traditional way. Cattle posts established near water points offer employment opportunities, albeit for minimal returns, and food, which is shared among both employees and non-working relatives (Hitchcock 1978; Guenther 1979, 1986; Vierich 1981).

Fencing is on the increase in many parts of the Kalahari, particularly veterinary cordon fences designed to prevent the movement of wild animals and livestock from areas affected by Hoof-and-Mouth (Foot-and-Mouth) Disease. These fences have affected the subsistence and incomes of Basarwa and other remote area groups both directly and indirectly. As Owens and Owens (1980, 1984) have noted, in times of drought large numbers of wild animals, many of them emaciated or dying, pile up against these fences. Large-scale die-offs of wildebeest and other animals have been noted historically, as was the case in the 1960s drought (Silberbauer 1965:20) and again in the early 1970s (Child 1972). Overall, the numbers of wild animals have declined over the years, reducing the availability of meat to peoples who derive part of their livelihood from subsistence hunting.

There has been an influx into the Kalahari of societies with different resource-use patterns. The combination of environmental, economic, social, and political changes has resulted in an increase in drought susceptibility of Basarwa and other Kalahari populations. Today, coherent social groups among the Basarwa are confined to specific and relatively limited areas of Botswana, particularly in remote parts of the Kalahari Desert and near the Namibian border. Small groups with a high degree of reliance on hunting and gathering still exist in the Central Kalahari Game Reserve, portions of Ngamiland, Central District, Kweneng District, western Ngwaketse District, and Kgalagadi District.

Hunter-gatherers in Botswana have lived traditionally in small groups which are linked together through kinship, marriage, and friendship ties. In the past, these ties extended over long distances, and they facilitated movement of people and goods (Marshall 1976; Wiessner 1977). A characteristic feature of the Kalahari Desert, in which many Basarwa reside, is that it lacks surface water except after rains. As a consequence, foragers have to move relatively frequently in order to obtain water and food. Table 2 presents quantitative data on the group sizes, mobility, and range sizes of Kalahari Basarwa populations in Botswana. It can be seen that average group size is small. It can also be seen that many Basarwa groups make residential moves during the course of the year. Range sizes are large, which is understandable given the fact that resource density is low in the Kalahari. Mobility and flexibility in the use of resource areas are key aspects of the Basarawa adaptation which have enabled them to adapt to drought and periodic shortages of resources (Lee 1968, 1969; Cashdan 1977).

It has been argued in some of the recent anthropological literature that, contrary to popular belief, hunters and gatherers such as the Basarwa do not live on the brink of starvation; rather, their nutritional intake is deemed to be more than adequate, even in drought periods. Indeed, this rosy picture of the foraging way of life has led some researchers to characterize traditionally mobile foraging populations as "the original affluent society" (Sahlins 1968). This view has been supported by data on subsistence returns and labor time which were collected during drought periods (Lee 1965, 1968, 1969, 1979).

Recently, the assumption that hunter-gatherers do not come under periodic subsistence and social stress has been called into question. Wilmsen (1978), working among !Kung at /ai/ai in northwestern Botswana, has found that body weights of adults change over an annual cycle, and that these changes are due to nutritional stress during certain periods of the year. The oft-cited "predictability" of Kalahari plant resources such as the mongongo nut *(Ricinodendron rautanenii)*, a staple food of the !Kung, may in actuality be an artifact of the timing of data collection. Wiessner (1977:54), for example, notes that the mongongo nut crop was completely destroyed in torrential rains in 1974 and that many of the !Kung in the /ai/ai area went hungry. Vierich (1981:3–4) points out that hunter-gatherer groups where patterns of sharing had broken down were adversely affected by drought in the southeastern Kalahari.

There are two kinds of responses to drought which relate to the structure and organization of labor, which we will define here as work related to subsistence. One is an intensification response, whereby people increase the amount of time spent doing subsistence tasks or they increase the number of laborers. On the other hand, there is an

Table II. Group sizes, mobility, and range sizes of Kalahari Basarwa populations in Botswana

Group name and location	Number of groups	Group sizes and average	Number of annual moves	Range sizes and average	Reference(s)
G/wi, Central Kalahari	6	21–85 57.17	6–15	457–1,036 779.67 km²	Silberbauer (1972:295–297, 1973:210, 1981a: 193, 196, 246, 1981b:460)
G/wi, Central Kalahari (!Xade)	9	7–57 22.89	11	4,000 4,000 km²	Tanaka (1976:100, 113, 1980:79, 81, 117, Table 20)
G/wi, G//ana, Central Kalahari	11	41–167 98.73	–	505–4,323 2222.64 km²	Sheller (1977:21, 34)
!Kung, Northwestern Kalahari (Dobe)	15	9–52 20.73	5–6	300–600 – km²	Lee (1965:47, Table 3, 1979:334)
!Kung, Northwestern Kalahari (Dobe)	15	10–24 16.67	37	320–3,000 1,000 km²	Yellen (1976:54, 1977a:54, 60, 237–353, Appendix C)
'Hüa, S. Kúa, Southeastern Kalahari (Kweneng)	13	10–42 24.23	0–15	250–3,500 1,100 km²	Vierich (1977:16, Table 1, 1981:138, Table 1, field notes)
!Xó, Southwestern Kalahari	6	18–48 33.17	0–7	1,000–2,200 1,660 km²	Lawry and Thoma (1978)
Nharo, Western Kalahari (Ghanzi)	–	8–40 + –	0–2	– 30 km²	Barnard (1979:140, personal communication)
Kúa, Eastern Kalahari	7	19–42 29.57	4–18	675–1,370 989.29 km²	Hitchcock (1982a: 179, 191, 1982b: 248)
Tyua, Northeastern Kalahari	11	14–88 39.27	0–4	87–400 199.91 km²	Hitchcock (1982a: 179, Table 9, 191, Table 11)

efficiency response, whereby people attempt to save labor. Trapping and snaring of small animals can be done in the absence of the person who set the trap, thus allowing him or her to do other work. Heinz (1967:2–3), for example, notes that during drought periods !Xõ Basarwa are forced to rely on traps as a means of obtaining food.

Studies of work effort have been undertaken among foragers in the Kalahari (Lee 1968, 1969, 1979:250–280; Draper 1976:210, n.d.; Tanaka 1976:115, 1980:75–78; Hitchcock 1982a:273–287). A major generalization drawn from these studies of forager work patterns is that relatively little input is necessary in order to obtain an adequate amount of food. The low number of work hours has led anthropologists to describe foragers as "remarkably leisured" (Draper 1975b:609). It should be noted, however, that there are both spatial and temporal variations in work effort. Draper (n.d.), for example, has shown that work input can be high at certain times among !Kung populations, and that there are regional differences in labor inputs. Tanaka (1976:115) indicates that the G/wi and G//ana of the Central Kalahari spend more time foraging than do the !Kung.

A traditional response to drought among Basarwa populations in Botswana was to expand the number of people in the labor force. Children, for example, were pressed into service as foragers. In some cases they collected gum from *Acacia* trees, while in others they helped their parents process plants for consumption purposes. In drought periods, resource depletion in the vicinity of residential locations meant that people had to either spend more time searching for resources or they had to switch to alternative foods. In general, Basarwa women gather plant foods every other day on the average. It was not uncommon for women to be out gathering on a daily basis during the droughts of the 1960s and the late 1970s and early 1980s. As the dry periods increased, more and more time had to be spent searching for food, and the work day expanded from a few hours to as many as nine or ten hours. The balance of the time was spent resting in the shade.

In an attempt to assess the differences between labor inputs of mobile and sedentary Basarwa groups in wet periods and dry periods, data were collected on the amount of time spent working. Table III presents information on subsistence work effort for both mobile and sedentary Basarwa populations in the Kalahari. In order to make our results comparable to those of Lee (1968, 1969:83–87, 1979:254–

Table III. Subsistence work effort for mobile and sedentary Basarwa populations in the Kalahari

Area	Observation period	Group size	Total days	Number of work days	Percentage of days worked	Number of days worked per week
Dobe[a]	1 (7/6–7/12, '64)	25.6 (23–29)	114	37	.32	2.3
	(7/20–7/26, '64)	34.3 (29–40)	156	42	.27	1.9
	(7/27–8/2, '64)	35.6 (32–40)	167	77	.46	3.2
/Du/Da[b]	1 (2/27–3/4, '69)	25.3 (16–29)	74	42	.57	3.99
	2 (3/27–4/1, '69)	32.0 (29–35)	142	62	.44	3.1
	3 (5/15–5/21, '69)	41.0 (34–43)	187	55	.29	2.0
	4 (6/1–6/6, '69)	54.6 (51–56)	173	35	.20	1.4
	5 (7/15–7/18, '69)	19.0 (19–19)	48	4	.08	0.6
	6 (8/15–8/25, '69)	56.5 (44–69)	439	142	.32	2.2
	7 (10/5–10/9, '69)	50.8 (44–59)	205	68	.33	2.3
!Koi!kom[c]	1 (4/10–13/10, '67)	16.0	160	54	.38	2.7
Khwee[d]	1 (1/28–1/30, '78)	28.5 (24–33)	57	29	.51	3.6
Uwe-Abo[d]	1 (2/14–2/17, '78)	26.5 (23–30)	44	21	.48	3.3
Bae[d]	1 (1/9–3/9, '78)	15.0 (11–19)	24	9	.38	2.6
Jubeetswipaa[e]	1 (3/8–3/14, '78)	24.9 (21–31)	232	144	.62	4.34
Mothatse[e]	1 (7/7–7/10, '78)	20.7 (17–24)	82	45	.55	3.84
Man/otai[f]	1 (2/3–2/6, '76)	7.0 (5–9)	32	24	.75	5.3
	2 (2/25–2/31, '76)	9.5 (9–10)	48	40	.83	5.8
	3 (8/2–8/6, '76)	6.0 (5–7)	37	25	.68	4.8

Man/otai[f]	1 (8/5–8/9, '82)	5.5 (4-7)	34	29	.85	5.95
	2 (9/13–9/15, '83)	5.0 (4-6)	15	14	.93	6.51
Masakwe[f]	1 (6/20–6/23, '76)	5.5 (4-7)	29	25	.86	6.02
Gogwane[f]	1 (10/27–10/30, '76)	10.0 (8-12)	38	11	.29	2.03

[a] Data from !Kung popuations in northwestern Botswana, taken from Lee (1968:38, Table 4, 1969:83–87, 1979:254–259, Table 9). Note that week number two in Lee's work diary has been deleted because he supplied people with food; see Lee (1979:256).

[b] Data from !Kung populations in the /Du/Da area of northwestern Botswana, taken from Draper (n.d.).

[c] Data from G/wi and G//ana populations in the !Kade area of the Central Kalahari Game Reserve, taken from Tanaka (1980:76–77 and Table 16). Note that the group size given is not the total but rather the number of male and female providers.

[d] Data from Kúa mobile foraging populations in the Western Sandveld region.

[e] Data from cattle post populations in the Western Sandveld region.

[f] Data from Tyua populations in the Nata River region.

259), Tanaka (1980:75–77) and Draper (n.d.), we have used only those cases in which producers were away from camp for purposes of subsistence procurement. It can be seen that there is variation in work effort among Basarwa both over the period of a year and from place to place. Mobile foragers worked as little as approximately half a day per week at /Du/Da in July, 1969 and as much as four days a week in the same area in late February and early March, 1969 (Draper n.d.). On the other hand, Tyua groups at Man/otai in the Nata River region worked as much as six and a half days a week in August, 1982 and September, 1983. Both of these years had less than average rainfall. Thus, one response of Basarwa to drought is to expand the amount of labor being done.

It should not be concluded, however, that labor intensification is always a response to drought conditions. Data collected among Kalahari foragers suggests that when resources are at their lowest point of availability during the year, labor efforts tend to be relatively low. This is often true among Kũa in drought periods as well. This pattern of work, in the eastern Kalahari, at least, is related in part to energy and body moisture factors. People attempt to conserve their energy and body moisture in the face of difficult conditions in dry periods (Silberbauer 1979; Hitchcock 1982a:281–282). A common response to severe moisture stress was to sit in the shade, sometimes in shallow holes in the sand in which people had urinated to increase the moisture levels.

There were cases in the central Kalahari of groups and individuals simply giving up their efforts at food collection. Some of them said that they simply sat in their camps and waited for the drought to break. In October, 1979, a group of Remote Area Development Officers came across a small group of Basarwa in the eastern Central Kalahari Game Reserve which had been abandoned by members who were able to walk. The elderly people and children had resigned themselves to their fate, saying that they did not anticipate that their kinsmen would be able to make it to a place with water and return in time to save them.

One of the reasons for the adaptive success of Kalahari hunter-gatherers was their wide knowledge of the environment and their efficient and sometimes unique methods for exploiting it. Wild plants provide the bulk of important resources for hunter-gatherer subsistence in the Kalahari. In addition, they provide the materials for building shelters, manufacturing artifacts, fuel, and medicine. Basarwa groups exploit a wide variety of plant resources. The !Kung, for example, were noted to have utilized 65 species in the Nyae Nyae area of Namibia (Marshall 1976:109–123); the G/wi and G//ana in the Central Kalahari Game Reserve used 78 (Tanaka 1976:117–118); the Tyua of the northeastern Kalahari exploited 83 species (Hitchcock 1982a:216). Some of these plants consists of roots and gums which are drought-resistant.

A major problem for Basarwa foragers in drought periods as well as during the dry season of the annual cycle is lack of access to moisture. Melons much as tsama *(Citrullus vulgaris)* are exploited as sources of fluids. Sometimes Basarwa groups will burn areas in order to promote the growth of melons and to reduce the grass cover so that they can see vines which indicate underground tubers and roots. When the melons are finished, Basarwa will fall back on roots such as bi: *(Raphionacme burkei)*. Table IV presents data on plants commonly exploited as sources plant parts utilized range from fruits to roots and tubers.

One of the ways in which Basarwa adapt to severe droughts is to exploit a wider variety of foods. They move down the food preference scale, exploiting items which are sometimes bitter or contain little in the way of digestible food. According to informants, it was not uncommon to see people picking the leaves off shrubs or stripping bark from trees in drought periods. In Botswana, virtually all groups have been noted to exploit wild plant foods as a buffer against scarcity during drought periods. Grivetti (1976, 1979), working among the BaTlokwa, a Tswana group in southeastern Botswana, notes that periodic food shortages saw people exploiting a wide variety of wild plants. Devitt (1977, 1979) points out that competition for wild plant resources increased in drought periods because more people depended on them. It is interesting to note that agropastoralists in Botswana exploit a wider variety of wild plant foods than do Basarwa foragers (Grivetti 1979:251).

Prolonged drought affects even the normally drought-resistant plant resources, thus threatening the very survival of Basarwa groups. A response to severe drought conditions was to utilize old skins, reins, and sandles as sources of food. Moisture was obtained from the rumens of animals which had been killed. In some cases, drought resulted in a reduction in the availability of grubs which are used for

Table IV. Plants commonly exploited as sources of moisture and food by Botswana Basarwa in drought periods

Scientific name	Common names	Description and uses	Seasonality
Acacia giraffae	camelthorn, mogotlo (Setswana), //ah (!Xo), go (Kũa), /una (!Kung)	tall tree (up to 10m); pods eaten, also gum	all year; pods fall in the dry season
Citrullus naudinianus	gemsbok cucumber, mokopane (Setswana), tsha (!Kung), nkxa (Kũa), ka: (G/wi)	melon on vine with long runners sprouting from a bitter meter long tap root; melon eaten raw or dried and pounded up; seeds are roasted	November-August with peak in February-May
Citrullus vulgaris Schrad. (or *Colocynthus citrullus*)	tsama melon, d/un (Kũa), n≠a (G/wi), n/an (G//ana), mokate (Setswana)	melons growing from 2–3 m runners attached to deep mass of roots; annual plant similar to the cultivated melon grown by Kalahari groups; cut into strips and dried for storage	ripens April-June, stored through August but sometimes longer
Coccinia rehmannii	magapa (Setswana), /a (G//ana), g/a: (G/wi), gaba (Kũa), /ga (!Kung)	vine with large tuber; tuber eaten as are small fruits from vine; tuber must be cooked	year-round but usually collected in dry season; fruits November-May
Cucumis hookeri	spiney cucumber, monyaku (Setswana), n/o'no (G/wi), n/enu (Naron), m/ibi (Kũa)	creeping annual vine with shallow roots; cucumber-like fruit eaten raw or roasted	April-June

Grewia flava	raisin berry; moretlwa (Setswana), kxum (Kūa), kxam (G/wi)	woody shrub with small berries eaten raw, sometimes pounded up and mixed with meat or porridge	ripens November-March, stored year-round
Hyphaene ventricosa	fan palm, vegetable ivory palm. mokolwane (Setswana), /hani (!Kung)	bushy palm which grows in clumps; sap made into wine, fronds used for basket manufacture; heart eaten roasted	October-December for fruit; other products available year-round
Ochna pulchra	monyelenyele (Setswana), kera (//Gana), !ara (!Xo)	small tree with shiny leaves; sour black fruits roasted and eaten	November-February
Raphionacme burkei	water root, leditsa (Setswana), bai (Kūa), //an (!Xó), bi (G/wi)	small, woody, slender-leaved plant with tuber	year-round; sometimes transported to camp and replanted
Sclerocarya caffra	marula (Setswana) gai (!Kung), !kaba (Tyua)	tall tree with yellow or green fruits; fruit eaten raw, dried and stored	fruit available December-January
Tylosema esculentum	tsin bean, morama (Setswana) //odu (Kūa), tsi !Kung, /xwi (G/wi) /oi (G//ana)	long vines growing from edible underground tuber; pods on vines contain bean which can be eaten after roasting	bean ripens in April-May; tuber used all year but mainly in dry season

arrow poison *(Diamphidia simplex)*, thus affecting hunting success. As Heinz (1967:2) notes people then turned to trapping strategies as a means of obtaining prey.

In severe drought periods, Basarwa had to withdraw from hard-hit areas. Vierich (1977, 1979, 1981) notes that some of the people in the northern Kweneng District had moved there from the Central Kalahari Game Reserve during the severe droughts of 1933, 1947, and the early 1960s. Tobias (1962:808, 1964:83) points out that in the late 1950s, as a result of seven consecutive years of drought, the movement of what he terms as "wild" Basarwa into the waterholes in the Ghanzi District had accelerated significantly. Silberbauer (1972:274) says that G/wi populations in the Central Kalahari Game Reserve fell back on the Ghanzi Fams in drought periods. Sometimes individuals and groups had to undertake forced marches to water points, leaving behind children and elderly people who could not stand the pace.

Under extremely arduous conditions, Basarwa foragers were known to resort to tying leather thongs around their stomachs. There is little, if any, evidence of cannibalism, and informants rarely discussed infanticide and senilicide as population control mechanisms in drought periods. Famines did occur, however, as noted by Central Kalahari Game Reserve residents who had survived the 1933 drought. In some cases, stock theft increased, as occurred in the Ghanzi Farms in the early to mid-20th century. Most groups, however, chose a dependency strategy as a means of getting through droughts. Ghanzi farmers described the tremendous increase in hungry people who congregated on their ranches in the 1960s. These squatters, as they were called, were not only deprived of access to traditional foraging areas but also were seen as having lost many of the skills and knowledge necessary to exploit a deteriorating environment.

Contemporary Responses to Drought in Botswana

Drought in Botswana is a persistent factor which with every group, whether hunter-gatherer, pastoralist, or even peri-urban, must contend in one form or another. Responses to this phenomenon vary in part according to the resource-use patterns and economic options of the group concerned. Urban dwellers with formal jobs may face little more than increased demands from rural relatives or higher prices in times of environmental stress. Those in the informal sector are likely to experience reduced demand from customers for their goods and services. This is particularly true for those people employed on a seasonal basis in the agricultural sector as well as those who brew beer, make handicrafts, and engage in itinerant trading.

Habitat deterioration, a declining water table, increasing overgrazing, and rising pressure from other groups are all causing greater hardship for Basarwa populations in Botswana. The penetration of the modern economy of southern Africa, particularly the livestock and mining industries, has brought about significant changes in the region. Boreholes have been drilled in large numbers; fences have been constructed; and cutlines have been laid out across the Kalahari in association with the rapid expansion of Botswana's beef export trade and the opening of diamond mines.

Declining foraging opportunities and reduced access to land pose a threat to the continued existence of hunter-gatherers. There is evidence of declining nutritional status and widespread poverty among those groups on heavily overgrazed ranches and on the peripheries of Kalahari villages and towns. Social deterioration is manifested in a number of ways, one of them being the breakdown in sharing which was so important to the survival of traditional foragers. Alcoholism and domestic violence are on the increase in some areas.

There has been a process of gradual migration to private boreholes and wells, some of which were drilled for drought relief purposes in the 1950s and 1960s. This has led to depopulation of some areas and a loss of critical labor among those groups who continue to forage in areas away from water points. The lack of development of social and physical infrastructure in areas such as game reserves has resulted in out-migration to other places where there are clinics and schools as well as employment and income-generating opportunities. The cohesion of hunter-gatherer groups has broken down, in some cases, and nowadays Basarwa live in family units on the peripheries of boreholes and villages.

Dispossession has increased as a result of the expansion in leasehold land in Botswana. In 1975 the Government of Botswana embarked on a major land reform and livestock development program. Known as the Tribal Grazing Land Policy (TGLP), this effort was geared toward the commercialization of the livestock industry, range conservation, and reduction of the gap in incomes between rich and poor in Botswana (Hitchcock 1978, 1985). An outgrowth of this policy has been a reduction in the amount of unfenced land in the Kalahari. Some Basarwa have been forced to move to what are known as communal service centers, small areas of land set aside for people who no longer have access to land leased out to cattle owners.

Partly because of the commercialization of the livestock industry, cattle owners are less willing to allow Basarwa and other people access to their herds for subsistence and draft power purposes. Cattle owners in the Kweneng District, for example, have requested that their employees not drink the milk of their cows, preferring that it be left for the calves instead (Solway 1980). Problems of cattle theft in drought periods have led to more and more calls for Basarwa and other people viewed as squatters to be removed to areas away from ranches and farms. One of the reasons for the popularity of settlement schemes among cattle owners and government administrators in Botswana is that supposedly these would aggregate hunter-gatherer groups and thus enable them to be controlled more efficiently. Fortunately, less than four percent of the Basarwa population of Botswana resides on specially-established settlements.

Facing droughts and reduced resources due to overgrazing, Basarwa groups have resorted to new strategies. In some cases Basarwa have begun to process and store food, such as *mmilo (Vangueria infausta)*. Food storage is a means of buffering against the risk of crop failures. Other Basarwa have obtained livestock, stating openly that they have done this in order to have something to sell in case of drought. Still others have turned to begging, as has occurred in the area of boreholes and camps operated by mining companies.

The 1960s drought saw widespread deaths of wildlife in the Nata area of northeastern Botswana. Tails of dead wildebeest were cut off and sold to trading stores in Nata Village. Bones, which littered the landscape, were collected and taken on donkeys to the bonemeal processing factory in Francistown. Basarwa had to compete with other people for access to foraging resources, and pressure on their subsistence sometimes led to ideological measures being utilized. Some Basarwa specialized in rain-making and were employed by Kalanga, Bamangwato, and other groups to dance and conduct rituals to bring rain.

A less common response among Basarwa hunter-gatherers has been for them to seek employment in the new towns of Botswana (e.g. Orapa, Jwaneng, Selebi-Pikwe) and the large Tswana villages (e.g. Maun, Serowe, Molepolole, Kanye). Some have continued to take contracts in the South African mines, although opportunities for this have declined greatly in recent years. A few Basarwa have become professional hunters, as seen, for example, in the Nata River region, the Mababe Depression, and the fringes of the Okavango Delta. Such responses have been essentially opportunistic, with strategies involving high costs in dislocation and risk being adopted only under more extreme conditions. A further example of a high-risk strategy is of the limited numbers who have joined the South African military in the war against the South West African Peoples Organization (SWAPO). This activity is far more common in Namibia than Botswana. While Basarwa are given food, clothing, and high cash wages, they expose themselves to battle conditions and risk the long-term animosity of people with whom they have lived for generations.

Faced with livestock and drought-induced environmental degradation affecting both wildlife and plant resources, Basarwa have been forced to enter into close socioeconomic relationships with cattle owners and villagers in an attempt to seek new sources of food and income. While foraging has generally not been abandoned entirely even in well-developed areas, reduced mobility has necessitated increased reliance on handouts and low-wage employment, sometimes in patron-client types of situations. These strategies allow Basarwa access to rations, trade goods, and cash. Cattle post employees are sometimes given a cow a year for their work in a system known as *sejara*, but in drought periods the payments of animals are reduced in number. The few animals that Basarwa have been able to accumulate often end up being sold or killed for meat in droughts. Thus, dependency strategies, which sometimes facilitate herd accumulation, do not always serve to enable groups to become pastoralists. Recurrent droughts have impacts on socioeconomic transformations through reducing access to livestock.

Low or poorly-timed rainfall initially affects agriculture and farm employment greatly, and livestock production to a somewhat lesser extent, depending ultimately on the severity and duration of the drought (Jones 1979). Wages and payments in kind tend to be reduced, and sometimes employees and hangers-on are cut off completely. Milk production, which has become increasingly important as a source of food for Basarwa in Botswana, is also curtailed significantly in drought periods.

Under these circumstances, Basarwa may attempt to revert to traditional strategies of foraging and mobility. Given the fact that populations have increased and development programs have expanded, however, these options are no longer as open to them as before. Wildlife populations have been affected by fences, competition from livestock, and overhunting by both subsistence and commercial hunters. Habitat changes have brought about shifts in the types of species existing in the Kalahari. Imposition of strict enforcement procedures by game scouts from the Department of Wildlife and National Parks has made many Basarwa afraid to hunt for fear of being arrested and going to jail. Groups in the Kalahari with members in jail are often worse off than others with a greater number of productive people in the labor force to sustain them.

Finally, resources available to Basarwa may be reduced in times of drought as a result of the fallback strategies adopted by other groups. Foraging is a common strategy among pastoralists, agriculturalists, and village dwellers in drought periods in Botswana (Grivetti 1976, 1978, 1979; Devitt 1977, 1979; Sheppard and Jones 1979; Vierich 1979, 1981; Hitchcock 1979). Added pressure on the resource base contributes to the decline of what has been described as a fragile ecosystem (Botswana Society 1971). In these situations, people sometimes resort to scavenging; in the eastern Kalahari, for example, Basarwa groups have risked serious injury or death by attempting to drive lions from their kills in drought periods. Competition over resources has sometimes led to fights. While the Basarwa are generally described as being non-territorial, droughts may lead to an increase in conflict over resource space.

Involvement of the State in Drought Relief

During the successive droughts of the 1960s the Botswana Government authorities began for the first time to accept a major responsibility for the relief of affected communities (Campbell 1979). Prior to that time, individual groups or sometimes the tribal chiefs or village headmen initiated drought relief measures (Hitchcock 1979). Although response of the state was fairly slow in the 1960's drought, livestock-related relief measures were instituted relatively early, and over a thousand boreholes were drilled between 1964 and 1966 (Campbell 1979:104). Efforts to alleviate the agricultural crisis did not begin until 1963 (Campbell 1979:106), and it was not until 1964 that the situation for people in terms of food availability was recognized as critical (Campbell 1979:105). Food relief deliveries on a significant scale were initiated; this amount doubled in 1965, when 23,000 people were fed. Food-for-work programs were run from 1965 through 1967, employing 27,000 people at their height, the vast majority being women. A total of US $3,900,000 was spent during this period on drought relief efforts.

In the subsequent drought years of 1969–1971 over $2,000,000 was spent, benefiting over 9,000 people. In 1973–74, another drought period, roughly $250,000 was spent on food-for-work. In most cases these projects were run through established villages which possessed Tswana-type authority structures and government extension workers. While intended ostensibly to assist those households without livestock or other visible means of support, the state largely neglected the considerable proportion of households living beyond the reach of villages.

The 1979–80 drought in Botswana was noted for its clearly negative effects on remote area populations. By March, 1979 there were indications in several districts that bush foods had declined significantly, and two districts reported severe malnutrition among Basarwa and other remote area dwellers. One response was a rapidly-implemented Government-sponsored survey in southeastern Botswana (Vierich 1979; Sheppard and Jones 1979) which showed the various strategies of households as having been undermined by environmental and economic changes in the region. A relief program consisting of the distribution of supplementary food was mounted for remote area dwellers in six districts where people were having difficulties meeting subsistence requirements. The relief efforts were organized by the District Councils, and were carried out by their Remote Area Development Officers, as private sources of transport were not always reliable.

In 1979 a special relief effort was mounted in North West District (Ngamiland), prompted by a combination of drought and Foot-and-Mouth Disease. The outbreak of the latter, which occured in Ngamiland in October, 1977 and subsequently in other northern areas, resulted in restrictions being placed on livestock movements and exports of animals and meat products from the affected regions and from veterinary 'buffer zones.' These restrictions, in turn, led to diminished access to livestock products (especially milk) in the villages as well as to lay-offs of employees or lowering of wage and ration payments on cattle posts. Against the background of forthcoming elections in 1979, the government quickly set up a loan facility for livestock owners against the security of the future marketing of hypothecated cattle (the Fifty Pula Scheme), but there was no comparable program for non-livestock owners. However, a small-scale income generation effort employed roughly 4,000 people on short-term cash-for-work projects in some remote areas of northwest Botswana. Due to the location of these projects, and the low wage rate, a higher proportion of participants were drawn from localities outside established villages than in previous relief works programs.

Meanwhile, the Government of Botswana, with the assistance of the World Food Programme (W.F.P.), had since Independence in 1966 continued a supplementary feeding program even in non-drought periods. This effort is intended to provide a meal to all primary school children through institutional feeding during the school term, and to provide monthly rations on the basis of medical selection to children under five years of age as well as pregnant and lactating mothers and tuberculosis patients. These programs are expanded in terms of ration levels and eligible groups in times of drought. The food delivery system has operated through the network of primary schools and health facilities, which has particularly low coverage in the remote areas of the country. Social service infrastructure is being extended to these areas at a relatively rapid rate, and this factor, together with special food deliveries organized by the Remote Area Development Programme in the Ministry of Local Government and Lands, now brings the bulk of hunter-gatherers and former foragers within range of government food supplies.

Effectiveness of Government Relief Measures in Remote Areas

Although earlier relief efforts left something to be desired, more recent measures appear to have been relatively effective in preventing widespread hunger and other problems. The 1979–80 drought saw food relief organized specifically for remote area populations. In practice, the remote area relief program often applied directly to Basarwa communities. Where these groups existed in ethnically mixed villages, as in western Ngamiland, a clear distinction in nutritional status was apparent between the Basarwa and non-Basarwa populations. As a result, programs were geared toward assisting destitutes, many of whom were Basarwa.

The Remote Area Development Program, founded in 1974 as the Bushman Development Program, is responsible for a wide range of on-going development efforts, some of which are geared toward increasing production and raising income levels of households in remote parts of Botswana. The officers of this unit were given the responsibility for identifying those people in need of special assistance. In 1979 the total number amounted to some 16,000 people out of a total population of about 60,000. The relief effort was hampered by an inadequate supply of transport and by a general lack of appreciation of the seriousness of conditions in remote areas among many government officials. Prevailing socioeconomic conditions and the shortcomings of the relief program induced widespread migration to villages. It was not surprising, therefore, that stock theft and crime levels generally rose considerably.

Where food deliveries were adequate, however, the question arises as to the nature of dependency which may be induced by such assistance from Government. Research data has indicated that, where sufficient food relief has been made available, willingness to invest effort in the search for traditional foods may be reduced drastically. The Government has made modest efforts as part of its Remote Area Development Programme to assist hunter-gatherers in adopting small-scale mixed farming, particularly cropping and small stock keeping, and has provided agricultural inputs in the form of seeds and implements for a number of communities. The indications both from the nutritional status of these groups and from the yields achieved in small-scale crop farming are that, while traditional methods of meeting subsistence requirements are indeed being replaced by new strategies, these new methods require long periods of learning and sustained capital inputs, and are also much more prone to fluctuations in the ecosystem and to outright failure in drought periods. Faced with urgent short-term needs among remote area dwellers arising from these serious failures, Government is obliged to supply relief in the form of immediate consumption goods, which in turn tends to further reduce the internal viability and productive capacity of these communities. Food relief, it should be noted, is an inherently unreliable method of guaranteeing the means of survival of rural populations over the long term, although the imperative of its provision in immediately-critical situations is clearly overwhelming.

In early 1982 the Botswana authorities were again forced by rainfall failures to declare an official state of drought, which has since lasted for a full four years. Now recognizing that the non-cattle owning populations in remote areas have particularly urgent needs for relief, special funds were provided to District Councils primarily for the purchase of food for these groups in advance of a nationwide relief program. This recognition has been prompted by increased reliance in drought monitoring on the gradually-expanding nutritional surveillance system first established in 1978: in the early months of drought in the 1981–82 season, many communities recorded malnutrition rates among children under five of 50% or above; Kweneng District in the southeastern Kalahari, for example, had high levels of children who were nutritionally at risk (i.e. below 80% of expected weight for age, on the Harvard Standard). Similar problems were seen in the ensuing 1982–1985 period, during which the increase in malnutrition levels was effectively limited by the various relief measures, but remained highest in the remoter settlements and the Kalahari districts. A further indicator of the stresses caused by drought was the rapidly rising numbers of people registered as destitutes with the District Councils or for the purpose of temporary relief feeding (over 36,000 by 1985). Again, many of these people were resident in or had migrated from smaller settlements in remoter areas.

A Botswana Government decision in 1983 resulted in the establishment of a specific Remote Area Dweller (RAD) relief program. As of mid-1985 there were approximately 21,000 people being fed under this program, with food being supplied through a combination of local purchases by District Councils and donations from the World Food Programme (WFP) through the Government's Department of Food Resources. A substantial number of load-carrying vehicles were purchased in order to service the food delivery operation. Special efforts were also mounted to provide food to populations in the Central Kalahari Game Reserve. Two districts were involved, Kweneng and Ghanzi, and trucks were provided to transport goods, including drums of water, to localities deep in the Reserve.

A second major component of the Government's relief effort was an employment-creation program which as of mid-1985 was serving some 70,000 persons in rural Botswana. People were paid P2[1] per day to undertake projects selected by their village organisations, such as clearing roads, preparing vegetable gardens, and building dams, storehouses and other community facilities. Since their inception in 1982, these labor-based projects have gradually expanded in scope and coverage, and by 1984–85 were able to reach a substantial proportion of Remote Area communities, thereby providing temporary cash-earning opportunities to complement the food deliveries described above. Such income confers an element of choice for those benefiting, and probably tends to minimise the dependency-creating effects of relief through encouraging working involvement in activities selected and partly organised by the community itself.

Botswana also has a related program which provides funds directly to local institutions (e.g. Village Development Committees). The money is used to provide materials for the building of teachers' quarters and other public facilities. In this way the village institutions have a longer term stake in public works. Other innovative programs include agricultural support measures such as cash grants for the clearing of fields and subsidisation of the hiring of draft power for poorer farmers. Free seed packages are also supplied throughout the country. Further, the Government has established a Direct Feeding Program in which money is given directly to personnel at health facilities, who then purchase food from local producers for use in the feeding and rehabilitation of malnourished children, and in nutrition education activities. In this way local agriculturalists or fishermen can earn some income for providing goods to the health posts, which are then redistributed to the most vulnerable groups. Finally, a sorghum-processing project at primary schools provides income to women in rural areas: P1.25 is paid for a bucket of stamped sorghum, which takes about four hours to process using traditional methods and equipment. This activity complements the employment-creating effects of the Labour Based Relief projects. In these ways, both income and food are distributed in rural areas of Botswana in response to drought conditions. In recognition of the underlying problems associated with

---

[1]Pula 1 = US$0.55 approximately (1985)

chronic poverty, income and food shortages, it is intended by the Government to retain most of these programs in non-drought years.

There are four critical elements to Botswana's successful drought relief program. First of all, it has an effective logistical (distribution) system, able to reach all parts of the country. Distribution of relief supplies is done through a combination of Government Departments, local authorities and private haulage contractors. There is little corruption, and food reaches those in need in a generally timely fashion. Secondly, there is a labor-intensive relief program which provides employment and income for rural and remote settlements. This program, and the related agricultural support measures, are production-oriented; destumping of fields, for example, increases the cleared area available for planting once the rains come, and the construction of dams helps to improve the accessibility of communal watering facilities for livestock. Another popular activity under the labor-based program has been the fencing of arable lands areas on a community basis to prevent encroachment by cattle on standing crops during the rainy season.

A third component of the government's drought relief program is a system of water provision, which includes delivery of water to areas facing chronic shortages and an expanded borehole drilling program. Finally, there is a well-established information and monitoring system which includes nutritional surveillance at health posts and clinics, and the collection and analysis of meterological, agricultural and range condition data. This is formalised in an Early Warning system monitoring both the incidence of drought and its effects on the human population. Additional information is obtained from extension workers and District Councils, data being sent on to Central Government, which has an Inter-Ministerial Drought committee that meets regularly and which is responsible for the co-ordination and design of all relief and post-drought recovery measures. The country has now embarked on a medium-term National Food Strategy, which is geared toward reducing vulnerability to drought at the household level and to increasing the level of national self-sufficiency in food production. Essentially, Botswana has gained in capacity to anticipate and respond effectively to drought through basing its monitoring and relief activities in already-established institutions, and by integrating them as far as possible with regular development efforts.

Conclusions

Whereas in the past drought relief efforts in Botswana concentrated heavily on livestock owners, expanding grazing land through provision of water points and establishing programs such as hammer mills to produce livestock feed (Campbell 1979), more recent efforts, particularly since 1979, have begun to pay more attention to households which possess few or no livestock and thus face significant constraints in terms of recovering lost assets or increasing production and incomes after drought (Vierich 1979; Sheppard and Jones 1979). Many of the early efforts at drought relief might best be described as crisis management. Even some of the recent programs were not started early enough to prevent severe nutritional stress and social hardship, as occurred in mid-1979, for example. When it was decided to terminate feeding in 1980, people in some parts of the Kalahari were forced to migrate to towns in order to beg for food and water. (A similar issue of whether or how to phase out special feeding programs for isolated communities will face the Botswana authorities at the end of the current drought.)

Part of the problem in organizing relief efforts in Botswana is that often Remote Area Development Officers in charge of the programs faced severe constraints, particularly in terms of transport. Other more recently-instituted programs, particularly Direct Feeding and Sorghum Handstamping, benefit such groups only to the extent that they have access to established social service infrastructure. Nevertheless, food and water have been delivered to many remote places, and significant funds have been injected through job-creation programs (Holm and Morgan 1985; Morgan 1985-c, 1986). Undoubtedly, a significant number of lives have been saved as a result. The improvement in the performance of relief operations continued during the 1982–85 drought period, as officials at all levels of government gained in experience and appreciation of the importance of drought relief.

As data on nutritional status of remote area populations improve in Botswana, it is becoming increasingly clear that chronic problems persist among certain groups. This is particularly true among very poor households, a significant percentage of which are Basarwa. These circumstances are not the product of seasonal or long-term rainfall deficiencies alone, but are also the result of political and economic processes which have brought about changes in traditional means of earning a livelihood. Strategies which in the past served to buffer people against severe stress, such as mobility and systems of delayed reciprocity, are no longer capable of sustaining people in the face of increased population pressure and declining food resources. There has been a reduction in access to productive resources such as land, labor, and livestock among Basarwa and other populations in the Kalahari and adjacent regions.

Palliative measures taken by the government to compensate Basarwa for their disadvantages, such as occasional or even sustained provision of food, temporary employment, and inputs such as seeds, can be seen objectively as an attempt to disguise the nature of the dispossession process which has led to dependency. To an increasing extent, Basarwa and other groups in remote areas are incapable of making the transition on their own to a self-sustaining economy which has the ability to withstand shortfalls in productive capacity and resource availability. Simply providing food and goods has served mainly to increase dependency and has not addressed the root causes of impoverishment and social stress. Greater effort needs to be made to promote economic development in remote areas. This can only be done through programs which are geared toward raising levels of production, incomes, and employment on a sustained basis, coupled with measures to conserve the environment. Without greater emphasis on long-term development and drought recovery programs, it will be difficult if not impossible to ensure the long-term viability of Basarwa communities in Botswana.

The Basarwa, like other indigenous populations in Africa, employ a wide variety of means of coping with drought (Hitchcock 1979; Vierich 1979; Fleuret 1986). Some of these strategies have become decidedly less viable in the face of increasing population and reduced land and resource availability. Foraging as a strategy is employed by virtually all groups in Botswana, not just the hunting-gathering Basarwa. At the same time, Basarwa resort to selling off livestock and eating their seed stocks in times of stress. In this context, it is difficult, if not impossible, to apply a rigid taxonomy of responses according to type of adaptation. Pastoralists forage, hunter-gatherers enter the wage labor market, and agriculturalists sell off their stock.

These societies, by their effects on the environment, have increased their own vulnerability to seasonal and longer-term rainfall shortages as well as to the incidence of drought itself. Competition between the resource requirements of forager and agropastoralist economies has been manifested particularly in the reduction of wild plant foods and the decline in the numbers of wildlife in heavily stocked areas (Hitchcock 1978, 1982a; Campbell 1986). There is a wide range of variation even among hunting-gathering Basarwa, as seen, for example, in settlement patterns (Barnard 1979). This variation is linked to differences in responses to resource stress, with some groups employing dependency strategies and others attempting to become self-sufficient.

Immediate issues facing decision-makers in Botswana in the context of these underlying problems are therefore centered around the difficult but important process of assisting a transition of sources of livelihood which derive primarily from state assistance to those of self-sustaining nature. These issues concern not only the extent or relief and subsidies needed, but also the form which they should take during the initial years of this transition. For example, to what extent is food distribution substitutable with, or should be complemented by temporary or seasonal employment creation? In the longer run, such types of assistance will only facilitate the transition of productive forces in Basarwa societies if there is a sufficient measure of integration with national and even regional developments in the economic and political spheres. The impacts of droughts and drought relief programs in Botswana suggest that integration is crucial in order to provide substantially widened options for Basarwa communities through improved access to productive assets and adequate control over resources.

References

Barnard, A. 1979. Kalahari Bushman Settlement Patterns. In *Social and Ecological Systems*, ed. by P.C. Burnham and R.F. Ellen. London: Academic Press. pp. 131–144.

Botswana Society 1971. *Proceedings of the Conference on the Sustained Production from Semi-arid Areas, with Particular Reference to Botswana. Botswana Notes and Records, Special Edition*, No. 1. Gaborone, Botswana: Botswana Society.

Campbell, A.C. 1979. The 1960's Drought in Botswana. In *Proceedings of the Symposium on Drought in Botswana,* ed. by Madalon T. Hinchey, Gaborone, Botswana: Botswana Society in collaboration with Clark University Press. pp. 98–109.

———— 1986. The Use of Wild Food Plant and Drought in Botswana. *Journal of Arid Environments* 11:81–91.

Cashdan, E.A. 1977. Subsistence, Mobility, and Territorial Organization among the G//anakwe of the Northeastern Central Kalahari Game Reserve, Botswana. Report to the Ministry of Local Government and Lands, Gaborone, Botswana.

Child, G. 1972. Observations on a Wildebeest Die-off in Botswana. *Arnoldia (Rhodesia)* 5(31):1–13.

Childers, G.W. 1976. *Report on the survey/Investigation of the Ghanzi Farm Basarwa Situation.* Gaborone, Botswana: Government Printer.

———— 1981. *Western Ngwaketse Remote Area Dwellers: A Land Use and Development Plan for Remote Area Settlements in Southern District.* Gaborone Botswana: Government Printer.

Devitt, P. 1977. Coping with Drought in the Kalahari. In *Drought in Africa 2*, ed. by David Dalby, R.J. Harrison Church and Fatima Bezzaz, London: International African Institute. pp. 186–200.

———— 1979. Drought and Poverty. In *Proceedings of the Symposium on Drought in Botswana*, ed. by Madalon T. Hinchey, Gaborone, Botswana: Botswana Society in collaboration with Clark University Press. pp. 121–127.

Draper, P. 1972. *!Kung Bushman Childhood.* Unpublished Ph.D. Dissertation, Harvard University, Cambridge, Massachusetts.

———— 1975a. !Kung Women: Contrasts in Sexual Egalitarianism in the Foraging and Sedentary Contexts. In *Towards an Anthropology of Women*, ed. by Rayna Reiter, New York: Monthly Review Press. pp. 77–109.

———— 1975b. Cultural Pressure on Sex Differences. *American Ethnologist* 2(4):602–616.

———— 1976. Social and Economic Constraints on Child Life among the !Kung. In *Kalahari Hunter-Gatherers: Studies of the !Kung San and Their Neighbors*, ed. by Richard B. Lee and Irven DeVore, Cambridge: Harvard University Press. pp. 199–217.

———— n.d. Regional Variation in Hunter-Gatherer Work Effort: Comparisons among Kalahari !Kung. Unpublished manuscript.

Ebert, J.I. 1978. Comparability between Hunter-Gatherer Groups in the Past and Present: Modernization versus Explanation. *Botswana Notes and Records* 10:19–26.

Fleuret, A. 1986. Indigenous Responses to Drought in Sub-Saharan Africa. *Disasters* 10(3):224–229.

Gooch, T. and J. MacDonald 1981. *Evaluation of 1979/80 Drought Relief Programme.* Gaborone, Botswana: Ministry of Finance and Development Planning.

Government of Botswana 1985. *Report of the Central Kalahari Game Reserve Fact Finding Mission.* Gaborone, Botswana: Government Printer.

Grivetti, L.E. 1976. *Dietary Resources and Social Aspects of Food Use in a Tswana Tribe.* Unpublished Ph.D. Dissertation, University of California, Davis.

———— 1978. Nutritional Success in a Semi-Arid Land: Examination of Tswana Agro-Pastoralists of the Eastern Kalahari, Botswana. *American Journal of Clinical Nutrition* 31:1204–1220.

———— 1979. Kalahari Agro-Pastoral Hunter-Gatherers: The Tswana Example. *Ecology of Food and Nutrition* 7:235–256.

Guenther, M.G. 1979. *The Farm Bushmen of the Ghanzi District, Botswana*. Stuttgart: Honschul Verlag.

———— 1986. *The Nharo Bushmen of the Botswana: Tradition and Change*. Hamburg: Helmut Buske Verlag.

Heinz, H.J. 1967. Conflicts, Tension, and Relief of Tension in a Bushman Society. *ISMA Papers* No. 23, Johannesburg: Institute for the Study of Man in Africa. pp. 1–22.

Hinchey, M.T., ed. 1979. *Proceedings of the Symposium on Drought in Botswana*, Gaborone, Botswana: Botswana Society in collaboration with Clark University Press.

Hitchcock, R.K. 1978. *Kalahari Cattle Posts: A Regional Study of Hunter-Gatherers, Pastoralists, and Agriculturalists in the Western Sandveld Region, Central District, Botswana*. Gaborone, Botswana: Government Printer.

———— 1979. The Traditional Response to Drought in Botswana. In *Proceedings of the Symposium on Drought in Botswana*, ed. by Madalon T. Hinchey, Gaborone, Botswana: Botswana Society in Collaboration with Clark University Press. pp. 91–97.

———— 1982a. *The Ethnoarchaeology of Sedentism: Mobility Strategies and Site Structure among Foraging and Food Producing Populations in the Eastern Kalahari Desert, Botswana*. Unpublished Ph.D. dissertation, University of New Mexico, Albuquerque.

———— 1982b. Patterns of Sedentism among the Basarwa of Eastern Botswana. In *Politics and History in Band Societies*, ed. by Eleanor Leacock and Richard Lee, Cambridge and New York: Cambridge University Press. pp. 223–267.

———— 1985. Water, Land and Livestock: The Evolution of Tenure and Administration Patterns in the Grazing Areas of Botswana. In *The Evolution of Modern Botswana: Politics and Rural Development in Southern Africa*, ed. by Louis A. Picard, London: Rex Collings and Lincoln: University of Nebraska Press. pp. 84–121.

Holm, J.D. and R.G. Morgan 1985. Coping with Drought in Botswana: An African Success. *Journal of Modern African Studies* 23(3):463–482.

Jones, D.B. 1979. Drought and Arable Farming. In *Proceedings of the Symposium on Drought in Botswana*, ed. by Madalon T. Hinchey, Gaborone, Botswana: Botswana Society in collaboration with Clark University Press. pp. 233–239.

Lawry, S. and A. Thoma 1978. *A Spatial and Development Plan for Remote Settlements in Northern Kgalagadi: A Supplement to the Kgalagadi District Development Plan 1977–1982*. Tsabong, Botswana: Kgalagadi District Council.

Lee, R.B. 1965. *Subsistence Ecology of !Kung Bushmen*. Unpublished Ph.D. dissertation, University of California, Berkeley.

———— 1968. What Hunters Do for a Living, or, How to Make Out on Scarce Resources. In *Man the Hunter*, ed. by Richard B. Lee and Irven DeVore, Chicago: Aldine. pp. 30–48.

—— 1969. !Kung Bushmen Subsistence: An Input-output Analysis. In *Environment and Cultural Behavior*, ed. by Andrew P. Vayda, New York: Natural History Press. pp. 47–49.

—— 1972a. !Kung Spatial Organization: An Ecological and Historical Perspective. *Human Ecology* 1(2):125–147.

——1972b. The !Kung Bushmen of Botswana. In *Hunters and Gatherers Today*, ed. by M.G. Bicchieri, New York: Holt, Rinehart and Winston. pp. 327–368.

—— 1979. *The !Kung San: Men, Women, and Work in a Foraging Society*. Cambridge: Cambridge University Press.

Lee, R.B. and I. DeVore, eds. 1976. *Kalahari Hunter-Gatherers: Studies of the !Kung San and Their Neighbors*. Cambridge: Harvard University Press.

Marshall, L. 1960. !Kung Bushman Bands. *Africa* 36(4):325–355.

—— 1976. *The !Kung of Nyae Nyae*. Cambridge: Harvard University Press.

Marshall Thomas, E. 1958. *The Harmless People*. New York: Random House.

McGowan and Associates 1979. *A Study of Drought Relief and Contingency Measures Relating to the Livestock Sector in Botswana*. Report to the Government of Botswana, Gaborone.

Ministry of Finance and Development Planning 1985. *Sixth National Development Plan, 1985–91*. Gaborone, Botswana: Government Printer.

Morgan, R.G. 1985a. Contribution of Labour Based Relief Projects to Drought Relief and Post Drought Recovery. Paper presented at a workshop on Labour Based Projects, Mahalapye Rural Training Center, Mahalapye, Botswana.

—— 1985b. An Overview of Food Relief Operations in Botswana During the 1982–1986 Drought. Paper presented at the 1985 Congress of the Medical and Dental Association of Botswana, Gaborone, Botswana.

—— 1985c. The Development and Applications of a Drought Early Warning System in Botswana. *Disasters* 9(1):44–50.

—— 1986. From Drought Relief to Post-Drought Recovery—The Case of Bostwana *Disasters* 10(1):30–34.

Owens, M. and D. Owens 1980. The Fences of Death. *African Wildlife* 34(6):25–27.

—— 1984. *Cry of the Kalahari*. Boston: Houghton-Mifflin.

Sahlins, M. 1968. Notes on the Original Affluent Society. In *Man the Hunter*, ed. by Richard B. Lee, and Irven DeVore, Chicago: Aldine. pp. 85–89.

Sandford, S. 1977. *Dealing with Drought and Livestock in Botswana*. Gaborone, Botswana Government Printer.

—— 1979. Towards a Definition of Drought, In *Proceedings of the Symposium on Drought in Botswana*, ed. by Madalon T. Hinchey, Gaborone, Botswana: Botswana Society in collaboration with Clark University Press. pp. 33–40.

Sheller, P. 1977. The People of the Central Kalahari Game Reserve: A Report on the Reconnaissance of the Reserve, July-September, 1976. Report to the Ministry of Local Government and Lands, Gaborone Botswana.

Sheppard, C. with D. Clement-Jones 1979. *Coping with Drought in Botswana: House-hold Strategy and Government Policy*. Gaborone, Botswana: Rural Sociology Unit, Ministry of Agriculture.

Silberbauer, G.B. 1965. *Report to the Government of Bechuanaland on the Bushman Survey*. Gaborones: Bechuanaland Government.

———— 1972. The G/wi Bushmen. In *Hunters and Gatherers Today*, ed. by M.G. Biccieri, New York: Holt, Rinehart, and Winston. pp. 271–326.

———— 1973. *Socio-Ecology of the G/wi Bushmen*. Unpublished Ph.D. Dissertation, Monash University, Clayton, Victoria, Australia.

———— 1979. Social Hibernation: The Response of the G/wi to Seasonal Drought. In *Proceedings of the Symposium on Drought in Botswana*, ed. by Madalon T. Hinchey, Gaborone: The Botswana Society. pp. 112–120.

———— 1981a. *Hunter and Habitat in the Central Kalahari Desert*. New York: Cambridge University Press.

———— 1981b. Hunter-Gatherers of the Central Kalahari. In *Omnivorous Primates: Gathering and Hunting in Human Evolution*, ed. by Robert S.O. Harding and Geza Teleki, New York: Columbia University Press. pp. 455–498.

Solway, J.S. 1980. *People, Cattle, and Drought in the Western Kweneng District*. Rural Sociology Report Series, No. 16. Gaborone, Botswana: Ministry of Agriculture.

Tabor, S. 1983. *Drought Relief and Information Management: Coping Intelligently with Disaster*. Ithaca, New York: Cornell University and UNICEF.

Tanaka, J. 1976. Subsistence Ecology of Central Kalahari San. In *Kalahari Hunter-Gatherers: Studies of the !Kung San and Their Neighbors*, ed. by Richard B. Lee and Irven DeVore, Cambridge: Harvard University Press. pp. 98–119.

———— 1980. *The San, Hunter-Gatherers of the Kalahari: A Study in Ecological Anthropology*. Tokyo: University of Tokyo Press.

Tanaka, J., K. Sugawara, and M. Osaki 1984. Report of the San (Masarwa) Investigation Carried Out During 1982–83. Report to the Government of Botswana, Gaborone.

Tobias, P.V. 1957. Bushmen of the Kalahari. *Man* 57:33–40.

———— 1962. On the Increasing Stature of the Bushmen. *Anthropos* 57:801–810.

———— 1964. Bushmen Hunter-Gatherers: A Study in Human Ecology. In *Ecological Studies in Southern Africa*, ed. by D.H.S. Davis, The Hague: W. Junk. pp. 68–86.

UNICEF 1983. *Report on the Evaluation of Botswana's Nutritional Surveillance System*. Occasional Paper No. 4, Social Statistics Programme, Nairobi, Kenya.

Vierich, I.D. 1977. Interim Report on Basarwa and Related Poor Bakgalagadi in Kweneng District. Report to the Ministry of Local Government and Lands, Gaborone, Botswana.

———— 1978. The Parameters of Hunting and Gathering in a Multi-Ethnic Setting: Adaptive Flexibility in the South Eastern Kalahari. Paper presented at the Conference on Hunters and Gatherers, Maisons des Sciences de L'Homme, Paris, France.

———— 1979. *Drought 1979: Socio-economic Survey of Drought Impact in Kweneng.* Gaborone, Botswana: Division of Planning and Statistics, Ministry of Agriculture.

———— 1981. *The Kũa of the Southeastern Kalahari: A Study in the Socio-ecology of Dependency.* Unpublished Ph.D. dissertation, University of Toronto, Toronto, Ontario, Canada.

———— 1982. Adaptive Flexibility in a Multi-Ethnic Setting: The Basarwa of the Southern Kalahari. In *Politics and History in Band Societies,* ed. by Eleanor Leacock and Richard Lee, Cambridge: Cambridge University Press. pp. 213–222.

———— n.d. Report on Populations in the First and Second Development Areas, Kweneng District, Botswana. Report to the Kweneng District Council, Molepolole, Botswana.

Vierich, H.I.D. and R.K. Hitchcock 1979. Kutse Game Reserve: Field Trip to a Drought-prone Environment. In *Proceedings of the Symposium on Drought in Botswana,* ed. by Madalon T. Hinchey, Gaborone, Botswana: Botswana Society in collaboration with Clark University Press. pp. 21–30.

Wiessner, P. 1977. *Hxaro: A Regional System of Reciprocity for Reducing Risk Among the !Kung San.* Unpublished Ph.D. dissertation, University of Michigan, Ann Arbor, Michigan.

Wilmsen, E.N. 1978. Seasonal Effects of Dietary Intake on Kalahari San. *Federation of American Societies for Experimental Biology Proceedings* 37(1):65–72.

Yellen, J.E. 1976. Settlement Patterns of the !Kung: An Archaeological Perspective. In *Kalahari Hunter-Gatherers: Studies of the !Kung San and Their Neighbors,* ed. by Richard B. Lee and Irven DeVore, Cambridge: Harvard University Press. pp. 47–72.

———— 1977a. *Archaeological Approaches to the Present: Models for Reconstructing the Past.* New York: Academic Press.

———— 1977b. Long Term Hunter-Gatherer Adaptations to Desert Environments: A Biogeographical Perspective. *World Archaeology* 8(3):262–274.

AUTHORS' DATA: (1) Robert K. Hitchcock is the Traditional Sector Specialist in the Community Development Section of the Ministry of Agriculture and Co-operatives, Government of Swaziland. Previously he was the Senior Rural Sociologist in the Division of Planning and Statistics, Ministry of Agriculture, Botswana. (2) James I. Ebert is a consultant in forensic, environmental, and archaeological remote sensing and an adjunct professor in the Department of Anthropology, University of New Mexico. (3) Richard G. Morgan is the Senior Emergency Program Officer at UNICEF in Maputo, Mozambique. Formerly he was the National Food Strategy Co-ordinator in the Rural Development Unit of the Ministry of Finance and Development Planning, Botswana and a District Officer (Development) in the North West District, Botswana.

INDEX

Printed in the United States
by Baker & Taylor Publisher Services